D0164023

Why Do You Need This New Edition?

- The new coauthor on this edition, David Shulman, has built upon the book's existing strengths of thorough coverage of key classic concepts in the study of symbolic interactionism.

- The new edition is thoroughly updated and rewritten to include new research and applications from the literature on symbolic interactionism (the ideas of accounts, "disneyification," dramaturgy and impression management, influence and persuasion, inferential heuristics, emotional labor, ethnomethodology, total institutions and trust).

- New applied examples of symbolic interactionist ideas are presented, including issues of the Internet, emotional labor, visual sociology, MTV, body image, consumer behavior, casino design, doublespeak, high school bullying, malls, and moral panics.

- A new postscript provides applied exercises for readers interested in working further with the book's ideas.

PEARSON

Self and Society

A Symbolic Interactionist Social Psychology

Eleventh Edition

John P. Hewitt
University of Massachusetts at Amherst

David Shulman
Lafayette College

Allyn & Bacon
Boston   Columbus   Indianapolis   New York   San Francisco   Upper Saddle River   Amsterdam
Cape Town   Dubai   London   Madrid   Milan   Munich   Paris   Montreal   Toronto   Delhi   Mexico City
Sao Paulo   Sydney   Hong Kong   Seoul   Singapore   Taipei   Tokyo

Publisher: Karen Hanson
Editorial Assistant: Alyssa Levy
Executive Marketing Manager: Kelly M. May
Marketing Assistant: Gina Lavagna
Creative Director: Jayne Conte
Cover Designer: Bruce Kenselaar
Cover Image: Getty Images
Production Project Manager: Clara Bartunek
Editorial Production and Composition Service: Nitin Agarwal/Aptara®, Inc.

Library of Congress Cataloging-in-Publication Data
Hewitt, John P.,
   Self and society: a symbolic interactionist social psychology/John
P. Hewitt.—11th ed.
      p. cm.
   Includes bibliographical references and index.
   ISBN-13: 978-0-205-63437-8 (alk. paper)
   ISBN-10: 0-205-63437-0 (alk. paper)
   1. Social psychology.   2. Symbolic interactionism.   I. Title.
   HM1033.H49 20111
   302—dc22

                                              2009045574

10 9 8 7 6 5 4 3 2 1 [DOH]   14 13 12 11 10

Allyn & Bacon
is an imprint of

www.pearsonhighered.com

ISBN-10:   0-205-63437-0
ISBN-13: 978-0-205-63437-8

Contents

Preface

When this book was first published in 1976, I could not have imagined that three decades later there would be an eleventh edition. Nonetheless, thanks to continuing support from students and their professors, it has endured and thrived.

This eleventh edition marks the debut of a coauthor, David Shulman of Lafayette College. David deeply appreciates the opportunity to become a part of this book's history and influence. He thanks John P. Hewitt and Jeffrey Lasser for their invitation to work with them and become a coauthor. This eleventh edition offers some significant new material. While staying faithful to offering a detailed presentation of the symbolic interactionist perspective, this edition also updates that treatment. There is now added coverage of the ideas of accounts, "disneyification," dramaturgy and impression management, influence and persuasion, inferential heuristics, emotional labor, ethnomethodology, total institutions, and trust. There are many new applications of symbolic interactionist ideas, including for celebrities, consumer behavior, casino design, doublespeak, high school bullying, malls, moral panics, and Web sites. This edition also includes a postscript with applied exercises for readers interested in working further with the book's ideas.

Thanks are due to many people: To reviewers Jennifer Dunn, Southern Illinois University; Clark Hudspeth, Jacksonville State University; David Marple, Loyola Marymount University; John Mitrano, Central Connecticut State University; and Steve Worden, University of Arkansas, who made suggestions for improvement; to Jeffrey Lasser, Sociology Editor and Alyssa Levy, Editorial Assistant at Pearson Education; to students at the University of Massachusetts and to readers elsewhere who have communicated with me about it; and to faculty who have honored me by adopting it.

Most of all, John owes thanks to his best friend and wife Myrna Livingston Hewitt; daughter, Professor Elizabeth A. Hewitt and her husband, Professor Jared Gardner; son Gary L. Hewitt and his wife, Mádère Olivar; and wonderful grandchildren Elijah, Gideon, Margaret, and John. He dedicates this edition to the memory of his late parents, John H. Hewitt and Anna D. Hewitt.

David Shulman thanks his colleagues in anthropology and sociology at Lafayette for their support and Lafayette students for their intellectual curiosity. It is an honor to write within a sociological tradition with so many interesting and compelling thinkers. Thank you also to Ted Knight from JL Hahn Consulting. David Shulman also wants to thank his best friend and wife, Susan Shulman, and their son Alex Shulman. David dedicates this edition to the memory of the late Dr. Sherry Blackman.

Introduction for the Reader

This book will introduce you to key ideas and applications of symbolic interactionist social psychology. We believe that acquiring a background in this tradition will help enhance people's ability to analyze social situations and their places within them. Sociologists and social psychologists address many interesting aspects about human behavior, such as the nature of emotions, creating a personal image, conformity, and people's senses of identity and self. We start by presenting some of those ideas and we then show their applications in everyday life.

Self and Society also emphasizes thinking sociologically, which entails focusing on how a person's social context can influence his or her behavior. Both sociology and social psychology are characterized by researching how larger social forces impact individual attitudes and behaviors. Investigating what individuals in isolation think about their circumstances is one level of analysis—examining what contributes to those thoughts and the patterns that they take across individuals is a more complex level of analysis. For example, a sociologist might research how advertisers consciously create and exploit social anxieties over physical appearances in order to build bigger markets for beauty or diet products. That conclusion offers a more multifaceted analysis than reporting survey results that some individuals feel bad about their bodies when they look at pictures of models with unrealistically good "photoshopped" looks.

A good maxim to describe thinking sociologically is "don't miss the forest for the trees." This wise saying is meant to warn people against failing to appreciate a social situation in its entirety because they get obsessed on just one aspect of that situation. By being too narrowly focused, people can miss important influences on and implications of their actions. Consider some cases in point. Athletes may play injured because they don't want to miss an important game, yet that decision can cause an athlete to risk a long-term injury that imperils their entire athletic career beyond that one game. Or someone may think that there is one quick fix to attain happiness, such as losing weight, undergoing plastic surgery, reading self-help books, or transferring to a new school. However, a focus on quick fixes neglects that several issues may explain happiness, and that obsessing just on one "answer" can prevent a person from seeing complex paths to happiness.

As an example, a television show on MTV called *True Life* once featured a story about a pompous man who thought that he was the "total package of muscles, looks, and personality"; yet he was still single. His analysis of this problem was that his calf muscles were too small. His answer: He needed to get "calf implants" to make those parts of his body as perfect as the rest—he was just a pair of symmetrical new calves away from attracting his ideal woman! Despite getting his perfect calves, he still ended up single, months later.

The scholarly traditions of social psychology and sociology are attentive to the impacts of missing the forest for the trees. People go through daily actions without always questioning and reflecting on why and how they do what they do. We get embedded in social routines and go through the motions without much thought, attending our classes, going to practices, having the same conversations over and over. We might embrace prefabricated labels to define what is good or bad, and not devote much effort to articulating why we hold those opinions. We expend tremendous effort trying to look good for other people by camouflaging our flaws. At the same time, we want people to view our actions as just how we naturally are, rather than have them think of us as being intentionally manipulative and calculating. What motives explain how we emphasize different aspects of social life?

Some people also do more than miss the forest for the trees. Instead, they do everything they can to avoid even seeing the forest at all. The simplicity of one-dimensional explanations has a straightforward appeal. They make social order and explanations unproblematic and people often prefer to hear what they want rather than to dissect issues. Can you think of a time when you urged people to think of a bigger picture and they resisted your arguments? As an example, think of how the calf guy might respond if you told him that lacking big calves might not be his cure-all. Why do many people tend to respond with such hostility to explanations that can counter their expectations?

This book explores how social expectations connect to specific social roles and institutions. Symbolic interactionists study the processes by which people create social meaning, how such meaning is self-referential (meaning how people see themselves as self-conscious images out there), and how people relate to each other. We present ways to understand the motives for people's actions and to understand how those motives for acting become powerful enough to influence behavior. We also hope to encourage people to better understand their own actions. In our view, sociology is not a storehouse of facts and formulas that people should apply mechanically to human problems. Instead, sociology offers tools for examining reality and the human condition.

We are confident that the ideas in this book are powerful tools for critical thinking. The ability to think analytically is important when we live in a world brimming with ideological movements whose leaders want to impose their own versions of utopias on the rest of us. There are also many professional reformers who underestimate the magnitude of their task and think the world yields to goodness easily. We think that the insights of sociology and social psychology are tremendously useful in helping individuals to appraise social situations in complex ways. An ideal that people should think deeply and independently about human behavior, and problems of human behavior, seems like a good idea to us. That is our book's goal and we very much hope that you will enjoy reading it.

CHAPTER
1

Introducing Social Psychology and Symbolic Interactionism

What's in a name? That which we call a rose
By any other name would smell as sweet.

These lines—spoken from Juliet's balcony in William Shakespeare's *Romeo and Juliet*—encapsulate the great power that names have in social life. Taken at face value, the names that we use to categorize people, objects, and beliefs appear to be mere labels of convenience. Thinking more deeply, however, it is easy to see that names have profound consequences for what people can, must, or must not do. Because Juliet, a member of the Capulet family, and Romeo, a Montague, are members of feuding families, they are forbidden from loving one another. Juliet urges Romeo, "O be some other name," knowing that if only Romeo were not a Montague, and she not a Capulet, they would be the same individuals but they could now marry. Juliet's melancholic words speak to the power inherent in the names that surround us, from the traditional importance placed on "continuing the family name" to the stickiness of nicknames. This book analyzes the wide range and impact of such psychological, social, and symbolic influences in our everyday lives.

Two distinct names—*social psychology* and *symbolic interactionism*—categorize both this book's subject matter and our scholarly orientations. Social psychology positions this book's content within a diverse body of research and theory that spans the disciplines of sociology and psychology. Symbolic interactionism situates the authors within a particular tradition of sociological theory and research. The first task in developing a symbolic interactionist social psychology is to explore the origins and implications of these names. We begin by differentiating symbolic interactionism from other perspectives in social psychology, and we then offer a systematic statement of its major tenets.

What Is Social Psychology?

Both psychologists and sociologists use the term *social psychology* to designate a field of specialization in their disciplines. The shared custody of this term began in 1908, when two books were published, each with social psychology in its title. One, written by the psychologist William McDougall, argued for studying the "native basis of the mind" in order to understand how society acts on those innate characteristics in human beings.[1] Like other scholars of that era, McDougall emphasized the concept of inherent instincts, and encouraged discovering the "innate tendencies of thought and action" that characterize human beings. The other book, by sociologist Edward A. Ross, prioritized explaining social forces and processes that come into existence because human beings associate with one another. Ross felt, for example, that the nature and structure of the individual mind alone could not explain why fads and fashions spread. Ross foregrounds a sociological approach by focusing on how human association creates behavioral processes that are cumulative, and whose study cannot be reduced to analyzing individuals in isolation.[2]

McDougall and Ross identify themes that still matter in social psychology. Psychologists, of course, acknowledge that social and cultural forces shape the environment within which basic psychological processes such as learning, cognition, or emotion occur. However, social psychologists make an individual the key unit of analysis. Sociologists, on the other hand, want to describe and explain patterns of conduct among larger aggregates of people—groups, communities, social classes, and even whole societies. Without denying the importance of individual instincts and other processes that operate at the individual level, sociological social psychologists prioritize the products of human association and make society the beginning point of their analysis.

Psychologist Gordon Allport defined social psychology as the "attempt to understand and explain how the thought, feeling, and behavior of individuals are influenced by the actual, imagined, or implied presence of others."[3] Studies of conformity, for example, explore how social groups shape the thoughts and actions of individuals. In Solomon Asch's historical experiments, subjects demonstrate social conformity by intentionally misjudging the relative lengths of lines. Asch's experiment used hidden collaborators who deliberately judged longer lines to be shorter in an effort to pressure a lone person to conform to a majority's erroneous opinions, which they did.[4] Likewise, in Stanley Milgram's studies of obedience, Milgram demonstrated that he could induce individuals to obey directions to inflict apparent harm on others, just for the sake of an experiment. Milgram created laboratory conditions wherein subjects administered what they believed were painful electric shocks to other human subjects, even over a victim's strong protests and vocal expressions of pain. The shocks were not real, of course, but the experiment was staged convincingly to create the impression that they were.[5] Milgram created a social situation that demonstrated that social pressures can cause sane, normally gentle people to engage in surprisingly brutal behaviors. In other words, a social situation can create brutal conformity in decent people; acts of brutality cannot just be explained as the work of sadistic individuals. Situations and individual dispositions must both be considered. Milgram's study, conducted in the 1950s in the aftermath of World War II and the Holocaust, is not a historical relic. Jerry Burger recently replicated Milgram's study, and using a modified experimental procedure, showed that people today are willing to administer painful shocks at about the same rate as they did in Milgram's study.[6]

More recently, psychological social psychologists have studied the cognitive processes that shape individual behavior in social settings.[7] In order to act, human beings must have considerable organized knowledge of themselves and of the social world. To explain what they do, therefore, social psychologists must study how people acquire, store, retrieve, and utilize this knowledge. As we note later in this chapter, the concept of the *schema*—an organized set of cognitions about a person, role, or situation—helps in this task. We humans do not meticulously catalog bits and pieces of information about others with whom we interact, about ourselves, or about the situations we encounter. Rather, we form schemas—composite pictures—that shape what we see, experience, and remember. People are apt to see homosexuals, for example, not as individuals in all their variety, but as representatives of a type—"homosexual"—and to act toward them as if these characteristics and behaviors represent them all. Such schemas—in everyday language we call them *stereotypes*—shape our actions in significant ways. In a sense, how we use schemas suggests that Juliet's assertion is erroneous: A rose by any other name may not smell as sweet to us.

The sociological approach to social psychology focuses on the social world itself rather than on the individual.[8] We examine social structure, culture, social roles, groups, organizations, and collective behavior as environments and levels of reality in their own right. Sociologists use concepts similar to ones that psychologists use—what cognitive social psychologists call a "schema" the sociologist is apt to call a "typification"—but with different purposes. For example, the psychologist is interested in how individuals use a "homosexual" schema to organize their understandings and actions toward that group, whereas sociologists are interested additionally in how a "homosexual" typification originates, is maintained, and functions to impose particular relationships between members of the gay and straight communities.

In our view, we gain nothing by arguing about which approach is better or which discipline has a prior claim on using a particular term. Psychologists and sociologists are not Capulets and Montagues, and their respective offspring are free to marry or not as they choose. The two disciplines are, nonetheless, two separate families, each with its own ideas about how to pursue the task of studying and explaining human conduct.

Our goal here is to present and develop a symbolic interactionist approach to social psychology. Symbolic interactionism is a general sociological perspective, and its theories and research extend beyond social psychology. Indeed, the basic concepts and theoretical insights of symbolic interactionism that we present here are important to sociology as a whole and not just social psychology. Sociologists take a distinctive view of the relationship between the person and the social world. Sociologists state that society is the source of human knowledge, language, skills, orientations, and motives. Individuals are born into and shaped by a society that will persist long after they are dead. While they are products of that society and its culture, that same society owes its existence and continuity to the conduct of its members. Neither "society" nor "culture" actually does anything, for both are abstractions. Only people act, and by acting, they create and perpetuate their society and its culture.[9]

This paradoxical relationship between an individual and society leads to some difficult questions: *How* does the individual acquire from a society the capacity to be an active, functioning member? Indeed, *what* does the individual acquire—what skills, knowledge, ideas, and beliefs? The social act of learning is crucial. While fundamental biologically programmed drives are the most important factor underlying human behaviors, an orderly and persevering society is guaranteed not only by biological programming alone, but also by what we learn as social beings. More than instinct guides individuals. They must rely on society and culture for their survival.

The simple assertion that culture primarily shapes behavior, however, begs the question of how cultural influences work. Human sexuality, for example, is part of our biological programming, yet it is profoundly influenced by culture. Human beings find a great variety of things—female breasts, male biceps, the size of genitalia, feet, spanking, leather clothing— sexually arousing. They engage in sexual activity in a variety of places—bedrooms, beaches, public restrooms, and in front of cameras. They have phone sex, virtual sex, and sex using the Internet to control mechanical sexual toys remotely, a practice known as "teledildonics." We have created a culture and commercial world of sex products that is so seemingly infinite that it is now a rich subject of parody, as in the example of *www.furnitureporn.com,* a Web site that features furniture pieces set next to each other in "pornographic" poses. Culture brings about this variety, not human nature. But how does culture shape these human sexual preferences and conduct? How does culture govern anything that human beings do?

Sociologists have adopted a variety of views regarding how society and culture explain actual conduct. In one view, which some criticize as *overdetermined,* culture and social structure dictate conduct so overwhelmingly that the question of what individuals actually think is moot. People perform the same tasks over and over again; the social situations and relationships in which people find themselves are pretty much the same from one day to the next; and cultures provide ready-made ways of behaving. As a result, explaining how culture and society actually shape conduct is less interesting and important than explaining the origins and persistence of cultural patterns and social structures. In other words, rather than study how people comply with norms or even whether they agree on what a given norm is, we are to assume that people blindly follow norms. In this perspective, we consider how norms emerge while taking their influence for granted.

This structural perspective has many attractive features. Human social life is highly repetitive, and we can transcend the details of individual behavior and its formation to see patterns and regularities. For example, the concept of social class references the fact that societies are divisible into segments whose members have a similar position in the division of labor, comparable education and incomes, and similar views of themselves and their places in the world. One social class, for example, might consist of small business owners, another of service workers, and another of corporate managers. In each case, the similarities are likely to be greater among the members of these classes than between the members of different classes. Class is a structural concept; its focus is on the patterned and repetitive conduct and social relationships that can be observed within and between various groups in a society at any given point in history. Moreover, although society ultimately depends on the conduct of individuals, their actions and interactions typically have consequences that they do not foresee or recognize. The everyday actions of people as they work, eat and drink, play, make love, socialize, vote, take walks, and attend meetings seem powerfully influenced by social class. Their actions maintain familiar patterns of behavior and they pass these patterns on to succeeding generations, who, in enacting these patterns, re-create the structures of social class.

Although it is crucial to study the reproduction of these social and cultural patterns, limiting attention to this analytic level has drawbacks. We should avoid accepting sweeping generalizing statements of what is "real" as taken-for-granted truths. First, even though social life is highly repetitive, it is not completely so, for patterns change over time, sometimes slowly and at other times, dramatically and quickly. Contemporary men and women in Canada or the United States, for example, inherit social roles and images of one another that were created during the nineteenth century but that have been periodically modified since. Although a small minority of people might still believe that women lack the political or intellectual skills to run for high political office, and that their talents and moral obligations should confine them to home and family, a majority of people, as evidenced in Sarah Palin's and Hillary Clinton's appeals in the American election process in 2008, now reject those beliefs. While criticisms of aspects of their candidacies may have veered into sexism, no group argued that sex alone was a valid basis for excluding either candidate from serious consideration by voters. The emergence of feminist movements and the economic facts of contemporary life have caused what were once perceived as unquestioned practices rooted in human nature, to now seem antiquated. Patterns that once seemed entrenched have changed—absolute seeming norms have been altered, redefined, rejected, and replaced. A structural approach is poorly suited to considering how norms evolve from a bottom-up perspective, such as examining how groups of individuals change society.

A second limitation of strictly focusing on patterns and regularities is that social arrangements are often matters of conflict and controversy and involve widespread disagreement. Assuming that people see all norms and compliance with them in uniform ways is erroneous. The contemporary United States, for example, is rife with battles over cultural values between very religiously conservative people and a majority whose orientation is more secular. Whether the issue is abortion, the Federal Communications Commission (FCC) issuing an obscenity fine for Janet Jackson's "wardrobe malfunction," the place of religion in public life, or the legality of gay marriage, fundamental disagreements over values are everywhere. To grasp how a society works and the place of individuals within it, we cannot just study a dominant secular pattern. We also have to examine the tension between the secular and the socially and religiously conservative resistance to the secular. What distinct interpretations of the world does each side associate with their deeply held views of what is absolutely "true?" Culture and conduct are in flux. We must look at them as shaped by the efforts of people who work within, and sometimes against, an inherited culture and existing social arrangements. People are not thoroughly and passively socialized to accept and reproduce culture and society, for under many circumstances they resist and rebel, finding ways to escape from the patterns of conduct that others urge them to follow. People are not merely agents of an existing social order. They are also active agents who create and change that order. Women did not just receive the vote. They fought for enfranchisement.

Many sociologists eschew concentrating on social structure and culture alone. They recognize the necessity for basic theories of action that account for how people actually form their conduct in everyday life in relation to cultural influences, and also for explaining how individual actions can sustain and/or modify those influences. The main task of sociological social psychology is to create such a theory of action. Its job is to examine the details of action and interaction, to show how society and culture influence people and also how their everyday actions both sustain and change these larger realities. To do so, the social psychologist concentrates on topics like socialization, the nature of the self and identity, and the actual formation of conduct in everyday life. Symbolic interactionism is centrally concerned with these topics, which have also preoccupied sociological social psychologists. Examining these issues—chief among them how the individual and the society are linked—are central to this book.

What Is Symbolic Interactionism?

Symbolic interactionism is a distinctively American sociological perspective with roots in the philosophy of *pragmatism*.[10] This philosophical tradition, identified with such scholars as Charles S. Peirce, William James, John Dewey, and George Herbert Mead, views living things as attempting to make practical adjustments to their surroundings. As philosophers, they are interested in fundamental questions of philosophy: What is truth? What is good? What is knowledge? How do we acquire knowledge? How do we know that we know the truth? In seeking answers to these questions, they argue that an idea's truth or a statement's meaning depends on its practical consequences. An idea, they say, is true if it works. Pragmatists see all living creatures as attempting to meet the demands of their environments in practical ways. They think that knowledge must always confront practical tests of usefulness, a view that emphasizes the consequences of ideas rather than their logical elegance or internal consistency.

Pragmatists see living things as probing and testing their environments. Truth is, therefore, not absolute, but is always relative to the needs and interests of organisms. An idea—for example, the idea that the sun rises in the east—is "true" if it leads to empirical predictions that help people adjust to the requirements and circumstances of their world. Questions of how members of a species know and interact with their environment are, for pragmatists, matters of great moment, not merely peripheral concerns. Knowing and acting, in the pragmatist's view, are intimately linked. We act on the basis of our ideas about the world. The reality of the world is not merely something that is "out there" waiting to be discovered by us, but is actively created as we act in and toward the world.

Philosophical pragmatism is an important forerunner of symbolic interactionism. Contemporary symbolic interactionism reflects the influence of Mead, Dewey, Peirce, and James, and various symbolic interactionists trace their ideas to one or another of these figures. However, George Herbert Mead is recognized as the single intellectual ancestor that all interactionists must honor. His theory of mind, directly or indirectly, profoundly shaped and continues to shape the work of symbolic interactionists. Mead's work comes to us primarily through his students at the University of Chicago, who assembled notes on his courses in social psychology into a book, *Mind, Self, and Society,* after his death in 1931.[11]

Mead's theory of mind attempts to account for the origins and development of human intelligence. He links mind and conduct, and shows that the origins of human mind lie in human society. For Mead, mind, body, and conduct are inseparable aspects of a process of evolution that has produced a unique human life form. All organisms come into existence and persist (or fail to persist) in interaction with their environments. Their physical structures and their capacities to act are created under specific environmental conditions. Organisms are not just passive receptors of stimuli that emanate from their surroundings. Each organism has a set of capacities to respond to its world. Bees, for example, are sensitive to the angle of light coming from the sun and use this knowledge in locating and returning to food sources. Humans are sensitive to the nuances of language and employ this capacity in everything they do. Such capacities have evolved over long periods of time as environmental conditions have changed and evolutionary adaptations have developed. An organism's capacities to respond to the environment help to make the environment what it is. The human child who learns how to react to a parental "no" is acting on his or her parents, obeying their demands in order to influence their acts, and thus secure personal needs for nurture or praise, every bit as much as he or she is being acted on by the parents.

In Mead's time, many social scientists explained human mind and conduct as being solely the result of instincts. If people cared for their children, resisted change, or sought novel experiences, social scientists argued that they did so because they were programmed with particular maternal, conservative, or novelty-seeking instincts. Mead argued that too much cultural diversity, novelty, and complexity exist for instincts to be a satisfactory explanation of human conduct. Thus, Mead rejected an instinctivist approach and the psychological theory that was the prevailing wisdom of the time. In doing so, he opened up new avenues for symbolic interactionist thinking.

Mead also criticized behaviorism, which insisted that the true path to explaining human behavior (or any animal behavior) lay in paying strict attention only to what the scientists could directly observe—both behavior and environmental events (stimuli) associated with the behavior. They emphasized that behavior was learned, and they sought to uncover the laws that governed learning behavioral responses to environmental stimuli. The behaviorists shunned any concept of mind. They stated that what is essential in conduct is not what people think they are doing but what they observably do and how they are rewarded for doing it. Mental events—thoughts, ideas and images—were for them mostly irrelevant because, they believed, such events are unobservable.

Mead felt that behaviorists are right to emphasize behavior, but he also thought that internal, mental events are crucial in explaining human conduct. Contrary to Watson, Mead argued that mental events are a form of behavior that can be observed. Human beings talk about inner experiences and in so doing, they make them observable. Moreover, behaviorism has far too individual a focus for Mead's taste. Although it is true that it is the individual who behaves, individual behavior is rarely disconnected from the acts of others. Human behavior is socially coordinated, often in very complex ways over extended periods of time, and any explanation of behavior that fails to take this fact into account is doomed from the start. Most individual acts are a part of more complex, socially coordinated activities involving several people. Shaking hands, for example, is not merely a bit of behavior in which one person extends a hand in response to the stimulus of the extended hand of another, but it is also a socially coordinated act in which the past experiences and future hopes of two individuals, as well as established social conventions, are important. Shaking hands to seal a business agreement differs from shaking hands in a situation where one of the individuals hoped for a kiss. To only assess the individual's part of an action within a more extensive social act is an attempt to explain far less than what we can and must explain in order to understand conduct. It was Mead's genius that he explained the nature and origins of human intelligence—the mind—that could deal with inner experience and simultaneously account for the social nature of human life. Although a full account of his theory and its application in contemporary symbolic interactionism is presented in Chapter 2 of this book, we sketch a brief outline of Mead's contributions here.

Many living things other than humans exist in association with others of their own kind and are affected by these associations. Other mammals vary in their gregariousness, for example, but all have at least some forms of association with one another, whether as members of a herd or of a small band of primates whose social organization and interdependence are more complex. Mead argued, however, that the basis for human interaction differs substantially from that of other animals, including our primate cousins. Among other animals, interaction takes a form that Mead called the "conversation of gestures." Each individual, in beginning an act, engages in overt and visible actions that can be detected by others and serve as stimuli to their responses. A dog, beginning a fight with another dog, bares its teeth and assumes an aggressive stance; its physical gestures are stimuli that key an aggressive response from the other. Interaction, thus, proceeds between the animals, with the control of each dog's behavior effectively in the hands of the other.

Humans are different. First, the most important gestures for people are lingual. Humans are animals that possess language and whose conduct occurs in a world of words. We are attuned to the overt bodily movements of others and also to a complex set of vocalizations that precede and accompany their acts and our own. Second, these vocal gestures—acts of speech—have the unique property of arousing in the one using them nearly the same response as they arouse in the others to whom they are directed. They are, in Mead's words, "significant symbols." Shouting the word "Fire!" in a public place, for example, does not merely elicit a flight response from those present. The word creates, both in the crowd and in the one who shouts it, a certain attitude—a readiness to act in a particular way, images of conduct appropriate to the situation, plans of action. Creating a common attitude in both the symbol-user and symbol-hearer makes the individual's control of his or her own conduct possible. For example, anticipating the possibility of people panicking if we hastily start screaming "Fire," we may decide instead to attempt to warn people in a subdued way, improving the chances for safe evacuation. Anticipating how other people might react influences our thoughts and conduct.

The significant symbol provides humans with a form of control over their own conduct that other animals lack: self-consciousness. Our capacity to use symbols in imagining how other people will respond to our actions allows us to be conscious of ourselves. We can think of ourselves in the third person—as objects out there in the social world. We can name ourselves, think about ourselves, talk to ourselves, imagine ourselves acting in various ways, love or hate ourselves, and feel proud or ashamed of ourselves; in short, we can act toward ourselves in all the ways we can act toward others. In this way, people have a motivating inner life that helps explain our external actions.

Mead's account of human behavior, mind, and self is a significant milestone in human self-understanding. His theory stresses explaining human conduct in scientific terms based on scientific observation. Simultaneously, he emphasizes inner experiences as being capable of observation, because we can report and communicate our private experiences and feelings to others using significant symbols. Mead's theory recognizes the sociability of human beings and puts the human experience of self on center stage. Human beings are conceived as creatures whose evolution has provided a capacity for self-control. Chapter 2 of this book builds on these basic ideas, developing a conceptual framework for a symbolic interactionist social psychology. To embark on this task, the remainder of this chapter develops a general overview of contemporary symbolic interactionism, first by identifying its major points of similarity to, and difference from other theoretical perspectives, and then by stating its major tenets.

Other Theoretical Approaches

Social psychologists have developed many approaches to understanding the link between society and conduct. Learning theory, psychoanalytic theory, exchange theory, phenomenology, ethnomethodology, social cognition theory, social constructionist theory, and postmodern theory are all part of contemporary social psychology, and all have impacted contemporary symbolic interactionism.

Learning Theory

John Watson's thinking provided the foundations for a school of psychological thought that is variously known as behaviorism, learning theory, or, in its more explicitly social psychological form, *social learning theory*.[12] Behaviorists typically refuse to consider "mental" and "subjective" phenomena as being observable. Instead they choose to emphasize direct measurement and observation of behaviors and environmental events. The basic ideas of behaviorism are familiar to students who have studied psychology and know something about classical (or respondent) conditioning and operant conditioning. Classical conditioning is often illustrated by referring to the work of the Russian psychologist Ivan Pavlov, who demonstrated that a response, such as a dog's salivating in the presence of food, could also be elicited by an unrelated stimulus, like the sound of a bell, as long as the bell was rung each time the food was presented to a hungry dog. After a certain number of trials in which food and a bell were presented together, the bell alone begins to produce the salivation response. This response is involuntary (the dog has no control over it), but the dog can associate it with a stimulus other than the one (food) that usually elicits it.

Operant conditioning focuses on more voluntary behavior—behavior that an organism controls and can produce in order to yield certain effects. In this form of conditioning, for which the psychologist B. F. Skinner is the chief architect of ideas, the stimulus follows the response. That is, some behavior (such as a pigeon pecking on a certain spot on its cage) is followed by a specific event (such as a kernel of corn being released into the cage). If the organism values the event (stimulus), the behavior is more likely to be repeated in the future. Under these conditions we would say that the behavior is positively reinforced.

How do principles of classical and operant conditioning provide a basis for social psychology? The governing idea is that an individual's environment, including other human beings with whom interactions occur, is the source of stimuli—both those that trigger classical, involuntary responses, and those that serve as positive and negative reinforcement, or as a punishment for voluntary activities. Thus, one might say that a child learns a repertory of behavior from his or her parents, who reinforce or punish the child's behaviors. The child learns to brush his or her teeth, or say "Thank you," for example, because he or she is positively reinforced for doing so and perhaps punished for not doing so. An important extension of learning theory is the observation that learning in social contexts is often vicarious: By observing the behavior of others and the rewards their actions earn, we learn what they learn without going through any trial and error ourselves. The child learns that he or she will receive praise for being polite to adults when he or she observes other children experience this reinforcement. The child can then enact the behavior, get the reinforcement, and thus experience model learning. This theory of social learning expands the basic ideas of learning theory and adapts them to the realities of social life as we observe it: People learn by systematic observation and imitation and not simply by blind trial and error.

Symbolic interactionists find much that is appealing in this perspective. Behaviorists, like symbolic interactionists, emphasize studying actual and observable behavior. Their perspective views learning as an important process, and symbolic interactionists agree that people learn their repertoire of conduct. Moreover, there is much in the behaviorists' ideas about operant conditioning that symbolic interactionists like. The idea that a future stimulus (the reward associated with an activity) can control a behavior is an important one, for it is a way of conceiving behavior as being goal-oriented. Much of what people do seems designed to produce some desired future effect.

But in the eyes of symbolic interactionists, classical behaviorism also has some serious flaws. Although both classical and operant conditioning can be found in human behavior, the symbolic interactionist also seeks evidence of processes that are not observed in other animals. The interactionist would say, for example, that people are aware of conditioned responses, whether they are respondent or operant. We can—and typically do—become aware of the relationship of present conduct to future events. Indeed, much of what we do is intended to influence what will happen to us in the future, whether in the next moment or the next year. Self-awareness and reflection is crucial to intentional behavior; for a person's capacity to be conscious of his or her own present and future actions makes it possible for these actions to be controlled. Becoming aware of the relationship between what I do at this moment and some future event is the first step in acquiring the capacity to control that response. The ability to govern my own behavior to secure goals depends on my capacity to imagine myself acting in multiple ways so that I can choose effective acts.

Moreover, although contemporary behaviorism conceives the social environment as an important source of stimuli, it still tends toward a microscopic view of behavior in which the complexities and real significance of that environment are ignored. Think of our earlier example of a child learning that politeness and obedience produce such rewards as praise and affection. To apply behaviorism in a very strict manner, one has to assume that the child—whether gradually on a trial-and-error basis or more quickly and vicariously—learns to behave in ways that produce the desired results. Symbolic interactionists argue that there is more to the process of learning than the reinforcement of specific acts. People seem to be guided not merely by rewards, but also by more general ideas of how their own conduct should dovetail with the conduct of others. Although in the earliest stages of our experience, these ideas may be fairly concrete ("If I eat all my food, my mother will be happy with me"), they gradually become more complex and abstract as the person ages. Our conduct comes to be guided more by general principles than by discrete reactions to concrete situations.

For the symbolic interactionist, an individual develops an awareness, not just of the specific behavior that will produce a particular result in a given situation, but more generally of one's place in the life of the group as a whole. One knows that he or she might get called on to play various roles, that the roles one enacts must somehow mesh with the roles of others, and that one must control one's own acts so that they fit in with the acts of other people. Thus, the interactionist conception of how people learn conduct is more global, complex, social, and dynamic than the simple learning model suggests.

Psychoanalytic Theory

Few social psychologists work explicitly from a *psychoanalytic perspective,* but Sigmund Freud and his intellectual followers have had an impact on the social sciences as a whole and also on our everyday, commonsense ideas about psychology.[13] Freudian theory has a distinct view of both the nature of society, and of the development and vicissitudes of the individual personality. Freud regarded the individual and society as being in conflict with one another. Freud's conception of personality divides it into three components. The *id* is the source of the individual's drives, instincts, and behavioral energy. The forces that move behavior—such as sexuality or aggression—are biological and universal and exceedingly powerful. These drives are a central force with which the individual and society must contend. The id, for example, is the source of both the sexual drive and images of sexual activities or partners that will satisfy that drive.

The second component of personality is the *ego,* which is a kind of operating mechanism that searches in the external world for opportunities to meet the organism's needs. The ego lives in the real world; that is, it confronts the external world and attempts to secure objects that will actually satisfy the person's drives. In a sense, the ego is driven by the id, for it attempts to accomplish what the id wants. In doing so, the ego must also cope with the third component of personality, the *superego.* The superego is the internalization of society and culture in the individual—many people refer to the superego as being "society's conscience." The superego represents what society stands for, as opposed to what the id wants, and it is as powerful and demanding a force as the latter. The superego represents morality, perfection, and the socially necessary as against the unremitting biological imperatives of the id. The ego can thus be thought of as the negotiator or manager that is caught between these two powerful forces, which are in conflict with one another. The ego has the difficult tasks of trying to satisfy both the id and the superego simultaneously. In doing so, the ego relies on many defensive techniques (*defense mechanisms*) whose objectives are to deceive the id and superego into thinking that their imperatives are being met. One of the more common mechanisms is repression, whereby potentially dangerous ideas or wishes are pushed out of the conscious part of the mind and into the unconscious. For example, if social values appraise sexuality negatively, the ego may deal with the insistent sexuality of the person by repressing it, and push sexuality out of consciousness.

Symbolic interactionists, like other sociological social psychologists, have either generally either ignored psychoanalysis or rejected it. In particular, most social psychologists reject Freud's biological and instinctual theory of motivation—they reject a depiction of human beings as seething pots of impulses that are barely contained by a thin veneer of civilization. Symbolic interactionists have felt that the relationship between society and the person is more cooperative, and that culture does not invariably battle biology. In their view, humans are animals without instincts; culture replaces the biological guidance that the human species has lost in the course of its evolution. As a result, culture guides human beings rather than restrains their antisocial impulses. If this version of events is true, much of the force of Freud's theory seems to be lost.

It is possible, however, to reject a theory of instincts and a theory of culture and biology as hopelessly pitted against one another without also rejecting some other important and valid insights that a psychoanalytic view offers. Donald Carveth argued that the instinctual basis of motivation could be rejected without discarding other aspects of Freud's theory. Indeed, according to Carveth, the theory of instincts must be rejected in order to get to the really important insights of psychoanalysis.[14] In a general sense, Freud's theories strongly caution against an oversocialized conception of human beings. Although culture does take the place of instinct, it does not automatically or mechanically dictate conduct. There is no lack of conflict between people or between the person and society, and what people do often seems unpredictable and inexplicable.

Moreover, in both psychoanalysis and symbolic interactionism, there is a basis for viewing the individual and society as in a natural state of tension with one another, although not in a constant state of war. Like Freud, symbolic interactionists say that acts have their beginnings beneath the level of consciousness. Psychoanalysis posits an unconscious with a life of which the individual is unaware and does not control. Symbolic interactionists are reluctant to adopt this conception, but they do acknowledge that people only become aware of the nature and directions of their acts after they have begun. Thus, they acknowledge that some part of mental life is unconscious. Symbolic interactionists also imbue individuals with the capacity to inhibit and redirect incipient acts—to say "no" to the impulses that arise within them, impulses that come from culture and from individual plans and purposes. The result is that the individual is no puppet of society, but is an active creature struggling for self-control, who develops plans and purposes that may run counter to what culture demands or encourages.

Exchange Theory

A third influential approach to sociological social psychology is the broad tradition known as *exchange theory*.[15] Drawing on intellectual sources as diverse as behavioral psychology and microeconomics, this perspective focuses on exchanges of goods or benefits between people. Exchange theory begins with a key social fact: People have to obtain much of what they want or need from others. Not only material things, such as food or shelter, but also such social goods as status or approval can be obtained only if the individual interacts with others. The resources and skills people need often lie in the hands of others who must be induced to give them up. People are, in other words, interdependent, and the nature, extent, and consequences of this interdependence are the focus of exchange theory.

Although there are several varieties of exchange theory, underlying most approaches is a common set of ideas about the nature of human conduct and the relationships that build up among people as they exchange benefits. Linda Molm and Karen Cook[16] have described three core assumptions of exchange theory, here paraphrased as follows:

- Relations develop among people within "structures of mutual dependence."
- People act in ways that tend to increase outcomes they value or desire and to decrease outcomes they dislike.
- Over time, social relationships develop and are sustained as people develop mutually beneficial exchanges.

Taken as a whole, these core assumptions portray a social world of interdependence based on the exchange of those things that people need or want.

Exchange theory argues that interdependence is structured socially. Exchange relationships develop when social arrangements dictate that actors must secure the things they value from one another. Exchange relationships develop between factory owners and workers, for example, because owners need workers' labor and workers need the money their labor earns in order to purchase goods. The interdependence may be unequal, where one participant is more dependent on the development of a relationship than the other. If there is a large unemployed or underemployed work force from which to hire workers, then owners are less dependent on any particular worker than workers are on owners. If jobs are plentiful and few workers exist to fill those jobs, the opposite is true. Nor must participants in an exchange be mutually dependent for everything. Workers, for example, may depend on owners for income, but they can seek other gratifications—confirmation of their worth, emotional support, and informal social contacts—elsewhere.

Exchange relationships develop in an established social world that shapes how people can depend on one another and exchange benefits. Some people have resources—money, land, tools, and knowledge—that others need, and the unequal distribution of these resources determines the conditions of social exchange. Established cultural definitions and expectations also structure relationships of dependence. In the nineteenth-century United States, for example, a popular ideal held that men ought to work outside the home to earn an income for their families and women should stay home to maintain the house, raise children, and nourish the family's emotional life. Women's rights to own and control property were restricted; men were expected to display strength and keep their emotions in check. These cultural definitions—the gender order—shaped patterns of dependence between men and women and thus also the character of exchanges between them. Men's labor at work provided the income needed to purchase the material necessities of life, and women's emotional labor provided men with a "haven in a heartless world" of occupational striving. These levels of exchange are abstract but they illustrate the basic mechanisms of exchange that these exchange theorists assume.

The basic motivational premise of exchange theory is that people act in ways that increase outcomes they value and decrease those they do not. In other words, over time, individuals will tend to do that which earns them benefits they want or need and to avoid doing those things that result in excessive costs. Consider how politicians will promise what they think will get them votes and try to avoid any positions that make voters hostile. Politicians may even lie to get votes if they value votes more than other goods—such as personal integrity or honesty—and if they can figure what lies will work best to get the most votes. Without besmirching all politicians, hardly a month goes by without a politician being condemned for being caught in a hypocritical lie. Who better to demonstrate a subterranean variant of exchange theory in politics than ex-governor of Illinois Rod Blagojevich, who allegedly attempted to trade a "golden" opportunity to appoint a senator in exchange for a variety of payoffs?

Exchange theory says nothing about what people are likely to value in any exchange, although we try to assess specifics through research. In other words, the theory predicts that if people value something, they will strive to achieve it and will tend, over time, to behave in ways that secure it. But the theory does not attempt to explain what people value—or why. Thus, the theory is somewhat less individualistic or egocentric than it seems, for individuals may value that which benefits particular others or the community as a whole and not just themselves. A child's values may favor hugs, videogames, or a bigger allowance for himself or herself, but they may also favor a happy or contented pair of parents. Or, in a worse case, the child may value parental actions that confirm the child's image of himself or herself, even if that image is negative and the confirming actions of parents are disapproving and punishing.

Do people consciously or unconsciously select behaviors that increase valued outcomes and decrease undesirable ones? Contemporary exchange theorists argue that the process may range from largely unconscious to very conscious. Exchange theory is based partly on the precepts of learning theory. That is, over time, action and reward become linked, even if the individual is not consciously aware of the connection. The more an action is rewarded, the more it tends to be repeated. Exchange theorists, however, are generally willing to consider what behavioral psychologists are not—namely, that people may consciously and rationally calculate what will get them the things they value. Thus, a child may not consciously construct actions that earn parental disapproval and thus confirm a negative view of self. However, the student who always agrees with the professor's opinions may do so in a calculated effort to earn the professor's favor and thus improve the chances of a good grade. Likewise, a person may turn to the same people for help with his or her problems without being conscious of doing so. But he or she may also calculate rationally that some people will give help, whereas others will deny it.

Taken together, these first two key precepts of exchange theory—socially structured interdependence and the tendency to repeat successful actions—imply a third basic idea: Over time, social relationships between specific partners will tend to stabilize. That is, as people find dependable sources of the things they value, they will tend to return to these sources over and over again. If two people meet and begin to provide each other with companionship, approval, and aid, their relationship as friends will gradually stabilize. Each will find the other a reliable source of those valued goods; the behavior of each will, in effect, reward the behavior of the other.

The development of a stable relationship depends on the fact that exchanges are contingent, both within a particular transaction and across time. A neighbor who borrows a tool receives the benefit of using the tool. This particular transaction also establishes expectations for the future: The lender will feel comfortable borrowing a tool from the borrower in the future, and the borrower is apt to expect this act to occur. In other words, an exchange conducted in the present has implications for exchanges to be conducted in the future. Social relationships endure so long as benefits continue to be exchanged. A neighbor who borrows a tool but expresses no gratitude casts a slight shadow on the relationship—a shadow that grows and becomes darker if the pattern continues. A borrower who refuses to be a lender casts an even darker shadow. To refuse to do a favor for one who has done a favor is to interfere with the expected pattern of exchange. If a person cannot receive a benefit from someone on whom he or she has bestowed benefits, that person is apt to feel cheated, to turn to other people to supply future needs, and to refuse to provide benefits to the person who has refused to provide them. Over time, if benefits are not reciprocated, social relationships cease to exist. In their everyday lives, people regularly extend one another interpersonal credit. That is, they bestow benefits without expectation of immediate return. But when interpersonal credit limits are exceeded, people tend to act very much like Visa, MasterCard, or American Express: The card is revoked and no more purchases are allowed.

Just as water is more valuable to a thirsty person than to one who has just drunk his or her fill, so it is with other wants and needs. People can become satiated with advice, tools, approval, or money, and find each increment to their supply to be of less use. As

Molm and Cook (1995) point out, both psychological and economic principles are involved here. One of the key findings of behavioral psychology is that the more a given reward is obtained, the less valuable (i.e., the less "rewarding") each subsequent unit of that reward becomes. When the pigeon becomes satiated with corn, the behavioral outcome of pecking is less valuable and the pigeon is less likely to peck. Likewise, diminishing marginal utility is a key precept of economics. The more of a good the actor possesses, the less useful each additional unit of that good becomes, and so the less worthwhile it is to expend resources obtaining additional units.

Valued things do not diminish in value at the same rate. One can only consume so much food or drink at a time, and the average person's need for tools is likewise presumably finite. These valued things have rather particular and finite use value, and when the actor can no longer use additional quantities of them, their value diminishes. In contrast, money tends not to lose its value so quickly. The reason is that money has exchange value. That is, money is a valued thing that can always be exchanged for other valued things. The actor can exchange money for food, but when needs for foods are met, he or she can exchange money for other things as well: housing, transportation, entertainment, and almost anything else in a society in which practically everything is for sale. Prestige also has exchange value. If association with someone of high social standing is valued, then prestige is exchangeable for the things a person desires from others. Celebrities from movies and sports may make personal appearances at individual parties for a fee. MTV ran a television show about sweet 16 parties in which the children of affluent parents had lavish parties with well-known celebrity performers. In these cases, the celebrity receives money (and adulation) in exchange for conferring prestige-by-association on the party-giver and his or her guests.

Symbolic interactionists are wary of assumptions about the motivation on which exchange theory is built. Rather than positing the same motivation to all cases, such as the inclination to maximize gains and minimize losses, symbolic interactionists examine what people say about their motives and the real contexts of social interaction in which they make exchanges. Instead of assuming that conduct is propelled by a single set of meanings, symbolic interactionists study the meanings people actually produce. Exchange theory may capture the meanings that people create within contemporary capitalist society, but this does not mean that people do or must produce such meanings at all times and in all places. To capture this complexity is a goal of symbolic interactionism.

Phenomenology and Ethnomethodology

Two other perspectives are closely related to one another: Phenomenology and ethnomethodology[17] deal more directly and explicitly with the meaning of human conduct than either learning theory or exchange theory. *Phenomenology* is a philosophical perspective whose founder was the German philosopher Edmund Husserl. As an approach to sociology and social psychology, its ideas have been adapted in the work of Alfred Schutz and Peter Berger and Thomas Luckmann. Phenomenological sociology takes the subjective standpoint of individual actors as the central focus of attention. Unlike a more "objective" approach that views the social world as a reality that exists independently of any individual's perception of it, phenomenology posits reality as constituted by people's view of it. In other words, there is not a single, objective social reality that can be analyzed in the same manner that a scientist might analyze physical reality. Instead, there are multiple realities. Pushed to an extreme, one might say that there are as many social realities as there are perspectives from which to view them. A phenomenological approach asserts that it is impossible to say that there is some objective reality called "American society" or "the Smith family" whose existence is so clear and straightforward that it can be literally described and explained. "The Smith family" is a different reality to each of its members, as it is to a variety of outsiders who come into contact with and perceive this family. To John Smith it may be a source of pride and satisfaction; to his wife the family may be a chafing set of restrictions; to the children the family may be a haven from a cruel world of teachers and peers. The family is a different reality to each member and to different outsiders, from neighbors, relatives, co-workers and different "friends of the family." The phenomenologist accounts for human conduct by attempting to "get within" and describe the subjective perspectives of people, on the premise that one can only understand and account for what people do by understanding the reality they perceive and act toward. A tradition that prioritizes what Max Weber labeled as "Verstehen," the need to value the subjective understandings of people in research, is a touchstone of symbolic interactionism and other interpretive sociological theories such as phenomenology and ethnomethodology.

Ethnomethodology is a variant of phenomenology. Like phenomenologists, ethnomethodologists are interested in the perspectives of actors, and how they view and act in their world as they see it. Ethnomethodologists are primarily concerned with the methods that people use to produce meaning. Ethnomethodologists assert that meaning lies in the accounts that people give of their experiences and interactions with others. These accounts are verbalizations, and they attempt to introduce order, sense, rationality, and predictability into the social world. For example, an ethnomethodologist might study how people are diagnosed as schizophrenic. The ethnomethodologist does not assume that there is some real disease called schizophrenia, or that its diagnosis is simply a matter of applying medical knowledge to ferret out the category of illness to which a given patient belongs. Instead, the ethnomethodologist suspends judgment on such questions and focuses on how the psychiatrist explains the diagnosis—the specific behaviors that he or she says are important, the rules he or she invokes to justify calling that behavior schizophrenic.

Underlying this approach is the belief that people are constantly engaged in a process of creating sense—making it appear that their behavior is correct or appropriate, that they are being sensible and normal human beings doing things in the usual way. This perspective argues that culture does not provide a specific set of rules that guide people in their everyday behavior, instead it provides the resources—including rules—that people can make use of in creating the illusion of normality and meaning in their everyday lives. Pursued to an extreme, ethnomethodology appears to take no interest at all in what people do, nor in explaining why people do what they do, but concerns itself only with how people make sense of what they do.

Ethnomethodologists place considerable emphasis on the detailed analysis of conversation. Given their perspective on the creation of social order, talk is of great importance. As people engage in conversations, they bring various resources to bear on their task of creating order. Moreover, they do so in very structured, regular ways. Conversations exhibit regular patterns of turn taking, for example, and frequently involve paired utterances, such as questions and answers or requests and refusals. Moreover, it is in mundane, everyday conversations that important social categories and distinctions are brought to life. If gender and social class are important ways in which people categorize one another, for example, they must be employed and reproduced in people's talk.[18] When a man calls a waitress "honey," or when men are accustomed to interrupting women speaking, or when people mimic ethnic accents, then sociological sensemaking is reinforcing broad gender, race and class dynamics in mundane, everyday conversation.

Symbolic interactionists find some features of phenomenology and ethnomethodology to be interesting and useful additions, and we will discuss some of these later in this book. Yet we do not consider these perspectives to be an adequate basis for a comprehensive social psychology. Although symbolic interactionism, like phenomenology, views a person's distinct perspective and perceptions as very important, symbolic interactionism avoids the extreme subjectivity into which phenomenology is prone to fall. Symbolic interactionists argue that people act on the basis of meanings, so that one's actions in a particular situation depend on the way that situation is perceived. If I believe the world is a hostile and dangerous place, I will interpret the actions of others in accordance with my belief and act accordingly. All the same, the world external to the individual does not simply become what the individual thinks it is. My view could be paranoid, and my actions may even cause other people to dislike me and to act in ways that confirm my paranoia, but the perceptions other people have of what I *really* should be paranoid about do not necessarily accord with mine. Someone worried about alien abductions might see a world full of extraterrestrial threats, but that does not mean that other people agree that they, for example, should cover their heads with tin foil to safeguard their thoughts and avoid driving on lonely country roads at night. The world, as an individual paranoid sees it, is different, and the paranoid's actions have different meanings for them than others would attribute to those actions. There is an external world that confronts and constrains the individual regardless of how he or she perceives or wants to perceive reality.

The major contribution of ethnomethodology is the insight that people construct meaning and sensibility through their conversations. Although symbolic interactionists emphasize the meanings that people share as they interact with one another, it is easy to overemphasize the extent to which meanings are fully and genuinely shared. Ethnomethodology emphasizes that shared meaning is often an illusion and not an actuality, that people have ways to convince themselves that they agree with one another, or that they share the same motives when, in fact, they do not. Beyond this insight, which is incorporated in this book, ethnomethodology is too limited in its scope to constitute an adequate foundation for social psychology as a whole. By reducing everything to the question of how people create meaning, it ignores such important matters as how people actually decide to act in particular ways, how interaction influences conduct, and how selves are formed. By paying attention only to what people say, ethnomethodology ignores a great variety of actions other than speech actions. Social psychology is necessarily concerned with all forms of conduct, not just talk. There is also an external world that acts upon us, regardless of how we want to make sense of it.

Social Cognition

Social cognition has been developed mainly by psychologists and is currently the leading approach to social psychology in their discipline. Nevertheless, this approach addresses questions of importance to sociology and some of its basic ideas are strikingly similar to—or at least compatible with—those of symbolic interactionism. As its name implies, *social cognition* focuses on knowledge—its content, organization, creation, and processing. What do people know about themselves and the social world? How is this knowledge organized? How does it get created? How is it processed or manipulated in order to solve problems or achieve other individual objectives? The theory of social cognition is not very much concerned with behavior; "what people do and why they do it" is not the central question. Nor do practitioners of social cognition focus much on emotions or on how people feel about themselves or others. In the social science trinity of thoughts, feelings, and actions, the emphasis in social cognition is almost exclusively on thoughts.

Although social cognition resists easy summary, its major ideas can be stated as follows:[19]

- People are "cognitive misers" who develop cognitive structures that enable them to process the vast amounts of incoming information about themselves and others efficiently.
- Structures assist cognitive processes, such as paying attention, remembering, and making social inferences.
- Structures and processes are socially formed and socially consequential.

These ideas illustrate a theoretical perspective that is not much concerned with an overall portrayal of the nature of the social world but that instead prefers to focus on the ways its members process information about it.

Social cognition theory postulates that the individual in the social world is constantly receiving far more information about others (and about the self) than he or she can process. Visual inspection may inform people about the age, gender, race, occupation, social class, or other characteristics of different people. People have wrinkles or gray hair, dress as men or women, have light or dark skin, and wear the uniforms of physicians or telephone workers. Likewise, their words and deeds are sources of information about them, their intentions, their interpretations of a situation, and their attitudes toward one another. People speak in the measured words of a college professor or in the slang of the street; they act toward others with sympathy, hostility, or indifference; they seem calm or anxious; they offer praise or criticism.

This potentially confusing jumbled mound of information, according to social cognition theory, must somehow be structured and processed if the individual is to know how to respond to it. In organizing information, human beings are miserly. That is, they attempt to be economical in their efforts to grasp and process information. They take shortcuts, assuming, for example, that someone with white hair is old (as opposed to prematurely gray) or that a person wearing a dress is female (and is not cross-dressing). They must take shortcuts because the alternative—inspecting the many details of the other's behavior or appearance—would make it impossible to act. Imagine how difficult it would be even to say hello to another person if one had to sift through the mass of information that the person presents in order to decide on the appropriate thing to say and how to say it.

The major concept invoked by social cognition theorists to explain how people organize or structure cognitions is the concept of the schema. *Schemas,* according to sociologist Judith Howard,[20] "are abstract cognitive structures that represent organized knowledge about a given concept or type of stimulus." The schemas that individuals develop and hold contain information about an object, ideas about the relationships among various cognitions of the object, and examples of the object. Schemas can focus on specific other people, situations, types of people, social roles, social groups, specific events, and even the self. Thus, a given individual might have schemas about a spouse, disciplining the children, office parties, workaholics, supervisors, fellow nurses, the war against terrorism, and self.

A schema is a kind of "picture" of any of these things. Parts of this picture are quite abstract: An individual's schema for a supervisor might include such abstract traits as superior knowledge and wisdom, willingness to listen, and capacity to make quick decisions. It may include negative and positive traits—for instance, insufficient knowledge, stubbornness, and indecisiveness. Other parts of a schema are more concrete, involving images of physical appearance, strength, clothing, or other material things. Thus, the schema for a corporate lawyer might include an expensive pinstriped suit, well-tailored shirts, and costly shoes, as well as such traits as intelligence, self-confidence, and the ability to articulate a strong position on behalf of a client.

A schema functions as a loosely organized theory that people use to make sense of their world, predict the behavior of others, and decide on their own course of action. People use personalized schemas to make sense of the behavior of specific other people, such as friends or spouses. They use role schemas to accomplish the same ends with respect to others whom they do not know personally but with whose role they are familiar. They use event schemas to grasp expected series of events in such routine situations as sitting in a college classroom or attending a wedding or funeral. They use self-schemas to make sense of and predict their own behavior, attributing traits, strengths, and weaknesses to themselves much in the same way they do to others. Particularly with respect to role schemas, people maintain the schema and make it more concrete by keeping in mind one or more exemplars of that schema. Thus, a favorite athlete might be the exemplar of one's athlete role schema, providing a concrete illustration of the more abstract traits that make up one's schema.

How do these cognitive structures aid in the processing of information about self and others? They do so first by shaping the individual's attention to stimuli, helping to determine what will be salient and thus receive attention and what will be ignored. Second, schemas are critical in the organization and functioning of memory. Third, schemas influence the way people make inferences about themselves and the social world.

The various schemas that people carry with them provide the background against which we perceive particular stimuli. A person's schema for a friend, for example, shapes one's responses to the friend's behavior because it defines what is normal or expected from that friend. If the schema constructs the friend as caring, gentle, and even-tempered, then conduct that violates the schema will be quite noticeable. If the friend acts in a way that seems indifferent, rude, or angry, those stimuli will be noticed. Similarly, if an event schema for a family dinner contains expectations of silence while eating, conversation will be perceived as an unwanted intrusion. Schemas thus provide the ground against which the figure of behavior is perceived.

The selection of stimuli as salient and, therefore, needing attention and response is not done consciously. That is, individuals are not engaged in a process of consciously selecting a schema and then consciously selecting the stimuli to which they will attend. Indeed, the "cognitive miser" view of cognition rests in part on an assumption that people could not act if they had to select schemas and stimuli in a conscious way. Instead, schemas operate in the background and the selection of stimuli is done preconsciously. The individual is not consciously aware, in other words, of the processes that cause him or her to notice that another person's behavior is out of keeping with a person or event schema. The individual is aware that something is unusual about the other's behavior but is not aware of the cognitive processing that leads to that awareness.

Behavior is highly dependent on memory—on the retrieval and activation of information that has been previously secured and stored. People know how to interact with their friends—what to say and do—because they have stored memories of their friends. They know their food preferences, the music they cannot stand to hear, and the others with whom they like to spend time. People know how to behave at a wedding or a Bar Mitzvah because they have information, stored in a schema for those events that they could retrieve and use as a basis for acting appropriately in the situation.

Cognitive schemas are also crucial to the retrieval of information. The schemas that organize the perception of those events shape memories of particular events. In other words, what an individual remembers about an event he or she has witnessed depends in part on the schema the person applied to it. Imagine that a person witnesses a crime—say, a mugging at night on a streetcorner—and organizes his or her perception of the event as a crime committed by an African American. In doing so, the individual may invoke social group schemas about African Americans as well as more particular schemas; say from media sources about black criminals. It is likely that the person's subsequent memories of the event will emphasize those aspects related to these schemas. He or she might remember the race of the mugger but not the victim, for example, or remember the victim as white when he or she was actually black. Group and event schemas might even supply remembered details that were not actually observed. The person might remember the perpetrator's clothing, for example, a black ski mask and leather gloves—not because those objects were observed, but because they are part of the person's schema for crimes typical of African Americans. What a witness to a crime scene remembers is in part a function of what he or she thought was occurring and not necessarily of what actually took place. Much of the approach to cognition perceives individuals as faulty processors of information because they use "inferential heuristics" that lead them to misperceive reality because of perceptual shortcuts that they take, often as a result of being cognitive misers.[21]

The structures and processes of social cognition are intensely social. Although individuals use them, their origins typically lie in the social world and in individual experience. Individuals form schemas, but they do so out of materials a social world provides and not exclusively on the basis of their own cognitive efforts. Schemas enable the individual to function in the social world in part because they are shared and used collectively in social interaction, not just in individual isolation.

The foregoing points are especially significant to sociologists who have worked within and favor a social cognition approach. For the sociologist, an important question to be asked is where schemas come from and how they apply in social situations. Clearly, the locus of the schema is within the individual mind—where else could it be? However, people build their schemas on the basis of shared experience with others, knowledge gained from others, and using ideas that are widely shared. Thus, an event schema that views street crime as predominantly involving black perpetrators assaulting or robbing white victims is both factually wrong and widely shared. In spite of the fact that black-on-black crimes far outnumber black-on-white crimes, event schemas emphasizing the latter persist. Initially, Americans widely viewed the 1995 Oklahoma City bombing as the act of Arab terrorists because of a schema of who is supposed to commit those crimes; the perpetrators were eventually found to be homegrown members of an American private militia group. How and why do we seem so certain in knowledge that is biased? Efforts to answer questions such as this take us beyond the fairly narrow limits of social cognition conceived by psychologists.

Many of the ideas developed within this approach fit well within an interactionist perspective. Indeed, for several concepts in social cognition—role schemas and event schemas, for example—there are parallel or equivalent concepts developed by symbolic interactionists. Indeed, students of social cognition have independently (though belatedly) discovered ideas interactionists have used for decades. At the same time, there are important differences. Symbolic interactionists are interested in actions and feelings and not only in cognitive processes. That is, they study what people actually do and how their emotions enter into their actions. Symbolic interactionists also much more commonly study thoughts, feelings, and actions in the real situations of everyday life rather than in the laboratory.

Social Constructionism

After the publication of Peter Berger and Thomas Luckmann's *The Social Construction of Reality* in 1967 (see Note 8), a new phrase, "social construction," came into widespread use and exerted a strong influence on the social sciences. The *social constructionism* that their book helped spawn, however, is less an organized theoretical perspective on the human world and more a set of questions that researchers ask about phenomena that interest them. As the philosopher Ian Hacking argues,[22] the constructionist perspective rests on a characteristic attitude toward the social world. Social constructionists look at existing social patterns or forms of behavior and try to show how they might have developed differently. Whether the phenomenon in question is juvenile delinquency, depression, child abuse, or even the concepts of physics, constructionists argue that the "reality" people see when they look at such phenomena is socially constructed. That is, they argue, the phenomenon is not an inevitable product of the laws of nature but is instead a human creation. Whereas common sense tells us that depression and quarks are facts of nature, constructionists argue that they are human products. Social scientists do social constructionist analyses because they want to reveal the social origins of what is commonly seen as "natural" rather than "social," a part of a given "reality" rather than a human creation.

What does constructionist analysis look like? The analysis of depression from their perspective provides a useful illustration. From a constructionist perspective, people generally take for granted that this mental illness is a medical problem to be treated by specialists in behavioral health (a term now often used in place of mental health). In other words, depression is the province of psychologists and psychiatrists, who use a variety of treatments, all founded on the notion that depression is a physiological illness. The constructionist argues that the contemporary conception of depression as an illness is widely assumed to be true because it has captured "reality." Therefore, the social origins of the idea of depression should be highlighted because they are less visible to people, including the diagnosed, their healers, and various relevant social circles and communities. In the constructionist view, depression is not an inevitable fact of human biology or psychology. There are alternative ways of defining or conceiving the phenomenon—that is, the behavioral or mental experiences or symptoms of depression—and some of them may be better than our existing conceptions. Moreover, the multitude of folk beliefs, medical practices, scientific findings, diagnostic categories, and the like that comprise "depression" have bad consequences. They expose people to antidepressant drugs whose long-term effects are unknown. Drugs make it cheaper for the managed-care system to prescribe pills rather than explore the psychological and especially the social origins of human problems. Psychotherapists treat patients at arm's length and pharmaceutical companies are enriched.

A variety of fields and topics have attracted the attention of social constructionists: quarks, madness, child abuse, weapons research, geology, and anthropology. Andrew Pickering[23] takes a strong constructionist stance in his book *Constructing Quarks,* arguing that even the discoveries of physicists are not inevitable products of the nature of things, but instead reflect the state of scientific knowledge and the questions scientists ask and can answer at particular times. Not surprisingly, physicists reacted with outrage to the idea that their theories and research could have led them to any other conclusions than the ones they reached. Sociological studies of child abuse have demonstrated how this phenomenon emerged as a social problem around 1961 and examined how the activities and claims of particular groups shaped its social definition.[24] Child abuse activists, again not surprisingly, also have reacted with some anger to suggestions that their conceptions of child abuse and the "facts" they propound may not be as real as they claim. The issue at hand is not whether child abuse is real, but when acting violently towards children became identified as abuse and a social problem. Unfortunately, this violence has been a consistent historical reality—it is the societal reaction to this violence that has changed in identifying this violence now as a social problem called "child abuse."

Whether a particular phenomenon is or is not "real" frequently becomes an issue in debates about the social constructionist approach. Natural scientists, not to mention most ordinary people, believe there is a "real world" and that science can discover solid and immutable facts about it. Quarks exist, and with the right ideas and techniques, they can be discovered. Constructionists say no: Quarks come into being as answers to the questions we raise about the physical world, as do phenomena such as depression or child abuse. As questions change or as the means of answering them become exhausted or new ones are invented, "reality" changes. Physics (and everything else), say constructionists, could have come out otherwise, had it asked different questions, developed other techniques, or been influenced by other historical circumstances.

How does the constructionist view of things relate to symbolic interactionism? From an interactionist perspective, human acts sculpt "reality" from "materials"—ideas, things, methods, knowledge—that people find as they seek to solve problems that confront them. Some of these materials people have already created, though they may not recognize their authorship when they find them. Other materials are not humanly created and lie beyond our control—or at least are out of our control at certain times. We respond to them on the basis of our ideas about them, but they do not respond to us on the basis of our ideas about them. What we sculpt this "reality" to be is probing and tentative, partial and incomplete, useful for some purposes but not others. Human beings doggedly pursue "reality," which refuses to sit or stay on command.

To go back to the example of depression, a symbolic interactionist might say—in partial agreement with constructionists—that a still-evolving body of ideas and practices has created something we now call "depression." The "materials" out of which past and contemporary people have sculpted the phenomenon of depression come to us from many sources: religious beliefs and concepts, the theories and practices of psychiatry and psychopharmacology, popular ideas about why people are sad and why they have the right to be happy. A variety of individuals and social groups—sufferers, healers, insurance companies, do-gooders, and government regulators—have created the concept of depression. Some symbolic interactionists would go further and argue that the sculpting and the sculptors encounter not just materials that other humans have created and foisted on the present, but that now and then they strike a hard place that does not so readily yield to their sculpted ideas about it. Therapists and their patients talk and talk and talk to no avail, but a few weeks of Prozac alters the serotonin reuptake process in ways not well understood that suddenly makes therapy effective. Sometimes, individuals know how happy they ought to be and know they are not, and discover they never can be, no matter what therapy they are given.[25]

Social constructionists and symbolic interactionists alike argue that it makes no sense to say that depression is "real" or "not real." It does makes sense to say that people have carved out the idea of depression as they have sought to cope with what appears to be a widespread human affliction. Human actions have created a set of ideas and practices, and some of these practices work some of the time, some work at other times, and some never do but persist nonetheless. The "reality" that psychopharmacology is beginning to carve out is gaining favor over the "reality" inherited from religion or psychiatry, for a host of reasons: Pills work as well as or better than talk, pills are cheaper, and taking pills and getting well is a major cultural script for illness and recovery. But it also makes sense to say that the "reality" carved out by those who treat depression with medication is itself incomplete and will remain so, however much psychiatrists take umbrage at this idea. Theories of how serotonin and other neurotransmitters affect what we call "depression" also encounter obstacles, in part because the socially constructed category of "depression" may combine a number of different problems in the brain. This is why, in fact, many students of so-called depression have concluded that it is not one disease but several, and that treating depression is the wrong way to conceive of and treat the affliction. Perhaps the most useful illness categories might be derived from various drugs and their effects. By this light, one would not be depressed, but rather one would have the disease that Prozac, Xanax, or Klonopin treats.[26]

Postmodernism

An influential perspective that has recently shaped the scholarly environment, not only for symbolic interactionism and social psychology, but also for most other perspectives and disciplines, is postmodernism.[27] This diverse and sometimes elusive set of ideas emerged from European philosophy and social theory starting in the 1960s. Its view of what the human world is like is accompanied by a strong critique of social science (including symbolic interactionism) as a way of producing knowledge. Though this perspective is difficult to summarize, some account of it is nevertheless necessary to understand contemporary symbolic interactionism.

Postmodernism is a broad effort to challenge the assumptions, theories, and methods that the social sciences take for granted. Its critique rests partly on the belief that the human world after World War II has been drastically transformed. Mass communications and the development of a culture of consumption, for example, have transformed everyday life. People are overwhelmed by such modern technologies as the computer, iPods, Blackberries, and cell phones. They have become obsessed with consumption, not (as they think) because they really want or need or will use the things they crave, but in order to assure themselves of their own reality and social worth. They live, according to French philosopher Jean Baudrillard, amidst a "hyperreality," having lost the capacity to distinguish between what is real and what is an illusion. Symbols, Baudrillard says, no longer stand for things, but only for other symbols. Postmodernists assert that the world had changed so greatly by the late twentieth century that social science became incapable of understanding it or communicating its understanding in ways that make sense to people.

Symbolic interactionism postulates a self-conscious individual who perceives situations, makes choices, and acts. In contrast, postmodernism views the active, deciding individual not as a reality that any theory must contend with, but rather as an illusion. It is a product of ideology—of our ideas about the social world and our belief in the individual. In other words, we—meaning symbolic interactionists and other social scientists as well as ordinary people—believe in the deciding and acting individual not because such a thing exists, but because our systems of ideas force us to believe in this kind of being. Postmodernists hold that the self, which is an object of great importance to symbolic interactionists, to other social psychologists, and to the modern culture that produced these disciplines, has disappeared—if, indeed, it ever really existed. To put it another way, the postmodern critique accepts the proposition, discussed earlier, that the individual is a social product but not the corresponding idea that society is a human product. In the contemporary world, this illusion is not only untrue but also irrelevant. That is, the idea of an autonomous and independent self—the term postmodernists often use is "the subject"—just cannot account for the way people live and experience themselves in the contemporary world.

One of the changes that most preoccupies postmodernists—and they view it positively— is the decline of what they call grand narratives. A grand narrative is any overarching account or story that seeks to explain the nature of the world or of human experience in sweeping and singular terms. A belief in progress—the idea that human history moves inexorably toward greater knowledge and power and better living conditions—constitutes a grand narrative. The theology of Judaism that sees the scope of human history leading to the advent of a messiah, and the theology of Christianity that states that the messiah has already come and we are awaiting his return are examples of grand narratives. Science itself—the conviction that human beings can know their world and assemble a comprehensive and true picture of it—is likewise a grand or master narrative. Such narratives direct us to perceive and believe in certain "facts"—that contemporary people live longer and better lives, for example, or that salvation requires the acceptance of Jesus Christ. But these so-called facts are significant—indeed, we only see them as facts—because we already believe in the truth of the theory on which they are based. Believing in progress leads us to see certain "facts"—such as people leading longer, healthier lives—and we then take those "facts" as evidence for the theory that has produced them.

For postmodernists, all narratives are essentially equal. That is, there is no basis for deciding that one narrative is true and the others are false. In their words, one narrative should not be "privileged" over any other. This attitude applies as much to scientific knowledge as it does to other forms. Hence, the grand narrative of evolution should be accorded no special place, nor should that of any particular religious tradition. Each claim to "truth," postmodernists argue, reflects what the German philosopher Nietzsche called the "will to power." Knowledge is not neutral, in this view, but always a source of power over others. To claim to speak "the truth" is to assert power, and typically claims by one group or another to know "the truth" conceal the goals and interests of such groups. The "truth" of religion or the "truth" of science, in other words, represents not just a desire for power in society but also the concealment of the interests of religion or science in holding power.

Claims to possess the truth conceal the interests of their claimants because they are embedded in what postmodernists call "discourse." Broadly speaking, the concept of discourse refers to characteristic ways of conceiving, speaking, and writing about things. We can think of science—or, for that matter, symbolic interactionism—as a discourse that entails a set of terms and concepts, ways of seeing and thinking about the world, propositions and ideas, and—perhaps most important—texts. The discourse of symbolic interactionism, for example, has produced such texts as George Herbert Mead's *Mind, Self, and Society* and Herbert Blumer's *Symbolic Interactionism.* These texts embody the interactionist way of seeing, speaking, and writing about the social world. Such texts always conceal an ideology, a set of beliefs that are not based on any empirical evidence, but only on the interests and preferences of people holding them.

Symbolic interactionists do share some suppositions with postmodernists, including the conviction that knowledge is relative; the belief that to understand narratives, we must "situate" them in the social contexts that produce them; and the understanding that discourses shape our views of reality and are not merely reflections of reality. Based on pragmatism, symbolic interactionism conceives of knowledge not as fixed and final, but as always evolving and changing, a response to the need to solve problems and overcome obstacles rather than a socially neutral quest for objective truth. Moreover, the postmodernist view that the self is an artifact of our ways of thinking about the social world to some extent mirrors the symbolic interactionist view of the self as an ongoing, mutable product of social interaction rather than a fixed entity. For interactionists, the self is not a structure located solely within the individual person but arises and exists in a social space that person shares with others. It is, in a basic sense, always something in the process of being created rather than something that gets created and then simply exists as an unchanging and invariant entity.

However there are also major points of difference between postmodernism and symbolic interactionism. First, interactionists argue that the self is an acting subject and a product of discourse. Postmodernism inclines toward a view of the person as nothing more or less than an artifact of modern discourses, whether those of religion or social science or consumer capitalism. If we see the individual person as making decisions or resisting social constraints, it is because our discourse and our ideologies force us to see things this way. In truth, postmodernists say, people do not create discourses; rather, discourses create people. Interactionists say, no, the person is not merely a fiction constructed by discourse but an active and creative constructor of that discourse. People confront obstacles and problems, they survey their circumstances, they consider alternatives, and they act to overcome these obstacles and solve problems. In doing so, they exercise creativity and do not merely speak the lines that discourse hands them.

Second, interactionists believe there is an empirical world that resists human actions. Interactionists grant that human ideas about the reality of this empirical world are inevitably imperfect and incomplete. In that sense, as social constructionists argue, "reality" is socially constructed, and there will never be a full or final knowledge of that reality, because as human interests and problems change, the "reality" they construct will change. Nonetheless, the empirical world is not merely a social construction founded on discourse. Problems do not disappear when we try to think them away. Religions that promise a better life in the hereafter nonetheless have followers in this world who have to be fed, clothed, and housed. Indeed, religions that seek to hasten the hereafter by encouraging their members to martyrdom or suicide end up with dead members but with no evidence that the hereafter exists. There is, in other words, an obdurate, resisting empirical world that does not roll over and play dead in the face of human constructions of it.

Symbolic interactionists do not claim to possess the absolute truth, nor do they think such a thing exists. Indeed, symbolic interactionists often argue that the postmodernist critique of the modern quest for absolute truth and morality represents a rather belated discovery of something pragmatists discovered a century ago. At the same time, many interactionists grant that postmodernism has developed some useful ideas and that its critique is worth attending to despite its decidedly extreme conclusions.

Major Tenets of Symbolic Interactionism

So, what is the essence of symbolic interactionism? Although there is more than one version of symbolic interactionism, most symbolic interactionists subscribe to the following general principles:[28]

- The task of social psychology is to develop a theory of action.

Like all sociologists, interactionists are interested in patterned regularities of human social life. Human conduct is social and cannot be explained merely as the result of idiosyncratic individual efforts. The fact is that our conduct does have a great deal of regularity; it is, as sociologists say, socially structured. But symbolic interactionists also believe that patterns and regularities cannot be fully grasped without understanding the social processes that create them. The regularities of social class or gender, for example, do not persist of their own accord or through sheer inertia but because human beings actively construct conduct in particular ways.

- Conduct depends on the creation and maintenance of meaning.

Unlike behavioral psychologists, who see meaning as either nonexistent or irrelevant, symbolic interactionists say that conduct is predicated on meaning. Unlike many sociologists who believe that culture and society dictate meanings to people, interactionists see meaning as variable and emergent. Meaning arises and is transformed as people define and act in situations; it is not merely handed down unchanged by culture. This emphasis on meaning "means" several things.

First, that people act with plans and purposes—that when they get in the car or speak words of love to someone, they do so with purposes in mind. Human conduct is directed toward objects and always looks toward some goal or purpose. People do not always pursue their purposes single-mindedly once they set their conduct in motion, for they are often deflected from their intended paths by obstacles or more appealing objects. Nor are people conscious of their purposes or of how they will attain them at every moment, for much of what they do depends on habit. When I get in the car to go to the store, I do not have to think constantly of the store or of the techniques of automobile driving I have learned. Habit takes over many tasks. I may sometimes speak words of love out of habit, not really intending what I am saying.

Second, the interactionist approach emphasizes that "meaning" and "intention" are two sides of the same coin. For symbolic interactionists, meaning lies in intentions and actions, and not in some ethereal realm of pure meanings or interpretations. Meaning is found in conduct, both in conduct that is overt and therefore visible to others, and in plans and purposes that are formulated and verbalized only silently and are not observed by others. Our conduct is meaningful because it is fundamentally purposeful; it can be purposeful because it rests on meaning.

Third, symbolic interactionists stress the possibility of meaning being transformed, and they recognize individual as well as shared meanings. Clearly, human beings are restricted to certain kinds of meaning by the words they learn, for words represent the objects they can imagine. People cannot act toward that which they cannot name. But symbolic interactionists say not only that humans live in a named world but also that naming is an activity that is central to the way they approach the world. People have the capacity to think of new ways to act by inventing new objects—new names. Although they may not do so frequently, they have the capacity to do so, and this guarantees that sometimes they will do so. Faced with novel situations or obstacles to conduct under way, human beings think of alternative goals and alternative methods. Thus, the meanings that inform how we act are never fixed or final, but emerge and change as we go about our affairs. These meanings—the objects of our actions—are personal as well as social, for human beings easily learn to pursue goals that are inimical to the goals that others pursue.

• Conduct is self-referential.

The individual human being is both an acting subject and an object in his or her own experience. Unlike other animals, who regard the world from the center of their own being, but can never themselves be fully a part of the picture, human beings have self-consciousness. They act toward themselves with purpose much as they act toward the external world with purpose. They take themselves—their feelings, their interests, their images of self—into account as they act.

The self is a valued and crucial human object, a major source of the purposes that people bring to their environment. Human beings do not merely wish to act in concert with others to secure the things they are taught by culture to value, but they also wish to find a sense of security and place—a sense of social identity—by integration into group life. They do not merely take themselves into account as they act, but also want to develop and sustain coherent images of themselves. They also want to attach a positive value to the self, to regard themselves favorably, to maintain and enhance their self-esteem.

Consciousness of self thus confers not only the capacity to exert control over conduct, but also to make the self an important focus of conduct. Human beings are capable of very precise social coordination, and can consider their own acts from the vantage point of the group as a whole and thus imagine the consequences of their acts for others. But they are also capable of considerable self-absorption and of putting their own interests before those of others. One can attain a coherent self and maintain self-esteem by cheerful cooperation with the organized life of a community, but one can also obtain these ends through more individualistic means.

• People form conduct as they interact with one another.

Psychologists, particularly the learning theorists, typically emphasize the individual's history of rewards and reinforcements as a way of explaining individual conduct. Many sociologists emphasize the determining effects of roles, norms, social class, and other aspects of our membership in society. The former often seem to depict a human being imprisoned within his or her own previous patterns of action and reward; the latter seem to depict an individual fully shaped and determined by society and culture. Without denying the importance of either individual histories of reward or of social and cultural variables, symbolic interactionists emphasize that conduct is formed in real time as people form plans and purposes, take themselves into account, and interact with one another.

Most human acts, interactionists think, are not individual acts but social acts, requiring the coordinated efforts of several individuals. Although individual capabilities affect the ability of individuals to perform their parts in social life, the actual performance of such actions as shaking hands or delivering a lecture is sustained not just by individual skills but also by their maintenance in a social setting. The audience is as important to the lecturer as his or her own speaking skills—a disinterested audience can flatten even the liveliest speaker. Although society hands down models for the social acts that we perform, these acts do not persist by themselves, but only because interacting people use their understandings of these acts as templates to reproduce them. A handshake exists not only in a name or an idea but also in the actual pressing of one sweaty palm to another.

Symbolic interactionists thus regard the actual outcomes of any given episode of social interaction as potentially novel. Most of the time, we human beings shake hands or deliver or hear lectures in a routine fashion. It is unusual for a social encounter to follow a truly novel course, but not impossible. Human beings do encounter situations they have not faced before; they find one obstacle or another blocks their paths; they misunderstand one another, failing to define situations as others do. In these and a variety of other ways, routine situations can become novel. People must find new meanings—new purposes and new methods—and they must reach into their stock of individual skills and socially acquired knowledge for general principles that can help them deal with novel situations. Thus, skills learned in other contexts are generalized as people encounter problematic situations; roles that cannot be performed in the routine way are performed in new ways.

• Culture shapes and constrains conduct, but it is also the product of conduct.

In common with other sociologists, symbolic interactionists emphasize the prior existence and impact of society and culture. We humans are born into an already existing society and culture, and we are quickly swept into its flow. We are surrounded by others who define reality for us, showing us the objects in their world and in some ways requiring us to make them our own. The child, for example, learns that there is a God, or that there are many Gods, and that one must tread carefully in his, her, or their presence.

We human beings however do not have to reproduce the society and culture that we inherit, and sometimes we do not. Regardless of what is at issue—belief in the powers of the Gods, or that to drink cold beer is important, or that we should be faithful to a spouse— the persistence of a belief or social practice rests on individual and collective action. Society is not a self-perpetuating, autonomous system of roles or social relationships. Rather, as Herbert Blumer said, society consists of people interacting with one another. Culture is not an invariant set of lessons from the past but an environment in which we all live, an environment composed of objects whose persistence depends on our continuing to take them into account, even as our survival depends on coming to terms with them.

Endnotes

1. William McDougall, *Introduction to Social Psychology* (London: Methuen, 1908).

2. Edward A. Ross, *Social Psychology* (New York: Macmillan, 1908).

3. See Gordon W. Allport, "The Historical Background of Modern Social Psychology," in *The Handbook of Social Psychology,* vol. I, ed. Gardner Lindzey and Elliot Aronson (Reading, MA: Addison-Wesley, 1968), pp. 1–80.

4. Solomon Asch, "Effects of Group Pressure upon the Modification and Distortion of Judgments," in *Groups, Leadership, and Men,* ed. H. Guetzkow (Pittsburgh: Carnegie Press, 1951), pp. 177–190.

5. Stanley Milgram, *Obedience to Authority* (New York: Harper & Row, 1974). See the documentary film Milgram made of these experiments if you want to see how the experiment in general (recommended) and how authentic the shocks appear to be.

6. See Jerry Burger, "Replicating Milgram: Would People Still Obey Today?" *American Psychologist,* 64 (2009): 1–11.

7. See Susan J. Fiske and Shelley E. Taylor, *Social Cognition,* 2nd ed. (New York: McGraw Hill, 1991).

8. For a survey of sociological social psychology, see *Sociological Perspectives on Social Psychology,* ed. Karen S. Cook, Gary Alan Fine, and James S. House (Boston: Allyn & Bacon, 1995). This book is the successor to an earlier book with similar goals; see *Social Psychology: Sociological Perspectives,* ed. Morris Rosenberg and Ralph H. Turner (New York: Basic Books, 1981).

9. Peter Berger and Thomas Luckmann discuss this issue as the dialectic of individual and society: "Society is a human product. Society is an objective reality. Man is a social product." See their *Social Construction of Reality* (New York: Doubleday Anchor, 1967).

10. The literature on pragmatism and symbolic interactionism is vast. For a review and analysis, see Dmitri N. Shalin, "Pragmatism and Social Interactionism," *American Sociological Review* 51 (February 1986): 9–29. For a discussion of Mead as a social reformer in the political context of his time, see Shalin, "G. H. Mead, Socialism, and the Progressive Agenda," *American Journal of Sociology* 93 (January 1988): 913–951. For other views of Mead and his ideas, see the commemorative issue on Mead in *Symbolic Interaction* 4 (Fall 1981) and another issue of *Symbolic Interaction* 12 (Spring 1989). Those interested in the relationship between pragmatism and critical theory should see "Special Feature: Habermas, Pragmatism, and Critical Theory" in *Symbolic Interaction* 15 (Fall 1992). For a historical review of Chicago sociology, see Berenice M. Fisher and Anselm L. Strauss, "Interactionism," in *A History of Sociological Analysis,* ed. Tom Bottomore and Robert A. Nisbet (New York: Basic, 1978), Chapter 12. For an excellent discussion of pragmatism and sociological theory, see Hans Joas, *Pragmatism and Social Theory* (Chicago: University of Chicago Press, 1993). See also by Joas, *The Creativity of Action* (Chicago: University of Chicago Press, 1996). For a review of developments in symbolic interaction, see Gary Alan Fine, "The Sad Demise, Mysterious Disappearance, and Glorious Triumph of Symbolic Interactionism," *Annual Review of Sociology* 19 (1993): 61–87; for a discussion of the emergence of a new "Chicago School," see *A Second Chicago School: The Development of a Postwar American Sociology,* ed. Gary

Alan Fine (Chicago: University of Chicago Press, 1995). Also see David R. Maines, *The Faultline of Consciousness: A View of Interactionism in Sociology* (New York: Aldine de Gruyter, 2001). For reviews of antecedents of symbolic interactionism, see Robert Prus, "Ancient Forerunners" and Larry T. Reynolds, "Intellectual Precursors," in *Handbook of Symbolic Interactionism,* ed. Larry T. Reynolds and Nancy J. Herman-Kinney (Walnut Creek, CA: AltaMira Press, 2003), pp. 19–58.

11. See George Herbert Mead, *Mind, Self, and Society* (Chicago: University of Chicago Press, 1934) and *The Philosophy of the Act* (Chicago: University of Chicago Press, 1938). Also see George Herbert Mead: *On Social Psychology,* ed. Anselm L. Strauss (Chicago: University of Chicago Press, 1964); Gary A. Cook, George Herbert Mead: *The Making of a Social Pragmatist* (Urbana: University of Illinois Press, 1993); David L. Miller, George Herbert Mead (Austin: University of Texas Press, 1973); John D. Baldwin, *George Herbert Mead: A Unifying Theory for Sociology* (Beverly Hills, CA: Sage, 1986); *Women and Symbolic Interaction,* ed. Mary Jo Deegan (Boston: Allen and Unwin, 1987); Hans Joas, *G. H. Mead: A Contemporary Reexamination of His Thought* (Cambridge, MA: MIT Press, 1985).

12. The major statement of social learning theory comes from Albert Bandura. See his *Social Learning Theory* (Englewood Cliffs, NJ: Prentice-Hall, 1977).

13. General discussions of Freudian theory and social psychology can be found in C. S. Hall and G. Lindzey, "The Relevance of Freudian Psychology and Related Viewpoints for the Social Sciences," in *The Handbook of Social Psychology,* 2nd ed., ed. G. Lindzey and E. Aronson (Reading, MA: Addison-Wesley, 1968), pp. 245–319.

14. Donald L. Carveth, "Psychoanalysis and Social Theory: The Hobbesian Problem Revisited," *Psychoanalysis and Contemporary Thought* 7 (1984): 43–98.

15. For presentations of exchange theory, see George C. Homans, *Social Behavior: Its Elementary Forms,* rev. ed. (New York: Harcourt Brace Jovanovich, 1974); Peter M. Blau, *Exchange and Power in Social Life* (New York: Wiley, 1964); Richard M. Emerson, "Social Exchange Theory," in Rosenberg and Turner, *Social Psychology,* pp. 30–65 (Note 8); and Linda D. Molm and Karen S. Cook, "Social Exchange and Exchange Networks," in Cook, Fine, and House, *Sociological Perspectives on Social Psychology,* pp. 209–235 (Note 8). For essays discussing rational choice theory, see *Rational Choice Theory: Advocacy and Critique,* ed. James S. Coleman and Thomas J. Fararo (Newbury Park, CA: Sage, 1992).

16. Molm and Cook, "Social Exchange and Exchange Networks" (Note 15).

17. In *Social Construction of Reality,* Berger and Luckmann (Note 9) present an essentially phenomenological perspective. For the work of Schutz, see *Alfred Schutz: On Phenomenology and Social Relations,* ed. Helmut Wagner (Chicago: University of Chicago Press, 1970). For a symbolic interactionist view of ethnomethodology, see Mary J. Gallant and Sheryl Kleinman, "Symbolic Interactionism versus Ethnomethodology," *Symbolic Interaction* 6 (1) (1983): 1–18. See also John Heritage, *Garfinkel and Ethnomethodology* (London: Blackwell, 1984); Douglas W. Maynard and Steven F. Clayman, "Ethnomethodology and Conversation Analysis," in Reynolds and Herman-Kinney, pp. 173–202 (Note 10).

18. For a discussion of conversational analysis and its relationship to symbolic interactionism, see Deirdre Boden, "People Are Talking: Conversation Analysis and Symbolic Interaction," in *Symbolic Interaction and Cultural Studies*, ed. Howard S. Becker and Michal M. McCall (Chicago: University of Chicago Press, 1990), pp. 244–274. For an analysis of conversational style and the self, see Susan E. Chase, *Ambiguous Empowerment: The Work Narratives of Women School Superintendents* (Amherst: University of Massachusetts Press, 1995). Also see Douglas W. Maynard and Marilyn R. Whalen, "Language, Action, and Social Interaction," in Cook, Fine, and House, *Sociological Perspectives on Social Psychology,* pp. 149–175 (Note 8).

19. See Judith A. Howard, "Social Cognition," in Cook, Fine, and House, *Sociological Perspectives on Social Psychology,* pp. 90–117 (Note 8).

20. Howard, "Social Cognition," p. 93 (Note 19).

21. See for example, T. Gilovich, *How We Know What Isn't So* (NY: Free Press, 1993); A. Tversky, & D. Kahneman, "The Belief in the Law of Small Numbers," *Psychological Bulletin* (1971): 105–110; A. Tversky & D. Kahneman, "Availability: A Heuristic for Judging Frequency and Probability," *Cognitive Psychology* (1973): 207–232; A. Tversky & D. Kahneman, "Judgment and Uncertainty: Heuristics and Biases," *Science* 185 (1974): 1124–1131.

22. Ian Hacking, *The Social Construction of What?* (Cambridge, MA: Harvard University Press, 1999). See also a review of this book by John P. Hewitt, "The Social Construction of Social Construction," *Qualitative Sociology* 24 (Fall 2001): 417–423.

23. Andrew Pickering, *Constructing Quarks: A Sociological History of Particle Physics* (Chicago: University of Chicago Press, 1984).

24. See Richard J. Gelles, "The Social Construction of Child Abuse," *American Journal of Orthopsychiatry* 45 (1975): 363–371. Also see John M. Johnson, "Horror Stories and the Construction of Child Abuse," in *Images of Issues: Typifying Contemporary Social Problems,* ed. Joel Best (New York: Aldine de Gruyter, 1995), pp. 17–31.

25. See John P. Hewitt, Michael Fraser, and L. B. Berger, "Is it Me or Is it Prozac? Antidepressants and the Construction of Self," in *Pathology and the Postmodern,* ed. Dwight Fee (London: Sage, 2000), pp. 163–185; Hewitt, "The Social Construction of Self-Esteem," in *Handbook of Positive Psychology,* ed. C. R. Snyder and S. J. Lopez (New York: Cambridge University Press, 2001), pp. 135–147.

26. Peter D. Kramer, *Listening to Prozac* (New York: Viking, 1993).

27. For a variety of views and arguments on postmodernism and symbolic interactionism, see Patricia T. Clough, "A Response to Farberman's Distinguished Lecture: A Closer Encounter with Postmodernism," *Symbolic Interaction* 15 (3): 359–366; Harvey A. Farberman, "Symbolic Interactionism and Postmodernism: Close Encounters of a Dubious Kind," *Symbolic Interaction* 14 (1991): 471–488; Norman K. Denzin, "Postmodern Social Theory," *Sociological Theory* 4 (1986): 194–204; Michael A. Katovich and W. A. Reese, "Postmodern Thought in Symbolic Interaction: Reconstructing Social Inquiry in Light of Late-Modern Concerns," *Sociological Quarterly* 34 (3): 391–411; David R. Maines, "On Postmodernism, Pragmatism, and Plasterers: Some Interactionist Thoughts and Queries," *Symbolic Interaction* 19 (4): 323–340; Ken Plummer, "Staying in the Empirical World: Symbolic Interactionism and Postmodernism," *Symbolic Interaction* 13 (2): 155–160; and Dmitri N. Shalin, "Modernity, Postmodernism, and Pragmatist Inquiry: An Introduction," *Symbolic Interaction* 16 (4): 303–332.

28. For a statement of an avowedly more social structural version of symbolic interactionism, see Sheldon Stryker, *Symbolic Interactionism: A Social Structural Version* (Menlo Park, CA: Benjamin/Cummings, 1980); Sheldon Stryker and Anne Statham, "Symbolic Interactionism and Role Theory," in *The Handbook of Social Psychology,* 3rd ed., ed. Gardner Lindzey and Elliot Aronson (New York: Random House, 1985); and Sheldon Stryker, "The Vitalization of Symbolic Interactionism," *Social Psychology Quarterly* 50 (1) (1987): 83–94.

CHAPTER

2

Basic Concepts of Symbolic Interactionism

We are all familiar with the signs near amusement parks and mall entrances that post directional maps with the markers "You are here." Those "You are here" markers situate visitors geographically by specifying their spatial relationships to adjacent locations. Given those bearings, people know where they are and where they might go. We have those maps to navigate physical environments, but what about when we confront situations where we could use equivalent guidance about how to act in social environments? What would "You are here" maps look like for social settings?

To develop those social maps, we would have to identify specific roles, values, and norms for social situations that would orient people about how to act appropriately within them. If we delineated values, norms, and roles for established social settings (like classrooms, parties, a job interview, a doctor's office, and workplaces), people could read those maps, and then choose among behaviors to direct them to their goals. Social "You are here" markers would be complex in having to describe the social expectations, appropriate demeanor, and understandings that different people would bring to settings. While we don't write out such social "You are here" maps for every social situation, there are settings where we do, such as when visiting sacred religious sites. However, we could hypothetically write out "You are here" maps for an almost infinite range of social settings. In doing so, we are delineating relationships between self (you) and society (here). Symbolic interactionists have developed an array of concepts that allow individuals to understand those relationships between self and society. Put into practice, these concepts expose the meanings and interpretations that people use to familiarize and situate themselves and their actions in various social settings. We introduce some of these concepts in this chapter and illustrate how people implement them in engaging in meaningful actions and behaviors.

George H. Mead, Herbert Blumer, and several subsequent generations of symbolic interactionists developed those aforementioned ideas and have provided a foundational perspective for conceiving social realities.[1] Grasping this bedrock of symbolic interactionist thinking will enable you to analyze social life in progressively higher resolution. We will base subsequent chapters on these foundational ideas in order to move from presenting theory to illustrating their contemporary applications in research by current symbolic interactionist scholars. To that end, we introduce the concept of the *symbol* in detail. People use symbols to act purposefully in and toward a world of objects (rather than merely responding to stimuli) and to define and redefine the situations that they encounter. Symbols are important aspects of interactions with others, of making roles that accomplish individual and collective goals, and in taking and enacting social roles, all of which enable people to imagine and anticipate the perspectives and reactions of others to potential lines of action.

Symbols

The vital conceptual building block that symbolic interactionists base their analyses of human conduct on is the concept of the *symbol,* or, as Mead called it, the significant symbol. To reiterate, a *significant symbol* is a vocal or other type of gesture that arouses the same response in the person using it as in people to whom it is directed. Symbolic interactionists are especially interested in how human beings interact with one another on the basis of perceiving similar meanings in symbols. How people respond to one another depends on making meaningful interpretations of symbols, and not just on enacting conditioned, biologically based responses to stimuli. We must interpret; we engage in symbolic interaction. To apply this perspective, we must explain the nature of symbols and the implications of using them in more detail.

The Nature of Symbols

We begin with the idea that signs influence behavior.[2] A *sign* is something that stands for something else—that is, an event or thing that takes the place of or signifies some other event or thing. Smoke, for example, is a sign of fire. If we see smoke on the horizon, we assume that there is an accompanying fire. When we hear a ringtone, we anticipate a text message or phone call. In both examples, a thing or event is important because it signifies some other thing or event.

A sign exists only when an organism is capable of perceiving and responding to the sign. Smoke is a sign of fire because various animals can perceive it, somehow relate it to fire, and then respond in some way. A human being might call the fire department or the forest service, on the theory that where there is smoke there is fire. Experience convinces us that when one event is accompanied regularly by another, that one can serve as a reliable sign of the other.

How do the signs that we learn influence behavior? The signs we learn to respond to often occur before or at a distance from the important events with which they are associated. A ringtone and/or a caller id allow people to prepare responses before the actual necessity to type, speak a response, or ignore the call. Signs enable us to anticipate and learn to act in ways that may well be more effective than if we relied only on spontaneous responses. People have more complex creative capacities concerning signs than animals do. We can create signs and produce things or events that are associated with other things or events. Our cell phones can beep, play classical music, or recite a poem as a ringtone.

Humans introduce a higher level of social complexity into signs because we have the ability to create signs that other groups can share and learn in a group context. We can teach, use and manipulate signs. We even create industries around them, as with ringtones. Socially complex signs differ from natural signs (smoke) and have important consequences.

Our socially constructed signs—more properly termed *conventional signs*—are what symbolic interactionists refer to when they mention symbols. A symbol does not have to have a natural connection with what it represents. The symbol has an entirely arbitrary relationship with what it represents, a relationship that is created and is shared among different cultures and peoples. Consider the vast number of nonverbal gestures that people use to swear at others. In Iraq, people point the soles of their shoes at you; in the United States, we raise just our middle fingers; in Greece, a thumbs-up accompanied with a sweep of the arm does the trick. These gestures have a contextual artificial relationship with what they represent—there is no universally accepted meaning. In the United States, a thumbs-up symbolizes the exact opposite of its Grecian cousin. We create and empower symbols with social meanings.

Human language constitutes the most important and powerful set of symbols. Words name various things, relationships, and events with no inherent, natural connection with the things whose place they take. *House,* for example, is a symbol that names a particular kind of structure that humans inhabit, but the sound of the word has nothing whatever to do with the structure. One might just as well call the house a *maison,* or a *casa,* or a *haus,* which is, of course, precisely what non-English speakers do. The particular word that denotes this structure is meaningful only within a community of speakers of that particular language, who share agreement about what the word signifies. The arbitrariness of naming is difficult to understand because we assume that the symbols that we use have a natural relationship to what they represent. However, the very ability of so many words to denote similar meanings implies that meaning can be associated arbitrarily, and accepting the word's meaningfulness involves agreement among people rather than an assessment of fact. A word has significance—or meaning—only if the individual speaker can learn to associate the word with the same things or events, as do other speakers of the language. As is the case with all signs, symbols elicit responses from those who have learned to respond to them.

Symbols have two additional characteristics that make them a particularly important form of sign. First, symbols have public meaning. When a word is uttered, it is heard by the one using it as well as by others who participate in its meaning. Hence, uttering a word in response to an environmental event has the effect of taking the individual's private response to the event and making it a public response. A second key aspect of symbols is that people can employ them even in the absence of the things they signify. Symbols do not have to be physically tied to their referents. We can use words—*fire, house, baseball*—even when the objects or events they designate are nowhere in sight. We can invoke symbols well in advance of the appearance of what they designate as well as after the objects or events have disappeared.

The Consequences of Symbols

Developing the capacity to use symbols, however it came about, is perhaps the single most important event in the evolution of the human species.[3] Although some scholars would argue that we can teach our primate cousins, the great apes, to employ rudimentary symbols, human beings remain the only species in which the development of symbols has gone so far that our very evolution as a species centers on this fact.[4] Our existence as a species depends on our ability to organize our responses to the environment using symbols. To understand how and why this is the case, we need to look in greater detail at the consequences of symbols for human conduct and the relationship of human beings to their environment.

Three facts are key to the impact of symbol using on human beings:

1. Symbols transform the very nature of the environment in which the human species lives.
2. Symbols make it possible for the behavioral dispositions, or attitudes, of one individual to be reproduced in another person.
3. Symbols make it possible for the individual to be a part of the very environment to which he or she responds.

Symbols transform the human environment, first, because they expand its scope both spatially and temporally. Animals can respond only to conventional signs that, for all practical purposes, are confined to an environment that is defined by how far and fast they can travel and by the nature and acuteness of their senses. Alternatively, human beings can use symbols as a means of imagining what is not present but might be or what was once present and may appear again at some point in the future. Because symbols are not tied to the actual presence of the things for which they stand, people can invoke them even when they are very distant in space or time. We can utter our children's names and thus evoke mental images of them and the feelings of affection they arouse in us, even though they are far away. We can remember scenes from childhood and also anticipate events that will, but have not yet, occurred. In other words, human beings can respond to things that are spatially and temporally distant because they can invoke the symbols for them. In doing so, they literally expand their world so as to encompass whatever they can imagine.

Symbols also transform the human environment by making it a named environment. In the simplest sense, names substitute for things and bring the external world inside our minds. Names also transform the environment from a relatively concrete and particular world into a relatively abstract and general one. Naming things, however, makes the environment considerably more general and abstract. To attach a name to a thing—to call a particular structure a "house," for example—is not only to label the thing but also to create a category into which similar things can be placed. *House* designates not merely a particular house, unique in the entire world, but also a category of things that share a set of attributes in common. The symbolic attitude, in other words, is a generalizing, abstracting attitude.

Symbols also transform the nature of the environment because they enable people to create things by creating names. The human environment does not consist of a finite set of tangible things to which language attaches names. Rather, the environment in which humans live and to which they must adapt includes a great many abstract and imaginary objects that have no tangible existence. *Love, liberty, responsibility,* and *respect* are names that English speakers use. But to what tangible things do they refer? We may take hugs and kisses as an indication of love, or meeting a deadline as an indication of responsibility, but clearly *love* and *responsibility* name something more abstract and far less tangible than these particulars. We speak of these things, and are convinced that they have a reality, but they do not have the same kind of existence as a dog or a house. The former are abstract, the latter concrete. The abstracting and generalizing quality of symbols, together with the fact that symbols are not tied closely or intrinsically to things, means that we can invent things by inventing names. Our social environments, as we know them, to a considerable extent, are the products of our names for them.

A second major consequence of symbols is their capacity to reproduce the behavioral dispositions or attitudes of one individual in one or more other individuals. Symbols are public and have meaning only because a community of speakers shares them. Moreover, because symbols can be invoked at will and even in the absence of the things they stand for, a symbol user may invoke a symbol, either as a way of imagining the presence of the signified or as a way of signaling its presence. As Mead pointed out, a significant symbol arouses in the person using it the same response as it does in the one to whom it is directed. When one person speaks a name and others hear it, they share a response to the symbol. The mental attitude of the symbol user is thus recreated in those who hear it.

A concrete illustration will help make this idea clear. Suppose a family is having dinner at home and one person says, "I smell something burning." In saying this, the individual symbolically designates or names some fact or condition in the environment to which he or she is inclined to respond in a certain way. In fact, the sentence itself strengthens and focuses the speaker's own response to the situation, for it is probably not until it is uttered that the person forms a clear inclination to act. But at the same time, the sentence arouses a similar inclination or range of inclinations in the others. They, like the speaker, feel a need to take action, that the source of the smell ought to be discovered and something done.

As this example suggests, symbolic communication consists of the arousal of shared responses among two or more individuals by using a symbol. In symbolic communication, the essentially involuntary sequence of responses of one animal to another is replaced by the voluntary use of symbols to arouse shared responses in a group of symbol users. Instead of merely responding to one another's acts, symbol users can respond jointly to a situation because the response of one can be recreated easily in another. Hearing someone say that something seems to be burning, I can adopt the same attitude of concern or urgency as the speaker did when he or she spoke. If I adopt the name a speaker uses, I can also adopt his or her disposition and orientation to act or not. I can share the cautious attitude of someone who alerts me to the possibility of danger by using the word *fire,* but I might also designate that person's response to the situation as a "mistake" or as a "joke." In other words, symbols make shared responses possible but do not guarantee them. It is precisely because people can invoke symbols without the presence of the things or events that they stand for, that we can be stuck distinguishing between truth and falsity, sincerity and deception, reality and illusion. Human beings participate in a world of shared meanings, a potentially tricky and deceptive world that often calls on them to interpret the symbols others use accurately. As we explore later in this book, people often try to persuade us to believe things that are not so; as a consequence, we must be wary to interpret the world more clearly than some might like.

Since organisms can create and use symbols to designate their external environment, they can also use them to designate (to name) one another as entities in their environment. Their propensity to do so leads to another tendency—namely, for individual symbol users to use their own names as designations for themselves. In this way, people have the symbolic capacity to make themselves a part of their own environment. Because an individual can name himself or herself, he or she can respond to and act toward himself or herself. We can conceive of ourselves as external objects in the environment. To use a name for oneself is to acquire a self and become one of the objects in the environment toward which the individual can act. The capacity to respond to oneself as a part of the world marks the dawning of self-consciousness. Because people are aware of themselves as a part of the world, they gain an important capacity for control over their own acts. Our ability to conceive of ourselves and other phenomena as external objects in the world links symbols and the actions people take on the basis of them.

Objects

Symbolic interactionists rely on George Herbert Mead's concept of the object to portray how people perceive and act on their environment. We experience an environment as a highly differentiated set of sensory experiences, not just as a microscopically perceived stream of stimuli. Human beings live in a world of nonmaterial objects—of symbolically designated things, ideas, people, activities, and purposes that extend far beyond the material world that we can see and touch.

What Is an Object?

Ordinarily, when we talk about an object, we mean something that has material existence—such as a table, a rock, or a screwdriver—that we can see or touch. The first definition of *object* found in the *Random House Dictionary,* for example, states that an object is "anything that is visible or tangible and is stable in form." After defining an object as something tangible, the dictionary lists four additional meanings:

> *2. anything that may be apprehended intellectually: objects of thought. 3. a person or thing with reference to the impression made on the mind or the feeling or emotion elicited in an observer: an object of curiosity and pity. 4. a thing, person or matter to which thought or action is directed: an object of medical investigation. 5. the end toward which effort is directed; goal; purpose.*

These additional definitions help convey an essential symbolic interactionist (and pragmatist) idea, which is that the intentions of acting human beings shape the very nature of the human environment. Human beings fashion a world of things and stimuli into a world of objects because they act with purpose toward them. Viewing objects as both created by human activity and as the goals of that activity has two important implications:

- People live in a world of objects, not of things or stimuli.
- People's conduct is oriented to goals and purposes.

In Herbert Blumer's words, from the standpoint of people acting at any given moment, "the environment consists only of the objects that given human beings recognize and know."[5] As this book is being read, the reader's environment consists of what he or she is immediately designating and acting toward, primarily these words—unless, say, it is a spring day and the reader is distracted or bored or daydreams. Distractions are always abundant, but only when people act purposefully and attend to a few of them do they get transformed into objects.

Physical things are only one category of object. Symbols, we stated, make it possible to designate things that are not present and even things that do not physically exist. A child, for example, can designate the shadows that play on the bedroom wall as ghosts and act toward them as if they were real—jumping under the covers or into his parents' bed for protection. The concept of an object is even more significant when we move from an individual to a social level of analysis. The child who treats shadows as ghosts has designated an imaginary object that is nonetheless treated much as any physical object. When the child acts toward the ghost by seeking parents' company and reassurance, the child and parents jointly create a new object. This new object—let us call it "reassurance"—is a social object created by a social act. The object comes into existence because parent and child act toward one another for the purpose of giving and receiving reassurance. The act is social because its object is social; that is, the parent and child coordinate their separate individual acts because each can keep the social object of "reassurance" in mind to represent the purpose of their conduct.

It may seem strange to think of something so abstract as "reassurance" as an object. Yet we indicate and act toward many such social objects in our daily lives, and we do so as if they were as real as any material thing. Jobs, marriages, political philosophies, love affairs, partiers, responsibilities, projects—the list could be extended indefinitely—are not material or tangible. Yet each exists and is made real in the coordinated actions of individuals toward it. "Responsibility" shapes our behavior, as when we work hard to fulfill an occupational obligation, even though no one can touch or taste responsibility.

This view of objects also shapes how symbolic interactionists view human motives and purposes. Both individually and socially, human action is typically oriented toward goals. More precisely, whether we speak of the individual as acting alone or in concert with others, actions typically "look toward" an end state or object. The child seeking parents' company on a windy night when the moon is full anticipates the completion of a joint action with them—namely, being reassured that the ghosts will not get him or her. Action generally moves toward an end state—toward the completion of an object. Bernard Meltzer, summarizing Mead's view of the object, wrote:

> *An object represents a plan of action. That is, an object doesn't exist for the individual in some preestablished form. Perception of any object has telescoped in it a series of experiences which one would have if he carried out the plan of action toward the object.*[6]

A world of objects surrounds the human being at every moment. These objects are not an inert set of things. They represent and remind us of a variety of experiences that we have and of motives and goals that we have. The objects that make up the human world embody the purposes and experiences human beings have in that world, and they invite us to act toward them in familiar ways.

Objects and Language

We are all born into a world of preexisting objects. The concepts of snow, automobiles, happiness, toothaches, beer, liberation, and thousands of others do not have to be freshly interpreted for the first time when individuals act. Rather, each person is born into a community of individuals who speak a particular language and who—by using this language to designate and act toward the world—also enclose us within it. When we learn the names of the things around us, we take it on faith that those things exist, that they are what they are called, and that they are important. This may not seem obvious in the case of concrete things, for many of our words seem simply to name the material things we can see and touch around us. The world of objects also contains abstract phenomena, such as the ideas of love and liberty, whose existence we must infer to believe.

Language is a repository of objects that have been important in the life of particular peoples. Despite that individuals are born into a world of preexisting objects, embodied in language and conversations, they are not imprisoned within this world. Objects are provided for us by language, but we can also create objects as we use language. Speech and written language give us the capacity to relate objects in the world to one another in ways that are familiar, but also in new and different ways. Language is not merely reproductive, but also creative of reality because we can coin and define new words. Language helps create new objects just as much as it embalms a world of objects that others created before us. Consider how the digital age has spawned a great many new words: DVD, iPod, MP3, tweeting, and blogging. The digital age has also introduced new objects and relationships into the world that require new language. Urban Dictionary (*www.urbandictionary.com/*) is a Web site that inventories some of the words that have been coined to describe experiences that technological innovations have generated. For example, they recently listed the term "social notworking" to describe people who busy themselves doing social networking at their jobs rather than their work, and "yellular" to describe when people think that raising their voices during a bad cell phone connection will somehow improve the reception. Of course, the continuity of a particular language and world of objects depends on us using that language. Objects exist through acts of speech; the objects that speech designate continue to exist only so long as they are discussed.

Acts and Social Acts

The concepts of acts and social acts represent the symbolic interactionists' view of how individuals organize their conduct in relation to objects in the environment. The act is an elementary unit of conduct that represents the smallest meaningful unit that we can abstract from the stream of human behavior. For behaviorists, as we pointed out in Chapter 1, the stimulus-response linkage is the basis for defining the basic unit of conduct. We suggested that this unit is too small, and that the symbolic interactionist's task is to specify a larger and more useful unit—the act. An act is a discrete unit of behavior. We may define an *act* as a functional unit of conduct with an identifiable beginning and end that is related to the organism's purposes and that is oriented toward one or more objects. An act is a useful definition that enables us to identify a slice of conduct to focus upon and whose structure we can describe.

Consider the example of the difficulties involved in trying to describe an individual's behavior during one day. That person's behavior involves constant activity, comprising a stream of conduct. We could describe the day that way, but an endless list of activity wouldn't be much of a description: "The person breathed in, then they breathed out. . . ." Instead, we make endless decisions about how to organize a description. We could start the description as a set of "things" the person did. We do this in describing our own individual behavior: When I got up this morning, for example, I first "went to the bathroom," then "washed and shaved," then "ate breakfast," then "checked e-mail," then had a "second cup of coffee," and then "went to my office" to write these words. In providing this description, I break up my stream of activity into a number of discrete acts and label each on the basis of some major purpose or object in relation to which I was acting. We take describing activities for granted but we actually do a great deal of organizing of reality in deciding what acts warrant description.

Phases of the Act

Acts begin and end, and our task is to examine what makes them begin, what moves them along, and what brings them to a conclusion. George Herbert Mead's analysis of the act provides a major foundation for completing this task. Mead found the beginnings of the act in what he termed *impulse,* and he examined acts as they proceed through stages of perception and manipulation to completion.[7]

An act starts with an impulse, which occurs when our existing adjustment or line of activity is disturbed. Imagine yourself in a social situation with a small group of people—perhaps a set of friends or acquaintances having pizza together while watching a television show. Everything is normal until you notice that the behavior of a group member seems unusual. Perhaps your eyes meet for a moment and a smile forms on the other's lips, or you detect what may be a glimmer of attraction in the other's eyes. When this happens, something is strikingly altered in your attitude toward the situation. Where you were previously focused on the game, your interest now shifts to the possible significance of the other's act. As you notice the other's smile or flirtatious glance, you experience an impulse to act. The other's act disturbed the situation for you—that is, a situation that was routine before is now disturbed. You feel an urge to act—to respond in some way to the other. You want to do something, and are ready—maybe to return the smile, to figure out what it might mean for your relationship with that person, maybe even to ignore it.

At any given moment, we are engaged in a particular line of conduct, but we have within us the capacity to respond to a great variety of stimuli, for there are many impulses striving to be released. The balance among our internal sensitivities changes from time to time; we may be very receptive to winks at one point but more interested in food at another. Sometimes we want sex; at other times erotic stimuli are less important and we wish to get a few hours of sleep. Given that a person becomes ready to act in response to a stimulus, what happens next? How do you respond to the other's smile or look?

Asking this question jumps the gun a bit, for we cannot talk about the results of an impulse until we examine how the stimulus is perceived. What object will you designate in response to the other's act? What is the goal of your own act, if any, toward the other? A stimulus alerts and sensitizes one to the need to act, but it does not itself define the object of the act. To act, you must interpret or designate the other's smile or touch in a meaningful way. You must attach a name to it and in so doing establish a goal for yourself. But doing so is at least potentially problematic. Does the smile have any meaning at all? Were you the intended object of the smile? Was the lingering look merely accidental?

How you respond to the other depends on your relationship to that person as well as to your internal condition. Suppose, for example, that you have a previously unspoken and unacknowledged romantic interest in the other. If so, you are likely to interpret the look as somehow indicative of the other's interest in you—and, therefore, as an act to which you should respond similarly. More generally, impulse and perception, as successive phases of the individual's act, are inextricably linked: The internal condition—in this instance your interest in the other—makes an external event a stimulus.

Assume, for example, that you are romantically or sexually interested in the other and that you interpret the look as an indication that the other is interested in you. The next phase of the act, which Mead labeled *manipulation,* requires an overt action. Suppose that you return the other's gaze, holding eye contact for longer than the usual time. This is the overt portion of the act—the external manifestation of a process that, until now, has gone on internally.

What happens next? It is possible—and from your perspective desirable—that the other responds positively to your look. Smiles deepen, the mutual gaze lengthens, and the two of you move closer together, or go off by yourselves, or hold hands, or do any of the countless things people do to confirm romantic interest. If this is the outcome, then the act has reached *consummation.* That is, your adjustment to the situation, which was disturbed by the other's look, is restored, and you can turn your attention back to the pizza or the game, albeit with a new hope for what might be in store later for the two of you. Or the two of you leave the situation and begin a new round of activity.

However, suppose your response to the other's look gets a different reaction. You lock eyes with the other only to find a quizzical, or worse, a disgusted look, in return. Uh Oh! Your adjustment is now problematic and it puts you on the track for another act whose object will be to get you out of this difficult situation. You quickly turn your eyes away, realizing that you have misinterpreted the other's gaze, and try to make yourself invisible.

For the person in this hypothetical situation, the other's look or touch is an object—something he or she must indicate to self and then act toward. The meaning of this object first lies in the individual's initial readiness to act toward it in a certain way. The meaning of the look or touch is not inherent, however, for it can be interpreted and acted toward in a variety of ways. Nor is one's understanding of another's look or touch merely a matter of remembering past occasions on which that person, or other persons, have looked and touched. We know from experience that looks and touches may have a variety of meanings. The other person in this example intends the look or touch in a certain way, anticipating a certain response to this act; but intent does not control interpretations.

For symbolic interactionists, then, meaning is anchored in behavior. The meaning of an act is neither fixed nor unchanging, but is determined in conduct as individuals act toward objects. As acts proceed, meaning can transform. Initial readiness to act toward an object in a given way does not mean that action will necessarily follow that course. One may change one's mind, redesignate the object, and act in a different way, or one may find that the act gets one nowhere, that one must adjust by getting ready to act differently. As the individual's actual conduct toward an object changes, the meaning of the object likewise changes.

In analyzing the individual's act in this way, Mead calls attention to the necessity of seeing human behavior in terms of both external manifestations and internal processes. The individual's act entails an internal process of control in which the individual directs conduct toward some goal or object.

In the preceding example, there are both individual and social objects, and individual and social acts. By attending to and acting toward another's look, one constitutes it as an object—it becomes something one's behavior must take into account. At the same time, one participates with others in the creation of a social object, which is an object created and sustained by coordinated or social acts. A conversation is such a social object—it is something toward which the attention of participants is jointly directed in a social act. They begin it, try to keep it going, and perhaps feel badly if it is interrupted. Likewise, in this example, two people may begin to "flirt"—that is, to engage in a set of actions both recognize as contributing to the object of "flirting."

People are social objects to one another as they interact. When you have to decide whether to treat someone who has given you the "look" as signaling a romantic interest, or just having something in his or her eye, you are really deciding what object that person will be. The reality of the other, at that moment, depends on how you constitute him or her as an object. What or who people are is a function of how we jointly designate them as we interact.

Social objects are created as people engage in social acts. In Mead's words, a social act is one that involves "the cooperation of more than one individual, and whose object as defined by the act . . . is a social object."[8] Social acts depend on social interaction and interpretation. Each person must take into account the possible response of the other to his or her own impending act and assume that the other will do the same. Such a process of mutual orientation in completing social acts is what we mean by social interaction—whether the social act in question has as its object flirtation, as in the preceding example, or something different, like a soccer game or a debate.

For people to engage in social interaction, and complete the social object of a social act, they must be able to interpret one another's acts (see Table 2.1). The individual engaged in interaction with another has to be able to assign meaning to other's acts so that he or she can act appropriately. An individual engaged in a conversation has to interpret—assign meaning to—what another person says so that he or she can reply appropriately.

To interpret other people's acts requires ascertaining their intent. There is nothing mysterious about the close association of meaning with intention. Meaning is *triadic,* to use Mead's term: When an individual acts (by making a statement or command, shaking a fist or turning away, or even by means of a facial expression), she indicates to the other what she plans to do, what the other is expected to do in return, and what social object is being created by them. The catcher signaling for a given pitch is indicating what the pitcher is to do, what the catcher is prepared for, and what he expects will happen as a result—a curve, a fastball, a change of pace, or an intentional walk.

The symbolic interactionist approach to conduct stresses that problematic events or situations require people to orient themselves self-consciously to objects and to try to interpret the meaning of one another's acts. So much of what we do in our everyday lives is routine—we awake and dress, make coffee, drive to school or work, and conduct a variety of activities in much the same way from one day to the next. Accordingly, we can explain a great deal of our activities in terms of habit. We do not have to invoke more complex conceptions such as those we have just been considering to explain them. Some habitual forms of conduct involve basic skills—such as standing erect and walking—that are so ingrained and repetitively exercised that we never think about them unless disease or disability interfere with our capacity to do them. Other habitual forms of activity, such as driving an automobile, are more complex and involve responding to the acts of others as well as the exercise of basic skills (see Table 2.2).

TABLE 2.1   Natural Signs and Conventional Signs (Symbols)

	Natural Signs	Conventional Signs (Symbols)
What do signs stand for?	Natural signs stand for (or signal) the presence of important things and events.	Symbols stand for (or signal) the presence of important things and events, but symbols also help create things and events because they refer to both abstract and tangible objects.
How are signs learned?	We learn natural signs through experience—the animal learns to associate the sign with that for which it stands.	We also learn symbols through experience, but humans learn a system of symbols when they learn language. They often learn the symbols before they experience the things and events for which they stand.
Are signs private or public?	Natural signs are private—they are learned anew, through experience, by each individual animal.	Symbols are public—the meaning of a symbol may be communicated intentionally by one person to another, and the response that a symbol creates in the user is similar to the response the symbol creates in the hearer.
When do signs appear?	Natural signs appear at the whim of the environment. They appear only when the things for which they stand appear.	People use symbols when the user wants to use them. The things that symbols represent do not have to be present in order for the user to use them.
How are signs connected to what they represent?	Natural signs have an inherent connection to the things for which they stand.	The connection between symbol and that for which it stands is entirely arbitrary.
What establishes the meaning of the sign?	The meaning of the natural sign is embedded in how the individual organism learns to respond to a particular thing or event that signals the presence of something important to the organism.	The symbol's meaning rests on a community of users agreeing to apply the symbol consistently to certain things and events and to respond in similar ways to the symbol.

However simple or complex the habit, it is when something interferes with the progress of an act toward its usual object that we become more keenly aware of the object itself and of the most appropriate ways of designating and responding to the acts of others. It is at such points that we are acutely aware of interpreting what we guess are the meanings and intents behind the acts of others. For a person responding to another's gaze, it is the ambiguity of the look that makes it necessary self-consciously to designate meaning. "What is going on?" we are apt to ask. "Why did the other person do that? What should I do?"

TABLE 2.2   Individual Acts and Social Acts

	Individual Acts	Social Acts
When does an act begin?	A new act begins when something occurs that disrupts the individual's ongoing act. Example: A student about to leave his apartment to drive to class for a scheduled examination discovers his car won't start.	A new social act begins when something interferes with an ongoing individual or social act. Example: The student fears he may miss the examination and contacts the professor to explain that he will try to find alternative transportation and may be late or may not be able to get there.
How is the object defined?	The individual imagines what must be done and then thinks of alternative ways of doing it. Example: The student tries to decide whether it would be better to take a bus to class or to borrow his roommate's car.	Several individuals cooperate to achieve a definition of the situation and thus an agreement on what social act is required. Example: The student talks to his roommate, who offers to let him use the car provided he brings the car back immediately after the examination.
Who does the acting?	The individual manipulates various objects in order to move toward the goal of the act. Example: The student gets his roommate's car keys, transfers his backpack to the car, and heads for the class.	Individuals act cooperatively to achieve a social object—that is, each contributes individual acts that are coordinated in such a way that they move jointly toward the social object. Example: The roommate lends the keys, explains how to work a stick shift, and wishes the student well for the examination.
When is the act complete?	The act is completed when the goal is reached and the individual can return to the act that was interrupted. Example: The student gets to class and takes the examination for which he had studied.	The act is complete when its goal is reached, which requires the explicit or tacit acknowledgment of all participants that this has been done. Example: The professor thanks the student for letting her know he would be late, and assures him it isn't a problem, and he thanks her for her understanding. After taking the examination, the student returns the car to his roommate.

It is thus true, in a limited sense, to say that human beings sometimes act as if we are just responding to stimulation from the external world. When we encounter red lights at intersections, we do not engage in a conscious process in which we designate the meaning of a red light. We more or less automatically and habitually respond by putting on the brakes. Yet at some point in the past, when we learned to drive, we had to designate the meaning of a red light and learn explicitly and consciously how to respond. Moreover, there are occasions when habitual responses are inadequate and we must actively designate the objects toward which we are acting. For example, other cars fail to stop as they should for red lights, traffic signals break, we fail to see a red light in time—in these situations we must decide what to do. It is in the face of problematic occurrences that our capacity to designate and interpret is crucial to the success of our actions.

Self and the Control of Behavior

The human capacity to control our conduct and coordinate our behavior with that of others, and to create complex social acts and social objects, is linked to a uniquely human phenomenon: possessing a self. Symbolic interactionists use this familiar word in a distinctive way to designate both an object that is created as we interact with others and the process we use to create this object.

Self as Object

The essence of the symbolic interactionist concept of *self* lies in the idea that human beings are objects to themselves. Each person is an object in his or her own experience; that is, an object that he or she can name, imagine, visualize, talk about, and act toward. One can like or dislike oneself, feel pride or shame in real or imagined activity, and, in general, act toward oneself within the same range of motives and emotions that shape actions toward others. This self-reflective capacity, for symbolic interactionists, is a fundamental fact of human existence.

How is it possible for people to constitute themselves as objects? How do individuals become conscious of themselves and so become a part of their own experience, of the very environment in which they live and act? Individuals can anticipate their own conduct, visualize themselves as a part of their environment, and see their own acts in relation to other people's acts. However it happened, the individual who first began to use the group's name for himself or herself managed to internalize the whole group of which he or she was a part. By naming self and others, the individual could internally represent others and their behavior *and* his or her own responses and their responses in turn.

By naming group members and themselves, human beings import the social process within the individual mind. As individuals participate in group life, each can represent the activities of the group within his or her own mind and act according to how he or she thinks others will act. We do more than symbolically represent a world of social objects—people— of which we are part. We also act toward (and interact with) those objects, including ourselves, which we consider in relation to others. By taking self into account as a factor in the situation, the individual is better able to control his or her own acts and better able to anticipate the outcomes of alternative acts.

However self-designation and self-interaction arose in the course of evolution, we see the operation of these processes in our everyday lives. "Talking to oneself" is an everyday experience. "Thought"—the name we give to such internalized conversation—cannot take place unless individuals treat themselves as social objects with which they can conduct a conversation. In conceiving of thinking as an internalized conversation, we are in effect saying that the human mind or consciousness is really the incorporation of social processes within an individual. People have conscious minds because they are able to act toward themselves, talk to themselves, and take themselves into account as they act.

When humans mind themselves, they constitute the self as an object. For example, a characteristic human response to situations is that people restrain themselves from immediately responding. They wait to construct a response that seems to "fit" the situation. Noticing another's prolonged gaze, one feels impelled to act, but generally he or she may hold a response in check until deciding what to do. We may consider several possibilities, select one, and then act. Each time we imagine ourselves doing something—whether saying "no" to a party invitation, achieving a promotion on the job, or getting a grade of A in a social psychology course—we act toward ourselves as objects. When I say to myself, "I'm going to work hard to earn an A in this course," I create and act toward an object— myself. This object, me, is a crucial object in my life, implicated in my every act. Although I may transform, modify, or revise this object as I interact with different people and find myself in different situations, this object always figures in my conduct.

The self as object does not refer to the body. People have corporeal existence, of course, but also, and more importantly, a great many intangible attributes and characteristics. People are mothers or farmers or criminals. They are moody or kind or capable or strong. They are self-confident or insecure, anxious or relaxed. They are, in short, whatever kind of objects their own acts (and, we will see, the acts of others) indicate them to be. When we constitute others or ourselves as objects with such attributes and characteristics, we are dealing in abstractions. We are talking about objects and not simply about the material thing that is the body. Grasping this point is vital. As generations of English teachers have pounded into our heads, nouns are the names of persons, places, and things. Very well, we are inclined to think, the self is a thing, a structure in the mind. The self is not; the self is an object we create and re-create through our actions and thoughts.

Self as Process

George Herbert Mead (as well as William James) used the personal pronouns *I* and *Me* to describe two phases of the process whereby the self is created and recreated. An act begins when the individual's adjustment to a situation is disturbed. The initial, impulsive tendency is to react to a disturbance in some way; if the telephone rings, if the significance of a glance is unclear, or if what someone says is not understood, the individual is spontaneously moved to respond. Typically, conduct already underway is interrupted, and attention is turned toward the new stimulus. If one is reading a book and the telephone rings, the impulse to react to the sound occurs because one is distracted from the activity of reading.

Mead intended the concept of the *I* to capture this immediate, spontaneous, and impulsive aspect of conduct.[9] The initial part of any act, whatever the source of impulse, involves an acting subject who is becoming aware of the environment and the objects within it toward which action must be directed. Action always is initially unorganized and undirected, so far as the conscious awareness of the person is concerned. The person cannot designate an object and begin an act toward it until he or she has become aware of the initial, impulsive response to a stimulus.

The individual's awareness of his or her own initial response to a stimulus signals the beginning of the *Me* phase of the self. Consider a mother disciplining her child: Deemed guilty of misconduct, the child is told she is banished to her room until dinner. She begins to protest her exile, but checks herself and goes off quietly. The child has begun to protest, has imagined her mother's likely response, and has realized that keeping quiet is the best way to avoid further difficulty. In such occurrences, we see the emergence of the "Me." The child in this example imagines the attitudes of the other (her mother) toward the child's possible response to the situation and doesn't like what she anticipates. Here the individual takes herself into account as an object. In taking the point of view of her mother, the little girl becomes a "Me." The "Me" here is the view of the child that the other will take. The child may even use the objective case of the personal pronoun, saying to herself, "She'll only be more angry with *me* if I object!"

The "I" and the "Me" alternate in ongoing conduct. At one moment, the individual responds as an "I" to a particular situation; at the next moment, that response becomes a part of the past and so is part of the "Me." For example, a parent sometimes shows anger toward his or her children, beginning to speak harshly to them; in so doing, the parent is acting as an "I." A moment later, becoming aware of this harshness by imagining how he or she looks from the children's perspective, the parent becomes a "Me," and then may respond to this "Me" by apologizing or by speaking less harshly. In doing so, the parent again becomes an "I," this time responding to an image of self rather than to something outside of the self. And so the alternation between "I" and "Me" continues.

This constant alternation of "I" and "Me," of impulse and reflection, is how human beings control their conduct. We can think of the alternations between "I" and "Me" as successive approximations to an act desired by the individual and the others present. As the father checks his temper and responds evenly to his son, the son relaxes, and the father, in turn, responds to this relaxation with fatherly advice rather than punishment. We see this process of self-formation also at work in the internal conversation that takes place when, for example, we feel caught between what we want to do and what others want us to do. Suppose a person gets invited to a party, but would really prefer to spend a quiet evening at home. "If I go," she might say to herself, "I won't have a good time, because I'm tired and I don't feel like partying. But if I don't go, I'll hurt his feelings. Well, maybe he'll understand if I explain that I'm tired. No, he'll remember I also refused an invitation last week. Perhaps I can go but not stay long. But that might also hurt his feelings or make him angry." In this internal dialogue, we also see the alternation of "I" and "Me." The person imagines how she will feel if she goes to the party, then imagines herself refusing to go, and then imagines various alternative responses and the way in which her inviter might respond to them.

The successive "Mes" that enable the individual to gain a measure of control over conduct are possible because the individual is able to imagine the perspective of another. In the moment-to-moment alternation between "I" and "Me," the person successively imagines his or her appearance in the eyes of the other and controls the direction of the act by responding to that imagined appearance. This control is more than just a way of showing how the individual conforms to social expectations. Perhaps with each successive "Me," the person appears to come closer to an act that the other expects and wants. However, matters are more complicated than this conclusion. Although the "Me" in a sense guides the person toward acts that are more or less in conformity with the expectations of others, human beings are capable of being more than conforming creatures. They are capable of considerable novelty, creativity, and sheer self-interest. There is tension in the relation between the accelerating impulse of the "I" and the brakes that the "Me" can apply.

The capacity to control conduct confers an ability to choose an act other than that which is socially expected and approved. Because human beings can inhibit their responses,

form images of themselves, and then choose an act, they can refuse to act as they are expected, choosing inappropriate acts instead. Put another way, because they have the capacity
for the self-conscious control of conduct, human beings also have the capacity to act in self-
interested ways and to choose alternative and even socially disapproved ways of doing so.

A person's capacity to exert control over conduct also depends on inhibiting an initial, impulsive response to a situation. The father who begins to respond in anger has to be
able to prevent the angry impulse from turning into an overtly angry word or deed. Clearly,
doing so is not always possible, for impulses are sometimes so powerful that they carry
forward into overt conduct before we can check them. To lose one's temper is to permit an
impulse to move forward, unchecked, into conduct. How many of us have lost our tempers
driving in heavy traffic, only to be embarrassed later at the string of obscenities that we un-
leashed, sometimes with our kids listening in the backseat? People are often doing things
they do not wish to do and that others do not like because their capacity to control conduct
is imperfect.

Moreover, people make mistakes in efforts to control their acts. They do so, for example, by misperceiving the expectations of others or of society as a whole. Each "Me" is
the result of an effort to imagine how we appear from another person's perspective, and can
fall prey to failures or errors of imagination. The father may fail to control his anger just
because he does not see himself as harsh; that is, he imagines himself as just in the eyes of
his misbehaving child, and so he feels no need to check his impulse to respond angrily.
Some mistakes in control also result from limitations of muscular control. A soccer goalie,
for example, knows that he is supposed to catch a ball hit close to him. However, if the ball
is hit very hard and its trajectory is good, the goalie just will not be able to react quickly
enough to catch the ball.

Roles and the Definition of Situations

The experience of self rests on the capacity to see ourselves from the vantage point of others. We know ourselves indirectly and socially by imagining how others will respond to us.
Likewise, we grasp situations that we are a part of by temporarily adopting the perspectives of others. How do we do this? Say, for example, that a daughter wants to stay out until
two in the morning for a big dance, but her dad is reluctant to let her stay out that late. Although her impulse may be to argue with him, or to stalk angrily from the room when she
hears "No," she imagines her father will respond negatively to that behavior and become
even more intransigent. Because she has the capacity to imagine herself acting in a way
that could destroy all hope of getting what she wants, she elects to try another approach,
this time engaging her dad in a calm and reasoned conversation about his reluctance to
allow her out so late.

How does the daughter anticipate her father's responses to her possible acts and predict his more favorable response to reason rather than anger? A small part of the answer
comes from the daughter having past experiences with her father. She has learned how to
ask permission to do things that he only reluctantly allows her to do. She knows which actions will anger him and which actions will appeal to his sense of reason and fairness.
While experience helps explain the daughter's behavior, experience offers an incomplete
answer to how people can anticipate each other's acts.

Remember that much human interaction occurs among people who do not know one another, who lack established funds of experience on which they can predict one another's behaviors. We interact successfully with store clerks, lawyers, students, and many others whom we have never met. Moreover, we interact with familiar others in novel situations, where we must rely on something more than past experience to enable us to anticipate their actions. People are able more or less successfully to anticipate one another's actions for two main reasons:

- At nearly every moment of our activity we are familiar with situations that face us. We know what we are doing, what is expected and forbidden, what is typical and what is atypical, what others are doing, and what we are doing with them, all because we have a *definition of the situation*.
- We know the others with whom we interact. We know what is happening and who is making it happen because we know the roles contained in the situation. We know which role is ours and which belong to others.

Situations

Conduct does not occur in a vacuum, but in specific, concrete, and usually well-known situations that present us with a familiar configuration of acts and objects. This configuration is termed the *definition of the situation*. The definition of the situation comprises an overall grasp of the nature of a particular setting, the activities that occur there and are likely to reoccur there, the objects that are sought or taken into account, and the others who are present. More formally, *a definition of the situation* is an organization of perception in which people assemble objects, meanings and others and act toward them in a coherent, organized way.

People act on the basis of how they define situations. When people are in a familiar situation and its configuration of meaning is known, they can organize their own conduct and their expectations of others in relation to its definition. Students and professors in a classroom, for example, usually act on the basis of a familiar definition of a situation. They know that the situation contains professors and students who act toward such objects as questions, explanations, lectures, exams, and grades. Where there is no definition of a situation to start with—where people find themselves without confident knowledge of who is present or what is going on—they must first focus on establishing a definition. If while driving along a highway one encounters stopped vehicles and people standing around, one attempts to define the situation—to decide, for example, whether an accident occurred and, if so, how recently—so that one knows what to do.

The concept of the definition of the situation stresses the idea that acts are not abstract, rootless, or mechanical. Human conduct is always situated. Our acts—along with the expectations and interpretations that they are based on—are rooted in our cognition of the situations of which we are a part. People know, for example, that there are limits on what constitutes a proper topic of conversation at a party—although their sense of what is proper will vary along such lines as social class or religion. In many circles, it might be permissible to tell off-color jokes, but revealing intimate facts about one's own sex life would not be tolerated. For some, promise rings are a way of life; to others, promise rings are a punchline for jokes. The point is that knowledge of what others will find tolerable or desirable is an important part of the definition of the situation. Knowing in advance who will be there, we can make more-or-less correct interpretations of others' acts and produce acts that they will find acceptable.

The definition of the situation allows us to anticipate or understand the actions of others and also provides an important basis for our capacity to see ourselves. Because we have a definition of the situation, we can see ourselves as a part of it. That is, because we know what is going on and who is making it happen, we have a basis for seeing not only who others are and what they are doing, but also who we are and what we are supposed to do. The "Me" that arises as we grasp the meaning and direction of our own acts is always a situated "Me." That is, we have a specific image of a "Me" that arises in specific situations. We see ourselves in classrooms, at parties, driving our cars, and in countless other concrete, defined situations in everyday life.

When we imagine ourselves in these situations, we use the definition of the situation as a platform on which to stand to view ourselves. Or, to shift to a different metaphor, the definition of the situation can be thought of as that map with the "You are here" prominently marked at the place where we should be standing. When one holds a map in hand and visualizes one's place on it, one does so in order to determine how to get where one wants to go. When one contemplates a definition of the situation and visualizes one's place in it, one does so in order to decide what one can or should do. In both cases, we rely on an abstract representation of the world as a device to locate our specific position in it.

Situations contain a great many elements, and their definitions convey a great deal of knowledge about them and us. Most important is what the definition of the situation conveys about the roles that the situation contains. No matter what situation we find ourselves in, we can grasp how its activities are socially organized. We know, more or less, who is responsible for doing what, who is allowed to do what, who must do what, and who cannot do what. We approach each situation with a sense of how it will be organized. This sense of organization is expressed in terms of roles. For symbolic interactionists, the concept of role provides a key link between the perspective and behavior of individuals and the social situations in which they find themselves.

Role

Role is one of the most widely used concepts in social science. Sociologists use the concept differently than symbolic interactionists do. Because of this divergence, we explain the conventional usage first, and then tackle how interactionists approach the idea of role differently.[10]

In the conventional sociological view, a *role* is defined as a cluster of duties, rights, and obligations associated with a particular social position (or, as it may be called, status). This approach emphasizes the normative requirements of a particular role. That is, a position such as professor obligates one to do certain things—to show up in class to teach students, to assign them work and grade it promptly, and to keep up-to-date in one's academic field. These normative requirements constitute the professor role. Just as there is a professor role, there is a reciprocal student role, with its own set of normative requirements—to attend class, take notes, participate in discussions, and show up for examinations. The conventional sociological approach to role sees these normative requirements as a guide for individuals as they construct their conduct. That is, one knows what to do—how to "play" one's role—because the norms that define the role provide a script for any given situation in which someone has to play a role. A role requires one to read the lines, doing and saying what one must in order to live up to the normative requirements of the role.

How people actually form their conduct and the significance of roles in this process is more complex to an interactionist. First, human beings follow and make use of norms, to be sure, but for the most part, our moment-to-moment conduct as we "play" roles does not depend on efforts to conform to norms, and our attention is not focused on obligations or rights. Our attention is ordinarily focused on objects and social objects and on our individual and collective efforts to reach them. Only occasionally—when we are uncertain of what to do or when someone challenges our conduct—do we focus explicitly on norms. Further, when we do think of what we ought to do in performing a role, we do so in hindsight; we act and then consider whether we did what we should, rather than starting with a norm and proceeding to construct our act. Moreover, a normative approach to a social role is unrealistic because even the simplest roles human beings enact would be difficult to capture, even with a full list of duties, rights, and responsibilities.

The symbolic interactionist approach to *role* does not emphasize a position with a fixed list of attached duties. Instead, interactionists emphasize three related ideas. These ideas stress the pragmatic and creative capacities of human beings rather than their tendencies to adhere to rigid schedules of conduct. First, we stress that participants cognitively structure situations into roles. Second, we perceive of a role as a configuration of ideas and principles about what to do in a situation. Third, we argue that people use roles as a resource for interaction in social situations.

When a situation is defined and participants know who is present and what will occur, they can cognitively structure the situation in terms of roles. Enter a college classroom, for example, and one knows to expect to see students and a professor. When a situation is defined (and thus also named), its participants are also known and named, and the names we use are the names of roles—like students and professor.

The second idea is that a role is a configuration—not a list of duties. Roles require a little more creative spontaneity and innovation. They are more than an organized set of ideas or principles that people employ in order to know how to behave. The role of a professor is more than a checklist of things a professor does; instead, there is more fluidity. The role is more a set of general ideas about how professors and students relate to one another in various situations where and when they interact. This sense of role as a whole rather than as a set of preconfigured parts is important. That is, to have a grasp of the situation as a whole and of the way its joint activities are parceled out to various participants (identified by their role names), is to have a grasp of several configurations—those of others and our own. The catcher in a softball game, for example, has a sense of the overall role structure of the game (as played by batters, pitchers, infielders, outfielders, catchers, and so forth), of his or her own location in that structure, and its implications for what he or she is expected to do, and of the locations and operating principles of others in the game. There is a cumulative whole that is more than just the sum of configured parts.

Third, a role is also a resource that participants in a situation use in order to carry out their activities. People use roles—that is, they bring into play their knowledge of roles in order to achieve their individual and joint goals. A pitcher uses his or her own role as a basis for acting in the situation; that pitcher also uses his or her knowledge of the roles of others in order to understand their actions. A situation provides a "container" for roles and makes it possible for participants to bring them to life, and in this sense roles are a property of the situation. But it is the participants who use the roles to bring the situation to life, and so roles are also the property of those who use them.[11]

To sum up the interactionist conception of role, we suggest that a *role* be defined as a perspective for constructing conduct. A role is not a concrete list of behaviors, but a more abstract perspective from which the individual participates in a social situation and contributes to its social acts and social objects. A role provides a perspective from which one acts—just as the roles of others, through our acts of imagination, provide perspectives from which we view both their conduct and our own. The catcher acts by grasping the softball game as a whole through the eyes of a catcher, but also by occasionally transporting himself into the perspectives (roles) of the pitcher or batter in order to anticipate and make sense of their acts.

This approach to role recognizes that roles constrain conduct, that a fundamental human tendency is to accept the guidance of a role, and also that people cognitively structure situations into roles. Our attitude toward social situations of all kinds is to organize or structure them in our minds. In other words, we look for order or meaning in the situations in which we find ourselves, and where we cannot easily find that meaning by assigning the name of a familiar situation, we work hard to create order. Thus, if we encounter a situation where it is unclear who occupies what positions and who enacts what roles, we attend to figuring out these matters. We are role-using and situation-defining creatures. We decide who around us has authority, to whom we are supposed to address a question, and who we are or seem to be in the eyes of the others who are around us. If we find ourselves in a situation that is so ambiguous that there is no structure, we create one. A newly formed group, for example, may be quite undifferentiated, but before very long, some people will become leaders and others followers, some will be active and some not, some will take on this task and others a different one. In short, we look for structure, and where we do not find it, we create it.

For symbolic interactionists, our knowledge of roles provides us with a grasp of structure and organization that is important. People act within their roles but in a manner that permits them far more latitude and flexibility than that provided by an actor's assigned role in a play. Although roles provide a sense of the structure of social situations, people are capable of altering the structure when it seems necessary or desirable to do so. Particular role structures do not have to lock us into actions; we have the capacity to create new possibilities.

Definitions of situations, together with the role structures associated with them, provide human beings with two important capacities:

- The capacity to anticipate or predict the actions of the others in interactions.
- The capacity to make sense of the actions of others, even actions that we did not anticipate.

Our knowledge of who is doing what permits us to make reasonably accurate predictions about the actual behavior of others. For example, we enter a physician's examining room. We know who the patient is, who the physician is, and who the nurse is. We know to expect medical talk and activity, that we may be asked to disrobe or to sit on a table, and to take deep breaths as the physician listens to our chest with a stethoscope. We can anticipate what the physician may ask us to do, what questions we will hear, and what his or her manner is likely to be. We do entertain at least some ideas about what may occur—we imagine what is going to happen—and we get our ideas about what may happen from our knowledge of the perspectives that roles and situations provide.

Our capacity for sense making is as important as our capacity to predict. Although much that actually transpires during a situation can be anticipated, we do not anticipate everything. Yet little often occurs that does not make sense in terms of the definition of the situation and its associated roles. Knowledge of situations and roles gives us a sense making and a predictive capacity. We can make retrospective "predictions," so that whatever does happen in a defined situation, we can make sense of it in terms of the definition of that situation and its roles. When we enter a physician's office, we assume the physician is acting within his or her role as physician and that we will act within our role as a patient. This is a very powerful set of assumptions, for it disposes us to interpret whatever the physician does as an instance of his or her role. The physician's behavior—the things he or she asks us to do, the questions he or she asks, and the comments he or she makes—makes sense to us (even though we may not have anticipated it) because we treat that behavior as an instance of appropriate physician role behavior. We interpret behavior as making sense from the perspective of a physician. Obviously, we cannot treat everything the physician does in these terms, for sometimes people fail in their roles—that is, they act in inappropriate ways for their role. As a rule, however, we expect that people will do what is appropriate for their roles. Those predictions can cover a considerable amount of variation in what people actually do. Behavior sometimes has to get very far out of alignment with a role before people challenge its propriety.

Individuals sometimes must act within or in relation to more than one role in a situation. Consider the case of gender, for no matter what other specific roles individuals have, they are almost always visibly male or female. As a result, gender is always available as a perspective on which to base one's own conduct or to interpret the conduct of others. Where occupants of a particular role—such as an occupational role—are predominantly or overwhelmingly of one sex, a special problem arises when we interact with someone whose gender is not typical of that role. In U.S. society, nurses are still predominantly women, and so the male nurse presents the patients with an atypical situation where they must, so to speak, expect intimate care giving from an unexpected gender. For women, accustomed to female nurses, this situation may be defined as "abnormal" to expose their body in this situation. The male nurse faces a different and more serious problem, in that he may be treated differently. Hospital patients, for example, may assume that a male nurse is gay or inappropriately effeminate and discriminate against them on that basis.

Role Making and Role Taking

Two concepts capture the essence of social interaction and conduct formation as shaped by social roles.[12]

- *Role making* is the process wherein the person constructs activity in a situation so that it fits the definition of the situation, is consonant with the person's own role, and meshes with the activity of others.
- *Role taking* is the process wherein the person imaginatively occupies the role of another and looks at self and situation from that vantage point in order to engage in role making.

These two processes are intimately linked. There is no role making without role taking. A person cannot construct a role without at some point occupying the perspective of the other and viewing self and situation from that vantage point. There also can be no role taking without role making. Each act observed in self and in others serves as evidence that the roles we think are being made are actually being made. Only to the extent that we are confident that we know the role of the other can we momentarily adopt their perspective in order to see ourselves as they see us.

Symbolic interactionists speak of role making, rather than role playing or role enactment, in order to stress two important aspects of the process. First, behavior "in role" is not a matter of routinely enacting lines in a script, where each action is well known in advance and where there is little latitude in what we can say and do. These situations can happen, but such forcefully conforming settings, where intense prescriptions about roles exist (like prisons) are rare. Roles are not typically packages or lists of mandatory behavior but are perspectives from which people construct lines of conduct that fit the situation and the lines of conduct of others.

Roles provide us with an organizing framework to use to construct a performance that will meet the needs of a particular situation. Each performance of a role must be oriented to the particular demands of the situation and to the social acts that are constructed there. There is tailoring to meet particular conditions. For example, a physician who encounters an automobile accident along the highway faces a different situation than he or she does when seeing a recalcitrant patient in his or her office. On both occasions, the individual is engaged in making his or her role as a physician clear, but how he or she does so must fit the situation and its demands. No single script provides all the required directions for action. Role making thus becomes a self-conscious activity in which persons are creatively engaged in making an appropriate role performance; there is not an autopilot that works for all role performances.

Second, role making is self-conscious. In order to make an adequate role performance—one that others will interpret as appropriate and that will be acceptable to the one making it—there must be a consciousness of self. The person must be aware of his or her own role performance in the making to adjust it to suit personal goals, the demands of the situation, and the expectations of others. This is where role taking enters the picture. To be conscious of one's own role performance, one must have a way of conceiving the performance. This consciousness is accomplished by assuming the perspective of others in anticipating reactions. To know where to throw the ball so that he or she can get the runner out, the catcher must know where the second baseman expects the ball to be thrown. If the catcher fails to grasp the infielder's expectations, he or she may throw the ball past the second baseman into the outfield, allowing a runner to advance. The catcher knows what the second baseman expects by taking the infielder's perspective and looking at the play from his or her perspective. Thus, seeing a runner on first making a move to steal, the catcher signals the second baseman, then gauges the latter's movement so that he or she can aim the ball appropriately. The catcher uses his or her grasp of the other's impending role behavior to control his or her own action.

Role taking always involves cognitively grasping the perspective of the other whose role is taken, and sometimes it also involves identification. Consider the child who responds to parental discipline. Say that the child apologizes and resolves to try to do better in the future after having been called to account for some transgression. The child here is role taking. The child makes a factual prediction that the parent will be pleased with an apology and a resolution to do better in the future. The child is identifying with the parent's perspective in making that assessment. That is, the child both grasps and accepts the parent's point of view, viewing what he or she did as inappropriate and viewing the parent's imposition of punishment as just. His or her subsequent conduct is thus an effort to rebuild and maintain a favorable conception of himself or herself as someone the parent will like. This sequence constitutes role taking just as much as the more neutral, factual conduct of the catcher in relation to the second baseman.

Role Taking as a Generalized Skill

An ability to see the world through a perspective other than one's own is a generalized skill. Human beings see things from the vantage points of others' roles, from perspectives the situation itself provides, by specific acts in the situation, and by using what Mead called "the generalized other." When we assert that a definition of a situation gives us a sense of how roles structure activities, we are in essence saying that the definition is a "platform" on which we stand to view the whole scene. We "take the role of the situation," as it were, surveying the events taking place before our eyes from the "perspective" of the situation as a whole. Moreover, specific social acts or sequences of social acts also provide us with a platform from which to view and assess what is taking place.

Consider two children constructing a scenario to persuade their parents not to give away a kitten that is destroying the household's plants and furniture with its claws. "When Mom says they're going to give the kitten away," one might say, "I'll start to cry, and then you come into the room with the scratching post and explain how you made it so the cat will leave the furniture alone, and then Mom will say that we can try it for a few days." The child constructing the scenario takes the role of the mother, to be sure, anticipating how she is likely to respond to a tearful child and the other child's act of building a scratching post. But the child also adopts the "perspective" of a social act, looking at what should or must occur in the behavior of each participant in order for the act to succeed. Here, the child's conception of the social act itself provides the perspective from which the situation can be viewed.

We are afforded a place to stand and a perspective on our own and others' conduct by the generalized perspectives of the groups to which we belong to or aspire to belong. Our behavior is always situated, shaped by the perspective of our role in a particular social situation, whether we are playing baseball, eating dinner with our family, or attending a lecture. Situations and roles are anchored, however, in a larger context of organized group life. Baseball games occur within such larger organizational contexts as Little League Baseball or Major League Baseball. Eating a family dinner presupposes the existence of a durable group called the family. Lectures are given and attended in larger organizational settings like colleges and universities. Furthermore, these groups and organizations themselves exist within the still larger context of community and society.

Situations, roles, and social acts provide us with perspectives and so do groups, organizations, communities, and societies. The physician examining a patient, for example, adopts the perspective not only of the patient and of the specific situation in which the examination occurs, but also of the profession of medicine itself. That is, he or she takes into account the patient's definition of the situation and also the views of other physicians, who have expectations about how to conduct examinations—of how to treat patients, what tests to order and what behaviors are inappropriate.

Mead used the idea of the *generalized other* to refer to a generalized perspective of the group, community, or society as a whole that people take into account in considering the reactions to their actions. The generalized other is, like a role, a perspective that the person must imaginatively adopt in order to take it into account in forming his or her own conduct. The generalized other is made up of standards, expectations, principles, norms, and ideas that are held in common by the members of a particular social group. The generalized other can also embed standards of appraisal that wreak havoc in our heads as we contemplate different lines of action and anticipate their positive or negative consequences. In a complex society, there is not one generalized other but many. Although some general ideas about conduct are held in common by all members of the society and represent the perspective of the society as a whole, others are confined to specific religions, ethnic groups, social classes, or even regions of a country. In their everyday lives, people may, at various times, take different generalized others into account in constructing their behavior. Each generalized other represents the unique perspective of some community, organization, group, occupation, religion, social class, or ethnic group.

The generalized others whose perspectives the individual assumes need not be limited to groups to which one belongs. *Reference groups*[13] exist. They are defined as social groups that provide generalized others and sets of standards for evaluating conduct. Reference groups may include groups of which one is not an actual member and groups to which one belongs. Thus, a working class person may use the upper class as a reference group; providing him or her with a generalized other whose views he or she takes into account. Persons with aspirations for upward social mobility typically take higher occupational or status groups as their reference groups, and use them to establish patterns of behavior that are appropriate to the kind of persons that they hope to become.

The Place of Emotions

We have emphasized the cognitive aspects of the self, defining the situation, role making, and role taking. Human behavior entails more than the cognitive activity in which people calculate and coordinate their conduct. People also respond *affectively* to one another and to social situations. Social life creates feelings of diverse kinds—fear, hate, love, empathy, and embarrassment—and these emotions play an important part in shaping conduct.[14] Emotions are an essential part of the self and the social world.

What is emotion? In everyday speech, people use the term to refer to a number of feelings—love, hate, or anger—that they think of as naturally or spontaneously aroused under particular conditions. They say that they "love" or "hate" certain individuals, or that in certain situations they are "afraid." The commonsense view of emotions often treats them as antithetical to rationality. When people are emotional, people say, they are being irrational, not in full command of themselves and their actions. Although emotions are a normal part of life, they are often defined as feelings that should be brought under a person's control. Thus, an individual who is frightened is urged to conquer his or her fear; a bereaved person is encouraged to stop grieving after a certain period of time. There are also occasions when people are supposed to vent their feelings and when others reassure them that crying or shouting in anger is acceptable. In any case, the emotion is thought to be a natural individual response to the situation in question.

The sociological conception of emotions differs from a commonsense view. Emotions are an important element of behavior that typically accompany and support cognition. People make roles or define situations with accompanying feelings, such as passion or dedication that enhances the effectiveness of their actions. Similarly, when human beings engage in role taking and form attitudes toward themselves, their attitudes are affective and cognitive. The self is also an experience of aroused feelings. People can cherish or despise themselves. Moreover, in a sociological view, emotions are embedded in the fabric of social life. They are meaningful experiences as much as any other form of behavior, and their origins and effects are likewise social and not merely individual.

Emotions have two major components. They are associated with physical sensations and they are physiological responses to situations. Fear, for example, entails an increased rate of respiration and pulse, as do several other emotions, such as anger, anticipation, or excitement. Similarly, sadness is associated with a depressed psychological and physiological state—tiredness, lack of interest or animation, and an inability to concentrate or sleep. Whether characterized by elevated or depressed physiological activity, however, emotions are grounded in noticeable physical states. We also name emotions and their names shape and sometimes determine how we experience them.

"Fear" and "sadness" are experienced as physical sensations and are also named and talked about, both by people that experience them, and by others who witness people experiencing them. One can have a physical sensation associated with a particular emotion without naming it, but in doing so, one experiences only a fragment of the emotion. To experience fear, one must not only have the sensations associated with fear, but also label those sensations as "fear." In doing so, people experience fear in a self-conscious way, seeing themselves as being "afraid" by taking the perspectives of others. One is afraid when one is followed on a dark street in an unfamiliar place, for example, because fear is a natural reaction to the situation, and because one takes the role of the person following one (and of the generalized other), and recognizes fear as an appropriate response and label for what one feels.

That emotions are both physiological and meaningful responses to situations has led to some controversy about the relative importance of each component. Some argue that there is an identifiable physiological state that corresponds to each named emotion; others argue that the same physiological states underlie all emotions, and that the only thing that differentiates one emotion from another is the label and implied expectations of behavior and feeling. The extreme physiological view ignores similarities in physical sensation between differing emotions, such as fear and guilt, and ignores variations from one culture to another in the labels we attach to emotions. The extreme social constructionist view tends to ignore differences in sensations between such emotions as fear and anger.

Theodore Kemper has advocated a compromise position.[15] According to Kemper, we can identify four primary emotions, each of which has evolutionary significance, is grounded in a different and identifiable physiological state, appears relatively early in individual development, and appears in every culture. *Fear, anger, depression,* and *satisfaction* are the four primary emotions. Fear, for example, is viewed as an evolutionary adaptation that energizes the animal in the face of danger. Fear is associated with the action of a specific neurochemical, epinephrine, on the sympathetic nervous system and can be identified quite early in infancy. Fear also appears in every culture. In contrast to primary emotions, Kemper says, there are more numerous and varied secondary emotions, such as pride, shame, guilt, love, and gratitude. These emotions are grounded in the primary emotions, but the specific experience of them depends on a set of shared social expectations. These expectations, and their names, are a product of culture and vary from one society to another. Guilt, for example, is based on the physiological responses of fear, but the nature and experience of guilt depends on our having learned to respond to certain social situations by labeling our physiological responses as "guilt."

Whether there are two, four or six primary emotions, all emotions have their origins in social life. We experience emotion because we participate in social interaction. The physiological states associated with various emotions can be induced by chemical means: We can increase pulse and respiration, for example, by administering epinephrine; and various antidepressant drugs, such as Prozac or Wellbutrin, have the effect of brightening or elevating mood. But these same states also—and more significantly—are induced by our normal involvement in social situations. Just as emotions originate in social interaction, they are regulated as people interact, and by the same general processes that regulate our conduct in general. Three facts are especially important to consider here.

First, emotions naturally arise in our efforts to complete individual and social acts. When an act runs successfully to its conclusion, it engenders feelings of satisfaction, or even elation, in those involved in completing it. The football player that runs 50 yards to a touchdown is excited by it. The parent who has just taught a child to ride a bicycle feels proud or satisfied as a result of this success. Likewise, when individual and social acts meet obstacles and are blocked off, people respond with feelings. A car that fails to start on a cold winter morning that ends up preventing a student from taking an important examination produces a feeling of anger or frustration, and a calculation of how to get to school and convince the professor to provide an opportunity for a makeup examination.

Second, our experience of emotions is an experience of self. Although bodily sensations—trembling, tightening of muscles, rapid breathing, or a feeling of supreme well being—are an important part of emotions, it is the attribution of meaning to these sensations that permits emotional experience. This attribution of meaning requires the objectification of self through role taking. We see ourselves—as happy, sad, afraid, or angry—as we imagine others see us in the social situation. The football player who feels elated when he scores a touchdown does so in a social context in which he shares the imagined judgment of others that his touchdown merits this feeling of elation. The student who misses an examination because her car won't start is angry with herself because she imagines and shares the views of others that she ought to have checked the condition of her car battery.[16]

Third, emotions are a regular part of the role-making process. When people construct performances that they think will make sense to others, mesh with the others' roles, and meet the requirements of the situation, they take emotional expectations into account. We are somber at funerals and happy at weddings because we grasp the fact that appropriate emotional expressions are a part of our role performances. We discuss how people construct the appearance or real experience of emotions appropriate to situations in Chapter 4.

Endnotes

1. Interactionists, as much because of their own pragmatism as because of the critiques of postmodern theory and social constructionism, use the word *reality* with caution. For a recent effort to reclaim the word *reality* (as well as *objectivity* and *truth*) for sociology, see Stephen Lyng and David D. Franks, *Sociology and the Real World* (Lanham, MD: Rowman & Littlefield, 2002).

2. Discussion is influenced by the classic work of Ernest Becker and Leslie A. White. See Ernest Becker, *The Birth and Death of Meaning* (New York: Free Press, 1952), especially chapters 2 and 3; and Leslie A. White, "Four Stages in the Evolution of Minding," in *The Evolution of Man,* ed. Sol Tax, vol. 2 of *Evolution after Darwin* (Chicago: University of Chicago Press, 1959). See also John P. Hewitt, "Symbols, Objects, and Meanings," in *Handbook of Symbolic Interactionism,* ed. Larry T. Reynolds and Nancy J. Herman-Kinney (Walnut Creek, CA: AltaMira Press, 2003), Chapter 12.

3. Classic portrayal of language evolution can be found in Charles F. Hockett and Robert Ascher, "The Human Revolution," *Current Anthropology* 5 (1964): 135–168. For another view, see Gordon Hewes, "Primate Communication and the Gestural Origin of Language," *Current Anthropology* 14 (1973): 5–24. A more recent theory of language can be found in Terrence W. Deacon, *The Symbolic Species: The Co-evolution of Language and the Brain* (New York: Norton, 1997).

4. Addition to Deacon, *The Symbolic Species* (Note 3), Part One, see Davydd J. Greenwood and William A. Stini, *Nature, Culture, and Human History* (New York: Harper & Row, 1977).

5. Herbert Blumer, *Symbolic Interactionism: Perspective and Method* (Englewood Cliffs, NJ: Prentice Hall, 1969), p. 11.

6. N. Meltzer, "Mead's Social Psychology," in *Symbolic Interaction: A Reader in Social Psychology,* ed. Jerome Manis and Bernard Meltzer (Boston: Allyn & Bacon, 1972), p. 15.

7. George Herbert Mead, *The Philosophy of the Act,* edited and with an introduction by Charles W. Morris (Chicago: University of Chicago Press, 1938), pp. 3–25.

8. Herbert Mead, *Mind, Self, and Society* (Chicago: University of Chicago Press, 1934), p. 7, p. 9, pp. 173–226, and pp. 273–281.

9. Dummy Text

10. Conventional sociological view finds its classic expression in the work of Robert K. Merton and William J. Goode. See Merton, "Sociological Ambivalence," in his *Sociological Ambivalence and Other Essays* (New York: Free Press, 1976), pp. 3–31; and Goode, "A Theory of Role Strain," in his *Explorations in Social Theory* (New York: Oxford, 1973). Others have argued that the conventional and interactionist approaches to role are more alike than they seem. See Warren Handel, "Normative Expectations and the Emergence of Meaning as Solutions to Problems: Convergence of Interactionist and Structural Views," *American Journal of Sociology* 84 (1979): 855–881; and Jerold Heiss, "Social Roles," in *Social Psychology: Sociological Perspectives,* ed. Morris Rosenberg and Ralph H. Turner (New York: Basic Books, 1981), pp. 94–129. Ralph H. Turner effectively rebuts their arguments. See his "Unanswered Questions in the Convergence Between Structuralist and Interactionist Role Theory," in *Micro-Sociological Theory,* vol. 2, ed. H. J. Helle and S. N. Eisenstadt (London: Sage, 1985), pp. 23–36. For a recent review of role theory and research, see Norman A. Dolch, "Role," in *Handbook of Symbolic Interactionism,* Chapter 6 (Note 2).

11. Wayne E. Baker and Robert R. Faulkner, "Role as Resource in the Hollywood Film Industry," *American Journal of Sociology* 97 (September 1991): 279–309.

12. Classic symbolic interactionist statement on role is by Ralph H. Turner, "Role-Taking: Process versus Conformity," in *Human Behavior and Social Process,* ed. Arnold M. Rose (Boston: Houghton-Mifflin, 1962), pp. 20–40. For another excellent statement, see also Peter L. Callero, "Toward a Meadian Conceptualization of Role," *Sociological Quarterly* 27 (Fall 1986): 343–358.

13. See Tamotsu Shibutani, "Reference Groups as Perspectives," *American Journal of Sociology* 60 (1955): 562–569; Shibutani, "Reference Groups and Social Control," pp. 128–147 in Rose, *Human Behavior* (Note 12); and Ralph H. Turner, "Role-Taking, Role-Standpoint, and Reference Group Behavior," *American Journal of Sociology* 61 (1956): 316–328.

14. For background on the sociology of emotions, see Steven L. Gordon, "The Sociology of Sentiments and Emotion," in Rosenberg and Turner,

Social Psychology (Note 10), pp. 562–592; and Lyn Smith-Lovin, "The Sociology of Affect and Emotion," pp. 118–148 in Karen S. Cook, Gary Alan Fine, and James S. House, *Sociological Perspectives on Social Psychology* (Boston: Allyn & Bacon, 1995). A more recent and very useful statement of the interactionist approach can be found in David D. Franks, "Emotion," in *Handbook of Symbolic Interactionism*, Chapter 32 (Note 2).

15. T. D. Kemper, "How Many Emotions Are There? Wedding the Social and Autonomic Components," *American Journal of Sociology* 93 (September 1987): 263–289.

16. Johnson extends Mead's theory of the self by including an emotional dimension. See her "The Emergence of the Emotional Self: A Developmental Theory," *Symbolic Interaction* 15 (Summer 1992): 183–202.

CHAPTER

3

Identity, Social Settings, and the Self

I n the preceding chapter we outlined the concept of the *self*. We emphasized the dual nature of the self as both a social process and a social object. In this chapter, we continue to develop this idea through exploring how people develop a self, manage impressions for others, and attempt to cultivate attractive social identities.

Learning the Social World

To recap, symbolic interactionists draw on G. H. Mead's key insight into the concept of the self: Individuals develop a sense of self through assessing the reactions that other people have to them. The advantage of this approach is avoiding two common oversimplifications. The first oversimplification is that the self is hardwired into a person biologically. The other is to accept an overdetermined view that people are just norm-driven robots that do everything that they are told to do and conform to all expectations. Alternatively, the symbolic interactionist perspective honors the creative agency that people have to respond to social norms, and acknowledges that people react to those norms in traditional, novel, and sometimes unanticipated ways.

A person's ability to act toward the self as an external object requires acquiring language. Our symbolic capacity also depends on facility with language.[1] Language is crucial to acquiring a self in two major ways. First, language provides a system of names for the self and others that make it possible for individuals to participate in group life and incorporate group life within the individual. Second, language enables people to identify and conceive of other important objects, so that children can be completely immersed in the environment in which they live. Language provides children with the ability to engage in the culture around them.[2]

All children are born into a social world that consists of an ongoing network of interpersonal relationships among parents, siblings, other kin, and wider circles of others. This world already exists and confronts the new child as a massive, natural fact. The individuals in this world are linked to one another in a variety of role relationships. Each such relationship is named. There are parents and children, brothers and sisters, husbands and wives, grandmothers and grandsons, cousins, friends, and many others. Just as the relationships among people in these networks are named, the individuals in these networks are named as well. Thus, "father" is also "Dad" or "Dave;" a "cousin" is also "Caroline" or "Andrew." As children first hear and then repeat the names of people in this social world, they make two important discoveries. The first is that things have names, and learning and using those names brings rewards and empowers them. For example, parents enthusiastically greet the first "Mama" or "Dada," conveying through tone of voice and facial expressions that something significant is occurring to the child. The second discovery is equally momentous: There is a name for me.[3] That is, the child learns to associate a sound with himself or herself, to repeat that sound and enjoy the social response that follows. When the child learns that he or she is an object to which others refer when they use a certain name, and that he or she can also use this name, the child is making a significant leap toward the full acquisition of a self. The child can now get outside his or her own perspective and view self from the perspective of others.

People develop a more complex capacity for self-reference with improvements in lingual facility and practice in referring to self and others. Children confront complex realities that they must decipher. For example, important social objects such as the child's mother and father have more than one name. There is "mom" and "dad" to the child, but also alternative personal names, roles, and titles. Gradually, children's usage becomes more accurate. They learn to use grammatically correct forms for pronouns (*he* or *she* as the subject of a sentence, for example, and *him* or *her* as the object), and more significantly, their usage comes to reflect the complexities of social relationships. That is, their pronoun usage comes to reflect a more sophisticated grasp of relationships between people, and of the variety of perspectives through which people can view those relationships.

Among the early facts about the social world that children learn to incorporate, as a basic part of their conceptions of themselves, is that the social world is gendered. They learn that there are several pairs of terms—boy and girl, male and female, man and woman—and that these terms refer to a fundamental principle of social classification. Children learn that this classification has a tremendous impact on his or her membership in society. As Spencer Cahill points out, adults speak and act as if babies "do not mature into 'big kids' but into 'big girls' and 'big boys.'"[4] No matter how children learn about gender, and at whatever speed, the selves they develop are, from the start, gendered ones.

The more the child masters these kinds of social classifications, the better he or she is able to represent these relationships internally and thus incorporate the social world into himself or herself. Because he or she can represent others and their perspectives symbolically (Mommy wants me to be a good boy), the child gains a capacity for self-control while also becoming more susceptible to social controls. The child can now represent to himself or herself the perspectives of others and take them into account as he or she decides on his or her conduct. Children become more adept at role taking, and as they do, they also become more successful role makers.

When children engage in meaningful communications, they learn a common set of objects—and thus a common culture (what a television or a fork is)—regardless of social class or the region of the country in which they live. They also learn about additional objects and define some objects in different ways, depending on whether their parents are wealthy or poor, farmers or factory workers, and so forth. Learning the names of things is one side of socialization. It is equally, and perhaps even more significant, that children learn the "things of names."[5] Many objects have names but are intangible. Thus, children learn meanings of words (e.g., *hot* or *no*) that are not labels for material things. For example, they learn something of their parents' conception of religion, even though for most people in our culture, there are not thought to be any directly visible manifestations of a deity, by whatever name he or she is known.

Learning the meanings for objects—the things of names—involves more than just the ability to talk about them. Fundamentally, meaning lies in the actions that people take, are prepared to take, or can imagine taking toward objects. Thus, to learn an object's meaning is to learn not only its name, but also, more importantly, how people will act toward the object. So, for example, children learn that the meaning of *hot* comprises not just a label for a certain sensation, but also that *hot* is a term that implies certain kinds of actions. People avoid "hot" stoves, drink "hot" coffee, wear clothes of "hot" colors, say they are "hot" when they feel warm, and use "hot" to describe someone who is physically attractive. A word's meaning expands as people discover the different behavioral possibilities inherent in that word's variable meanings.

Objects present several behavioral possibilities and are intrinsic to a variety of social acts. A major part of the socialization process entails learning what these acts are and how to decide in any given instance what act is most salient. Linguistic socialization transcends learning words, their definitions, and their possible grammatical relationships; it involves learning the relationships between words and deeds, between the system of labels for objects (and the rules for combining these labels into sentences) and the range of social acts that are possible in the world in which the child lives. In short, the child learns how to represent his or her own conduct and that of others linguistically. They also learn how to represent the world linguistically and how to link themselves and the world together.

Learning the meaning of objects applies to the self. The self is an object grasped from and through the perspectives of others. Children learn the meaning of this very crucial object, the self, on the same basis as they grasp the meaning of any other object. That meaning is found through the ways that others act toward the self. The child is, after all, an object to other people. Beliefs about a child's attributes and characteristics stem from two major sources. First, they emerge in a particular family on the basis of a history of interaction with the child. The second and more important source of beliefs and attitudes toward children is culture. Each culture depicts the child as a different kind of object at various points in the life cycle, just as each culture objectifies men and women in distinctive ways. Thus, in one culture, children are defined as special objects, with qualities and characteristics that differentiate them sharply from infants and adults. In those societies, children are viewed in a special identifiable category in which children should be free from adult cares and always happy. Other groups in different societies treat children and childhood differently, seeing children very much as miniature adults or as easily influenced and coercible beings to exploit. They may work to prevent childhood from being a carefree and pleasant time of life and make children assume adult responsibilities.

As an example, in *A Long Way Gone,* Ishmael Beah offers an autobiographical account of having been a child soldier in Sierra Leone.[6] Starting at the age of 12, Beah was indoctrinated to become a child soldier and a killer. Adults drugged these children with amphetamines and liquor, used their hunger against them, and cultivated a killing mentality within them. There are thousands of child soldiers in the world. The culture that produces a child soldier treats children as one kind of object; an environment that prolongs childhood innocence treats children as a different kind of object.

The nature of socialization and what kinds of human beings get produced depends on the cultural definitions of such objects as child, childhood, adolescence, male, female, and human nature. Whether a particular individual experiences childhood as a pleasant time of play or as a time of intense panic and upheaval depends on cultural and familial influences. Whether originating in culture in general or in unique family experiences, social definitions shape self-definitions. However, children do not just see themselves as others see them. Children develop defense mechanisms to insulate themselves from definitions they dislike. They strive for autonomy from others. They reflect upon their experiences with others. Crucially, in acquiring a sense of the self as a social object in a world of social objects, children acquire the capacity to control their conduct as others wish, and also the potential to say no to social demands. Beah, for example, eventually learned to see himself as other objects; as a student, a victim, and an author. He changed his self-perception from that of a child soldier and a killer to that of an advocate. The process of moving to different lines of self-definition is fluid. The process of role taking is central to the acquisition of self, including a self that is capable of resisting definition by others.

Stages of Socialization

In what Mead called the *play stage* of socialization, the child "plays at" various roles. That is, a child imagines being and acting like someone else. At first, perhaps, the child plays at a role in a rudimentary fashion by animating a toy—moving it about, giving it actions to perform. Later the child plays in a more organized way, such as pretending to be a mommy, a professional wrestler, or Hannah Montana. Having observed the activities of these characters and roles, the child duplicates their words and deeds in play. They comfort imaginary babies, get revenge on bad guys, and mimic performing a Hannah Montana song. Playing at roles, Mead wrote, "is the simplest form of being another to one's self. It involves a temporal situation. The child says something in one character and responds in another character, and then his responding in another character is a stimulus to himself in the first character, and so the conversation goes on."[7] In this form of play, the child is an object to itself, but always by responding to and imagining himself or herself to be a particular other.

As children move through elementary school and beyond, peer influence becomes stronger as the amount of time a child spends with peers increases. Some degree of tension between children and their adult mentors occurs because of the development of peer cultures. When members of any social group interact more frequently with one another than they do with outsiders, they tend to develop what Gary Alan Fine calls *idiocultures*.[8] Children, for example, develop activities, beliefs, norms, knowledge, and social practices that, while derived from the adult world and ostensibly under the control of adults, are transmitted and maintained by children themselves. Whether in Little League teams or just through hanging out with other kids, they develop and sustain distinctive ways of being that are transmitted from kids directly to other kids, rather than through adults. These forms of conduct—ranging from ways of defining and enforcing standards of "masculinity" or "femininity," to ideas about loyalty, serve to bond group members to one another as well as to separate them from others. The peer group itself becomes a generalized other with its own standards of conduct.

As an example, C. J. Pascoe recently completed an ethnographic study of the power boys manipulated through calling other high school boys a "fag."[9] She writes that other boys use the "specter of the fag," the threat of this label, to control other boys. The fear of being called this name led boys to conform to particular ways of acting out their gender. Many people have powerful memories of how people bullied others in high school by tossing around labels like "fag," "slut," "freak," or "nerd." The generalized other is a powerful determinant of self-definition that people seek approval from or hope to mitigate. William Corsaro has shown, for example, that even nursery school children resist the demands and rules of adults by engaging in "naughty" talk, playing in ways that are forbidden, or avoiding cleaning up after play.[10]

The interactionist approach to socialization emphasizes that children are active interpreters of their world and not merely passive sponges that mindlessly absorb lessons. Socialization is, in the last analysis, symbolic interaction. Once the capacity for self-reference develops, socialization occurs on each social occasion in which a child finds himself or herself. Indeed, socialization is not confined to childhood. One is always in a state of becoming socialized throughout their lives.

Everyday Experience, Self, and Impression Management

Human beings think, feel, and act toward themselves. This classification—thoughts, feelings, and actions—delineate three aspects of self that we now examine. When people act toward themselves and others act toward them, they jointly create various forms of identity. We are constantly engaged in locating ourselves in relation to one another—as student to teacher, friend to friend, adversary to adversary, Catholic to Protestant, and in countless other ways. As we locate ourselves, we gain the capacity to interact.

In order to really grasp how we think of ourselves as external objects out in the social world, let's move from abstract-seeming terms to specifics. Recall a concrete situation when you felt that your self-consciousness held you prisoner. Think of times when you worried intensely about your physical appearance. Maybe you ducked into a bathroom to check the mirror, anxious to scrutinize and fix up your appearance? Did you make faces, check your teeth, brush your hair, or see if you had sauce stains from lunch around your mouth? What about situations when you worried about an upcoming date or job interview or when you would be making a presentation? Without implying that all of this book's readers are excessive neurotics, we think we can safely imply that most of you can pinpoint some anxious moments where you worried about how others would perceive you. Of course, we do not keep those worries locked up in our heads and ignore them. We often act on them, and in doing so, act on ourselves as objects that we anticipate people will appraise. Anticipating judgment, we try to manipulate those appraisals.

Sociologists use the term *impression management* to describe the strategic actions that people take to manage both the impressions that other people will have of them and how other people will then react to them. Thinking about occasions of self-consciousness clarifies the concreteness of impression management, since at such times we are acutely aware both of having to engage in impression management (a social process) and of our marked sensitivity to how much we think about ourselves as social objects. Sociologist Erving Goffman wrote a book, *The Presentation of Self in Everyday Life,* that is a landmark contribution to advancing symbolic interactionist thinking.[11] In this book, he analyzes how individuals and groups of people present images of themselves to others. To tackle the analysis of how people manage their impressions, Goffman suggests that we adopt a dramaturgical analogy. Doing so means examining individual and collective social behaviors as if people are actors performing characters onstage for an audience. These actions reflect how we locate ourselves to others and act out identities.

Placed into the context of symbolic interactionism, *The Presentation of Self in Everyday Life* analyzes how people convey a personal identity and definition of the situation by managing the impressions that they express to others. Other people can only understand what we think of as individual and personal identity (the jumbles of characteristics that we think define us), when we enact them and put on a show to demonstrate them. Goffman offers five dramaturgical principles to help analyze impression management. These principles are that (1) people engage in performances to present themselves to others; (2) people work in teams or collectively to express the characteristics of a social situation; (3) people distinguish between different types of social space in which to perform. There are front-stage regions where we offer performances and backstage regions where we prepare our performances; (4) people must worry about the credibility of their performances; and (5) people must avoid communication out of character. They must not express sentiments that are at odds with the requirements of a performance. When someone communicates out of character, he or she must try to repair the damage to an image (or an audience may choose to overlook such divergences).

The idea of people giving performances or acting in teams makes intuitive sense. The concept of regions requires more explanation. Conventional social life demands that people perform particular roles and performances in particular venues. For example, we primp and rehearse answers backstage in order to ready a successful presentation of ourselves for job interviews. All the practicing of answers in advance and examining of our appearance is done out of sight of the interviewer. At the job interview, we are on the front stage. On the front stage, we are supposed to seem naturally who we are without appearing insincere or fake. To get to that good impression, we might rehearse what we will say and how we look in front of a bathroom mirror, in advance, in the backstage, out of sight of the audience. Then on the front stage, we can perform for our intended audience with more credibility.

To conceive of projecting a desirable identity as a social process, and not as a naturally occurring, unconscious behavior is an important motif in *Presentation of Self.* Goffman offers many examples of people enacting a self in the front and back stages. He quotes from George Orwell's description of a waiter's impression management in *Down and Out in Paris and London*:

> *I remember our assistant maitre d' hotel, a fiery Italian, pausing at the dining room door to address an apprentice who had broken a bottle of wine. Shaking his*

fist above his head he yelled (luckily the door was more or less soundproof): Tu me fais chier. *Do you call yourself a waiter, you young bastard? You a waiter! You're not fit to scrub floors in the brothel your mother came from.* Macquereau! *Words failing him he turned to the door, and as he opened it he farted loudly, a favourite Italian insult. Then he entered the dining room and sailed across it dish in hand, graceful as a swan. Ten seconds later he was bowing reverently to a customer. And you could not help thinking, as you saw him bow and smile, with that benign smile of the trained waiter, that the customer was put to shame by having such an aristocrat to serve him.*[12]

Backstage, the assistant maitre'd is vulgar and gruff in chewing out an apprentice. However, on the front stage, when the waiter puts on a polished and deferential appearance for a customer, he transforms from a vulgarian into an aristocrat. Who among us cannot relate to a workplace situation in which we had to put on "service with a smile" that we did not really mean?

Goffman wrote, "We tend to see real performances as something not purposely put together at all, being an unintentional product of the individual's unselfconscious response to the facts of the situation."[13] We want our performances to appear naturally who we are. We attempt to look as if we comply authentically with social and cultural norms in our performances, even if we actually do not. As Goffman notes: "When the individual presents himself before others, his performance will tend to incorporate and exemplify the officially accredited values of society, more so, in fact, than does his behavior as a whole."[14]

Goffman recognized that people have creative potential that they use to manage their impressions. As we noted earlier, situations and roles have fluidity; people do not fulfill all of their roles or act in situations using absolutely scripted and dogmatic actions. Consequently, Goffman does not argue that we act only according to scripts. For example, Goffman does not argue that people go to a party, unfold a paper, and read off a set of instructions of things to say to other partygoers. Instead, we have a sense of how we want to come across, and of how we might talk and act to deliver a desirable impression. Definitions of situations are loosely prescriptive. Goffman identifies the mechanics of how we perform, keeping in mind that we can depart from a script, and improvise how we will come across to others, depending on what we think best under the circumstances, and our own physical and mental ability to perform.

A key contribution that *The Presentation of Self* makes is to provide a conceptual framework for analyzing how people present their "selves" to others. As part of presenting ourselves favorably, we must control what information we emphasize about ourselves and what information we keep secret. Here Goffman's ideas reflect the classic symbolic interactionist argument that people project a desirable definition of the situation to others and have a socially derived sense of self. *The Presentation of Self in Everyday Life* emphasizes that reciprocal relationship between self and society in two important ways. First, Goffman connects consciousness of self and social behaviors in social interaction. Second, he links people's resulting impression management with larger order issues of social order and norms.

To label people as self-conscious is ironic. People commonly understand this term as being inner-directed, but what the term actually refers to, is being hyperconscious of societal expectations, and of what other people might think of you. Self-consciousness puts us on the social stage, where we do things to attempt as ideal a match to a desirable self-image through the *self-reflected appraisals of others* that we possibly can. A wonderful example of the linkage between self-consciousness and an attempt to direct the appraisals of others is in Goffman's example of Preedy, a vacationing Englishman at a Spanish beach.

> *The beach might have been empty. If by chance a ball was thrown his way, he looked surprised; then let a smile of amusement lighten his face (Kindly Preedy), looked round dazed to see that there were people on the beach, tossed it back with a smile to himself and not a smile at the people, and then resumed carelessly his nonchalant survey of space.*
>
> *But it was time to institute a little parade, the parade of the Ideal Preedy. By devious handlings he gave any who wanted to look a chance to see the title of his book, a Spanish translation of Homer, classic thus, but not daring, cosmopolitan too—and then gathered together his beach-wrap and bag into a neat sand-resistant pile (Methodical and Sensible Preedy), rose slowly to stretch at ease his huge frame (Big-Cat Preedy), and tossed aside his sandals (Carefree Preedy, after all).*[15]

Notice in this extended example the link between self-consciousness and focused attention to how Preedy wants other people to perceive him. At times he is "Carefree Preedy" or "Kindly Preedy" or "Big-Cat Preedy". Consider how often we act as Preedy does, conscious at all moments of how we want to appear to others and how we will act and plan to give off those impressions. Perhaps we practice an air of nonchalance (above-it-all Shulman), or we suck in our stomachs (not-as-fat Shulman) or throw a big word into a conversation (intellectual Shulman). Our self-consciousness is linked to social appraisal, and Goffman skillfully illustrates our efforts to portray selves that we desire over ones that we hope remain hidden.

Performances as Cumulative Expectations

Teams of people perform on front and back stages in daily life. It is important to analyze the types of control that people exercise over information in attempts to offer convincing performances and identities. Consider the array of institutions (school, family, and workplaces) where people expect us to act in particular roles. Those sites become theaters where people have prescriptive interactions. The performances that these venues demand have a history of expectations that constitute cumulative patterns. To symbolic interactionists, many of our behaviors in social institutions comprise sets of role characteristics and coordination among performance teams that produce orderly and predictable interactions. For example, Liverpool soccer club fans have been singing "You'll Never Walk Alone" for decades. Prisoners learn routines of how to act around guards and other inmates and they form gangs. Spelling bee participants understand the rules of the competition and act accordingly, almost always asking for the language of origin, alternative pronunciations and for the word to be used in a sentence before attempting to spell a word. The contestants understand that they are to proceed in numerical order, go up to a mike, not heckle other contestants and act with decorum.

Workplaces are also clear locations for examining coordinated dramaturgy between service workers and clients. Have you been to a Disneyworld anywhere in the world? If so, you have seen friendly garbed figures dressed up as cartoon characters help guide thousands of people through an amusement park. They build a consumption experience for guests; likewise guests know what to expect and how to act when at the park, cheering on heroes and hissing at villains. Alternatively, strippers create a definition of the situation and emergent reality that comprised choreographed physical routines, feigned interest in customers and hidden gestures between bouncers, bartenders, and other dancers about patrons.[16] In both situations, the performers hide any behaviors that challenge the impression that they are paid to create. They must avoid showing any discrepancies between image and reality evident. Goffman distinguished between *expressions given,* which are behaviors people present to others that they intend to communicate, and *expressions given off,* which are typically physical communications that people cannot control but that could contradict an image. For example, a person at a job interview might try to act very calm and composed, but if he is anxious and starts sweating, the sweat exposes his nervousness.

Gender, race, religion, and family background all help determine the range and complexity of how we choose to interact with one another. Job interviews are a common experience but the range of how people act within that routine interaction is variable. Cultural and economic backgrounds, for example, can determine how well people do in job interviews. In a book called *The Working Poor,* David Shipler described how a woman's inability to pay to fix the poor appearance of her teeth ended up hurting her in job interviews, which then added to her economic hardships.[17] An ability to alleviate stigmas with backstage resources, experts, and help demonstrates that money can impact the quality of someone's performance and thus the effectiveness of their presented identity. Plastic surgeons, tutors, cosmetic dentistry, and internships are all examples of economic resources that can help give someone an edge in upward mobility.

Conning Consciousness and Individual Agency

Goffman wrote that people might offer overly cynical or sincere performances. When individuals or teams enact identities, they want to create impressions that appear as credible as possible in what they claim to be, say, as the loyal employee, affectionate wife, or nurturing mentor. A sincere person believes so much in a performance that he or she truly loses himself or herself in believing that he or she is that character even when he or she is not. A cynical performance is one where the actor does not really believe in the impression that he or she is presenting but tries to pass off that persona as authentic.

When people take social behavior for granted, they may not account enough for cynical or sincere performances. Instead, they may see behavior as authentic and natural, just how people are. Goffman's ideas that people labor to make their performances credible should make us wary that people's behaviors sometimes attempt to persuade rather than show just how they "are." We must have a healthy skepticism as an audience. Symbolic interaction attunes us to attempts to develop a self in response to feedback from others. Yet how authentic are these selves or the feedback that we are getting from others? We live in an age of self-help books, of guides on how to pick up men and women, how to dress for success and control our nonverbal behavior because "first impressions are everything."

Goffman alerts us to the scheming that can lurk behind impression management, and raises alarms that what could appear to be natural and authentic personas are not. Because individuals have fluidity in performances, they can attempt to shape definitions of the situation through a variety of machinations. As children grow up and they become more aware of attempts to con them, they grow to have a greater appreciation for the impact that impression management has in the world. Erving Goffman's work inspires sociological thinking because he encourages us to "reverse engineer" social interactions. He introduces concepts and a dramaturgical perspective that appeals to the interest that people have in trying to figure out what makes other people tick.

The Nature of Self

Derived from experience, self-images reflect cultural ideas about human nature and about what people can and should be. People have self-focused feelings that the concept of self-esteem captures. They like or dislike what they are, love or hate themselves, and feel energized or depressed by their own real or imagined actions. Three terms that social psychologists use for studying the person—*identity, self-image,* and *self-esteem*—provide a good foundation for understanding the nature of self. Each is a lens that people use to view their relationships to one another and to the social world as a whole.

Western culture, in particular, fosters a view of the person as "separate" from others. This cultural tradition encourages adherents to think of the self as an entity that really and truly exists solely within each person. From this vantage point, the self resides only in an individual and consists primarily of thoughts, feelings, and actions. The symbolic interactionist view of self, as we have noted, however, emphasizes the social nature and origins of the self. We are skeptical of the notion that each person has a "real" and unique self. Although there are commonalities in experiencing a self, symbolic interactionists assert that people living in different cultures vary considerably in how they conceive of a sense of self.

A simple experiment will help to understand how people experience themselves in everyday life. Try writing down the various ways that you have been conscious of yourself in the last few hours. We cannot perform this experiment for you, of course, but we can share an example from Dave as a starting point:

> I woke up this Sunday morning at nine. I know that if I feign that I am still sleeping, maybe I can stick my wife with walking our dog, who is starting to whine for her morning walk. I feel like sleeping even longer, since I am up so early during the workweek, and last night's staying up late and having a few glasses of Merlot isn't helping me get out of bed any faster. I don't drink very much, but how do I have a mild hangover from just a few glasses of wine? What a wuss I've become! I really need to get stuff done today. I think about my teenage son who likes a girl that I think might be playing him—I don't want him to get hurt. Teenagers are so oversensitive at this age. I need to call my father and mother. My mom is recovering from a mild stroke. They live 3,000 miles away and convincing them to move closer so that my sisters and I can help them is going to be an impossible pain in the ass. I am going to have to do some house stuff today too—go food shopping with my wife. The dog is clamoring for

a walk—my wife is going to walk the dog. Yes! Chalk one up for laziness! I get up, hit the bathroom and get some water. My son is still asleep. My wife gets back and I ask her if she wants to go out for coffee and bagels. We drive to the store. I catch a glimpse of myself in the mirror—ok, I need to shower and shave when we get back—I look like crap. My wife and I talk about planning summer activities for our son. He is a gifted soccer player and I am really proud when I watch him play. I like watching him outplay other kids and then I feel bad that I am not the kind of dad who is noncompetitive about that stuff. Am I just another jerky sports parent? At least I don't run my mouth during games. During the drive, my wife and I talk about money as our retirement savings got hammered from the market plunge. I see how the sun catches her face and makes her eyes even bluer. I am still so in love with her after decades. When we get back home, I am first to the computer. I sit down to read my e-mail. All the e-mails waiting for me are reminders of things I have to do. I have e-mails from students about awarding course credit for classes taken abroad (oh the joy having to sign paperwork as a department head), from two different colleagues about meeting to do committee work, and e-mails from retailers—like anyone can afford to buy things right now. Our kitten wants to roughhouse. Time to have Chill (the kitten's name, chosen by my kid) scratch my hands to shreds. Okay, I can respond to these e-mails now, or work on writing, or hit some good Web sites and load up a podcast and then get to work. Who am I kidding—I know I am going to procrastinate. It's time to read the news on the Web for a while.

This mundane account illustrates several features of the experience of self. Taken together, let's conduct an overview of a social psychological experience of the self.

- The self is intermittent.

The experience of self does not involve uninterrupted self-absorption. Most of the time, our attention has to be directed elsewhere. When Dave drove to the store with his wife, for example, he paid attention to driving and wasn't spending the whole time thinking about how he looked in the rearview mirror. When he talked money with his wife, he listened to what she had to say about their debts, her workplace, and an opportunity that she was pursuing for a promotion. When playing with the cat, Dave absent-mindedly roughhoused with him with one hand while spacing out looking at the computer screen.

The experience of self is intermittent, not continuous. Human beings catch glimpses of their thoughts, feelings, and actions. When Dave wrote the self-consciousness passage, he felt briefly self-conscious writing about himself and then he didn't think about it. People cobble together a sense of continuity and sameness—to feel that the self they experience at this moment is the same as the one they experienced a moment, or a day, or a year ago. But they do so on the basis of intermittent and often fleeting glimpses of themselves. Our days are just too full of mechanical acts and routines. We cannot direct our attention everywhere at once. Attention to self is interspersed with attention to a great many other things. For the sake of economy of effort and ease of information processing, we attend to some things and ignore others.

The experience of self is also intermittent because thoughts, feelings, and actions are inaccessible until after they start. A stimulus occurs, and then a response is released. For example, a husband sees his wife give him a dirty look (Why don't you walk the dog in the morning for a change?), and then he begins to feel uncomfortable. Only as the phase of perception gets under way does the husband interpret the look on his wife's face as a "dirty look" and his own feelings as a mix of shame and giddiness at getting out of the task. An act has to begin for it to become a basis for the experience of self.

- The self is indirect.

The glimpses that we do have of ourselves are indirect rather than direct. When Dave felt briefly ashamed about being selfish, he imagined himself from his wife's vantage point. Shame is an individual and personal feeling, to be sure, but in order to experience it, one must imagine oneself from the perspective of another. The experience of self depends on the capacity for adopting the perspective—the role—of the other. Dave sees himself as a "nonjerk sports parent" by momentarily adopting the perspective of the generalized other toward crazy parents who become enraged by bad referee calls, aggressive tackling, or mistakes made by players. Dave doesn't yell at referees and players, so he can define himself positively. Role taking requires knowledge of the role of the other and of role expectations in general. That is, knowledge of the roles of "jerk sports parents" or "nonjerk sports parents" enables a person to look at self from the other's point of view.

- Consciousness is imaginative.

The everyday experience of self is as much a product of our imaginations as of the actual words and deeds of others. Dave imputes to other people and to himself an attitude, but his experience of both them and himself is located in his imagination. He doesn't know that his son is going to end up having his feelings hurt by the girl that he likes. Maybe he is playing her and Dave ought to worry about whether he is going to be the player and not the playee. Maybe his colleagues asking to meet about committee work are motivated to meet to do work collectively rather than to pass off their work at the meeting. Maybe they are sincere rather than seeking to get out of work. Maybe Dave is too distrusting and should change.

Since the self depends on imagining what is going on in the other's mind, the self is a more tenuous and uncertain construction than common sense tells us. Even though we participate in a social world of shared meanings with other people, ultimately we must interpret their words and deeds to know what they think of us. We can be wrong. An experience of John's in graduate school vividly illustrates the point. During a required and much-dreaded oral examination, a professor listened gravely and impassively to his answers to the other examiners' questions. When it came his turn to ask questions, he said without expression, "I have no questions." John struggled inwardly to make sense of this turn of events while outwardly keeping his cool. Was he doing so badly that this professor felt it better to spare him any further embarrassment? Or was John doing well enough that the professor felt it pointless to ask more questions? As it turned out, the latter was the case, and John passed the exam. But for a short while, John's sense of self was, to say the least, uncertain, for he could not be sure what was happening to him. The self is in flux, caught in a process of imagining how the self is being assessed and in turn should be understood. Is a "self" coming across well or poorly?

- The self requires naming.

Consciousness of self typically depends on naming oneself and others. In the illustrations Dave provided, he named himself in a variety of ways: husband, father, department head, wussy and the like. These names are integral to the experience of self and to the capacity to think, feel, and act. Naming of self is always tied, implicitly or explicitly, to naming others. To see oneself as "department head" is implicitly to imagine "students" and "professors" as partners in interaction. To name and thus imagine the self is to name and imagine the other.

Moreover, names motivate actions. When Dave labels himself as looking like "crap," he plans on showering and shaving to avoid criticism. An image of looking like crap is consistent with being unshaven and having sleep lines and uncombed hair. Since Dave labels people with that appearance as "looking like crap," he can scarcely expect to look that way and avoid being labeled as crap himself. Naming oneself puts one into a social context of obligations and expectations, and thus exposes one to their influence, which can then control the person's actions.

- The self arises from self-control.

The experience of self is acute when we act with purpose. Self-consciousness arises from efforts to exert control over our behaviors. Self-consciousness gives human beings their generally refined and precise capacity to choose (within limits) the directions that their conduct will take.

Every act begins preconsciously as an impulse whose nature and direction can become evident and governed only after it has occurred. When a friend you haven't seen in a long time greets you coldly, your response begins before you are aware of it. You feel something—a readiness to act, a sense that you must do "something"—before you know what you will do. Only by taking the perspective of another—of the friend, for example, or of a bystander who sees an emergent look of hurt on your face—can you assign meaning to the friend's act and decide how to respond. Viewing yourself from the perspective of another, you might see that your initial response is one of being hurt and that your face will make that hurt evident. Your response to your own forthcoming act may be to put on the behavioral brakes and formulate an alternative act. In place of a "hurt" response, you can imagine yourself putting on an "unconcerned" face. Seeing that as a more desirable act, you conduct yourself in that way, not letting on that a cold "hello" hurt your feelings. As Goffman might note, you are on the front stage and may not want to reveal how you really feel.

As this illustration suggests, we do not see ourselves aimlessly, but with purpose, and the purpose is usually one of self-control. We are especially conscious of ourselves in those circumstances where we want to shape our conduct to our own purposes or to the expectations of others. For example, you may treat your friend's slight as confirming a suspicion that this person no longer sees you as a friend, and you conceal your feelings as a way of showing that you don't care.

- Consciousness is socially situated.

Much of the everyday experience of self involves establishing a clear situational relationship between the self and other people. Is the person you thought was a friend still your friend? Is someone to whom you are strongly attracted also attracted to you? In these examples, what we later call a *situated identity* is at issue. That is, at least one person in a situation is uncertain of how he or she stands relative to the other. Not knowing how one stands, in sociological terms, means that one does not know who one is in the eyes of the other.

In many routine situations of everyday life, of course, social location is not much of an issue. In the classroom, professor and students know who they are. The professor knows who the students are and the students know who the professor is. Their situated identities as student and professor are firmly established. To put the matter another way, each participant in the situation can name the others, at least by their roles if not by their personal names. They know how to act toward one another and what kind of social object the other is.

Whether problematic or not, a sense of actual, possible, feared, or hoped-for positions relative to others is always a key aspect of experiencing self. We can participate in social situations only by knowing at some level how we fit with the others who are present. Sitting in an automobile repair waiting room, for example, a customer observes (but cannot hear) a conversation between a mechanic and the service manager. Naturally, the customer wonders whether they are discussing her car and worries about how much money their discussion might cost her. When the service manager approaches, she suspects her fears are about to be realized. Even in situations where we clearly know who we are relative to others, our sense of self depends on what we take for granted. With close friends, for example, we take our relationship for granted, and in doing so feel an assured, secure sense of who we are. However, if something happens to that assurance to raise a question about it, our sense of self is doubted right along with it. When we don't know where we stand in a situation, we don't know who we are in that situation.

- The self relies on narrative.

Finally, human beings experience the self through narratives—that is, through stories told and retold, polished, embellished, trimmed, and refurbished.[18] People do not merely act, but tell others of their doings. They tell their life stories when they fall in love or interview for a job. They tell their teachers what they did on their summer vacations. They recount their athletic or sexual exploits to friends, reveal their innermost secrets to those they trust most, and construct more socially palatable accounts of their activities for parents and grandparents. Our symbolic species is a story-telling one.

Occasions for narrative occur almost daily, and when they do, they put the person in the spotlight and require him or her to formulate a plausible account of self. If you apply for a new job, for example, you have to explain why you left or are leaving a previous job. You must sell your qualifications for the position and state your salary requirements. Job applicants that succeed must learn the right things to say about themselves. "I left my previous job because my boss is a jerk and fired me for no good reason" could be true, but "I am a professional who wants to work in a more serious professional environment" is more palatable.

Self-narratives also exist in informal settings. A couple falling in love, for example, exchange narratives, which become progressively more intimate as their relationship grows. The stories they tell each other attempt to portray themselves in a favorable light. That these stories are fashioned for the occasion does not mean that these narratives are inauthentic or insincere. People can convince themselves to believe sincerely in their own presentations of self, whether they are true or not. Moreover, as relationships develop, the narratives of two people are linked. "My story" and "your story" become "our story." When these narratives are linked, experiences of self are as well.

The narrative quality of the self underscores an important point: The self is always in a process of becoming. The self is an emergent reality—an object brought about over time as people tell and retell stories about themselves. It is periodically revised and edited. Although many people are inclined to think of "the self" as unchanging bedrock, the self is constantly being shaped, inscribed, discarded, and polished up.

Identity: The Self as a Social Object

Symbolic interactionists view the self as a primarily social experience. We have been examining in detail how the self arises and how everyday social interactions sustain the self. Erving Goffman's dramaturgical approach offers one means of analyzing how people act socially to convey a public sense of self. We now examine cognitive and affective lenses for concepts of self-image and self-esteem. In order to explore the origins and impact of identity, we must simplify. We do so by focusing on a typical, routine, and relatively straightforward nature of identity in everyday life. Each of the following three illustrations of identity at work involves at least two individuals interacting in terms of named roles in a familiar and relatively short-lived social situation. They differ from one another in the kinds of roles that each represent and in their goals, but all have a similar underlying structure.

Patient and Physician

Alonso arrives at the physician's office on crutches and checks in with the receptionist, who expresses concern about his broken foot and makes sure Alonso's insurance coverage is current. At this point, Alonso becomes a patient in the hands of different medical personnel: nurses, aides, x-ray technicians, and physicians. They weigh him, check his blood pressure, ask questions, probe, prod, examine, pull, push, inject, wrap, caution, instruct, and perform a variety of other tasks. Alonso is swept into an office routine, moved from place to place by others, and told what to do next, and in general made the focus of a medical team that has treated hundreds of broken feet. Along the way, he answers questions ("I broke it when I fell off a ladder"), listens dutifully to instructions about how to care for the cast ("Keep it dry"), and tries to ignore the pain as the broken bones are set and the cast applied. In general, he acts as a patient is supposed to act.

Father and Kids

Harry promised to take his daughter and son fishing. They wake early, eat breakfast, and set off in the car, canoe on top, gear in the trunk, for the drive to the lake. They arrive, unload, launch, and begin their quest for bass and blue gill. Hooks are baited, with friendly and helpful dad showing the kids what to do. Lines are cast, retrieved, untangled, recast, and untangled again. Hooks get stuck on snags or clothing or in trees and have to be replaced. Kim, 8 years old, and Will, aged 6, focus determinedly on the task of catching fish. Harry looks around, sees others catching fish, and thinks he might throw in a line himself. But there is another hook to be baited and a tangled line to be retrieved and fixed, and so his own fishing will have to wait. Then Kim hooks a fish and follows her father's instructions on how to reel it in. More fixing of tangles, baiting of hooks, casts, retrieving lines from trees, and eventually a fish for Will. After a few hours, they set out for home, tired, happy, and sunburned, the kids planning for the next trip, Dad happy with the day, but also secretly thinking of when and how he might go fishing and actually catch something himself.

Just Friends

The phone rings as we finish eating; it's Fred and Carol. They want to meet up, have a few drinks, and then arrive at a party with us. They come over to our place and then we all sit in the living room and chat for a while. We talk about the Dark Knight movie, gossip about mutual friends, and make tentative plans to have dinner together. The occasion is spontaneous and purely sociable: The conversation accomplishes no particular tasks, other than a dinner arrangement, and has no particular topic. We tell jokes, discuss popular culture and our mutual friends. After we hang out for a while and have a few drinks, we walk over to the off-campus party.

These simplified illustrations of everyday interactions gloss over many details of what actually occurs in such situations. Broken feet really hurt intensely and are apt to make patients irritable, especially when nurses and physicians act like it is "no big deal" and seem to ignore a patient's pain. The fishing expedition has the character of a 1950s situation comedy, and doesn't mention the fact that Dad has finally taken the kids along and that Mom will be truly angry with him if he doesn't make it a good day for them. Friends might have come over to our place not to hang out, but because by being there we can leave together and they don't have to arrive alone at the party.

Nevertheless, these illustrations offer a basis for exploring identity. Each illustration portrays people interacting with one another and experiencing each other and the situation from role-based perspectives. That is, there are patients, physicians, fathers, sons, daughters, and friends. In each situation there is a common focus of activity—a goal or object toward which their interaction is mutually directed. Setting a broken foot, learning to fish, and enjoying friendly conversation provide a basis for experiencing the self and to orient oneself toward interacting with the other. Each situation also has a more or less known duration—a beginning, middle, and end that participants understand. Whatever experience of self such situations provide, the experience is finite.

Each of these illustrations demonstrates the presence of a *situated identity*. That is, in each case people experience themselves primarily from perspectives that a situation and its roles provide. These perspectives direct conduct and social interaction, and they also give form to the experience of self. A patient with a broken foot knows what to do in the social setting of a physician's office because he or she grasps the situation as a whole and the various perspectives of the others in it. But the person is also thereby provided with a way of experiencing the self in that situation—not a self with generalized attributes or characteristics, but a "patient" self, one given meaning by the experience of being a patient to the other's physician, nurse, or x-ray technician. A father teaching his children to fish likewise derives a sense of self as a "father" from the specific situation in which he instructs his children in this activity and receives their appreciation and the tacit approval of others for doing so. People talking with friends earn the identity of "friend" by talking with them in situations where friendly conversation is the only object.

Identity is primarily a matter of establishing and maintaining a situational relation between self, roles, and location. Situations and their roles (and other perspectives) provide a way for people to locate themselves relative to one another. The social space within which they do so in the foregoing illustrations is that of the situation—hence the term *situated identity*. What is the meaning of a situated identity? We answer this question in two ways, each of which is important to a full understanding of identity. First, we examine how situated identities are established or produced. Second, we ask what a situated identity "feels like"—that is, what the experience of self as situated identity means to the person in the situation.

How We Produce Situated Identities

When people come together to interact in a situation, they generally establish situated identities without much difficulty. In fact, they ordinarily do not need to think much about doing so. We enter a clothing store and can usually identify the salespeople. They wear nametags with the store logo, dress in a particular way, and they are busy occupying themselves with such tasks as straightening racks of clothing. They also act as clerks should, approaching customers with a "May I help you?" The same is true in a variety of social situations—medical offices, fishing trips, visits from friends, classrooms, post offices, restaurants, libraries, family dinners, and so on. We readily identify other people and place them in relation to us.

The relative ease of identifying self and others in routine social situations depends on a social process that is invisible though familiar. As Gregory P. Stone points out, people regularly make announcements of their own situated identities and placements of others in their situated identities. Indeed, Stone defined identity as a "coincidence of placements and announcements." A person with identity, Stone said, "is situated, that is, cast in the shape of a social object by the acknowledgment of his participation or membership in social relationships."[19] A situated identity emerges when one person's announcements coincide with how others place him or her. This consistency marks an identity.

An identity announcement is anything that another person can potentially interpret as an indication of the role that an individual intends or wants to enact in a situation. Merely to walk onto the showroom floor of an automobile dealership is to announce one's potential situated identity as a "customer." To wear a gold band on the third finger of the left hand is to announce to the world that one is married—and that, in certain circumstances, one should be treated as a married person and not as a potential mate. Likewise, to set up a portable electronic keyboard and begin to play on an urban street corner is to announce one's identity as a "street musician." We make announcements of identity through what we say and do and through our appearance. An identity placement occurs when another person treats the individual in accordance with the announcements that the person has made—when a car salesperson approaches and offers to help or when people stop, listen to the musician and then leave some money. People make announcements and placements with such ease that they are typically unaware that they are doing so.

Perhaps the best way to see the importance of the correspondence of announcements and placements is to examine what happens when they do not exist. Imagine approaching a store clerk who ignores you and keeps up what is evidently a personal telephone conversation instead of offering to help you. This all-too-familiar experience is irritating, to be sure, but in social psychological terms it is more. The clerk's actions not only frustrate your line of activity—you want to make a purchase and leave—but also turns you into a nonentity in the situation. You come with an announcement of a customer identity and are put into a kind of limbo. The clerk, talking excitedly with a friend on the other end of the line, seems to look right through you. It is as if you don't exist. In terms of a situated identity, you actually don't. As this illustration suggests, the capacity to act rests on establishing situated identity. Lacking a response from another that acknowledges one's possession of a situated identity is problematic. Without acknowledgment from the store clerk, one can't act as a customer or get the clerk to act as a clerk.

What makes announcements and placements coincide? A patient and physician that are jointly focused on the patient's broken foot, for example, display mutually congruent announcements and placements. Two other social facts underlie the correspondence: First, two individuals have acknowledged their presence together in a social situation that demands their joint activity. They are—and they know they are—co-present in the situation together. They have mutually recognized that the situation calls for their interaction. Second, acknowledging co-presence means that each accepts the other's right to be in the situation and to make requests or even demands. The physician acknowledges the patient's presence and right to medical treatment; the patient grants the physician's right to touch his or her body and issue commands.

Co-presence and mutual recognition of rights help explain more deeply why having a store clerk ignore you is so irritating and unsettling. These ideas also explain why the clerk must studiously ignore the individual in order to carry on a personal phone conversation in the customer's presence. To be ignored makes one a nonentity. Acknowledgment of copresence is a fundamental condition for situated identity and corresponding action. Without this acknowledgment, there is no identity, nor is there any acknowledgment by the other of one's right to act in terms of it. The store clerk implicitly understands that as soon as he or she recognizes the presence of the customer, the telephone conversation must end. The professor in an office earnestly talks with a student and carefully avoids noticing the student standing outside (whom the professor has, in fact, noticed and must, therefore, make a show of not noticing). To acknowledge the presence and rights of another is to begin the process of placing the other in accordance with his or her announcement.

The Experience of Situated Identity

The experience of situated identity is paradoxical.[20] When announcements and placements coincide, a situated identity is like clothing that warms and protects even though one is scarcely aware of wearing it. Patients having broken parts fixed, father and children spending a warm summer day together, and friends hanging out together are not highly or constantly conscious of being patients, parents, children, or friends. Once these situated identities are established, they provide the framework within which people act. They are important, for the capacity to act depends on their establishment, but for the most part, they are invisible and we take them for granted. They are powerful yet tenuous and short-lived experiences.

To grasp the power and the limitations of situated identity, we must look in greater detail at two ideas—integration and continuity—that help explain how situated identities function.

- Situated identity provides for the integration of the person's thoughts, feelings, and actions in a single situation.

The word *integration* refers to "joining" or "bringing together" something—but what? A situated identity concentrates the mind, keeping distractions at bay and enabling the individual to fully engage with the activity at hand. Concentration is important in maintaining a focused identity in social life. Identity puts a set of blinders on the individual, making it possible for him or her to attend only to those stimuli that are relevant to the activity at hand. We can recognize these signs when norms are disturbed, such as in the case of the clerk that ignores us.

While people try to concentrate on their situated identities, others may do things to undermine their efforts. Mothers interrupt children watching television or doing their homework and ask them to take out the garbage. Students knock on professors' doors and interrupt their deep thoughts. Even when others are not distracting them, people distract themselves. A student thinks of her upcoming soccer game instead of focusing on the lecture. We daydream. We stress. For example, a professor teaching in the classroom remembers that later that day, he or she will have to chair a difficult and contentious faculty meeting.

How do people respond to such distractions? Sometimes they simply get distracted—a male administrator is transfixed by a shapely leg and momentarily forgets about the request of the woman attached to that leg. A real estate salesperson forgets a client's name. But whether the distraction is real or merely possible, a common response is a verbal one. The man tells himself, "don't stare!" The real estate salesperson reminds herself that she needs to make a sale to get a commission. These verbal responses have several things in common: First, they directly or indirectly name the situated identity that the person seeks to recover or reinvigorate (or they name the situated identity of the other): "She's staff, for heaven's sake!" "I can sell any piece of real estate!" Second, they reaffirm the person's attachment to and embracement of the role. The verbal self-reminder is a way to get "psyched up" for the task at hand. Third, somewhat paradoxically, these announcements also remind one that at other times and places one is firmly attached to other situated identities. The very act of reaffirming a situated identity reminds us of other situated identities that we have.

- Situated identity creates a feeling of continuity. Unifying the person's thoughts, feelings, and actions for a limited period of time enables a sense of events and actions to flow logically and meaningfully from one point to another.

Situated identities organize conduct over time. Sport provides many illustrations of the look and feel of this continuity. When things are "clicking" on a basketball team, for example, each player moves in easy coordination with the others, positioning himself or herself in just the right spot to receive a pass or attempt a shot. A golfer on her game confidently judges the lay of each hole, calculates the effects of wind and weather, and plots a strategy to achieve the fewest number of shots. A tennis player on a good day seems able to anticipate an opponent's every move. Moreover, these experiences feel good. Movement seems fluid and easy and the individual feels in control of self and situation. Like integration, continuity is subject to disruption. People make mistakes. They may misjudge responses. Sometimes they don't have the ability to do exactly the right thing. A jumbo jet passes low overhead, the house shakes, and the dismayed real estate agent sees the unmistakable look on her client's face: This house is not for me! The bell rings, the class ends, the game is over.

The response to disruptions is, again, partially verbal. Just as people remind themselves who they are in a situation in an effort to regain their concentration, they do so in an attempt to restore the flow of activity. The pitcher reminds himself that he has pitched many complete games and in doing so tries to summon the energy to keep a no-hitter going. A resident who gives the physician the wrong instrument utters a brief "sorry" and shakes his head in disapproval of his mistake. Doing so is an implicit promise to self and others to redouble one's efforts so that the expected routine won't be disrupted again. The real estate agent shrugs inwardly and reminds herself there are other houses she can show the client.

Such efforts to sustain a situated identity and the situation as a whole remind the person that he or she has a life outside this situation. An athlete may overcome tiredness or distraction and talk himself or herself back into the game. Even so, the individual may wonder whether fatigue is an indication that a career is nearing its end. To think such thoughts is to evoke an image of oneself with a life beyond a particular situated identity. When people—athletes, professors, and airline flight attendants alike—contemplate retiring and thus severing their active ties with an occupation, they think of what else they will do with their lives. To think in such terms is to imagine a self that will continue even when one of its mainstays is no longer present.

Social and Personal Identity

Discussion of the "person beyond the immediate situation," as Sheldon Stryker[21] puts it, leads us to consider other ways that people locate themselves and one another in social life. In addition to the situated selves that are produced in each context of interaction as situated identities are created, there is an ongoing process that produces what we sometimes call a biographical self. Two additional forms of identity—personal identity and social identity—also provide for the integration and continuity of the person and are the main components of this biographical self. To understand why personal and social identities exist and how they function, we must examine another pair of ideas.

- *Identifying* self with others is a major driving force in human conduct, encompassing feelings of attachment to others, common purposes in interaction with them, and likeness or similarity. Such identification is associated with positive affective responses to others and to situations.

This identification is conceived best as a by-product of social interaction. People must share a definition of the situation in order to interact. They must recognize that they are in the same place, that a particular range and sequence of activities are required, and that they are linked to one another in particular ways. To purchase a new car, for example, one goes to a new car dealer, finds (or is set upon by) a salesperson, looks, tests, negotiates a price, and signs a sales agreement. These activities entail a shared definition of the situation, and to that extent, a limited perception of similarity and common purpose between seller and buyer.

Identification is an affective and a cognitive experience. To identify with another person, the members of one's team, or even an abstract category of people ("the human race") is to respond with positive affect to the object of identification. The presence or even the thought of the object creates positive feelings, a hopeful and optimistic mood, and a sense that life is good. A conversation with a dear friend not only enhances a sense of how much one shares experiences and attitudes with the friend but also how much the presence of the friend makes one feel good. Moreover, identification involves positive affect and good mood and also a variety of positive emotions: happiness, joy, excitement, and satisfaction, to name a few.

- *Differentiation* is also a major force, entailing an individual perspective, a feeling that the person has a particular part to play in interaction with others, that he or she is in some ways distinctive, and that there are individual goals worth pursuing. Differentiation is also associated with positive affect.

Thomas Scheff argues that although identification is an essential part of the healthy social bond, so is differentiation.[22] Identification cements people together through their mutual cognition of similarity and positive affect. In contrast, differentiation bonds people through their sense of separateness. A healthy bond, in Scheff's view, does not exist when people are joined at the hip to the extent that each cannot think, feel, or act without taking the other into account. Rather, the bond is healthy when each person can maintain a sense of individuality in relation to the other. People naturally seek to develop and maintain healthy bonds, Scheff says, and they seek to balance the pleasures of identification and differentiation, to be attached to the other without being overwhelmed.

Just as situated identities help individuals develop a sense of integration and continuity, they contribute to identification and differentiation. Playing in a softball game, for example, enables the person to identify with his or her team and feel a bond with others.

Winning feels good, of course, but so does just playing. At the same time, the game and a situated identity of "pitcher" or "infielder" provide for a sense of difference from others. One makes a distinctive contribution to the team effort because one is a "pitcher." One also feels distinct from members of the opposing team.

However, a situated identity is limited as a basis for a social bond, just as it is limited in providing for integration and continuity. When the game is over, team members disperse and interact with other role partners. In these other situations, the person acquires a new situated identity and new others with whom to identify or differentiate. Moreover, some situations are more suited for purposes of identification than differentiation and vice versa. In a crowd aroused to a fevered pitch by a charismatic speaker, such as an evangelist, people strongly identify with one another but they may lose some of their capacity for self-control. They are, we sometimes say, swept away by their feelings. The same may be true of people in the throes of romantic love. In contrast, situations like that of a real estate agent are better suited for the differentiation of self from other. The sales agent is keenly aware of the differing interest of self and other and of buyer and seller. The agent and the seller want the best price they can get for a property; the buyer wants the lowest price at which the seller will sell. Far from being just an economic transaction, the situation fosters a heightened awareness of the differing perspectives from which participants act.

People develop a sense of themselves as whole beings (integration) acting purposefully and effectively in their social world (continuity) by developing forms of identity that transcend a particular situation. We call these forms of identity social and personal identity. People identify with particular others in immediate and short-lived situations and also with others that they interact with over longer periods of time. They include such particular others as friends and family and larger groups and categories, such as communities and even abstract categories. These kinds of others provide for a sense of individual difference and similarity. Table 3.1 presents a systematic comparison of situated, social and personal identity.

Social Identity

Social identity locates the person in a social space larger and longer lasting than any particular situation. A player has a situated identity within a game—pitcher, catcher, batter, and the like—but also thinks of himself or herself as an "athlete." To claim a social identity as an athlete is to place oneself in relation to others in the social world, specifically those who are or are not athletes. The social identity of athlete is larger in scope and longer in duration than the particular situated activities on which it is based.

Social identity also depends on identifying with a social category. To be an athlete— or Jewish or a born-again Christian—is to identify with others who are perceived as like oneself and whose real or imagined presence evokes positive feelings. Identification with others implies that the group shares beliefs, values, and purposes. One person may believe in "achieving my personal best," and another may believe that developing a "personal relationship with Jesus" is a vital measure of individual accomplishment. In either case, identification means that members of one's social category share such beliefs and goals. Fellow athletes want to excel at a sport and members of congregations are expected to agree on the basic tenets of their faiths.

TABLE 3.1   Forms of Identity

	Situated	Social	Personal
What is the basis of the identity?	A role is required (e.g., student, priest, friend, and professor).	Membership in or identification with a community is needed (e.g., fellow students, the gay community, and a neighborhood).	A life project or life story is required (e.g., becoming famous, being a nonconformist, and being oneself).
How long does the identity last?	The identity lasts for the duration of the situation in which the role is located (e.g., as long as one is in class or interacting with a friend).	The identity lasts during the span of membership in or identification with the community (e.g., as long as one lives in or identifies with the neighborhood).	The identity lasts until the narrative of the life story changes (e.g., as long as one is doing things designed to achieve fame or establish differences from others).
What kinds of announcements are made?	Announcements are expressive and instrumental actions that show identification with the role and/or perform activities of the role (e.g., taking notes, wearing a priest's garb).	Announcements are about one's identifications, especially announcements made on narrative occasions (e.g., telling others about the importance of family or friends).	Announcements are about plans, projects, and individuality, especially announcements made on narrative occasions (e.g., wearing distinctive clothing, piercing bodily parts).
What kinds of placements are made?	Placements are expressive and instrumental actions by others that confirm the acceptance of the individual's appropriation of role and his or her willingness to interact in terms of the role (e.g., answering a student's questions, confessing to a priest).	Placements are expressive actions by community members and/or outsiders that confirm legitimacy of identification and willingness to accept claims of membership (e.g., treating a claimant as a friend or a family member).	Placements are expressive actions that confirm the legitimacy and desirability of the life story (e.g., expressing agreement or admiration).

Identification also converts social categories into functional (if not necessarily functioning) communities. In a sociological sense, a functioning community is comprised of people that live in close proximity to one another over a prolonged time. The English village (such as Arkengarthdale in North Yorkshire), the American small town (Casey, Iowa) or the ethnic urban neighborhood (Boston's heavily Italian North End) are examples. In these places people know one another and lead their lives to a great extent in one another's presence. They feel a sense of shared purpose and are likely to develop well-defined and enduring relationships with one another. Those who identify with a social category relate to members of that category like a community in the classic sense. That is, they come to feel that they know other members even if their "knowledge" of others is indirect and impersonal, and that those others are "present," even if typically only in imagination.

Identification with a category as if it were a community in the classic sense does not make it so in fact, but from the individual's perspective it functions in the same way. That is, the imagined community provides an encompassing social place to which the person can attach himself or herself, providing a set of beliefs, values, and purposes that the individual can share with others, even if only in the mind. Common beliefs, values, and purposes transcend the goals and roles of a particular situation.

Social identity also provides for differentiating the self from others. Within the real or imagined community, a person can carve out a distinctive place in relation to others even while identifying with them. A star quarterback in professional football is a distinguished athlete, perhaps also a model for others. Others may view a woman who identifies strongly with her company and makes it one of her communities as distinctive because of her commitment, leadership abilities, and capacity to solve problems. Even though identification is at the core of social identity, there is an evident need for some degrees of separation and difference from others.

Identification with a particular community is also a way to differentiate oneself from people who are not members. In many instances, social identity establishes a sense of difference that looks on others with pity, condemnation, avoidance, or even violence. Evangelical Christians feel a strong need to bring others into the fold. The old-order Amish restrict and regulate contact with outsiders, who are viewed as potential threats to the community's survival. For many gays and lesbians, identification with the gay and lesbian community provides the security of a social identity and also a sense of legitimate and valued difference from others.

Social identity, like situated identity, relies on the announcement/placement process. In other words, a social identity is more than a private experience, something carried within the mind as a way of thinking about oneself in relation to others. Rather, when the individual announces a social identity, that identity does not fully exist until others place him or her in it. As tempting as it is to think of social identity as primarily a matter of interest to the individual, other people also take it into account and use it as a basis for acting toward the person.

Social identity is accomplished when announcements and placements coincide. Athletes tell others of their accomplishments, get their pictures on cereal boxes, endorse products, and go on talk shows. These public presentations of self as athlete constitute claims about who they are and how others should treat them—as great athletes or role models for high school athletes. The television host who shows respect or lavishes praise on this athlete honors that claim and places the athlete's social identity.

Placements of people into situated identities usually involve positive responses from others, but not always. Members of socially marginalized groups, for example, honor one another's claims for membership, because nonmembers often treat them with hostility. The hostility of outsiders strengthens, rather than undermines, the solidarity of the group and the identification of members with it.[23]

Although announcements typically precede placements—someone makes a claim and then someone else honors that claim—the reverse can also be true. Dissatisfied with the reckless behavior of some male star athletes, a variety of people—women, sportswriters, politicians—have called upon these men to clean up their acts and serve as better role models for young people. These calls for better behavior are, in fact, efforts to place the athletes whose behavior is being criticized in the "role model" role and confer the obligations attached to the situated and social identities that go with that role. Famous athletes can also reject this call and attempt to negotiate such placements by countering, as the famous basketball player Charles Barkley did when he stated, "I don't believe professional athletes should be role models. I believe parents should be role models."

Finally, there is an important exception to the rule that social identities depend on the coincidence of placements and announcements. Sometimes a social identity is intensely desired, but the individual knows that he or she cannot reveal that identity without being drastically transformed and perhaps rejected by others. Gays and lesbians have felt historically that they often must remain at least partially "in the closet" because those whom they know or with whom they work would reject them if they knew their sexual orientation. They may stay closeted because there is no one to whom a claim of a social identity based on sexuality may be made safely. Individuals in contemporary society can now access a wide array of ideas, facts, opinions, and ideologies through mass media. As a result, gays can now learn about other gays and lesbians, and about being gay or lesbian, without openly contacting other gays and lesbians and exposing the secret to friends or family. The person can read the personal narratives of gays and lesbians and participate in discourse about sexual orientation vicariously. In short, social identity can emerge without specific placements and announcements, because society exists in the mind and the imagination and not just in concrete interactions between people. Also, other people can now learn more about homosexuality and change their views. Eventually, more social acceptance can emerge of that social identity, as many people argue is now occurring with the increasing public presence of many gay celebrities in a variety of professions.

Personal Identity

By focusing on the individual's life story, personal identity locates the person in a social space that is larger and longer lasting than any particular situation. Where the social identity of "athlete" entails identification and similarity, the personal identity of a particular athlete rests on distinctive accomplishments and characteristics, such as with Tiger Woods. Personal identity stresses uniqueness and difference. The amazing success of Tiger Woods interests other athletes and sports fans, of course, but someone who has dominated a familiar and traditionally racially exclusive sport unlike any other golfer in history also impresses a wider audience. Personal identity depends on the person's construction and maintenance of an autobiography—a life story that is built, told to (and by) others in various contexts, and from time to time revised to fit changing experiences or preferences.

The life story around which personal identity is constructed typically has one or more main themes that give meaning to the individual's actions. One person may emphasize an especially strong work ethic and show up at the job day after day, ready to go to work, even at times when he or she could easily find an excuse to take a day off. Another may define himself or herself as a seeker of religious or philosophical truth, exploring first one, and then another system of beliefs, in an effort to discover the most plausible one. Others may seek fame or celebrity wishing to become a "household name," someone everybody knows. Tens of thousands of people crowd *American Idol* auditions to attain this individual acclaim. Others seek full autonomy and a desire to be unique and independent. Some get full body tattoos or remove themselves from society and live solitary lives. Such themes are a basis for the person to interpret his or her own acts and have others interpret them. The steady employee that thinks of himself or herself as totally committed to work never takes a sick day. He or she thinks of normal aches and pains as "not serious enough" to stay home from work. The person seeking full autonomy is likely to interpret urges to connect with others as a threat to his or her independence. Recognizing this aloofness, other people may refrain from making overtures because they know they will be rejected.

A personal identity is considered something that the person creates, owns, and is entitled to modify as he or she sees fit. Avoiding change can even be considered a source of pride or stubbornness, depending on the beholder. For example, a dedicated worker that others urge to "take it easy" might respond, "This is me!" A religious seeker who has committed to a belief system, when confronted by people with differing opinions, might say, "These are my beliefs and my truth, and no one can take them away from me." The autonomy seeker acknowledges as few obligations to others as possible, arguing, "My first obligation is to myself." In more general terms, personal identity involves a sense of ownership of "the self," a belief that one owns the rights to one's body and mind, and should not cede these rights to others.

Every personal identity rests at some point on the individual's participation in a cultural world shared with others. A star athlete like Michael Jordan, for example, had a truly distinguished sports career; he was a unique basketball player, one whose name almost everybody knows, who inspires unusual respect for his accomplishments. But his very distinctiveness is defined by the fact that he exceeded the typical expectations of a career in basketball. Basketball players, professors, plumbers, and police officers all orient themselves to careers typical of their fields. Professors have a six-year probationary period as assistant professors before they are evaluated for and possibly awarded tenure and promoted to associate professors. Police officers strive to advance through a set of defined ranks and duty assignments, and they know approximately on what schedule they might do so. Careers are culturally and socially standardized. Individuals can achieve a personal identity by meeting expectations in distinctive ways. Even people seeking as much autonomy as possible do so against a background of cultural definitions and social arrangements. For such an individual, cultural definitions of the good life or of correct behavior are likely perceived as wrong, and social arrangements as overly restrictive—the individual defines himself or herself personally against those standing conventions. People that rebel define themselves as rebels by what they rebel for and against.

Personal identity depends on announcements and placements like situated identity and social identity do. The adolescent striving for autonomy from parents announces his or her emergent personal identity as an independent being in various ways. He or she might test or break the rules that parents impose, reject parental authority, or openly break with the family's religious or political affiliations. Parents, in turn, place their adolescent son or daughter into a more autonomous identity, as they slowly modify the rules, look the other way when they are violated, or react strongly to transgressions.

The three forms of identity—situated, social, and personal—are not mutually exclusive. Each person acquires and exercises a variety of situated identities in his or her daily life. But the individual also develops a personal identity and one or more social identities. Sometimes a personal identity is strong enough to dominate and diminish the person's social identities. Some individuals rely on one or two mainstay social identities, whereas others manage several. Some cultures make a virtue of strong personal identity and make attachment and commitment to others quite difficult. Other cultures discourage individuals from developing any personal identities, by always defining the person in relation to others. In all cultures and social settings, however, situated, social, and personal identities are an inevitable product of the social organization of personal life.

Self-Image: Knowing the Self

How is identity related to self-knowledge? A situated identity means that the person knows where he or she stands in relation to other people—as father to daughter, student to professor, friend to friend. One or more social identities tell the person where he or she is placed in the social world—as a dedicated worker among less-committed colleagues, a Jewish person in a predominantly Christian society, as a resident of an urban neighborhood, or perhaps all of these. Personal identity provides a basis for knowing oneself as a person with a life story and who has goals or qualities that distinguish one from others. Individuals categorize themselves as they announce identities and are placed in them by others. They use abstract ways of defining people—as introverted or extroverted, athletic or clumsy, flexible or rigid—that culture provides to characterize them. People use the generalizations they learn or create as a basis for understanding themselves.

Psychologically oriented social psychologists use the concept of the self-schema to study self-knowledge—how people know themselves, what they know, and how they use their knowledge. More formally, a *self-schema* is a "cognitive generalization about the self, derived from past experience, that organizes and guides the processing of self-related information contained in the individual's social experiences."[24] Individuals who see themselves as possessing a particular trait are said to be "schematic" for that trait. Thus, one may be schematic for athleticism, extroversion, or unhappiness. Individuals to whom a particular domain is unimportant are said to be nonschematic.

A self-schema, like any schema, contains information about an object (in this case, the self), ideas about how the object is put together and functions, and examples of the object. So, for example, an individual's self-schema may contain information about his or her traits and characteristics (intelligent, strong-willed, compassionate toward others, ambitious, outgoing). Likewise, the same individual may have formed ideas about how these elements do or do not fit together: "I am ambitious because I want to use my intelligence and willpower to good effect." "Sometimes my ambitions get in the way of my desire to be caring and sensitive to others." A self-schema may also contain images of an ideal self, and perhaps also images of others whom the person idealizes.

Self-schemas "theorize" the self just as schemas in general "theorize" the external world. That is, self-schemas create a theory of the self that combines categories, abstract ideas, and propositions about how things relate to one another. People create these assemblies of facts, ideas, and propositions—or adopt them from others—for practical reasons.

Self-schemas reduce the incoming flow of information to manageable dimensions. They help people make sense of themselves so that they can decide how to act. They focus memory on relevant information and help the person process that information and shape how people see the others with whom they interact.

According to Markus and colleagues,[25] being schematic on a particular trait is like being an expert in a particular field. Experts quickly recognize relevant information in their field. For example, a plumber will see evidence of a leaking pipe more readily than will a homeowner. Experts can organize incoming information readily and relate it to what they already know. A plumber will quickly observe that the leaking pipe is probably a drainpipe and remember repairing such pipes previously. Experts use contextual clues to fill in missing information and adjust their processing of information to the task at hand. A plumber notices the location of stained wallpaper or a wet ceiling and treats these facts as clues to round out his or her picture of the situation. He or she can shift attention from the trees to the forest. They can see that although the drainpipe is leaking, a greater problem is that the floor is about to collapse because water has caused it to rot.

An individual that is schematic on a particular dimension develops expertise in that area. For example, a person who thinks of himself or herself as having a tendency toward depression reads about it, talks about it with others, or seeks professional help. As a result, this individual knows how to recognize the signs of an impending depressive episode more than a nonschematic person would. He or she is better able to remember past episodes of depression and relate this one to those experiences. Contextual clues—the perplexing behavior of others, difficulty getting going in the morning—enable the individual to get a good picture of the impending episode.

The sociological significance of self-schemata is in how schematic information about the self influences perceptions. Others that share and use an existing set of categories, ideas, and propositions surround people, in all societies, from birth. In contemporary societies, people not only encounter others with whom they directly interact but they also confront a seemingly omnipresent mass media communicating a vast variety of ideas and propositions. Magazines, radio, television, movies, and the Internet make available great quantities of information about human beings and their characteristics. The possibility of being schematic regarding a trait is now more detailed and nuanced than at any other historical moment. Whether the source of categories, ideas, and propositions is one's family, teachers, MTV, or writings from a wall on Facebook, the result is the same. People learn what images of self are possible. Their schemas reflect what culture makes available.

Self-Esteem

People respond to their experiences with their hearts as well as their heads. Their relationships with others engender emotions and feelings—of love or hate, satisfaction or frustration, security or fear—and these emotional responses are crucial to understanding the person. These feelings are directed toward the self as much as toward others and social situations. We love or hate, feel satisfied or frustrated with the type of person that we believe we are, and feel secure or anxious in our identities.

This emotional or affective dimension comprises what people refer to as self-esteem. We take pride in a job well done or feel shame when we make mistakes. We experience feelings of joy, sadness, anger, dismay, and other emotions in our everyday lives. When the focus of those sentiments is the self, we are in the realm of self-esteem. Self-esteem arises in us when we think and feel about ourselves in connection to how we think others see us.

When considered as an affective dimension of the self, self-esteem appears to be just an individual phenomenon. Yet self-esteem, just like identity, is a complex product of co-ordinated social activity. Self-esteem is a product of situations and also something people bring to situations. Self-esteem is a property of individuals that also emerges from a social context of role making and role taking. Sociologist Charles Horton Cooley used the metaphor of a looking glass to depict the nature and sources of images of the self.

> *A self idea . . . seems to have three principal elements: the imagination of our appearance to the other person; the imagination of his judgment of that appearance; and some sort of self-feeling, such as pride or mortification.*[26]

According to Cooley, our feelings about ourselves emerge from a process of imagining how we appear in others' eyes.

> *The thing that moves us to pride or shame is . . . an imputed sentiment. . . . This is evident from the fact that the character and weight of that other, in whose mind we see ourselves, makes all the difference with our feeling. We are ashamed to seem evasive in the presence of a straightforward man, cowardly in the presence of a brave one, gross in the eyes of a refined one, and so on. We imagine, and in imagining share, the judgments of the other mind.*[27]

People develop images of one another through interaction. They bring schemas for one another to those interactions. Those images—of bravery, refinement, tact, competence, intelligence, kindness, cruelty, stupidity, deviousness, and the like—become established, and people then imagine their own appearance in terms of the appearances of others. That is, the person forms an image of the other, then imagines his or her appearance to the other from the standpoint of that image, and then feels good or bad accordingly.[28]

This approach to self-esteem emphasizes the appraisals of others, as the individual perceives them in situations.[29] When people mince no words telling us exactly what they think of us, we have direct access to their opinions of us. Their words of praise or condemnation encourage us to form specific images of ourselves. Much of the time, however, we must rely on role taking, and imagine our appearance to the other. In either case, the result is an affective response. Whether other people tell us directly how they feel about us, or whether we impute their sentiments concerning us, the result is that we develop an attitude toward ourselves.

Our responses and feelings of self-esteem vary depending on the importance we attach to different people. We put more stock in what our long-standing friends think of us than in a stranger's opinion. Some situations also carry more impact than others. We filter the self-sentiments that arise in each situation through our existing conceptions of self, after which they add to or subtract from our overall self-esteem.

In an American culture that emphasizes competitive individual achievement, we ruthlessly compare our own activities and accomplishments to what other people have done. We look over our shoulders and worry about what we have done compared to others of our age or in a peer group. When we are younger, we might care more about who is better looking or popular. We might then graduate into worrying about who has better chances of getting into a good college or university or more respect. As we age, we can compare ourselves into happiness or despair by assessing who has more money or has achieved a more impressive career. We can then move into comparing whose children or grandchildren are doing better in school or sports. These comparisons impact our self-esteem. From a cynical perspective, we might become depressed, unless we can explain away or rationalize having a worse social status than another person. For example, we can think that someone got that great job because they know somebody. In contrast, we might pay special attention to other people who we think are doing less well than we are and be happy because we are doing better. In this cynical vein, as Gore Vidal once stated: "It is not enough to succeed. Others must fail."

While important, we cannot state that the determining nature of group standards and judgments is the only game in town. Symbolic interactionists stress that human beings are naturally active and self-conscious creatures that acquire some degree of autonomy along with the self. We act to earn the approval of others. We also act in ways that let us approve of ourselves because we act in ways that others would have us act. But we also develop individual goals and aspirations. We seek social identities that situate us comfortably in the bosom of community but also develop personal identities that entail projects and goals of our own that will put us in opposition to others.

People also derive self-esteem to the extent that their pursuit of personal identity is successful. Viktor Gecas and Michael Schwalbe have argued for the importance of what they call "efficacy-based" self-esteem, which is a positive sense of self a person derives from effective action.[30] Self-esteem is achieved in part through exercising our capacities to take effective actions—to solve problems, create new things or ideas or demonstrate our autonomy from the social world.

In seeking positive appraisals, people may consciously seek to deceive others. While people sometimes genuinely and spontaneously adapt their behavior to social standards, at other times, they will just create the appearance of doing so. We cannot always emulate others or live up to their expectations. Instead, we may use a variety of techniques of impression management to mislead them. As an example, consider clothing and cosmetics as props and not just as fashion items. Corsets and girdles created artificial narrowness. Men dye their hair to avoid grey and wear toupees to cover up baldness or a receding hairline. Men wear lifts in their shoes to appear taller and women purchase bras designed to enhance the appearance of their busts. Tabloids continually identify movie stars that are alleged to have had plastic surgeries (that they routinely deny—more impression management) to appear younger than they really are.

In another example, consider how often employees hide shirking their work. In *From Hire to Liar,* Shulman identifies many examples of this deception in the workplace.[31] Consider what you might have seen yourself. Have you observed someone call in sick to take a day off work, surf the Web or send text messages instead of work, or play solitaire on a computer while having a fake work screen ready with a quick pressing of the ALT-TAB buttons? In the romantic realm, men and women feign sincere interest in and respect for one another in quests for one-night stands. David Grazian documents these techniques in his ethnography of college men and women "on the make" in the Philadelphia nightlife scene.[32] For example, he describes how men are on a "girl hunt" that often ends up in a show of masculine bravado for male peers. Women, in turn, use maneuvers to attract men, such as trying to look older, or they may adopt defensive techniques to ward off unwanted suitors. One amusing example of such a tactic is a fake number that some women give to rid themselves of unwanted suitors. The number is (215) 618-1505 and leads to a message service called the Philadelphia Rejection hotline that plays a recorded message for callers, explaining all the potential reasons why his advances are being rejected.

An individual who acts deceptively may find himself or herself inwardly alienated from this presented self. They may be able to convince themselves, as well as others, of the validity of their performance. Erving Goffman points out that people may be "taken in" by their own performances, so that what was initially a "false" presentation of self becomes a sincere one.[33] He also acknowledges that people are also self-aware of putting on a show that they know is false, and that they may just resolve themselves to offering a "cynical" performance.

Our own appraisals of our performances influence our self-esteem. In the classic formulation of the psychologist William James, our self-esteem is influenced by a "ratio" of success to pretension. The more someone aspires to a particular accomplishment or other standard of self-worth, the greater one's successes must be in order to feel worthy. How we feel about ourselves results from what other people tell us and also from what we want to be. If you see yourself as someone who could be a champion athlete, mere athletic prowess or modest success is not enough; you have to win in order to live up to your aspirations. As James's formulation suggests, the feelings we have about ourselves are weighed against our aspirations. If your goal is to be a professional tennis player and you have defeated a third-rate club pro, the thrill of victory should be tempered by a sense that this particular victory does not really count for much.

Self-esteem is the product of a continual process of reflection in which the person decides what standards and people are significant influences. At any given point in a person's life, we learn that a person has an organized sense of what is important and what is not, of whose appraisals to take seriously and whose to disregard. Some identities, for example, are more psychologically central than others. A lawyer who falls short of a previous aspiration to make a fortune can adopt a revised version of occupational identity in which the new goal is to do well enough to be respected in the community and provide for family needs. A person that is good at academic tasks but lacks athletic talents emphasizes the academic identity and downplays the athletic one. People thus maximize the chances of feeling positive about self by emphasizing those activities where they experience more favorable appraisals and comparisons.

Finally, although much social psychological theorizing treats self-esteem as variable according to the person's social experiences, there are limits to how much self-esteem can vary in a person from one occasion to another. Each person may have a particular "set-point" for self-esteem—a level of self-esteem that is customary and normal for him or her and which does not fluctuate much. Moreover, self-esteem is closely linked to mood—the person's overall sense of whether things are going positively or negatively. The same things that affect mood can also shape self-esteem. These include positive and negative occurrences in the person's life and also internal organic and psychological factors that elevate or depress mood regardless of external events.

The Self, Motive, and Motivation

Why does one child conscientiously do what her or his parents expect while a sibling rebels at almost every opportunity? What makes one person ambitious for wealth and power while another is content with less? Why do some people obey the speed limit on the highway and others break it? Why do some people always feel good about themselves while others apparently never do?

To answer these "why" questions, social scientists and lay people alike frequently invoke two terms: motivation and motive. The psychologist, for example, might explain that a child's disobedience in school is motivated by a need to get the attention of teachers, or that a person's ambition is shaped by the need to please demanding parents. The explanations that people routinely construct in their everyday lives often invoke motives that they presume underlie their own and others' conduct. That is, people are supposed to have a variety of motives for their actions: love, revenge, profit, altruism, and the like. The motive for donating a healthy kidney to an ailing spouse is love, we might say, or a student's motive for giving a professor a bad rating on a course evaluation is revenge for receiving a low grade.

Both motivation and motive have their roots in the Latin verb *movere*—to move. To explain why people do what they do, social scientists and ordinary people alike examine what "moves" conduct. If a person acts in a particular way, it must be, we think, because something pushes, impels, drives, prompts, stimulates, induces, or provokes the person to act in that way. Social scientists and ordinary people alike recognize that external influences and internal ones shape behavior. However the terms *motivation* and *motive* refer specifically to internal states. A crucial part of what moves conduct is thought to come from within the person.

We must distinguish carefully between motivation and motive (see Table 3.2). *Motivation* refers to drives, needs, urges, and other states that shape responses to stimuli at any given moment. In other words, to cite motivation is to identify an internal state of the individual that influences how he or she responds to the environment at a particular time. To say that a person is "hungry," for example, is to say that he or she is particularly sensitive to food stimuli and that the impulses most likely to be released are those linked to food. A "hungry" person is more alert to a sizzling steak on a grill or the enticing look of a salad than, say, to other things and events that may be present, and under other circumstances, might be more appealing. In other words, motivation shapes impulses and is thus most closely related to the "I" phase of conduct, in which the individual initially responds without conscious thought to a relevant stimulus. A "hungry" person smells food and begins to respond in ways appropriate to securing it. The mouth waters and the other senses become alert to the source of the smell, even before the person is conscious of doing so.

Motive, in contrast, references meanings that people attach to their conduct and is linked to the "Me" phase of conduct in which the person self-consciously grasps the direction in which an impulse is taking him or her. The smell of food cooking is apt to lead a "hungry" person to announce, to self or to others, "I'm hungry." The essence of motive lies in such verbalizations: motives consist in what people say about their actions, as opposed to internal states (motivations) that shape their responses to the world around them. To announce a motive is to constitute a "Me"—a hungry, ready-to-consume-food "Me"—and to

TABLE 3.2   Motive and Motivation

	Motivation	Motives
How are people conscious of motivation or motives?	People are not conscious of motivation at all. Motivations lie beneath the surface of consciousness.	People are explicitly conscious of motives. Motives are consciously announced as people name the reasons for their conduct.
How is it related to the self?	Motivation shapes the "I" phase of conduct.	Motives shape the person's view of self in the "Me" phase.
How is it related to phase of act?	Motivation shapes impulses.	Motives are employed in the phase of perception and manipulation to direct conduct and to grasp the nature of conduct of others.
What is its relation to role making and role taking?	Motivation, by shaping impulses, provides the initial material with which the individual shapes appropriate conduct.	Motives are invoked in the shaping process, as people interpret their own and others' conduct by imputing motives.
What are its sources?	Motivations reflect the individual's history of conditioning; his or her situated, personal, and social identities; and previously avowed motives in the situation.	Motives are socially standardized expressions of reasons for conduct, applied in specific situations and in response to particular audiences.

begin to organize conduct with "food" or "dinner" as its object. Motivations and motives thus offer differing, intrinsically related explanations of what "moves" conduct. To say that "hunger" and "sex" are motivations is only to say that at a particular moment, the individual's awareness of and sensitivities to his or her surroundings are shaped by one of those particular drives or needs.

Many factors can influence the particular sensitivities of an individual at any given moment. There are organic states such as hunger or sexual deprivation. There is also previous conditioning to various aspects of the environment, ranging from picking up the telephone when it rings, to responding to stimuli of which one is scarcely even aware, such as others' tone of voice or body language. Motivations such as these operate at a preconscious level, and they determine the impulse but not the whole act. As the person experiences his or her impulsive response, they become a part of the "Me"—the person takes the imagined attitudes of others toward the act. At this point the determining influence of motivation temporarily ends, and the person can bring the act under voluntary control.

Motives, in contrast, exist in the things that people say about their conduct. In everyday life, we frequently speak of people's motives for their actions and ask people why they behaved in a particular way. We explain to others and ourselves what reasons explain our actions and what we hope to accomplish in taking them. Motives are verbal phenomena; they exist because people talk about what they do. They exist as visible markers of the existence and importance of self-consciousness. To claim a motive for oneself—"I'm starving!"—or to attribute a motive to others—"She hates me!"—is to experience the self.

Motivation and motive are linked to the "I" and "Me" phases of the self in another crucial respect. Motives can reshape motivation in the same way that the individual responds ("I") to a particular image of self ("Me"). Verbalized motives organize the person's sensitivities to the environment and its social objects. If the internal state of hunger (as motivation) leads a person to snack between meals, he may explain (to self or others) that he is "hungry" (a statement of motive) because he didn't eat much for lunch. As he says this, he may respond to his own words by recalling that he also had a snack before lunch and after dinner last night. He might start thinking that perhaps he is starting to get hungrier because he is a nervous eater and he has an upcoming performance review. After the review, he may not snack as much. Here, a motive has become a motivation—what a man has said about his act has shaped his sensitivities to his surroundings (including his own actions) and thus influenced future impulses. In Mead's terms, the "I" has responded to a "Me."

Maintaining a clear distinction between motivation and motive is important for at least two reasons. First, it is always tempting—as much for the social scientist as for the lay person—to assume that each act can be explained by linking it to a particular underlying motivation or motive. People eat, we might say, because they are hungry, or they work hard in school because they are motivated to achieve. This assumption is flawed, because the conditions that move most human acts are more complex and less obvious than they appear on the surface. We eat "because" we are hungry but also for other reasons: "because" it is noon and we ordinarily eat lunch then; "because" we are restless and wander to the refrigerator to graze; "because" eating makes us feel better when we are anxious about something. Few acts are explained by a single motive or motivation, and typically even the person whose behavior is under the microscope has only a limited grasp of what uniquely moves him or her to act in a given way.

Second, efforts to explain why people act as they do run the risk of what C. Wright Mills called "motive mongering," which substitutes an observer's accounts of what moves conduct for the real reasons that shaped what a person does. Social scientists motive monger when they try to explain complex forms of conduct in terms of such presumably universal motivations as a "quest for self-esteem" or the "rational maximization of advantage." Even a simple explanation of a child's misconduct as the result of a need for attention or a "cry for help" attributes to the child a state of awareness that may not exist, even as it fails to distinguish between unconsciously selected impulses and consciously constructed acts. We engage in similar forms of motive mongering in everyday life when we summarize a person's action by attributing it to a particular motive, such as "love" or "revenge." It may well be that "love" is a motive for generosity, but people act generously for many "reasons" and under a variety of circumstances. A wife who donates her healthy kidney to her spouse may despise him yet fear the social disapproval that would ensue if she refused. Perhaps the student pans the professor on a course evaluation out of revenge; but perhaps the professor just deserves the criticism.

Symbolic interactionists argue that to explain conduct we must look at the circumstances around which conduct is formed and at the meanings people construct as they go about their affairs. These circumstances include the internal states of individuals at various moments; and the meanings people construct are shaped crucially by what they say about their own and others' conduct. In other words, both motivations and motives are important in explaining conduct. In Chapter 4, we will devote considerable attention to the avowal and attribution of motives in everyday life. The focus in this chapter, however, is on motivation—that is, on how identity and self-esteem affect conduct at the level of impulse.

The guiding principle of this analysis is that the person's conceptions of self will influence motivation. They affect a person's state as an organism and thus influence impulsive responses to various objects and events. They shape the person's dispositions, level of anxiety, moods of depression or elation, feelings of joy or sadness, and sense of competence or incompetence. These motivations in turn affect conduct by shaping the person's sensitivities to the acts of others, to the world of objects, and to the person's own acts. How people respond to various circumstances at the level of impulse—the "I"—is affected by motivational states that the self shapes.

Identity and Motivation

How is identity implicated in motivating conduct? In general terms, situated identity is the master organizer of a person's sensitivities to events that transpire within the situation. Social and personal identities are more deeply rooted motivational states that shape how we respond to situated roles and form situated identities.

Consider a patient and a physician interacting within the situation of a medical examination. Each is motivated by his or her respective identity—one person by the identity "patient" and the other by the identity "physician." To say that each is motivated by an identity is to say that of the large set of responses each could make to the situation, a subset pertaining to identity is selected and activated. The patient, for example, has a great many wants, needs, desires, and inclinations. However, only some pertinent to a patient's identity are activated as the patient interacts with the physician. Others—being hungry for food or affection, wanting a new car, longing for a vacation, or wishing one could understand the behavior of a rebellious child—are for the moment given a much lower standing in the person's internal hierarchy of impulses. Events within the examining room that are relevant to the patient's concern about what ails him or her will be attended to closely, but those that relate to other stimuli will be noticed less quickly or perhaps not at all. Thus, the patient is alert to the physician's facial expressions, but much less interested in the advertisement for new cars in the magazine lying on the table.

It is partly the capacity of an identity to organize attention and impulsive responses in a situation that accounts for its impact on conduct. Having assumed a particular role, one has an identity that organizes relevant impulses and excludes those that are less important to the activity at hand. To make the role of patient, for example, one needs to attend to the physician's words and deeds. The patient identity provides the motivation to do so.

Ordinarily, the process whereby the person assumes a role and its associated identity is a swift and almost unconscious one, and the identity itself becomes taken for granted. The patient submits to a physical examination with considerable consciousness of self, for he or she must interpret the physician's directions and govern his or her conduct accordingly. This consciousness of self occurs within a given identity—one does not have to think of the identity itself, only of what one must do from that perspective.

People are conscious of their situated identities when they are uncertain or undergo change. Young couples that see one another socially a few times may at first think of themselves as "just friends" but gradually come to take a romantic interest in one another. At some point they will become conscious of the change and announce that change publicly to themselves and others.

When people consciously reorganize their situated identities—whether by expressing doubts or announcing a new identity—they also reorganize or transform motivation. The new couple will start to pay attention to one another in new ways. Sexual impulses that were ignored earlier become more important. Also, characteristics of the other that seemed less important—such as religion or occupational plans—now become matters of intense interest as the couple begins to think of their potential future together. In these examples, consciously verbalized identities shape motivation both in some concrete ways and in some other ways that are less easily identified.

Social identity and personal identity also are significant as motivation and motive. One may throw one's energies into parenting while doing the minimum one can get away with at work. You can participate actively in local political affairs but be content to be a bystander in the affairs of your church or synagogue. Some identities energize us much more than others and so we invest in them more.

Situated identities are always linked to social and personal identities. Suppose someone has a social identity as a musician. That social identity makes other potential affiliations more salient than others. Given an identity as a musician, particular situated identities will interest a musician to the extent that they have an affinity with that social identity. Thus, aspiring to musical fame and fortune may mean jumping at the chance to audition for the television program *American Idol,* even to the extent of passing up other identities (e.g., quitting your job) in order to go for the big prize. If a personal identity based on academic success in college dominates an individual's sense of self, however, he or she may perceive auditioning for *American Idol* as far less important than preparing for final examinations. Our tendency to choose situated identities often depends on how they contribute to our chosen social and personal identities.

The effects of social and personal identities occur through both motivation and motives. On one hand, we carry social and personal identities with us at every moment, although well beneath the surface of consciousness. These identities organize our receptivity to various kinds of events. The ears of a community leader prick up at hearing that a political office will be vacant, not because the individual thinks of himself or herself as a "community leader" at each and every moment, but because previous designations of self in those terms have organized his or her sensitivities to the world in a certain way. These identities form predetermining influences that then shape action and perception in conscious ways. The eyes of a would-be best-selling detective novelist light up when he or she hears of a particularly gruesome crime, because that crime represents an opportunity to write a new book. One does not need to think "best-selling author" at every moment in order to have this response, but at some point in the past that self-objectification was made, and it now helps shapes one's conduct.

In some circumstances, people emphasize announcing their social or personal identities to themselves and others. They also may focus inwardly on social and personal identity. A person is apt to do so, for example, when the situated identity he or she has is a socially devalued one. In a study of the homeless, David Snow and Leon Anderson discovered a number of efforts with the object of maintaining a more honorable social and personal identity in the face of bearing a socially denigrated label of being home-less.[34] A homeless person is placed in a devalued situated identity, and is thus, in a sense, stripped of any legitimate social place.

So how do the homeless try to sustain a sense of dignity in the face of their predica-ment? Snow and Anderson found that some homeless people do so by distancing them-selves from other homeless people or institutions, in effect claiming that their situated identity does not reveal their "real" or "authentic" social or personal identity. A person might maintain that he or she is not really like other homeless people; or that homelessness is only a very temporary condition and the person is about to return to a normal life; or that unlike other homeless people, he or she fends for himself or herself and does not depend on shelters or other institutions for the homeless. Others among the homeless adopt an op-posite tactic, making their homelessness into a virtue as best they can by embracing the sit-uated homeless identity and claiming it as the basis of a valued social or personal identity. One might, for example, point to how homeless people stick together and help one another, thus claiming a valued place in society by virtue of one's commitment to the important cul-tural value of aiding others. Finally, some of the homeless essentially retreat into fantasy or tell stories designed to create and maintain the appearance that they once really had, and that they hope will soon have again.

The performance of every situated identity has implications for social and personal identity. Playing an organized sport, for example, provides people with opportunities to assume situated identities as athletes. If they achieve particular success at sports, they solidify and validate other personal and social identities The small-town high school football hero, for example, who in the last game of the season in his senior year, scores the winning touchdown to upset a favored rival, achieves not only praise at the moment but also a durable place in his community. Others recognize him for that accomplish-ment on a lasting basis, and he may make it a central feature of his social identity. Such "trophy case" stories that participants repeat to each other help shape people's identities and interactions.

As Raymond Schmitt and Wilbert Leonard suggest, sports are a particularly effective social context for "immortalizing" the self.[35] Sports fans talk about sports, rate athletes and their accomplishments, and legitimize sports as an activity worthy of attention. In a small town, the accomplishments of a high school athlete may be the talk of the whole commu-nity. In these kinds of examples, personal and social identities inspire efforts to talk about situated identity in the best possible light. Confronted by degrading social conditions, peo-ple wish to have a valued place. Exceptional performances or accomplishments, such as in the world of athletics, become a way of "immortalizing the self" and making a permanent place for oneself in some community.

Personal and social identity also produce a phenomenon that Erving Goffman called "role distance."[36] Goffman noticed that even in the midst of serious situated role performances, such as a surgeon in the operating room, people sometimes made light of their roles, acted playfully, and engaged in self-deprecation. Surgeons and nurses, for example, might joke about the sterility of surgical instruments, even though that topic is no laughing matter. As Goffman pointed out, this type of conduct, known in common as "gallows humor" has the important function of easing tensions and enabling people to maintain high standards of performance without making the atmosphere oppressively heavy. Humor is an effective means of social control, a way to remind people of their responsibilities without directly accusing them of falling short. Jokes about sterility also serve to remind people in a subtle way about the importance of ensuring that tools are sterile.

Recently, Blake Ashforth and his colleagues examined how people "normalize" their identities when they work in jobs that are conventionally considered "dirty."[37] Those jobs involve unpleasant or disreputable tasks, such as messy social problems (debt collecting), labor in dirty conditions (garbage, septic tanks, manure spreading) or working with socially taboo subjects (undertaking). Their research found that people mitigate the "taint" associated with those jobs by either focusing on unheralded virtues of the job as an ideology (helping people deal with grief); forming associations as buffers to make them more professionalized; being more confrontational and fighting back; or adopting defensive tactics that explain an attraction to that work, such as an exterminator seeing himself as a specialist that knows more about insects than scientists do. People learn tactics to help them distance themselves from the criticisms associated with their work. Working in potentially discrediting dirty jobs leads people to adopt techniques to "normalize" their identities.

Role distance also arises because social and personal identities loom in the background of every act. Taking oneself with less than full seriousness in a role is a way of reminding self and others that there is more to one than just the current situated identity. When that identity requires much involvement from the person, role distancing is a way to reassert the significance of other components of a person's identity.

Social identities also surface when an event occurs that is significant for social identity but not a situated one. When a professor delivers a lecture, he or she may be engrossed in that situated identity and role, and be scarcely conscious of his or her ethnic, racial, or religious identity at that time. However, if a student makes a prejudiced comment during that lecture, one or more of these social identities may quickly rise to the fore. If so, the professor will suddenly become aware of being, say, Jewish, and then approach the situation on the basis of that social identity rather than in—or in addition to—his or her identity as a professor.

Each time a person announces a social or personal identity, he or she reorganizes the self at a motivational level. That is, a person reorganizes impulses and alters the environment to be sensitive to that particular identity. The parent who announces that his or her career requires the rest of the family to make sacrifices attempts to redefine the situation to determine how others will act and also transforms the self. By announcing the importance of a career identity, the person seeks to rationalize subsequent conduct in his or her own eyes as well as in the eyes of others. If one tells oneself that career comes first, one makes career impulses most important and career stimuli most significant, and at the same time makes it easier on him or her to ignore other stimuli.

Self-Esteem and Motivation[38]

Like identity, self-esteem is a motivational state that affects a person's sensitivities to the surrounding social world. Social scientists propose a variety of ways that self-esteem shapes conduct. The linkage we propose here represents just one of several approaches that a symbolic interactionist can apply to this topic. We suggest that self-esteem influences what a person does by shaping his or her imaginations of self and others in social interaction. In other words, self-esteem impacts role taking in powerful ways. In particular, low levels of self-esteem interfere with role taking.

The ability to engage in successful role taking—that is, to grasp the perspective of others sufficiently well to enable one to coordinate one's conduct with theirs—depends on three conditions. First, the role taker needs a cognitive map of the situation and its role structure and to know what activities will take place and who will do what. To take the role of a physician, the individual must know he or she is in a medical situation and that the other is a physician. Second, the role taker must have a situated identity—the person must know not only that the other is a physician but also that he or she is a patient. As a rule, these two conditions are readily met in the situations in which people interact. People go to physicians, know who is going to perform what part, and identify with the parts they are to perform.

The third condition for adequate role taking is more elusive but no less important: The role taker must trust the definition of the situation and the identities of self and other. In other words, the person must have a reasonable degree of certainty that a given situation is what it appears to be and that the others present are who they claim to be. We go to physicians trusting that they are really who they claim to be, that they will act toward us as physicians, and that their motives are those of physicians. Indeed, one of the reasons people can identify with their own situated roles is that they feel assured that others are identifying suitably with theirs. There are occasions on which doubt arises. A patient thinks that his or her physician has lost interest in the case or that the physician's competence isn't what it should be—but these are exceptions rather than the rule. Trust is in large part a function of people's actions. We trust doctors because they do what they are supposed to do. Doctors trust their patients because they act as patients should act. People act in good faith, or at least appear to do so, and trust is maintained.

However, trust also depends on the attitudes that individual participants bring to situations. Sometimes, people come to situations reluctant or unable to trust others. They bring anxiety or suspicion, doubting that things will go as they ought, feeling unable to rely on the good faith of others. Self-esteem is a major factor that shapes the trust—or lack of trust—that people bring to social situations.

We can explore the impact of self-esteem on social interaction by examining the effects of low self-esteem, which is associated with two painful psychological conditions—anxiety and depression—that undermine the trust on which role taking depends.[39] First, low self-esteem is associated with relatively high levels of anxiety—that is, with a psychological state of apprehension or psychic tension. People with low self-esteem are more anxious than people with higher levels of self-esteem. They worry more about their performances, are more concerned that they might fail, and more keenly interested in what others think of them. They are more nervous, more likely to bite their fingernails in anxious anticipation of an event, and approach the world with a sweaty-palmed reluctance to engage with other people. In contrast, persons with higher self-esteem are a lot less worried about social encounters. They are more likely to take things as they come. They worry less about possible failure. They seem to exude confidence in their abilities and to take it for granted that they have a right to be where they are and do what they are doing.

Second, low self-esteem is associated with—indeed it is a clinical symptom of—depression, a disorder of mood characterized by overwhelming feelings of sadness, lack of energy, hopelessness, and worthlessness that drain their capacity to function in everyday life. Depressed people may be responding to particularly distressing circumstances but they can also experience sadness and internal feelings of guilt or lack of self-worth even when things are going well and they have objective reasons to feel good about themselves. Although individuals typically feel depressed in the face of traumatic events—such as the death of a loved one—depression also occurs in the absence of such events. Depression is an additionally painful experience when people are unable to attribute their feelings to external events that can explain why they feel so bad. Absent such circumstances, they can explain their depression more personally and attribute their situation to personal failings. People who are not depressed have higher levels of self-esteem. They are more likely to feel worthy and hopeful in general. They also recover more quickly from traumatic events that do occur.

Anxiety and depression undermine people's confidence in the social world. Those feelings allow affected people to imagine any given situation in negative and distrustful terms rather than positive or at least neutral ones. Albert Ellis, one of the founders of tremendously influential therapeutic approaches in psychology called cognitive behavioral therapy and rational emotive therapy, described this tendency among people as "awful-izing."[40] That is, whenever a person entered into a situation, they could only imagine the worst possibilities occurring instead of more likely outcomes. They also tended to overestimate the negative consequences of events rather than to assess outcomes in less than dire circumstances. For example, a person might "awfulize" when they imagine a response to their speaking in public as being that the audience will openly start jeering their performance or walk out in the middle of their talk. That awful possibility impairs that person's ability to actually prepare for and deliver their talk. The person who is "awful-izing" is unable to accept that an audience might listen politely, if at worst, in a slightly bored way, or at best in a very appreciative way. They consistently frame situations in the worst possible ways, which means that they cannot trust in social situations enough to take up roles. They also will not tend to believe that others will define situations in a productive way for them.

When people enter situations with their self-esteem more or less intact, we trust in the others who are present as well as in ourselves. We believe in their authentic embrace of the roles that they are playing. We walk confidently into the physician's office or a classroom, and in doing so, we imagine a social situation in which others can be counted on to act in good faith according to their roles and identities. However, the person who enters a situation laden with anxiety and self-doubt will imagine others who cannot be trusted—who are perhaps hostile or have hidden agendas, or who are incompetent. This person will assume that others have motives that are not as they are supposed to be. Under ordinary circumstances—that is, where self-esteem is more or less adequate—we interact with people primarily on the basis of their roles and identities. Where self-esteem is low or under some threat, we are more apt to interact with others on the basis of doubts and suspicions about their intent.

Someone with low self-esteem tends to imagine that others are making negative judgments of them when in fact those people may not be. He or she is oversensitive to the opinions of others, engages in needless comparisons of self and others, and is often unable to do the very things that might earn the approval of others. As the psychiatrist Harry Stack Sullivan wrote, the person with low self-esteem finds it difficult to "manifest good feeling toward another person."[41] People with low self-esteem tend to react to others' efforts as if they want to pour salt on their wounds rather than salve. That suspicion closes a vicious circle, as people with low self-esteem act in ways that make others not want to give aid and comfort, even though that comfort might benefit the person with low self-esteem.

Hopefully, most individuals have self-esteem that is high enough to keep anxiety from paralyzing them, but that is low enough to make them receptive to others' evaluations. As this formulation suggests, both exceptionally low and exceptionally high self-esteem may have important implications for the individual. Very low self-esteem makes it difficult for the person to do things that would improve self-esteem. Very high self-esteem is equally consequential because it works to insulate the person from the appraisals of others. The person who approaches every situation with customarily high self-esteem may impulsively select images of others in such a way that only favorable conclusions about self can be reached—the person may always see himself or herself as an object of admiration, regardless of how others actually feel. People with very high self-esteem can thus fall beyond the control of others' judgments.

We want to also offer one last important caveat. While we have focused on how self-esteem unconsciously shapes impulses within social situations, we do not want to imply that self-esteem is a basic or primary human motivation that trumps other motivations.[42] Affective responses—to self and to others—are very important in social life. However, so are the cognitive responses—the thoughts—on which role taking and the assignment of meaning to self and others depend. The actions that human beings undertake are also critical. In the trinity of thoughts, feelings, and actions, no term is more important to appreciate than others.

Indeed, symbolic interactionists would view assigning some particular significance to self-esteem, as a human motive, is to engage in motive mongering. Human beings are culturally diverse and we label, understand, and emphasize the phenomena that we see as self-esteem in diverse ways. This point is especially important for contemporary students to understand, for Western culture—and that of the United States in particular—has created a set of ideas that treat self-esteem as if its attainment is the most important human goal and the means of solving a host of personal and social problems. We make no such claim here. Rather, we emphasize a more modest point: How people see themselves affects how they see others. That perception then shapes their capacity to engage in role taking and also role making.

This discussion of self and motivation must also integrate the larger social context within which social interaction occurs. We write of identity and self-esteem as if a person is free to go wherever he or she chooses in the social world and to present a self as he or she sees fit. Realistically, however, culture and society influence the others with whom a person interacts, what identities are available, and what conduct is possible. To complete our account of the person, we must move to the forest from the trees.

The Self and the Social Order

Many cultural and social factors constrain the nature and development of the self. The identities people can assume in specific situations are only partly open to their own choosing. People often have no choice about a situated role. Likewise, people are not entirely free to choose with what people they can interact. In many situations in life, people are designated to interact with specific others, regardless of anyone's wishes or the appraisals they expect to receive from them. In addition to these fundamental constraints, people are pulled in different directions by conflicting expectations. People are subject to the influences of the communities to which they belong, and by the special nature of modern life. In the following pages, we consider some of the ways through which culture and society constrain the self.

Limitations on the Choice of Roles

Sociologists distinguish two different ways through which people come to enact various roles. On the one hand, many roles are ascribed, which means that others assign the person a role on the basis of biological considerations (such as age or sex) or birth into a particular family (identified, for example, by ethnicity or religion). Gender is a clear example of ascription (leaving aside physical abnormality or surgical change of sex). A person is born with the genitals of one sex or the other, and that fact alone assigns the person to a sex category. In any situation in which people define gender as a relevant part of the role structure (and that probably includes most situations to some extent), role making and role taking are influenced by specific ideas that people have about proper, normal, and expected conduct for boys or girls, and men or women. Similarly, religion, age, and sometimes even political affiliation are ascriptive. A person is perceived as having a set of characteristics or dispositions by virtue of having been born into a family that others see as having those characteristics.

Often referenced as ascribed statuses, these roles have an involuntary component. They are imposed upon people from birth and constitute role demands that herd large numbers of people into specific behaviors. In most situations, taking on a role requires a person to act from the perspective of the role while also doing so in a way that others will regard as appropriate to his or her gender. For example, the assertive, relentless spewing of vulgarities from a male sports fan might be viewed as unduly aggressive or pushy coming from a female fan. Gendered expectations are powerful in part because they are taken for granted as a natural feature of the social order. From the earliest stages of socialization, children learn to scrutinize the differences between males and females, in order to enact gendered performances and inspect the conduct of others from a gendered perspective.[43]

Alternatively, some roles are achieved. Achieved roles do not depend on birth. Instead, they are voluntary and require attaining a specific set of qualifications. People achieve these roles, such as getting particular grades or working in a particular job. For example, in modern societies, occupational roles are largely achieved. Not many families require individuals to assume a particular occupation merely because they were born into that family. Further, no legal sanctions are available to force an individual to become what parents want. People can seek out and attain achieved roles and the identities within them.

However, people cannot pursue all achieved identities with equal power. No legal restrictions prevent the child of a factory worker from aspiring to become a college professor, but social and economic circumstances make such mobility a comparatively uncommon occurrence. Higher education may be financially beyond a person's reach, and it may be difficult for a working-class child to imagine himself or herself as the kind of person who would have such aspirations. Where middle-class culture may confer on the child a sense of entitlement to education and a rewarding career, working-class experiences may define such aspirations as unrealistic.

A person's identity, whether in a specific situation or in a larger biographical sense, is in many ways not within the person's control. In the United States, historically and presently, the role of an African American is often fixed by race rather than by characteristics that pertain to ongoing interactions. In many circumstances, people react differently to men and women, even though gender may be unrelated to the particular activity at hand. In these situations, an ascribed characteristic that is not germane to an activity is used as a basis for establishing situated identity. An extreme example is a hospital patient who assumes that all African American people working in the hospital are orderlies. In thus establishing the situated identity of a particular person as someone who must be an orderly because he or she is African American, the patient approaches interaction with him or her with a preconception of the role structure of the situation. Even when the patient learns that this particular individual is a physician or a nurse, the interaction that takes place is still likely to be influenced by this patient's preconceived ideas about race.

Even a role that the individual has achieved the right to enact by acquiring the appropriate qualifications—such as an occupational role—subsequently constrains and shapes the self. Acquiring the training necessary to be a history professor, for example, means that one forgoes the opportunity to acquire the skills of a pharmacist. People have to invest so much time and money in preparing for one profession that changing those roles is almost precluded. Moreover, to develop a conception of oneself as, say, a physician or a farmer, also will mean being regarded as such by others, and to become entangled in a web of social relationships with others. People are constrained by the identities that they develop in the course of learning and enacting an occupational role, and also by the fact that a significant part of one's self-esteem depends on the successful performance of the role. Patricia and Peter Adler demonstrated, as an example, in their study of college basketball players, that a role performed with great success and cheered by others can overwhelm the self. Adler and Adler studied the roles and what they termed the "gloried selves" of college basketball players. Engulfed by the athletic role, and facing pressures from coaches, fellow students, and boosters to define themselves almost solely as athletes, the players they studied found themselves confronting strong pressures to define themselves in the same terms. They concentrated mainly on the athletic role to the detriment of other present and future roles. They became almost totally defined by a role they had achieved. In a sense they were diminished as persons by their very achievements as athletes, as other aspects of their identities were buried under the athletic one.[44]

Limitations on the Choice of Others

Social life also limits a person's choice of others with whom to interact and his or her ability to define their appraisals as important or unimportant. These limitations also stem in part from the facts of birth and ascription. We normally cannot choose our parents—parents and their children are typically stuck with one another, at least initially, as are siblings. Furthermore, to be born black or white, male or female, rich or poor, is to be constrained to some extent to particular networks of social relationships within the world into which one was born. In some cultural groups, the worlds of men and women may be far removed from one another such that the others with whom women interact may be limited (often very rigidly) by custom, knowledge, or rules and sanctions dictated by men. De facto segregation of housing and schools, patterns of hostility between groups, community sentiments, and sheer racism are among the factors that constrain or limit contact between blacks and whites.

Moreover, as individuals in a modern society move from infancy through childhood, and adolescence into adulthood, they encounter a series of others whom they do not choose, but whom they interact with because of their social position. Teachers, other children, members of the extended family, gang leaders, social workers, Boy Scout leaders, police officers, college professors, and employers are others with whom individuals interact, sometimes by choice, but often on the basis of chance or the decisions and actions of others over whom they have little or no influence.

The ongoing social order that confronts individuals at birth is in many ways an unyielding reality to which people must adjust. Beliefs about what is normal behavior for boys and for girls, the practice of starting school at age six, a propensity to mentally place certain ethnic groups in particular jobs—are given features of the social world from the individual's standpoint. A variety of attitudes exist in the social world into which the person is born, and they shape the formation of the self. They exist only because people form their conduct on the basis of particular beliefs, ideas, and knowledge—because, for example, they have learned to act toward certain ethnic groups, girls, or six-year-olds as particular kinds of social objects. But from the standpoint of individuals confronting the social world for the first time, this world of objects is real. It is there as an objective, factual set of conditions that must be taken into account in his or her conduct. That little girls are to be avoided is simply a fact for some little boys, a matter of what is "obviously" real and important.

In order to account for self-development, therefore, we must know the person's location in the social order. That is, we must know the world of objects and the social arrangements of the family and community into which the person is born. We must know the beliefs and values found in the family, the attitude taken toward the child in school, the kinds of peers with whom the individual associates, and the sort of job attained or college attended. All of these outcomes are also strongly influenced by the person's social position, for example, by whether the person is black or white, male or female, rich or poor, Catholic or Protestant, urban or rural, or of Italian or Norwegian descent.

How does this obdurate social world influence self-conceptions? Both consciously and unconsciously, people arrange presentations of self in various situations so as to manifest the qualities and characteristics valued in their social worlds. By manifesting valued qualities, the person is able to imagine his or her own appearance in the eyes of the other more favorably. The social order has a considerable impact on this process. The adjustment of conduct—which is what the presentation of self is all about—always is to a specific set of others and to particular standards of evaluation, and these are a preexisting part of the world, at least so far as much childhood experience is concerned. As one grows older, of course, one may discover that the standards by which people evaluate one another are matters of human creation, not absolutes, and that a variety of other people in the society hold different views of what is natural and proper.

Some important constraints on the adjustment of conduct to valued images of others occur when the child moves out of the exclusive confines of the family and encounters a more diverse set of others. In a complex society, which divides the labor of socialization among various agents and agencies, what parents expect may well not coincide with the views of teachers. If the child imagines his or her parents to emphasize street savvy and toughness, while teachers want refinement, sensitivity, and attention to schoolwork, the child, only with great difficulty, may be able to manifest both sets of qualities, if at all. If the child perceives teachers as protective or restrictive, and has already developed a self-image that emphasizes self-reliance and independence, the child may rebel against their efforts to impose controls.

Such conflicts between selves fostered within the family and those encouraged in public contexts, such as schools, are common in a society as ethnically, racially, and religiously heterogeneous as the United States.[45] Ideal conceptions of the person differ across Christians, Muslims, and Jews, including within the membership of each of these groups. Contradictions between family and public expectations are inevitable. From a personal standpoint, these contradictions impose limitations on self-development and are a major project to which impression management is dedicated. It is difficult to live up to parental images or to those among an enclosed ethnic community, while at the same time manifesting qualities valued by outsiders whom the person may have to please if his or her goals are to be achieved. An African American or Jewish American in U.S. society may resonate best to a particular ethnic "soul," and yet find it advantageous or necessary to strip away or conceal peculiarly ethnic qualities of manner, dialect, or belief while on the job and in interactions with nonminority individuals. Sometimes thinking that you must be a different person within the family or the ethnic community as opposed to in the world outside, leads to a bifurcation of social worlds and of the self.

As a quick example, consider the world of celebrities. Many entertainers change their names in order to conceal their ethnic origins or to emphasize them for a particular market. Did you know the original names of the celebrities identified below?

FIGURE 3.1   Changing Names to Seek Fame

Birth Name	Celebrity Name
Carlos Estevez	Charlie Sheen
Farrokh Bulsara	Freddie Mercury
Criss Sarantakos	Criss Angel
Carlton Ridenhour	Chuck D
Shawn Carter	Jay Z
Phillip Clapp	Johnny Knoxville
Ned Holnes	Carlos Mencia
Natalie Hershlag	Natalie Portman
Chaim Klein Witz	Gene Simmons (Kiss)
William Drayton	Flavor Flav

Selves are shaped by ideal conceptions of what the person ought to be, and these vary by gender, ethnic origin, religion, region, social class, and other kinds of social differentiations. Many definitions of the ideal person are linked to group memberships. They also depend to some extent on we-they contrasts between groups. The selves fostered among Asian Americans, Jewish Americans, white southerners, or Polish Americans are defined, not just by the beliefs and values of the group itself, but also by the particular contrasts between themselves and outsiders emphasized by members of the group. To be Jewish, for example, is to live up to a set of images of what Jews ought to be like, as defined by Jewish people, and also to avoid certain patterns of behavior or belief presumed to characterize gentiles.

There are also occasions when a child or an adult confronts images that he or she cannot emulate in their conduct. No matter what people wish, they may be unable to offer a presentation of self that represents a good adjustment to other people's expectations. Situations where race or class is a significant base for distinguishing among people and evaluating them invidiously are particularly problematic. No presentation of self can avoid the fact of race, and class is also very difficult to overcome, as the child may be distinguished by patterns of speech or dress that clearly mark him or her as different. In such contexts, a person may form an image of what is desired and present an impression of self accordingly, but to no avail, for negative appraisals will still occur.

This circumstance raises an interesting question: What strategies are available to people when self-presentation makes little or no difference? When others base their appraisals on grounds (race and gender) that have nothing to do with what someone actually does or is capable of doing, that person can define a critical public as insignificant and their evaluations as irrelevant. However, there are limits to being able to ignore this lack of acceptance. A child whose teachers persist in appraising him as stupid can avoid taking their judgments seriously. She or he may even invert their images and regard as positive whatever they see as negative. The child who comes to see herself or himself as artistically creative may withdraw from emotional attachment to parents if they see this creativity as unimportant or even undesirable.

Limits do exist on a person's ability to define others as significant or insignificant as he or she chooses. A child must endure critical parents and teachers even if their appraisals are painful to the child. Emotional attachment will not develop with teachers who act negatively toward the child, but such attachment to parents occurs to some extent regardless of what they do, since the child's earliest experience of the social world has been with them. A teacher also gets to assign grades and write comments no matter what the student wishes. Similarly, an employee may see his or her boss's standards as wrong, but it is still the boss who calls the shots at work and writes the paycheck. As often stated in customer service, the customer is never wrong; yet anyone who has worked in service jobs can think of occasions when the customer was certainly not right, even though they cannot be wrong.

We can dismiss the painful opinions of others as being insignificant to the self, as a way of protecting our sense of selves, but this strategy comes at a cost to a person. Though we label the negative appraisals of others as insignificant, they will continue to have an impact on us because they raise doubts, particularly among children. A child may define teachers as insignificant, but their appraisals may raise doubts about competence that will endure long after the child has forgotten the teachers themselves. An individual with a positive conception of self may, from time to time, encounter others who do not share that image. Some continued interaction with critical people, perhaps coworkers or a family member, is unavoidable. That inevitable contact offers an unwelcome constant reminder of the fact that other people hold you in low regard. One may encounter fellow workers who are very supportive and others who hold one's work in very low esteem. The former will be seen as more significant to self-image and self-esteem, but the latter cannot be completely ignored, for they are present from day to day, and they may be in a position to affect one's advancement on the job.

Withdrawing recognition is also costly because doing so may shrink a person's associations with other people. As Hans Gerth and C. Wright Mills noted, the avoidance of interaction with negative others leads to a retreat to a circle of "confirming intimate others."[46] As the person moves through successive stages in the life cycle, he or she may encounter so many negative images of self that he or she decides that more and more people must be seen as insignificant. Eventually, that person may choose to limit himself or herself to a small circle of confirming others because those people provide the only company where he or she can sustain a positive self-conception. In extreme situations, people may retreat to a private fantasy world where they avoid encounters with real people. Instead they prefer sticking to imaginary others who always give positive feedback.

Limitations on the Choice of Stories

There is yet another way that the social world constrains the self, which is by limiting the kinds of stories that people can tell about themselves and in which contexts they are permitted to tell them. We have suggested that the self is in part a narrative construction—an object created and modified by what people say about themselves and by the autobiographies they tell and edit in a variety of circumstances in their everyday lives. Cultural materials and social arrangements deeply affect this process.

When people tell others about their lives, they draw not just on their own experiences but also on cultural models of self-narration. From an individual's point of view, talking to other people about oneself seems to pertain mainly to reporting biographical facts: "First I went to college, then started on this teaching career that I wanted so much, and now I feel tired and burnt out and stuck in a job I despise." Or, on a more positive note, "I put myself through college and medical school, trained as a surgeon, did my residency at Massachusetts General Hospital, worked long and hard hours to perfect my trade, and I'm now Chief of Surgery at the leading hospital in our state." These accounts report experiences, but also contain interpretations within them, and the latter are less individual inventions and more the result of culturally standard ways of giving meaning to experience. "Burnout" is a relatively recent cultural idea, a way of labeling and understanding a cumulatively enervating frustration and anger that people experience in demanding jobs that they have held for a long time. Burnout reflects a cultural belief that people have the right to enjoy their work (not every culture has this belief) but also a tendency to interpret individual experiences in psychological terms. Likewise, the successful surgeon's story draws from the cultural ideal that hard work and effort is followed by success.

Cultural models for interpreting and narrating experience vary and change over time. The surgeon's story is a variation of an old and familiar theme in the culture of the United

States: A talented and persevering individual overcomes obstacles, works hard, and in the end reaps the rewards of money, social standing, and professional recognition. The "self-made person" may be a myth, especially to people (such as spouses) on whose efforts the success also depended, yet the story nonetheless seems entirely factual to the individual who claims it as a life story.[47] Those whose hard work brought only failure or limited success also can turn to cultural models: "I would have been a success if only I had been able to get an education," for example, or "I could have become company president, too, if I had married the boss's daughter."

Narrating the self occurs in socially structured and often obligatory occasions. Co-dependents tell their stories to one another in weekly group meetings.[48] The prospective employee does so in job applications and job interviews, where the task is not only to present a competent self to a human resources interviewer but also to construct a plausible account of a job history and of aspirations for the future. The college applicant does so in the personal essay, attempting to convince an admissions committee that he or she possesses talents, skills, and virtues required for success in college. Reunions likewise provide structured occasions for people to recount their life stories to others, or to bring their life stories up-to-date. The high school reunion, for example, periodically reunites individuals who were together earlier in their lives. As individuals anticipate attending a reunion, they imagine how they will present themselves and what accounts they will give of their successes and failures since graduation. They also imagine how others will tell their stories.[49] For example, an illness provides an occasion for the construction of a biography. As individuals anticipate recovery, ongoing struggle, or death, they are forced to confront the meaning of their lives.[50]

Individuals do have choices in such narrative occasions. People attending a high school reunion can make up wild stories about their successes, as did the characters in the movie *Romy and Michelle's High School Reunion,* or, more likely, they can find ways to emphasize their accomplishments and draw attention away from their failures. Job applicants find many ways to explain a history of frequent movement from one job to another. However, those choices are constrained by the discourse available and the likelihood that others will accept a preferred narrative.

The Self in Contemporary Society

People form selves by making and taking roles, by constructing narratives within particular situations and by imagining themselves as members of larger social entities. One way to portray this process is by examining the role that community plays in the creation and maintenance of the self. Contemporary societies are creating communities in ways that differ considerably from those of past societies.

The classic communities of the past were in many respects self-sufficient entities. The European peasant community of the Middle Ages was in important ways a world unto itself. The community produced the food and fiber on which people depended, and a person could live their entire life without ever leaving the community or encountering members of other communities. Thus, in effect, this historical community was also a society—a more or less self-sufficient and self-reproducing entity with little reliance on a world outside itself.

In contrast, contemporary society contains a great many communities, few (if any) of which are economically self-sufficient, and most of which depend on other communities and on society as a whole. The rural small town and the urban ethnic neighborhood, for example, have some of the characteristics of classic communities: They are important in the lives of their members and are composed of individuals who spend their lives together. But these communities are not self-sufficient and generally not self-reproductive. The residents of a neighborhood live their lives together and identify with one another, but many of them must work outside the neighborhood and interact frequently with strangers. Small-town dwellers may feel great loyalty to their town, but the town is dependent economically on other towns and on structures of government and economy of the larger nation and increasingly, in an age of globalization, of the whole world.

As a result, contemporary community provides a psychological world and a place of identification for its members, but not the same kind of enclosing and secure world as the community of the past. The individual is keenly aware of the existence of a society whose economic and political significance transcends that of the local community. Moreover, the surrounding society offers a tempting field of opportunities, where other communities exist with which a person might choose to identify. Larger society is a constant reminder that the community within which one resides is not the only option. A popular song of the World War I era wondered, "How are you going to keep them down on the farm after they've seen Paris?" This is, in fact, the common dilemma of communities in modern society—how to retain the loyalties of members who are tempted by the glamour and opportunities of the outside world.

The departure from being immersed completely within a small world to the possibility of embedding oneself within many worlds represents a vast social change. The modern age has witnessed technological change that means dramatic changes in possibilities of self-identification. We live in an age of mass travel where someone can travel to other countries and continents in a day. We can find ourselves not just in different real worlds, but we can also immerse ourselves in virtual worlds where our selves can create new communities that are unlimited by scientific or practical constraints, such as in *Second Life* or *World of Warcraft* on the Internet. Virtual communities reduce distances of space between people and represent the emergence of new virtual societies. While people may not choose to join these virtual worlds, they are just a click away on a computer, whether you live in Eastern Europe or Lawrence, Kansas. The world has gotten much smaller yet more full of societies than at any other time in human history. Rather than having to pursue a clear traditional form of existence, we now are overloaded with possible communities for self-identification. We can even manage multiple situated selves in a real world and a virtual one, having social relationships with people we never physically met through the Internet.

Another major difference between past community and contemporary communities is the basis on which people form a sense of communities and identify with one another. Contemporary communities are based on many different grounds and not just on a basis of sharing territory. To be sure, urban ethnic neighborhoods and rural towns retain some of their importance as communities in the member's lives. Life within those communities still centers on the association of people who know one another well and who are bound by a sense of obligation to one another, as well as by their sense of similarity. But contemporary people, because they frequently rub elbows with others who are very different from them, also must narrow their focus in order to feel a sense of likeness and identification. Many people live and work near others who are very different from them. In order to find a sense of community, they must either overcome these differences or identify with others who, although they may not be nearby, are similar in some respect.

For each member of a contemporary, heterogeneous society, there are many possible grounds on which he or she can identify with others. For some people, a shared commitment to a set of religious beliefs provides the basis for identifying with a community. Christians who have had a "born-again" experience, for example, have a strong mutual identification based on this experience. For others, membership in a social class may provide the same sense of likeness and common purpose. Modern people may find community in a social movement, for example, with the environmental movement and "going green;" with their professions; and even with their nuclear or extended families. Many ways now exist for people to develop and feel affinity with certain others.

The kind of community that develops from a sense of identification with similar others is a rather narrowly defined community, though often based on quite abstract criteria. For the person whose community consists of those who have been "born again," the sense of similarity is limited to religious conviction and experience. Persons who may be quite dissimilar in social background, ethnicity, formal religious affiliation, occupation, race, and other social characteristics can feel a sense of similarity with one another because they define these differences as irrelevant in the light of their similar and strong religious outlook. They identify with one another on the basis of this one characteristic, or master status, that makes them alike and they downplay the significance of other differences. The members of such experiential communities do not have to interact frequently with one another. They can rely on correspondence, revival meetings, or "televangelist" programs that feature preaching or talk about the "born-again" experience. Just these shared experiences are enough to confirm the existence of a community and an identity grounded in that community.

A new wave of anthropological theory has emerged to counter the assumption that people can only find an authentic culture within a distinct geographic territory.[51] They no longer believe that if someone wants to study Irish culture, that they can only do so by studying a community in Ireland. We now live in an age where people assert that the Polish population in Chicago makes it the largest Polish community in the world. More Jewish people live in New York City than in Tel Aviv, and Montreal is the second-largest French-speaking city in the world (Paris is the largest). Persons of Irish ancestry who have never visited Ireland have come to perceive themselves as more Irish than a person living in Ireland. Cultural identities and practices are seeping across geographic borders more than at any other point in history. The existence of culture beyond a single territory, such as eating sushi in Iowa City and country music bars in Japan, is generating new ways to appreciate how culture and community can be porous. Anthropologists are now exploring how a sense of community identity and culture can exist in space and time in different ways than have ever occurred before. You can now have people who are more "Irish" than people in Ireland and people who can see themselves as kindred born-again individuals that have never met and only share a relationship of "community" through watching the same preacher on television. We can include Internet communities and see people forming associations and shared identities who will never meet in person yet who feel extraordinarily close through e-mails and postings in their virtual worlds.

Contemporary communities can now rely on people's imaginations as much as on a mundane social life. Contacts with fellow community members may be infrequent, and a self-conscious imagining of the nature and scope of the community must sustain the sense of community. This case is less so for communities where there is an existing organizational structure. Individuals who identify with a professional community, for example, usually have concrete social organizations to support their identification. Professional groups, boards, journals, and meetings provide opportunities for those who identify with the community to meet one another and to reinforce their sense of community membership.

Many observers argue that contemporary society is drastically transforming the nature of the self. Where classic community flourishes, the self is a stable object defined by a strong sense of social identity grounded in and certified by the community. The direction of the person's life seems fixed, the self is given continuity and integration by its place in the community, and people need not devote much energy to securing or maintaining their identities. People know who they are, and thus they know what to do. Their sense of personal identity is subordinate to their social identity as community members.

Where communities have to be constructed by finding some basis on which to identify with others, the nature of the person is transformed as much as the nature of the community. The creation and maintenance of identity requires more self-consciousness; people must decide or discover who they are in order to know what to do. They can, within certain limits, choose who they are, but they are also faced with some degree of doubt as to the choices they make. The person who chooses one community with which to identify is always aware that his or her choice could have been different. There is also a strong temptation to identify with no community. In doing so, they can seek to subordinate community to a personal identity that places the person ahead of any community. We live in an ironic time where a variety of communities are more available to us than ever before, yet we can also be more isolated than ever before as we have an unprecedented freedom not to belong to any community.

Ralph Turner has argued that modern people are becoming more inclined to look within themselves and to define as the "real self" those impulses and inclinations they feel are genuinely and spontaneously theirs rather than the external dictates of society.[52] Turner's view can be readily interpreted within the framework of social and personal identity. Those who identify strongly with a community tend to feel comfortable with themselves when their impulses and actions live up to the standards of the community. But those who do not have a community-based social identity, who feel confined by community or torn between the demands of several communities, may feel that the only authentic expression of themselves is in a personal identity that permits a considerable degree of autonomy. When they feel they are doing what they want to do, and thus pursuing a personal identity, they feel true to themselves.

Social identity in contemporary society is much more likely than in the past to be based on a more or less self-conscious selection of a community as its main support. Whatever the basis on which such a community is constructed or imagined, it performs some of the same functions as the monolithic community of the past. The modern community still provides the person with a set of similar others who can support—or be perceived as supporting—the person's definitions of self. Even when a community is based on rather narrow criteria of similarity, spatially dispersed, and significantly a product of the person's own imagination, it provides for a sense of continuity and integration, linking various situated identities to the social identity that the new community provides.

People construct social identity through these contemporary forms of community in a variety of ways. Some seek to construct a community that resembles as closely as possible the community of the past. The old-order Amish, who maintain very traditional farming communities in Pennsylvania, Ohio, and Indiana, for example, attempt to enclose their members' lives in a way that is very much like the historic Amish communities of old. The whole of life is lived within the boundaries of the community, which rests on commitment to a traditional set of religious ideas about how people ought to live. Those who live in such communities have some contact with the surrounding contemporary world, of course, but their identities are almost exclusively grounded in the community itself, which provides a basis for identification with similar others. The outside world is important mainly for providing a contrast—it confers distinctiveness on the person by virtue of his or her membership in this distinctive community, and serves as a reminder of what the person should not be and how he or she should not live.

The contemporary person who seeks to ground social identity exclusively in one community need not, however, attempt to construct a classic community. Some participants in social movements, for example, have lives that are exclusively centered in the movement. For them, every act is seen as meaningful in relation to the movement and its goals. The committed member of a women's movement, for example, may lead a life that is as centered in the movement as is that of the Amish person in that community. Yet, whereas the Amish community has many of the attributes of a classic community, the social movement does not; it is not a context within which all of life's needs can be met.

Most people have a more tenuous relationship to the community (or communities) with which they identify. The person may identify with one community—such as a profession or neighborhood—but not so exclusively that everything the person does must somehow be linked to the community. Most people, perhaps, fit this pattern, finding limited forms of community in professions, neighborhoods, religious experiences, or social movement participation, but not devoting themselves exclusively to any of them. The person may thus identify mildly with several communities rather than exclusively with one. The person may also migrate from one community to another, identifying with a number of communities over the course of a lifetime. The person may stand on the margins of two communities, unable either to identify fully with or to ignore either. Presumably, there are persons who may be unable to find any community with which to identify or who will not be accepted in any community. Some people are also forced into a community that is not of their own choosing, such as people who are incarcerated and thus have particular community boundaries forced on them.

Where identification with a community is less than total, personal identity is a more salient component of the self. Community identification produces social identity, but the coherence and continuity of the person must also be found in the goals, ambitions, dreams, and projects that define personal identity. Thus, people must make plans, assert themselves, keep their eyes fixed on a clear image of what they want to be, and, in general, self-consciously construct themselves as autonomous persons. Some will carry a quest for autonomy to an extreme, eschewing any social identity, but most will seek some kind of balance between social and personal identity.

The contemporary person is thus in many ways a more self-conscious being than the resident of a traditional community. The self is not simply a spontaneous product of a fixed community that surrounds it from birth and that assigns it a place. The modern self is, instead, something that must be found, constructed, or cultivated. The person must find or make a community, as well as supplement social identity with personal identity.

Endnotes

1. For a theoretical elaboration of the relationship between language and the self, see Michael L. Schwalbe, "Language and the Self: An Expanded View from a Symbolic Interactionist Perspective," *Symbolic Interaction* 6 (2) (1983): 291–306.

2. The term *culture,* as used here, refers to the world of objects shared by those members of a society or one of its constituent social entities. Culture is thus environmental to conduct. For elaboration of this view, see John P. Hewitt, *Dilemmas of the American Self* (Philadelphia: Temple University Press, 1989).

3. Norman K. Denzin, "The Genesis of Self in Early Childhood," *The Sociological Quarterly* 13 (Summer 1972): 291–314.

4. E. Cahill, "Language Practices and Self Definition: The Case of Gender Identity Acquisition," *The Sociological Quarterly* 27 (Fall 1986): 302.

5. A. R. Lindesmith, A. L. Strauss, and N. K. Denzin wrote in *Social Psychology* (New York: Holt, Rinehart, and Winston, 1977) that children "discover that names have things—that is to say, that the words they learn correspond to aspects of the real world. In complex types of learning especially, the progression may be from word to things rather than the reverse" (p. 289).

6. Ishmael Beah, *A Long Way Gone: Memoirs of a Boy Soldier* (New York: Farrar, Straus and Giroux, 2007).

7. George Herbert Mead, *Mind, Self, and Society* (Chicago: University of Chicago Press, 1934).

8. Gary Alan Fine, *With the Boys: Little League Baseball and Preadolescent Culture* (Chicago: University of Chicago Press, 1987), pp. 191–192.

9. C. J. Pascoe, *Dude You're a Fag: Masculinity and Sexuality in High School* (Berkeley: University of California Press, 2007).

10. William A. Corsaro, *Friendship and Peer Culture in the Early Years* (Norwood, NJ: Ablex, 1985).

11. Erving Goffman, *The Presentation of Self in Everyday Life* (New York: Doubleday Anchor, 1959).

12. Goffman, *Presentation of Self,* p. 122.

13. Goffman, *Presentation of Self,* p. 70.

14. Goffman, *Presentation of Self,* p. 35.

15. Goffman, *Presentation of Self,* p. 5.

16. See Carol Rambo Ronai, Carolyn Ellis, "Turn-ons for Money: Interactional Strategies of the Table Dancer," *Journal of Contemporary Ethnography* 18 (1989): 271–298; Kari Lerum, "'Precarious Situations' in a Strip Club: Exotic Dancers and the Problem of Reality Maintenance," in *The Production of Reality: Essays and Readings in Social Psychology* 3rd ed., ed. Peter Kollock and Jodi O'Brien (Thousand Oaks, CA: Pine Forge Press, 2001), pp. 279–287.

17. David Shipler, *The Working Poor: Invisible in America* (New York: Knopf, 2005).

18. The study of the self as "narrative" is a relatively recent development but has accumulated a vast literature. For useful discussions using this approach, see Jerome Bruner, "Life as Narrative," *Social Research* 54 (1987): 11–32; Susan E. Chase, *Ambiguous Empowerment: The Work Narratives of Women School Superintendents* (Amherst, MA: University of Massachusetts Press, 1995); Arthur W. Frank, *The Wounded Storyteller: Body, Illness, and Ethics* (Chicago: University of Chicago Press, 1995); Jaber F. Gubrium and James A. Holstein, "Narrative Practices and the Coherence of Personal Stories," *The Sociological Quarterly* 39 (1998): 163–187; James A. Holstein and Jaber F. Gubrium, *The Self We Live By: Narrative Identity in a Postmodern World* (New York: Oxford University Press, 2000); David R. Maines, "Narrative's Moment and Sociology's Phenomena: Toward a Narrative Sociology," *The Sociological Quarterly* 34 (1993): 17–38; Robert Zussman, "Autobiographical Occasions," *Contemporary Sociology* 25 (1996): 143–148.

19. Gregory P. Stone, "Appearance and the Self: A Slightly Revised Version," in *Social Psychology through Symbolic Interaction*, 2nd ed., ed. Gregory P. Stone and Harvey A. Farberman (New York: Wiley, 1981), p. 188.

20. Analysis of the self relies heavily upon John P. Hewitt, *Dilemmas of the American Self* (Note 2), especially Chapter 5: "A Theory of Identity."

21. For Sheldon Stryker's views on the nature of self and identity, see his *Symbolic Interactionism: A Social Structural Version* (Reading, MA: Benjamin/ Cummings, 1980).

22. J. Scheff, *Microsociology: Discourse, Emotion, and Social Structure* (Chicago: University of Chicago Press, 1990), especially Chapter 1: "Human Nature and the Social Bond."

23. This idea is a consistent tenet of functionalist social theory. See Lewis Coser, *The Functions of Social Conflict* (Glencoe, IL: Free Press, 1956).

24. Hazel Markus, "Self-schemata and Processing Information about the Self," *Journal of Personality and Social Psychology* 35 (1977): 64.

25. Hazel Markus, Jeanne Smith, and Richard L. Morland, "Role of Self-Concept in the Perception of Others," *Journal of Personality and Social Psychology* 49 (1985): 1494–1512.

26. Charles Horton Cooley, *Human Nature and the Social Order* (New York: Scribners, 1902), p. 152.

27. Cooley, *Human Nature and the Social Order,* p. 152.

28. Cooley did not view the individual as a passive participant in the reflected appraisals process. See David D. Franks and Viktor Gecas, "Autonomy and Conformity in Cooley's Self-Theory: The Looking Glass and Beyond," *Symbolic Interaction* 15 (Spring 1992): 49–68.

29. A classic sociological study of self-esteem is Morris Rosenberg's *Society and the Adolescent Self-Image* (Princeton, NJ: Princeton University Press, 1965); summaries of research and theories can be found in Viktor Gecas and Peter Burke, "Self and Identity," Chapter 2 in *Sociological Perspectives on Social Psychology,* ed. Karen Cook, Gary Alan Fine, and James S. House (Boston: Allyn & Bacon, 1995); *The Social Importance of Self-Esteem,* ed. Andrew M. Mecca, Neil J. Smelser, and John Vasconcellos (Berkeley, CA: University of California Press, 1989), and *Extending Self-Esteem Theory and Research: Sociological and Psychological Currents,* ed. Timothy J. Owens, Sheldon Stryker, and Norman Goodman (Cambridge: Cambridge University Press, 2001).

30. Victor Gecas and Michael L. Schwalbe, "Beyond the Looking Glass Self: Social Structure and Efficacy-Based Self-Esteem," *Social Psychology Quarterly* 46 (1983): 77–88.

31. David Shulman, *From Hire to Liar* (Ithaca: Cornell University Press, 2007).

32. David Grazian, *On the Make* (Chicago: University of Chicago Press, 2009).

33. Goffman, *Presentation of Self* (Note 11).

34. A. Snow and Leon Anderson, *Down on Their Luck: A Study of Homeless Street People* (Berkeley, CA: University of California Press, 1993).

35. L. Schmitt and Wilbert M. Leonard, "Immortalizing the Self through Sport," *American Journal of Sociology* 91 (March 1986): 1088–1111.

36. Erving Goffman, "Role Distance," in *Encounters,* ed. Erving Goffman (Indianapolis, IN: Bobbs-Merrill, 1961).

37. B. E. Ashforth, G. E. Kreiner, M. A. Clark, and M. Fugate, "Normalizing Dirty Work: Managerial Tactics for Countering Occupational Taint." *Academy of Management Journal* 50 (2007):149–174.

38. The most up-to-date and sophisticated summary of research findings on self-esteem can be found in Owens, Stryker, and Goodman, *Extending Self-Esteem Theory and Research* (Note 29).

39. See the excellent characterization of low self-esteem in Timothy J. Owens and Morris Rosenberg, "Low Self-Esteem People: A Collective Portrait," in Owens, Stryker, and Goodman, *Extending Self-Esteem Theory and Research,* pp. 400–436 (Note 29).

40. Albert Ellis, Windy Dryden, *The Practice of Rational Emotive Behavior Therapy* 2nd ed. (New York: Springer, 2007).

41. Stack Sullivan, *The Interpersonal Theory of Psychiatry* (New York: Norton, 1953), p. 351.

42. For critical views of the self-esteem literature see John P. Hewitt, *The Myth of Self-Esteem: Finding Happiness and Solving Problems in America* (New York: St. Martin's Press, 1998); and Hewitt, "The Social Construction of Self-Esteem," in *Handbook of Positive Psychology,* ed. C. R. Snyder, and Shane J. Lopez (New York: Oxford University Press, 2001).

43. Candace West and Don H. Zimmerman, "Doing Gender," *Gender and Society* 1 (June 1987): 121–151.

44. Patricia A. Adler and Peter Adler, *Backboards and Blackboards: College Athletes and Role-Engulfment* (New York: Columbia University Press, 1991).

45. For an analysis of the problems of mixed ethnic identity, see Cookie White Stephan, "Ethnic Identity among Mixed-Heritage People in Hawaii," *Symbolic Interaction* 14 (Fall 1991): 261–277.

46. Hans H. Gerth and C. Wright Mills, *Character and Social Structure* (New York: Harcourt Brace, 1953).

47. Irvin G. Wyllie, *The Self-Made Man in America: The Myth of Rags to Riches* (New York: Free Press, 1966).

48. Leslie Irvine, *Codependent Forevermore: The Invention of Self in a Twelve Step Group* (Chicago: University of Chicago Press, 1999).

49. Vered Vinitzky-Seroussi, *After Pomp and Circumstance: High School Reunion as an Autobiographical Occasion* (Chicago: University of Chicago Press, 1998).

50. W. Frank, *The Wounded Storyteller: Body, Illness, and Ethics* (Chicago: University of Chicago Press, 1995).

51. Akhil Gupta and James Ferguson, "Beyond Culture: Space, Identity and the Politics of Difference," *Cultural Anthropology* 7 (1) (1992): 6–23. See also Arjun Appadurai, "Disjuncture and Difference in the Global Cultural Economy," *Theory, Culture & Society.* 7 (2) (1990): 295–310.

52. H. Turner, "The Real Self: From Institution to Impulse," *American Journal of Sociology* 81 (March 1976): 989–1016.

CHAPTER

4

Defining Reality and Accounting for Behavior

S ymbolic interactionists explain human behaviors as the result of situated social interactions. Just pointing to social and cultural norms to explain people's actions does
not satisfy them. They go beyond simply identifying the motivations that people
offer for their actions. The symbolic interactionist perspective examines people's conduct
through focusing on the concrete contexts where behaviors take place. They investigate
how people interact in specific social situations, such as going to a class, attending a party,
dating, or working on a term paper. Symbolic interactionists seek out everyday situations
and explore people's definitions of them, how people make and take roles, and how they
form and enact individual and social actions. In this chapter, we examine those processes
of situated social interaction.

The Definition of the Situation

In Chapter 2, we stated that people construct their actions based on how they define situations. We now examine this complex process further. To start, the sociological concept of
defining a "situation" is more nuanced than just referencing how people use the word "situation" in everyday life. When people speak of or identify a "situation" in everyday talk,
they often refer to a particular occasion such as a party, an argument, a predicament, or an
event. They might say, "It was an embarrassing situation" or "I got out of that situation as
soon as I could." Symbolic interactionists integrate two aspects of this everyday usage of a
situation.

First, symbolic interactionists agree that the word *situation* locates an activity temporally in relation to other activity. When we speak of a particular situation, we mark off a

particular portion of time and give it a name. A "party" may consume several hours during which people engage in a great many particular acts—dancing, drinking, laughing, flirting, conversing, and the like. When we call a particular situation a "party," we subsume, under that single label, all those activities that occur during that particular interval of time. The second aspect is that situations locate those events spatially. The event that we call the "party" occurred in a defined place—at someone's home, for example. People assembled for parties conceive of themselves as being in the same place, and they are cognizant of one another's presence there. They are acutely aware that they are in a particular physical location together, and further, that they are there in a situation of "partying."

Symbolic interactionists transcend the commonsense understanding of a situation by emphasizing how people define a situation from their social perspectives as actual or potential participants. People have shared ideas about the meaning of events as they occur in time. Place is likewise defined in social terms. A party is a place where there are "partiers." Symbolic interactionists attend to how roles, acts, and objects found in places make them constitute a particular "situation."

George Herbert Mead identified an important idea called *emergence*.[1] He used this idea to refer to how the meanings of a situation—and of the events that take place within it—are not fixed, but emerge over time. The present—the here and now of any particular moment—is experienced in terms of both a past and a future. What is happening at this moment is understood in relation to what has already occurred and what is expected (or hoped) will occur later. Mead said that the "present" is actually fluid and ephemeral. By this, Mead means that people experience something that we call "the present" or "now," although the present does not really exist, for our consciousness is always moving through time, always focused either on what has occurred (or on the self as it has acted) or on some imagined future event or act.

Consider, for example, how people construct an event like going to a themed fraternity party. Before even going to the party, students will anticipate and prepare for the event, perhaps—imagining who they will see there or how people will react to what they are wearing. They often engage in what college students refer to as "pregaming," which is drinking in a dormitory room with friends before leaving for the party. At this point, going to the party as a concrete, situated activity is part of the future; yet as the outcome exists in the imagination, that future is shaping present acts. As the party gets going, people might start playing drinking games or flirting with other partygoers. Seeing those activities, a student might remember past parties when the same people beat him at a game of beer pong or that he flirted with someone he liked at a previous party and was looking forward to seeing that person at this party. Here, past events flow into and help shape the meaning of the present. Today's party might offer an opportunity to get revenge in the drinking game or to try to make a romantic connection with the person from the last party. The meaning of the situation is progressively transformed and in flux over time in relation to expectations for future and past experiences.

The symbolic interactionist is interested in engaging a deeper social analysis of a situation rather than simply detailing an event in space and time. Meaning is an emergent property and is never absolutely fixed or established. A party where someone was hopeful of finally seducing someone becomes a disappointment when the seduction fails. At no point is the meaning of "the party" fixed, even though the situation has the same name throughout. Rather, meaning alters with the passage of time. What is expected for the future shapes the meaning in the present. As events do or do not occur as expected, a past is created, and the meaning of the present is transformed.

Just as situations have a "place" in a larger social context, they also have a place for the individual participants within it. Knowing their roles in the situation provides a sense of place. People locate themselves—that is, they maintain a cognitive grasp of "where" they are—relative to the situation and to the larger social context in which that situation exists. A cognitive map of the situation itself is given by one's sense of its arrangement of roles—of the variety of perspectives from which participants act and of their relationship to one's own perspective. One has a role in the situation relative to the roles of others. One's cognitive map of the situation as a place in the larger scheme of things depends on the fact that we routinely imagine situations as elements or fixtures of groups, organizations, and other social units. A "class" is situated within a university relative to other situations—other classes, having lunch, writing papers, going to parties, and numerous other situations of college student life.

Under some conditions, the relative social and temporal locations of participants in a situation, as well as the larger context within which the situation is embedded, can be drastically and swiftly transformed. When professional or university sports teams win championships, many of their fans crowd public spaces in celebration. Sometimes those situations of collective jubilation suddenly and unpredictably change into mob violence. A celebratory crowd suddenly transforms the situation so that it is dangerous for all, as there is a progression from shared congratulations to rioting and mayhem. Melees break out, with people who had been "fans" now becoming "rioters," "looters," and "victims." The situation is transported wholesale from one conceptual domain to another—from one framework of social space and time to another—even while the participants remain in one physical place.

What, then, is the definition of a situation? Who has it? Where is it? How do we know that a shared definition exists? What happens when people do not understand or share a definition of the situation? To answer these and similar questions requires a detailed analysis of situations and their definitions.

The crucial fact about a definition of a situation is that it is cognitive—it is our idea of our location in social space and time that constrains how we act and interpret. When we have a definition of a situation, we cognitively configure acts, objects, and others in a way that makes sense to us as a basis for acting. We have a definition of a situation, for example, when we "know" that we are at a "graduation party." We "know" that there will be a graduate and that his or her family, friends, and party guests will congratulate her or him and celebrate in familiar ways. Our definition of a situation consists of what we "know" about what will happen and what persons will make it happen.

Definitions of situations thus exist in the minds of the individuals who participate in them. Definitions do not hang from invisible wires in midair nor do they exist in a mysterious "group mind." Instead, people act on the basis of their "knowledge" of the situation. They make and take roles in terms of the situation's sensed role structure, acting toward familiar and expected objects, cooperating in the performance of social acts. Participants share their definitions of situations in the sense that each person acts on the basis of a definition that more or less resembles the definition that others hold.

There are limits, however, to how much participants fully share the definition of a situation. Take the common situation of a college classroom. A professor and students at one level have a shared definition of this situation. They are in a physical space where the class is held and they share a sense of its role structure and joint activities. The professor is lecturing on a topic and the students look in the professor's direction with occasional head nods and the appearance of diligent note taking. However, the students in the class may actually be restless and bored. They may hide cell phones underneath their desks and text their friends while looking up occasionally to nod their heads. The professor may see students whispering to one another but not say anything to avoid losing face and risk shifting the definition of the situation to one where the professor has to acknowledge disrespect. Instead, the professor and the students might settle on a silent working agreement: As long as the students pretend to listen and learn, the professor will pretend that the students are actually listening and learning.

At one level, the professor and students share a definition of the situation. Each person, by acting on the basis of a definition of the situation of "what being in class involves," constructs acts that fit with the expectations that others have in this situation. Each person can employ his or her definition of the situation and its role structure to make sense of the acts of others. At another level, however, they do not conform to the ideal definition of the situation. Students, acting on the "knowledge" that they are bored in class, sit through the lectures without saying anything. The professor, acting on the "knowledge" that the students at least look like they understand everything being said, takes their silence as an indication that things are going well, or that he or she doesn't have to take reparative actions for being dull. Definitions of the situation can be somewhat incongruous and still serve as the basis for meaningful, predictable, and organized interaction.

Definitions of situations imply roles and identities. Therefore, incongruous definitions of situations imply misidentifications of self and others in relation to the definition of the situation. For example, a man may invite a woman to dinner thinking his strong feelings for her are reciprocated and begin to talk about their future together, only to discover that she does not hold similar feelings for him. Incongruous definitions of a situation can persist for some time before they are discovered.

These situations are important to examine, as such misunderstandings may not be accidental, but result from an effort by one party to manipulate and misrepresent a definition of reality to suit their interests. There are important stakes in how people interpret situations and thus define what they think is real. The understandings of the man and woman mentioned above may represent an unfortunate but innocent misinterpretation, or conversely, an effort by the woman (or man if the roles are reversed) to gain some reward by leading on the other party.

As an example, some companies currently hire what are called "guerilla marketers." In guerilla marketing, a group of people in a social setting does not announce that they are promoting a product or acting as an advertisement while they engage in everyday behavior that in fact does promote a product. For example, a guerilla marketer might pay people who post praise for a restaurant or hotel on a travel or review Web site. They might hire particularly attractive men and women to hang out at a nightclub as if they represent the kind of people that just naturally happen to be there. Films and television shows feature a plethora of what are called "product placements," in which characters use products during what is supposed to be a story in order to promote those products to potential consumers. What is ostensibly a cultural product to be evaluated on merits of performance can also be considered as a series of micro-advertisements, such as the use of Reese's Pieces in *ET*,

BMW cars in recent James Bond movies, Federal Express in *Castaway,* and the plastic cups with the Coke logo in front of the *American Idol* judges.

Consider the interesting case of Cameron Hughes, a professional fan.[2] Hughes is paid $2000 a night to perform the role of a maniacal sports fan at pro sports games, screaming at referees, exhorting the home team on at the top of his lungs, whipping T-shirts around, and doing ludicrous versions of dances like the electric slide and the robot. His job is to get home crowds riled up by heightening a situation of excitement at the game. His goal is to be a spectacle drawing attention and involvement in the game. He is creating "atmosphere." However, the bottom line is that he is a paid fan and his performances are choreographed and approved by client teams beforehand. He might love sports, but he is not just another spontaneously enthusiastic fan. Stefanie Cohen's article published in the *New York Post,* on Hughes states, "Teams, such as the [New Jersey] Devils don't like to discuss Hughes's work for them, believing people would be disappointed to learn he isn't a die-hard fan." Those teams have a commercial interest in the public defining the situation so as to heighten their commitment to the product (the game/team). They also want to cloak that they are manipulating the definition of the situation by bringing in a pseudofan, who in reality, is just as likely to be working at a rival's home arena putting on the same show of dedication the following week.

As we will see later in this chapter, mutual awareness of roles, identities, and purposes is not always fully open, and when it is not, there are consequences for social interaction that are important to recognize. There are stakes at hand in getting people to believe in particular versions of reality. For the time being though, we will concentrate our analysis on situations where there are genuinely shared definitions of what is real.

Routine and Problematic Situations

Most of our everyday behavior occurs as we participate in routines. Our behavior emerges in situations with familiar and congruent definitions, such as when we sit down for dinner, attend a class, drive a car, go to a movie, write a paper, play football, and do our jobs. These situations have recognizable expectations. We can easily name them, anticipate the objects they will contain, and know what roles people will assume and who will assume them. We expect those activities to strongly resemble past similar activities.

Everyday life consists of many habitual actions. When we are accustomed to having dinner at the same hour each day, sitting down and eating at that time seems virtually a matter of reflex. Things are in their accustomed places, appropriate others are present, and food is served on time. Many such situations are so routine that we appear to be creatures of habit, or perhaps actors enacting a script, rather than self-conscious human beings making our roles. Definitions of situations seem to provide general guidelines of what to expect and what to do. Thus, when two acquaintances exchange greetings, inquiring about one another's health and families, they seem just to be behaving in a ritualistic, habitual way. Many presuppose that routine situations wholly categorize all of people's conduct.

One could argue further that culture ultimately provides our definitions of situations. In this view, during socialization, we learn a large number of definitions, along with rules for applying them to the concrete repetitive situations that we encounter. Thus, our culture seems to anticipate so that we will know how to act, provided we have been socialized appropriately to apply correct definitions of the situation.

However, matters are not so simple. Although we do learn the definitions of many situations in advance, we do not learn all possible definitions, nor does each episode of interaction merely require us to apply a preestablished definition. The cumulative experiences of human beings as they grow from infancy through adulthood provide them with many scripts, scenarios, and frames from which they can more or less easily construct their conduct, but people are also confronted continuously with unexpected and novel events.

Every concrete situation can differ at least slightly from expectations. Moreover, openness to new situations and meanings is an inherent characteristic of human conduct. The need to interpret new meanings and lines of action, although sometimes minimal, is always present to some degree, and always potentially significant. Language provides a useful analogy. In the process of learning our native language, we do not learn every possible combination of words that we will eventually use. We learn language in such a way that we can say new things. We can create sentences that are, to us, completely novel, since we have not previously heard them spoken. Definitions of situations also involve learning many seemingly fixed and preestablished meanings that are roughly analogous to words that we can use to form these definitions. However, as with language, we can also learn to create new meanings, to consider the possibility that our interpretations of a situation might be wrong, and to face unexpected events that constantly intrude themselves into human affairs. A situation may be defined well enough so that there are few surprises, and habit can account for the bulk of what we do. However, even in routine situations, people misunderstand one another, fail to get jokes, behave in selfish or unpredictable ways, disagree with one another, seek conflicting goals, and compete for scarce resources.

Most unexpected events in everyday life are problematic within the boundaries of a defined situation. As Mead pointed out, we can see an event or circumstance as problematic only by contrasting it with something that is not problematic.[3] Suppose that a dinner guest criticizes the host's cooking in front of other guests. The momentary shocked silence that likely follows signifies that the others see this outburst as an unusual and problematic form of behavior. The dinner guests share a clear understanding that such opinions are best kept politely to oneself, no matter how bad the food is. Even though a guest's rude conduct in this instance elicits a response from others—the host will be hurt and the other guests will express strong disagreement—the rudeness will not make the definition of the situation itself untenable. The common expectations offer an unproblematic background against which the problematic event of rudeness is viewed.

In contrast, some situations are themselves problematic or become so. Situations that were defined in one way are redefined; situations that were defined clearly can become undefined; and situations that were defined congruently can become defined less congruently. A party can degenerate into a brawl or an intimate dinner can transform into an argument. People can behave in thoroughly unexpected ways, as, for example, when they are under the influence of drugs, and by their baffling acts, come to challenge the very definition of a situation. People fall into or out of love with one another at different rates, and so their definitions of social situations can be incongruous. When such disruptions occur, at least some participants will be baffled until they can reconstruct their definition of the situation and thus their place in it. We will emphasize problematic situations in Chapter 5. At present, we note that routine and problematic situations represent two end points on a continuum. They comprise ideal types, for no situation is either fully routine or completely problematic; actual situations fall at various points between these extremes.

Role Making and Role Taking in Routine Situations

Role taking, we noted, occurs when people momentarily and imaginatively adopt the perspective of others. They do so to enact a role performance that will be in coordination with the role performances of others. But how does someone adopt another person's perspective? How does one know what that perspective is? What does a person need to know in order to take the role of the other?

Answering these questions should start through examining the attitudes that people bring with them to situations and how those attitudes impact how people begin to construct the conduct that follows. People approach situations with the attitude that they are routine situations—that objects, acts, and others will be much as they usually are and that nothing unusual will take place. Basing his analysis on the work of Alfred Schutz, Peter McHugh suggested that people bring three fundamental assumptions to routine situations:[4]

1. People assume that the prior conceptions that they have of situations are valid—they take for granted that what they "know" as the situation is actually what is taking place. People ordinarily trust their understandings and impressions of what is going on around them.
2. People assume that others in the situation share their conceptions. That is, although people generally make due allowance for the acknowledged fact that no two people experience a situation in exactly the same way because they occupy different positions in it, there is still a basic assumption of shared perspectives and experiences.
3. People rarely bother to check their assumptions about a situation. So long as their definition of a situation works—so long as it allows meaningful conduct to take place—they do not need to question it.

Some care must be exercised in referring to "assumptions" that participants bring to routine situations. An "assumption" sounds like a self-conscious formulated thought or announcement. But such assumptions are only occasionally formulated in words. People rarely say to themselves before entering a classroom: "I assume this is the place where Symbolic Interaction 211 meets, that others are here for the same reason, and that I can act on that basis until there is some reason not to."

According to McHugh, people organize meaning in a thematic way as they role-make and role-take in situations. When a student enters a classroom and assumes that a symbolic interaction course is being offered, the student assigns meanings to acts, objects, and people by linking them to the central theme of that course. This theme provides the basis for interpreting the meanings of acts and events within the situation, each of which serves to "document" the theme. Thus, if the professor distributes a syllabus that is titled "Symbolic Interaction" and begins to explain what this social science perspective is, these acts offer supporting evidence for the theme. They reinforce the student's sense of the role arrangements of the situation—that here is a "sociology professor" talking to "sociology students."

As social interaction moves forward in a routine situation, people fit together various acts and objects as they develop their individual lines of conduct. This process, as we indicated, is a temporal one—what took place a moment ago has a bearing on what is now occurring or is about to occur. Students assume, for example, that the outline the professor put on the board a moment ago will serve as the framework for subsequent comments and discussion. They interpret the professor's statements as if they are linked to the headings on the outline. So long as this process of interpretation occurs, where each event can be fitted to the central theme of the situation, the definition of the situation is unproblematic.

Problematic events do occur within defined situations, though, because people can act in unexpected or seemingly nonsensical ways. Professors brag about their grandchildren or go off on non sequiturs, and their students wonder what relevance these comments have to the class. Within limits, students will seek ways to interpret the professor's talk as relevant to the course, for example, by waiting to see if a link between seemingly irrelevant comments and the lecture topic develops. If they find a connection, then the relationship between theme and events is revealed and the definition of the situation is preserved. If not, the definition of the situation becomes incongruous.

The more that objects and events in a situation are problematic (because they cannot be readily fitted to the supposed theme), the more strenuously and self-consciously people search for patterns of meaning. This aspect of the definition of the situation—its authorship by members—cannot be stressed too much. Defining situations and maintaining meaning in situations is not merely a matter of responding to objectively present objects and events, to things that are merely there, and waiting for people to understand their true meaning. Rather, defining the situation is a process in which we create meaning. Human beings author the meanings that form the basis on which they act.

In a larger sense, we are claiming that social reality and shared meaning are not objective, natural, or to be taken for granted. People define what are objective, nonphysical truths, often—though not always—in concert with how other people see them. We come to accept things as true if we agree they are, without openly acknowledging that we have agreed to accept something as true. The meanings that we attach to events and actions are not inevitable or to be taken for granted. They take ongoing work through interaction to maintain. We have said that human beings create objects in their environment by acting toward them. Objects do not merely exist; they exist by virtue of people's defining efforts. Thus—within limits—reality is created by intentions. Of course, this proposition should not be carried to absurd lengths. A flat tire is a flat tire no matter how much one wishes it was not or pretends that the tire is okay. But in many situations of everyday life, the definitions on the basis of which people act create the reality.

Yes—Reality Is Not Just There—We Define What Is Real

The point that people *make* meaning rather than just *accept* an objective reality is difficult to grasp. However, grasping this point is vital for understanding the insights of the symbolic interactionist perspective. Symbolic interactionists see reality as socially constructed by people's beliefs and socialization. This view does not mean that symbolic interactionists deny "real things" that make common sense and are physical facts. For example, we would not argue that people can breathe in outer space without spacesuits or that slamming our head into a reinforced wall would be painless. The levels of reality that we have in mind are more the realm of beliefs and nonmaterial culture. For example, people have many beliefs about what is real that are not matters of empirical science. Whether someone thinks ghosts exist, whether the "hot hand" in basketball is real, or whether something is fashionable or funny or cool (or not) is actually a matter of argument and perspective.

Their status of being real becomes an issue of what people choose to believe and/or agree to believe under particular circumstances; they are not objective real facts. Once we become committed to certain beliefs about what is real, we work very hard to convince others and ourselves that the belief we have about what is true is actually objectively true out there in the world. Though we might consider our own beliefs in this regard as absolutely true and factual, we have to confront that we make up this objectivity and that the factual nature of those beliefs might be more neutral than we want to admit. In this sense, as some have written, what is real is "up for grabs."

Consider how vulnerable we are to people's attempts to convince us of what is real or false. We have many biases in waiting: People and organizations want us to believe that particular things are real, and dubious advertising claims are present at every turn. How many social groups consistently work at encouraging us to believe that their particular claims are true? Governments want citizens to believe in their policies; salespersons trumpet claims about what using their products will really do for us; some religious practitioners tell us that if we do not act as they instruct then we will be damned; family members tell us that our crazy relative is not so bad; and astrologers tell us that the stars and our horoscopes reveal our fates. The notion that we actually *choose* to believe that some things are real, and then that we transform our accepting claims of what are real into an objective fact that they are real, is a significant implication of the symbolic interactionist perspective. Examining how people work to claim things as real gives us a deeper analytic insight into the culture and influences that act upon us.

David Shulman gives a quiz about what is "real" versus false to his classes (based on the results of published research). We reproduce this quiz below (along with answers).

Q1. An experiment is designed to test whether 100 research subjects are willing to electrocute a stranger to the point of death. What percent of research subjects are willing to do so?
A. About two-thirds, depending on variations in experimental conditions.

Q2. You design an experiment to get 16 sane people to fake their way onto a psychiatric ward. They claim to "hear voices." Afterwards, the 16 people act normally while they are on the ward. How many of these "pseudopatients" does the staff detect?
A. None.

Q3. What percentage of participants in a recent gubernatorial primary in California grew up speaking English at home?
A. 40 percent

Q4. What percent of crime do police officers catch in the act?
A. 1 percent

Q5. Has the United States ever invaded Russia?
A. Yes, under President Woodrow Wilson, American troops landed on USSR territory.

Q6. What percentage of American families are conventionally married, heterosexual couples with children under 18?
A. According to recent U.S. Census data, 24 percent of families fit this category.

Q7. The wealthiest 5 percent of all Americans own what percentage of all the wealth? What percentage does the bottom 20 percent own?
A. The top 5 percent of all Americans own around 24 percent of all the wealth. The bottom 20 percent owns 2 percent of American wealth.

Q8. What percentage of heterosexual marriages is dissolved within five years? What percentage of the 958 same-sex marriages granted to Vermont residents since July 2000 have been dissolved?

A. 20 percent and 3 percent.

Q9. What is the chance that a movie released last year was pornographic?

A. Nine out of ten.

If some of these answers about what is objectively real surprise you, ask yourself, why didn't you know that answer? What assumptions do you carry with you that made you comfortable with what you had previously taken to be real? When and where did you learn that conventional wisdom could be wrong? When you think of history textbooks, radio shows, political advertisements, old wives' tales, and family traditions with a critical eye, you can appreciate how much work people engage in to sustain beliefs about what is real that are erroneous while manufacturing what we will take to be "true" or "real." While we will develop a more nuanced analysis later of how others manipulate definitions of the situation to engage in what Howard Becker described as *moral entrepreneurship* (efforts to convince people about the correctness and legitimacy of particular moral constructions of issues), we must first consider how we ourselves work to embed ourselves in constructing what is real.

A common means through which we experience constructing reality involves an important concept called the self-fulfilling prophecy. First coined by the sociologist Robert K. Merton, a *self-fulfilling prophecy* refers to an "assumption or prediction that, purely as a result of having been made, causes the expected or predicted effect to occur, and thus confirms its own accuracy." In other words, when people have a prior belief about what is true, they interpret information or actions that pertain to that belief to be evidence that confirms the prior belief and "makes" it come true. For example, suppose someone believes that a person is antisocial and unfriendly. They may treat every action by that person as being intended to be nasty, and in turn, give off an unwelcoming vibe to that individual. Where the person might actually have not been an "angry outcast," how people act on the belief that the person is an angry outcast comes to make the person feel alienated and angry at being treated in an unfriendly way, such that the person retaliates by becoming antisocial and unfriendly. People's actions cause the prior belief to become true. Sometimes those expectations also entrap people, such as when people's behaviors are always interpreted to confirm expectations, even when they do not.

There are large-scale institutional level consequences to self-fulfilling prophecies. For example, when large groups of people act on the basis of their definitions of the situation—even if their definitions are in some respects erroneous—there is a possibility that their actions will bring about the very conditions they thought existed. Consider gas shortages. If drivers believe that gasoline is going to be in short supply because of a refinery explosion or a pipeline break, they are apt to visit gas stations with great urgency in order to keep their tanks topped off. Lines at gas stations will become longer and more gas will be hoarded in individual cars. As a result, spot shortages will result, even when gas is actually plentiful. Acting on the basis of their definition of the situation, drivers helped to make gas shortages real and made their prophecy of a shortage come true.

We will examine problematic events that threaten the definition of the situation more closely later in this chapter and show how participants cope with such events. To do so, however, we must first examine the process of defining the situation in greater detail.

The Cognitive Bases of Role Making and Role Taking

People's actions are grounded in both thoughts and feelings. To perform a role in coordination with the actions of others, a person must have a definition of the situation—or find one—and understand which possible acts will work successfully and which will not. To engage in successful role taking, one must have a cognitive grasp of what another person is thinking—how the other defines the situation and what the other might be expecting you to do. Affect plays an important part in these processes. Typically, situations have an expected emotional tone—we expect to witness and express laughter at comedies and joy at weddings—and successful role making and role taking depend on an individual's capacity to share these feelings. Moreover, role taking is a cognitive process and an affective one. By attempting to grasp the perspective of the other, one identifies with that perspective. Role taking can generate empathy in the sense that people try to assess what feelings others have that are appropriate in that situation.

Definitions of situations, together with the role structures associated with them, provide human beings with two important capacities. First, we gain the capacity to anticipate or predict the actions of the others with whom we interact. Second, we gain the capacity to make sense of the actions of others, even actions that we did not anticipate. People must have grounds for deciding among alternative possible actions in order to control their conduct when they interact with one another. How does an individual determine, for example, if a person encountered on the street is friendly or hostile, and thus whether the proper approach is wariness or trust? How do people anticipate what others might say next in a conversation? Clearly people do make predictions about how other people will act in order to govern their own conduct. The problem is to determine how they do so. What do people know that enables them to grasp the perspectives of others?

Powerful research questions that are associated with the symbolic interactionist perspective emerge from unraveling this process. The capacity to know enough about how others might act requires that people can share a common set of meanings about the world, at least enough to understand how people might respond to particular statements or actions. Shared meanings are also linked to sustaining social order. The capacity to predict a response means that responses can be organized and follow an order that can also organize social interactions. If people lack shared meanings, we can explore what social characteristics enable some people to have more useful knowledge and an increased ability to adjust their "reality" to situations. If we can predict responses, we can also try to manipulate them, which in turn allows us to study how people attempt to influence the interpretations that others might make. As seen in the classroom example earlier, there are also dynamics of power. Some people have more power to negotiate how people will have to "pretend" to accept certain definitions of the situation; students cannot state that they are bored directly to the professor without risking potential retaliation. Symbolic interactionists also understand that meanings of a situation are relative and culturally dependent, such that gestures in one country might be interpreted very differently in another. Therefore, the importance of predicting responses can necessitate investigating social identities and how they vary by culture.

In order to specify how knowledge informs the processes of taking and making roles, we must analyze the important contributions of the *phenomenological tradition*. The analysis that follows is based on that body of work.[5] The basic premise is that the members of a society share a common stock of knowledge, which is not a random assortment of facts and ideas, but a very structured body of knowledge and procedures for using that knowledge. This knowledge is not "true" in a scientific sense, which is to say that it has not been produced or tested according to the accepted standards of a community of scientists. But it is "true" in a practical sense, which is to say that it serves effectively to help people decide what to do and how to interpret what others are doing (see Table 4.1).

TABLE 4.1   Cognitive Frames for Role Making and Role Taking

	What Is the Key Question asked by Role Maker/Taker?	When Is the Frame Used?	How Is the Frame Confirmed?	What Is the Role of Negotiation?
Typification	Who am I and who is the other?	Typification occurs early in situations.	Predictive or "postdictive" confirmation occurs. The typification makes past or future behavior comprehensible.	Actors try to control typification of themselves and may try to negotiate more favorable ones through aligning actions.
Probability	What is likely to happen? Or Was this a likely occurrence?	Probability generally follows the establishment of a typification.	Predictive or "post dictive" confirmation occurs.	Ideas about probability are invoked in discussions.
Causality	Why is this happening or did this happen?	Causality generally follows establishment of a typification but may reflect some uncertainty about typification.	Some predictive or "postdictive" confirmation occurs.	Ideas about causality are invoked in discussions.
Means and ends	Is this an effective way to achieve a purpose?	The means and ends frame generally accompanies or follows the establishment of a positive typification.	Some predictive or "postdictive" confirmation occurs.	Ideas about effectiveness are invoked in discussions.
Normative requirements	Is this right, appropriate, moral, correct behavior?	Normative requirements generally accompany or follow the establishment of a negative typification.	Self-establishing confirmation occurs. Normative labels define conduct by fiat.	Norms are negotiable through aligning actions.
Substantive congruency	Am I defining the situation in the same way as others?	Substantive congruency occurs when typification and other frames fail.	Predictive confirmation occurs. New effort is directed to redefine the situation.	Redefinition may require open and explicit negotiations.

Typification

Alfred Schutz described typifications as a crucial form of knowledge.[6] Typifications have important implications for conduct. A *typification* is an image or picture that people maintain with respect to a particular role, situation, person, or object that organizes or catalogs their knowledge of it. On the first day of class, students ordinarily have no difficulty identifying the professor, because that person both looks and acts "like" a professor. If someone thought to be a professor takes a seat with the class, the identity of that person as the professor is undermined, and students will seek a new typification of the person. They may, for example, identify the individual as a "nontraditional student." That is, because the individual does not look "like" a typical young college student and also does not act "like" a professor, they may decide this person is someone that fits into a category of an older mature college student.

As this example suggests, typification relies on visible and auditory cues. According to Gregory Stone, all interaction involves two levels.[7] We observe and respond to one another's words and deeds, to what Stone called *discourse*. These serve as bases for typification and subsequently affect the course of interaction. We also observe and respond to appearance—to manners of dress, physical appearance, and demeanor—and these clues also shape the course of interaction by providing us with typifying cues.

Very little about people is actually visible to observers. Physical appearance (expressed in dress, posture, and facial expression) and a few overt words and deeds constitute all that is directly accessible to others. Thoughts and motives are hidden, and most situations provide an opportunity for people to display few of their talents. There are vast blank spaces in the selves people present to one another. Yet appearances, acts, and words serve effectively as cues on the basis of which others establish an identity for a person and thereby typify his or her acts. For example, it is only on the basis of such minimal physical and behavioral cues as facial recognition, manner of dress, and a few fragmentary acts that one identifies the person who is the physician in a medical office. Yet on the basis of such cues, a vast array of knowledge about what physicians do, how they speak and act, and what is usual and unusual in their conduct is made available as a basis of our conduct toward them and the interpretation of theirs toward us.

Appearance is important because it provides us with the cues we need to typify someone initially and also because it assists us in maintaining and refining that typification as interaction proceeds. We assign identity to the physician on the basis of appearance—by dress, demeanor, and conduct in the examining room—but we continue to rely on appearance for other cues that will refine the typification. On the basis of tone of voice, body posture, and facial expression, we may typify the physician as cold or warm, self-confident or uncertain, interested or distracted, about to deliver bad news or good news.

People act in given situations on the basis of typifications. They can predict the conduct of others because they identify them as types of people who are likely to behave in ways similar to others of their type. The very process of role taking depends on the ability to typify. People are able to grasp others' attitudes toward themselves only because they can typify their own acts from others' point of view. If people regard conduct as typical of certain roles, groups, or categories of people, they also are aware that others typify them— that whatever they do themselves shapes their situated social identity.

Seen in this light, role taking is a process in which people attune themselves to the typifications others use to interpret their behavior. Likewise, role making is a process in which individuals seek to devise conduct that will induce others to make desired typifica-tions. Since some typifications are more desirable than other ones—better to be an interest-ing professor than a boring one, for example, or an upstanding citizen rather than a crook—people will seek to present themselves in ways that give others cues on the basis of which to make favorable typifications. This concerted effort emphasizes the importance of impression management, as we discussed in Chapter 3.

There are many circumstances when people contemplate acts that they know or fear will lead to their retypification in undesirable terms. Yet they perform these acts anyway, perhaps because the significance of the loss from a possible negative retypification is less than the probable gains from an act others might regard as untoward. A person may steal even though this conduct makes him or her a thief in the eyes of others, if what he or she steals has a high enough value or if being thought of as a thief by others does not matter greatly. Moreover, as discussed earlier, a person's control over conduct is often imperfect, so that many acts do not have the benefit of prior reflection about the possible responses of others. Often, people do not control the circumstances under which they act—mistakes and accidents affect what they do—and sometimes their impulses produce acts they wish they could recall. As we will see, controlling the typifications others form of us is a common focus of our role-making efforts in everyday life.

Cognitive Theories and Inferential Heuristics

Typifications refer to how people impose interpretations on environmental stimuli and use the resulting categorizations to select, interpret, and store information about how to act in situations. A booming field in psychology focuses on what are called *inferential heuristics*. This perspective began as an investigation into how people make judgments and decisions in situations of uncertainty, such as when they do not have enough information to fully know how to act. Psychologists Amos Tversky and Daniel Kahneman argued that people make those decisions using sets of simple rules for making inferences.[8] Those heuristics, or rules, enable people to use typifications, even though using those rules can sometimes lead to making inferential errors. Though the inferential heuristics or rules that people use can work well to reduce complexity, they also can be inaccurate in terms of leading people to make sound probabilistic decisions about people. These psychologists (and others) have identified many heuristics that people use to make inferences. We discuss a few in order to develop a sense of the bases upon which typifications depend.

One heuristic is called *representativeness*. Tversky and Kahneman argue that people make interpretations of whether a person represents a category by the degree to which a person resembles the stereotypical categories associated with that category. So, to use their example, if a person is described as "very shy and withdrawn, invariably helpful, but with little interest in the world of reality," and people are asked to assess the probability of whether that person is a librarian as opposed to a lawyer, people will state that the person is a librarian.[9] However, simply resembling a stereotype does not mean that this person is a librarian in practice. The correct answer to this question is really, who knows if that per-son is a librarian? However, what happens is that a stereotype is used to make a judgment with limited information, and while that process makes typifications possible, it is also fraught with the possibility of making erroneous judgments.

People use stereotypes to select relevant information in making inferential decisions. They also use several other heuristics in making typifications. Harvey Sacks, for example, discusses two cognitive rules that people use to organize information to construct social reality. One is *the rule of consistency,* which suggests that once people have categorized events and persons, they organize past information and future perceptions consistently with these categories. For example, upon defining someone as a homosexual, people tend to search for and remember confirming cues—all of which would have been ignored and organized differently if they had not initially categorized the person. This rule is a practical variation of the self-fulfilling prophecy. A second rule is *the rule of economy,* which refers to a tendency people have to "lock in" categories. That is, once a general category is selected for interpreting a situation, people tend not to reorganize situational cues to test the application of alternative categories. The first heuristics uses just one blueprint to organize the future actions of categorized people; the second heuristic never considers nuances or alternatives to that first blueprint.

People operate in a world of complex and overwhelming information about how to act and about what other people think. Confronted by this complexity and uncertainty, it only makes sense that people want to use interpretive rules to reduce complexity and filter only enough information to have a basis for deciding how to act. An inferential heuristic such as representativeness or others provides those simple bases for making decisions and taking interpretive actions. Relying on them also has many implications for daily life. For example, how often do we make inferential errors about people based on judging books by their covers? Research has found that people almost automatically categorize attractive people as being more intelligent, brave, and noble than people they perceive as less attractive, even in the absence of any information.[10] It is valuable to think about how these inferential directives can produce consequential judgments in everyday life that affect people's quality of life. While typifications can work well, they can also lead us to making errors. It is important to pay attention to the lessons that cognitive theories offer that we must study people as inference makers. When we adopt a particular perspective, we gain strength in focus. However, adopting a perspective also limits our awareness of reality by allowing only some of what is out there to be seen. Perspectives and typifications both sensitize and desensitize us to what can be real, rendering detail to one view but leaving us with blind spots in others.

Causality

Our stock of decision-making tools also includes propositions about causality. We assume that an event has a cause, and to act appropriately or effectively we must first establish the cause. If an ordinarily cheerful child becomes anxious or depressed, for example, a parent will respond to that atypical or unlikely conduct by asking "Why?" Did something happen to upset the child at school? Is the child getting into drugs? Why is the child behaving in this new and unusual way?

The causal propositions we apply in such instances will vary considerably from one society or community to another. Many use religious teachings to explain and interpret conduct. A child's anxiety could reflect a struggle with temptation or be a consequence of sinful behavior. Others will view that anxiety in scientific or quasi-scientific rather than theological terms. Here, the child might be anxious because of a learning disability that makes schoolwork difficult or because of involvement with drugs. In another society, the same conduct could be interpreted and explained as the result of witchcraft or of spirit possession. Wherever our propositions about causality come from—and whatever their truth as judged against some scientific standard—they still are a way to make sense of conduct when faced with a problematic event.

Means and Ends

People rely on knowledge in everyday life that phenomenologists categorize as "recipe knowledge."[11] Recipe knowledge, just like with cooking, consists of regular procedures that people follow in order to secure their ends. Knowledge of relationships between means and ends is crucial for negotiating everyday affairs and interacting with one another. Knowing how to study effectively, how to take a book out of the library, how to get along with professors, and how to write a good term paper are examples of means and ends knowledge that students must employ regularly.

Recipe knowledge has a double function in social life, as do all forms of knowledge. First, this knowledge provides a basis for individuals' abilities to act toward various objects in their world and to secure their goals. A student who knows how to study, for example, will find passing a course easier than the student who does not know how to study. Recipe knowledge also provides a frame through which we can interpret and predict the conduct of others. Role taking is made possible to a great extent because people can examine one another's conduct as means undertaken in pursuit of ends. In a physician's office, for example, many activities are unintelligible to the patient because they depend on technical knowledge that the average person does not possess. Yet people permit physicians to engage in activities that they do not understand because they can attribute purpose to what the physician does. The act makes sense as a means to something the physician wants to accomplish, even if bystanders do not know why.

Normative Standards

People use their knowledge of social norms to appraise other people's conduct. As people interact with each other, taking and making roles on the basis of what they know about typicality, probability, causality, and means and ends, they make judgments about others' acts in terms of what they feel is morally appropriate or necessary. These moral codes can also vary in intensity. Thus, an act of homicide may arouse very powerful feelings of outrage, whereas a small lie or even theft might be received far less intensely (even though people define them all as wrong in their moral code).

Norms enter into consciousness under problematic and unusual circumstances. They do so, for example, when someone's conduct is questioned. When someone acts in a manner that others find strange, unexpected, or untoward, it is likely that someone will invoke a social norm or rule. We invoke the norm through implication. For example, we might ask: "Why are you upset?" Posing this question in response to unexpected or odd behavior offers a challenge to conduct and it also speaks to a norm but is not a direct statement encouraging conformity. If someone, instead, declared, "You should be calm," that statement could ruffle feathers, although that point is the premise of the prior question. Another circumstance in which social norms are stated (if only in a conversation with the self) is when there is some uncertainty about what to do or about whether other people will perceive a contemplated act as socially acceptable.

This approach to social norms makes them a less significant aspect of social life than many sociologists portray them. For a symbolic interactionist, rather than being the major criterion people employ to regulate their own and others' conduct, social norms are one of several forms of knowledge that people use in their everyday conduct. Norms are not typifications or encoded instruction manuals for behavior. They are organizing routines. Thus, the formulation of normative statements is a part of role making and role taking, but only a part. People take the roles of others and respond to their own conduct in normative terms. They also guess whether others will use norms to act in a contemplated way. However, norms are not constantly implicated in all acts nor do people choose how they behave by just finding the appropriate norms that govern each and every social situation.

Substantive Congruency

Finally, the definition of the situation itself is a form of "knowledge" that we routinely employ when we attempt to determine whether other people's acts seem to be based on the same definition as the one we hold. *Substantive congruency* refers to when various participants in a situation can regard one another's acts as sensible in terms of their own understanding of what is going on in the situation, what objects are present, and who the actors are. Substantive congruency is like a test that people apply to one another in the process of making and taking roles. One avenue of role taking is to say to oneself, "What does the situation look like from the other person's point of view?" Here the focus is on the nature of reality itself, and particularly on the question of how a view of reality imputed to another squares with one's own view.

For example, the common situation where one individual sees smiling as just a friendly behavior and the other sees the smile as an invitation to romance illustrates how substantive congruency comes into play. Although the two may interact for a time with incongruent definitions of the situation, eventually the realization that different definitions of the situation exist will become clear to both people. The romantically inclined participant will be disappointed; the friendly socializer will find the other person's misinterpretation uncomfortable. In these kinds of examples, role taking becomes a form of reality testing, and role making may then focus on making definitions of the situation more congruent.

Each of these ways of knowing comes into play as roles are taken and made in social situations. Lacking instincts of any consequence and faced with a complex social world, human beings must simply know a great deal in order to interact with one another. The potential complexity of interaction seems enormous in view of the alternatives open to participants in many situations—the possibilities for misunderstanding and misinterpretation, and the sometimes tenuous relationship between outward appearance and inner intentions.

Symbolic interactionists have developed concepts that analyze how people cope with this complexity through efforts to give some order and continuity to the apparent fluidity and precarious nature of social interaction. Taken together, these concepts all deal with various forms of aligning actions—that is, with how human beings attempt to maintain alignment or consistency among their individual and social acts, important cultural objects, and their own conceptions of themselves. These aligning actions constitute the next important topic in our analysis of social interaction and conduct formation.

Aligning Actions

Assuming that people share similar definitions of the situation and a congruent stock of knowledge, a person should be able to predict and interpret what conduct to expect from other people. He or she can then perform his or her role appropriately in interactions with others. However, three factors can make this coordination problematic. First, people act in unexpected ways. Whether they are late to meetings, tell lies, exceed expectations or fall short of them, these surprises can interfere with the routine flow of social interaction. When unexpected conduct occurs, people now have to reconcile incongruent behaviors. Second, each individual act has implications for a person's sense of identity and self-esteem, and for the person's pursuit of his or her own goals. Those individual goals can diverge from the goals of collective behavior, as individual interests can clash with those of other organizations and individuals. Finally, people are conscious of culture and ideal dictates for how to act and may not be able to make their conduct meet those standards. "Truth," "freedom," "duty," and other cultural ideals are an important component of the environment from which human beings form their conduct. Social interaction is complicated because acts that meet the situated expectations of others, further individual goals, and enhance the self may not accord with cultural ideals. When such contradictions occur, people have to associate their acts with cultural ideals successfully so that other people will accept their actions.

These three factors create the need for aligning actions. *Aligning actions* are verbal efforts to place social interaction in alignment by reconciling individual conduct and prominent cultural ideals.[12] The use of aligning actions pervades everyday life. As a category, they include accounts, explanations, apologies, disclaimers, and other verbal techniques that people use when they talk about unexpected and problematic behaviors, seek to protect or defend themselves from accusations, and attempt to make their conduct appear sensible and appropriate.[13]

An important theme of symbolic interactionist research is dissecting the processes through which people carry out these moral deflections. Symbolic interactionist and other social scientists have identified and studied many types and features of aligning actions. Erving Goffman conceptualized different remedial strategies that people use to fend off various forms of stigmatization.[14] Other sociologists have identified "accounts," "aligning actions," "disclaimers," "discounts," "misunderstandings," "techniques of neutralization," and "vocabularies of motive" as just some of the techniques that people use to reconcile behaviors that conflict with prevailing ideals.[15] Recent reviews of this literature identify literally dozens of preemptive and post hoc actions that people use to avoid or repair a potentially spoiled identity.[16] Among those most often employed are motive talk, accounts, disclaimers, and other aligning actions like apologies. Each technique attempts to define individual conduct in culturally acceptable, or at least tolerated, terms. Ongoing scholarship continues to advance our understanding of how individuals and groups attempt to sustain their situated identities when these are threatened by discrediting past, present, or future conduct.

We cannot overstate the importance of aligning actions in reconciling the relationship between culture and conduct. Aligning actions attempt to "sustain a relationship between ongoing conduct and culture in the face of recognized failure of conduct to live up to cultural definitions and requirements."[17] People are imperfect, and pressures to act in culturally ideal ways at all times are difficult to comply with in a world where faultless means are in short supply. Using aligning actions "implies an actual effort of some kind to bring conduct more into line with normative culture."[18] Doing so can also smooth out social interaction. No one is exempt from having to—at some point—reconcile some of his or her actions with cultural ideals.

C. Wright Mills kick-started this research direction when he developed the notion of *vocabularies of motive*.[19] Mills argued that individual motives ought to be considered as more than inherent psychological states. Instead, motives are constituted in the vocabularies of social explanations and justifications that individuals know they can offer to explain their actions. Mills wrote: "A motive tends to be one which is to the actor and to the other members of a situation an unquestioned answer to questions concerning social and lingual conduct. . . . Motives are accepted justifications for present, future, and past programs or acts."[20] The need for motives arises when someone interrupts a line of conduct with a stated or implied question. Behind the question lies someone's view that what is taking place is "questionable"—that is, unexpected, unclear, and perhaps undesired or untoward. Questions about motives challenge identity and the relationship between the conduct and culture. Motives must address actions to make them seem less problematic, to repair the person's identity in his or her own eyes or the eyes of others, and to find cultural support or justification for the conduct in question.

Building on Mills, Scott and Lyman developed the concept of accounts. They define an *account* as "a linguistic device employed whenever an action is subjected to valuative inquiry."[21] Accounts include excuses and justifications that reconcile untoward actions and social expectations. Each manifests a particular attitude toward the questioned act and the person's responsibility for it. Excuses acknowledge that a particular act is undesirable or wrong but deny that the individual was responsible for his or her conduct. Excuses are an important social lubricant. People who use excuses acknowledge committing a negatively viewed act but they disclaim personal responsibility for their actions. Everyday examples of excuses include: "It was an accident" or "I did it, but I was drunk." People who use justifications acknowledge committing a discreditable act but claim that extenuating circumstances legitimate that behavior. Everyday examples of justifications include: "I was following orders" or "Those people had it coming to them."

Within symbolic interaction research, much empirical scholarship on accounts focuses on highly stigmatized groups, such as male hustlers, juvenile delinquents, disgraced professionals and convicted criminal offenders, such as white-collar criminals and rapists.[22] Another strand of this literature examines how people use "accounts" in the narratives that they tell in association with various life events, such as marriage and stressful situations.[23] Implicit in any use of accounts are the following questions: How do people know what to say about why they did what they did or are doing? From what sources do people acquire a set of reasons for their acts—reasons that they can cite on appropriate occasions and that others will accept as answers to their questions? What makes the difference between an acceptable and an unacceptable motive? What determines whether others will accept or reject an avowed vocabulary of motive?

People learn that in given situations their choices of conduct and motives are limited by what others will treat as legitimate. Particular sets of motives hold more or less sway and are treated as more or less legitimate (whatever the specific situation) by various social groups and categories. The existence of vocabularies of motive that are specific to situations or categories of situations helps explain how people are able to compartmentalize their lives by separating motives important in one sphere from those important in another. In an example from popular culture, consider the images of Mafiosi (or, for that matter, corporate executives engaged in criminal behaviors) who seem to lead double lives. They act with ruthless self-interest in their occupational worlds but with great tenderness and selflessness toward their families. They separate these worlds into distinct sets of objects, and acts, and vocabulary of motives.

A group's capacity to attract and keep members is determined partly by its vocabulary of motives. The more a group provides and supports motives that accord with a person's established or desired lines of conduct and self-conceptions, the more the group can bind that person. Families, organizations, social movements, workplaces, and other social groups provide contexts in which people talk about their reasons for conduct and have their reasons confirmed by others. Thus, a group of alcoholics (such as an Alcoholics Anonymous group) are bound together by similar experiences and because they share a common way of talking about themselves and their activities. They share a vocabulary of motives that focuses on accepting personal responsibility and maintaining complete abstinence. Motive talk is a common feature of everyday life and arises whenever people are uncertain about the meaning of others' acts or of how others will interpret their own acts. Other forms of aligning actions—such as disclaimers, accounts, and apologies—also arise in response to problematic conduct.

Disclaimers

A disclaimer[24] is a verbal device people employ when they want to ward off the negative implications of an impending act—something they are about to do or say that they know or fear will result in a hostile response. Typical disclaimers include "I'm not prejudiced, because some of my best friends are Black, but . . ." "Maybe some people on welfare want to work, but . . . ," or "I'm no expert on psychology, but . . ." A disclaimer prefaces an act or statement that ends up contradicting the disclaimer. People claim not to be prejudiced and then make racist statements. Self-proclaimed nonpsychologists offer diagnoses that someone else is acting mentally ill that only a licensed psychologist should be trusted to make.

Actions either do or do not fit with particular situations. Acts also have positive or negative implications for people's identities. A racist remark could fit with the theme of the conversation, be in proper sequence with the statement of a previous speaker, and express a commonly held sentiment. At the same time, people that hear a racist remark are likely to interpret that remark as defining the speaker's identity. People know that their acts can typify them in other people's eyes, so they are often careful to disclaim the implications of acts that could get them typified in terms that they do not like.

Therefore, disclaimers constitute efforts to carry out an intended act—in this case a racist remark—without damaging your identity in the process. By acknowledging that he or she knows that an impending remark could be construed as racist, the disclaiming person hopes to avoid being considered one. The person uses the disclaimer to kill two birds with one stone—get away with a racist remark without taking a hit for the remark. If the audience accepts the disclaimer, conduct can proceed unimpeded and situated identities remain unchallenged. Disclaimers also align conduct with culture, since they establish that those present are not acting out of prejudice, at least in their own eyes. The disclaimer can exculpate both parties.

Disclaimers are prospective aligning actions. People employ them when, through role taking, the individual anticipates how others will respond to a contemplated act. In effect, then, a disclaimer attempts to control a definition of a situation and the identities of those present in advance. In contrast, another type of aligning action, accounts, is retrospective, and focuses on actions that have already taken place.

Accounts

What happens when an untoward act occurs without an anticipatory disclaimer? Marvin Scott and Stanford Lyman argued that when the course of social interaction is disturbed by rule violations, unexpected or inconvenient activities, inconsiderate or rude behavior, and other problematic acts, a process of demanding and giving accounts occurs.[25] In this process, someone who commits an untoward act is asked to account for it—that is, to explain the act satisfactorily to others. Although we may demand accounts explicitly, we also sometimes request them indirectly or by implication. People also may volunteer them when individuals think that they will be asked to account for their acts or words.

By enabling troublesome situations to be passed over, put aside, and treated as unfortunate past history, accounts can prevent each and every untoward act from becoming a major issue. Since much does go wrong in everyday life, excuses make it possible for many definitions of situations and identities to be maintained, and for people to see themselves and to be seen by others in positive ways. At the same time, excuses help preserve the rules, standards, and expectations by means of which people ordinarily judge one another's acts. Excuses lay the blame for untoward conduct on someone or something other than the individual held to account, but they unmistakably preserve the definition of the conduct as undesirable. Saying something offensive is still offensive, even if the particular person is not blamed for this bad act because he or she is drunk or mentally ill.

Accounts lubricate social interaction and reflect attempts to protect identity. Although social norms and laws forbid certain activities, either categorically or under certain circumstances, the status of any particular act as proscribed is never a matter of absolute certainty. As addressed in Chapter 6, untoward conduct is not automatically alleged to be a rule violation or representative of deviance. Rather, there is flexibility, both in everyday life and in the formal procedures of the law, to determine whether a particular act is or is not a violation. The existence of a vocabulary of justifications is one basis for this flexibility. Justifications provide a means through which people can decide whether particular acts constitute infractions. Equally important, the outcome of a particular effort at building a justification for an act—whether it is successful or not—bears on the kind of identity that a person can claim. If an act is justified, then the person's identity is not transformed; if not successfully justified, then a new identity, perhaps as a deviant or troublemaker, may be in store.

All account giving reflects attempts to negotiate the level of punishment that is attached to an individual's action. At their core, accounts often represent an individual's attempts to assign responsibility for their discrediting actions to other actors or social forces, such as alcohol, scapegoats, or a superior's orders. That being stated, it is also important to point out that both individuals and social groups, professionals and organizations, use accounts.

How are accounts different when organizations, groups, or collectivities put them forth? Little research exists on how an organizational or group context for account-giving differs from private individual contexts, such as accounting for deviant acts in one's personal life. Lawrence Nichols identifies failing to consider the collective or group use of accounts as an "elementary omission" in scholarship on accounts.[26] Potential differences exist between how groups construct and honor accounts according to their aims, power, and stakeholders. A sharper analytic focus is needed to discern the distinctive qualities of offering accounts within a professional context. Further, many groups have much more power to put behind the credibility of their accounts than individuals do.

We also need to consider who offers accounts and the different contexts in which people offer accounts. For example, how does a professional affiliation also impact a person's ability to give a successful account? A key theoretical attribute of accounts is their cumulative power. This cumulative power refers to the capacity that a particular account has to legitimate or excuse repeatedly engaging in a kind of controversial or contested behavior. For example, if someone knows that saying "boys will be boys" will always justify male aggression, that particular account can come to assume a cumulative power. Citing this account may allow males to act more aggressively because the account sustains those actions.

Cumulativeness is important because knowing that an account is cumulatively honored means that a power exists to exonerate repeated incidents of potentially discreditable behavior. The potential cumulative power of accounts is highly relevant to occupations, because professionals involved in adversarial work have to engage in potentially discreditable behaviors consistently for their livelihood. Accounts function to excuse and justify behaviors as social facts; they do more than rehabilitate individual reputations. A "cumulative" account preserves the capacity to engage in discrediting behaviors by successfully mitigating norms against engaging in those behaviors.

Other Aligning Actions

Motive talk, accounts, and disclaimers are just some of the aligning actions people employ in everyday life. Another common form is the apology, in which the person who commits a contested act admits the untoward nature of the act, accepts responsibility, and expresses remorse: "I'm sorry I lost my temper—it was wrong of me to act that way and I sincerely regret it; please forgive me." This kind of apology honors cultural values and attempts to maintain social interaction by assuaging the anger or irritation of offended parties. Apologies also attempt to restore the offender's good identity by reminding the audience of his or her knowledge of the untoward nature of the act. Implicit in any apology is the claim that one who readily acknowledges an offense, sincerely expresses regret, and begs forgiveness should not be treated the same way—that is, retypified and given an undesirable identity— as someone who neither recognizes the nature of the offense nor tries to make amends.

Consider, for example, drivers that acknowledge making an error when driving their car with an apologetic wave of their hand to another driver. We are quicker to forgive that person's offense than we are when a driver who cuts us off or almost backs into our car will not acknowledge the misdeed. The act can be the same but a hand wave apology or lack of one can make all the difference to the aggrieved driver. As Nicholas Tavuchis pointed out, an apology places the offender's fate and his or her identity in the hands of the person to whom the apology is offered. At that abstract level, the offended person can bestow forgiveness and thus restore the offender's identity and his or her place in the social world.[27]

In his classification of aligning actions, Christopher Hunter pointed out that aligning actions can focus on unexpected desirable acts as well as on undesirable acts.[28] Human beings may sometimes fall short of what is expected of them, but occasionally they do much better. They perform heroically, do good deeds and special favors, and in other ways do more than one would expect of them in their assigned roles. Actions that go "beyond the call of duty" also lead to aligning actions. That is, they have unanticipated consequences that have to be assimilated to the situation and its definition; they alter established situated identities; and they stand in contrast to cultural objects by demonstrating more than is ordinarily expected.

Take, for example, someone who goes out of his or her way to help a colleague at work, perhaps by pitching in at a time when the workload is especially heavy. That person has created a situation in which alignment processes may now have to occur. The helper may, for example, want to have the act defined by others as central to his or her identity as "someone who can be counted on when the going gets tough" or "someone who has the interests of others constantly in mind." If so, the helper may use what Barry Schlenker called an entitling acclaimer, which is an effort to emphasize his or her contribution. The helper may now say, "Remember, I was there for you when no one else cared!" The helper may also use an enhancing acclaimer, which is an effort to stress the importance of the contribution: "You'd have been in real trouble without my help!"[29] As with other kinds of aligning actions, these acclaimers represent efforts to maintain the flow of interaction, to sustain or enhance identities, and to link conduct to important cultural objects.

Moreover, acclaimers illustrate another important property of aligning actions—namely, negotiating meaning in the situation. Those who use acclaimers typically want to put the best face on their conduct, as do those who use accounts and disclaimers. But the audience for these aligning actions may resist efforts to define the nature of the questioned conduct or the perpetrator's identity. A professor, for example, may refuse to accept the excuse of a student who is repeatedly late to class because of problems with transportation, arguing that the excuse is used too frequently and is therefore worn out. The professor may fear that accepting the excuse too readily deprives him or her of any leverage over the student's future conduct. If there is no penalty for coming late—not even an altered identity—then the conduct is likely to recur. Likewise, the recipient of extraordinary help may want to minimize the importance of that help or to downplay the key role of the helper. To accept the latter's claims about the crucial character of his or her help could incur a debt that might have to be repaid.

Emotions and Social Interaction

While the cognitive aspects of social interaction are crucial, we must also examine the importance of emotion and affect in social interaction. People try (consistent with impression management and dramaturgy) to display emotions that are consistent with expectations for a particular situated identity and definition of the situation. Definitions of situations specify what emotional tone people should express and register. From the symbolic interactionist perspective, feelings of emotion should align with views of self, context-dependent identities, and social interactions.[30] When other people's responses verify an identity, a person is more likely to experience positive emotions. When other people's responses do not verify the projected identity; a person is likely to experience negative emotions. Roles also have an affective component. As an example, emotional typifications carry into the occupational sphere. We expect counseling therapists to be "caring," football coaches to offer angry displays at poor officiating, and police officers to be emotionally neutral and project authority.

Departures from emotional expectations will precipitate aligning actions. People must explain why they are sad when others expect them to be happy or to apologize for losing their tempers. As an example, when a person demonstrates much more anger than seems appropriate in a particular situation, and he or she does not offer an account, people will often say that he or she needs to take an anger management class. Shulman once watched a training DVD on the psychological treatment of patients with anger management issues. The first patient wrote a four-page, single-spaced letter of complaint about a deli worker who didn't put enough mayonnaise on her sandwich and about how much this poor customer service had impacted her at a personal level. To her, the lack of mayonnaise was a purposeful and intentionally injurious act, but for most people, the situation would be no big deal. Stories about "overreacting" or "hardly registering an emotion" speak to when people's emotional displays are out of synch with a situation. We are wary of people who don't seem to feel the right way about things (or at least the right way in terms of what we expect). Think of a time when you encountered people that "just didn't feel right" because they displayed emotions that were out of place. As you do so, you can appreciate how our emotional "reads" of social environments are crucial in shaping our interpretations of others and for decision-making. Just as we rely on inferential heuristics, we can also consider how informal "emotional" heuristics exist that also help us make social inferences.

Sociologists studying the role of emotions in everyday life owe a debt to Arlie Hochschild, who developed this field of inquiry in sociology. In a landmark paper, she coined the concept of *feeling rules* to describe the types of feelings that people expect in particular situations.[31] People's private feelings may also contradict or be consonant with the feelings people are supposed to display in public. *Surface acting* refers to feelings that someone learns and performs for public display. In high school, for example, students may display "disgust" when they encounter an unpopular teen. When flirting, people may put on a smile and fake laughing at a lame joke told by someone they like. Hochschild also described another aspect of experiencing emotion, which she referred to as *deep acting*. Deep acting occurs when an individual expresses a feeling that is intended as authentic rather than just put on for a performance. With deep acting, people remember stimuli that trigger genuine, deep-seated emotion that allow them to truly feel in public what they are stating that they feel, as opposed to just acting on the surface how they are supposed to feel. For example, people might not feel very angry about how someone treated them, until a third party mentions, "If I were you, I'd be totally pissed." In response, people may remember similar situations where they thought they were egregiously mistreated, and start transforming their internal emotional states into anger or rage. They then work themselves up into an angry frenzy. The difference between deep and surface acting is that deep acting is not an act just to suit the third party, as surface acting would be. Instead deep acting reflects true feelings. Hochschild thus distinguishes two ways that people manage and express emotion.

Many social interactions demand surface acting. They involve public displays of emotion, feeling rules and even work displaying particular emotions as part of the job. Having to manage emotions is a task confronting people in their occupations just as emotions form part of their associations with friends or family members. In some occupations, as Hochschild demonstrated in her study of flight attendants, a considerable amount of emotional labor is required in day-to-day work. Airlines expect flight attendants to be cheerful and attentive to passengers, for example, and to remain calm when facing possible crises. They must maintain their emotional composure and work hard to avoid producing the "wrong emotions"—even when passengers are unpleasant or demanding. Like waiters and waitresses, sales personnel, and others who are in regular contact with the public, they must learn to put on a face that often betrays their true underlying feelings. Their capacity to do so is a part of their personal labor that they sell to their employers.[32]

When you hear someone described as good with people or having great "people skills," someone's emotion management skills are recognized as a commodity in the labor market. From this perspective, when an employer hires someone, they also hire a "working personality" that accompanies the job. For example, bodyguards are supposed to deter strangers or crowds through emanating an aura of intimidation. When people act in an emotionally inconsistent way at their jobs, other people may accuse them of acting "unprofessionally," such as if a doctor or nurse makes fun of a patient's weight. When people work in sales, the success of the commercial enterprise may depend on how deferential or attentive a service worker is. In some jobs, such as river rafting or being a tour guide, a worker's emotional performance is a key aspect of the product that a client buys, with the worker being someone who has to help produce "fun." When you think back to a job that you had or have, think of whether a particular display of emotion is supposed to be a part of performing your work successfully.

When workers display emotions that are inconsistent with what they really feel, they may over time develop a sense of self-estrangement or distress that Hochschild called *emotive dissonance*. Emotive dissonance threatens self and identity and can lead to a feeling of alienation. Having to consistently feel things that people do not feel can be debilitating and draining. People writing within the symbolic interactionist tradition have expanded on studying emotional labor on the job.[33] Robin Leidner examined what she called "the routinization of emotional labor" in service work. She observed workers at McDonalds and at an insurance company and examined how the routine scripts on those jobs demanded consistent emotional labor by workers. Ceaselessly following routine and scripted behaviors, where the customer is always right and procedures are unchanging, requires people to summon up emotional performances of deference that they will resent, an experience that could be as stultifying as completing endless routine mechanical and physical actions at a factory job.

Emotional demands can be alienating, such as in the fast food context, or someone can have more privileges in terms of emotional labor on the job. Orzechowicz has described "privileged emotion managers" who have more emotional autonomy on the job, as opposed to those that are the "emotional proletariat." One interesting avenue for further research is to consider how one privilege of occupational hierarchy is the range of emotionality that a worker is allowed to have on the job. Gendered, ethnic, and racial stereotypes also impact what emotions people can expect in social situations.

Whatever the specific situation or social context, the experiencing, display, and regulation of emotions are a key aspect of social life. People's actions are guided not only by cognitions that focus on definitions of situations and on role making and role taking; they are also strongly influenced by their affective responses to situations, others, and themselves. Seen from a symbolic interactionist perspective, affect impacts social behavior in powerful and unanticipated ways. Jack Katz offers an illustration in his analysis of how emotions motivate people to commit crimes.[34]

When people invoke explanations for criminal behavior, they often casually cite causal factors like education, poor role models in the family, media or peer influences, or poverty and social class. People discuss these factors as if they operate simply and their influences are crystal clear. Most researchers also examine crimes either in terms of identifying "big" causes of deviance (e.g., family, tainted souls, and economic inequality) or in studying societal reactions to deviance, which address how people should control deviance (as illustrated by studies of policing or psychopharmacology or penology).

Katz offers a different approach, asking, what are the sensual rewards of deviance? What about "crimes of passion?" In his view, we must examine the experiential and emotional qualities that are associated with committing crimes. For example, someone may experience committing a crime primarily as a set of emotionally driven responses to perceived offenses by others. One may experience deviance as a conscious effort to maintain appearances. For example, people may appear as being "up to no good" or act to embody a trait, such as expressing threats to appear menacing before fights. One might experience deviance as addictive and intoxicating, thinking of shoplifting, for example, as an emotionally driven fun "sneaky thrill." One also may experience deviance as a means of mastering the world, in terms of exerting an ability to control others and the situation. How and who is likely to feel these emotions can differ by race, class, education, and other factors. However, at the heart of Katz's efforts is the point that any adequate analysis of crime must take into account the experiential qualities of committing crime in order to provide good motivational explanations for crimes.

Katz thus offers distinct guiding questions for understanding the sensual dynamics or "seductions of crime." How does the person empower the world to seduce him to criminality? How is responsibility, within the very act itself, shifted to encourage the criminal act or to stem it? What are people trying to "accomplish" when they commit crimes? What are the dynamics, the rewards that people create, as being a sensual seduction into committing deviant acts? A common theme of these questions is the impact that emotion has on behavior.

We will consider Katz's answers to these questions for two examples: murder and shoplifting. Katz offers a three-part theory to describe some murders as "righteous slaughter." For the most part, these murders involve individuals who know one another. The stages are that: (1) a murderer sees himself or herself as defending some "good" or "value" that is being grievously offended by the future victim, (2) the murderer then undergoes an emotional process from being humiliated by the offense against good (and him or her) into a righteous rage, and (3) a final act of "righteous" slaughter occurs in which the murderer acts against the offense and offender. Here, Katz describes a serious of escalating patterns within this form of deviance. For example, murderers often experience a "crisis" event preceding the actual murder, in which pent-up history explodes into a rage so sudden that a murderous act occurs, an event powerful enough to blind the perpetrator to the consequences of murder. Some forms of rage come in defense of either female or male identity. For example, an enraged man might kill his wife after she insults him for "not being a man." A significant aspect of this theory is its connection to particular physical evidence that helps criminal profilers solve murders. For example, a murder that involves much more damage to the human body than is needed to commit the crime, as coined in the word "overkill," points to particular suspects. Crime procedural dramas, such as *CSI,* illustrate this approach in popular culture.

In analyzing shoplifting, Katz discusses a three-stage model of (1) being seduced into the crime, (2) a necessity to maintain normal appearances during the crime, and (3) a euphoric thrill felt after accomplishing the crime. In identifying these stages, Katz offers many examples of "a magical object" that calls out to be taken; a thrill in challenging observers and getting away with something while not appearing to do so; and accounts of intense "sneaky thrills" from carrying out the act. Katz discusses different symbolic abstractions associated with the experience: A sense of boundary between self and others; a metaphor of being involved in a game; thrill from "defiling" another world or property, as occurs in cases of vandalism accompanying theft; a sexual rush from the thrill of stealing; a sense of gaining charisma through being a center of attention and being fully self-conscious. Katz associates these experiences as having a particular affinity with emergence from adolescence. The importance of managing a normal appearance or playing a deviant identity to the hilt reflects impression management and surface acting. Clearly, Katz argues that there are deep connections between emotionally based motivations and crime.

The emotion of grief offers another illustration of a symbolic interactionist analysis of emotions.[35] Death is the loss of a member of society but for those who have been close to the deceased, the death is much more meaningful. A spouse's death means the loss of a companion, lover, and friend and also the loss of a part of the self. When people that are close to us die, we lose the supports for our own self-conceptions that those people provided. We lose part of our identity; part of what had buttressed our self-esteem.[36] Lyn Lofland suggested that "threads of connectedness" that attach people to one another determine the impact that a death has. We are linked to others by the roles we play, by the help we receive, by the wider network of others made available to us, by the selves others create and sustain, by the comforting myths they allow us, by the reality they validate for us, and by the futures they make possible.[37] When these linkages are spread widely among a large number of people, the loss of any single other may have little impact on the individual's membership in the group or on everyday activities. But, where a few others command the greatest share of our attention, providing role partners, definitions of reality, and validation of ourselves, each other person is likely to be of very great significance and thus losing that other will occasion more intense grief.

As Lofland points out, the extent to which people feel a sense of loss depends on their typical definitions of the situation of death. In the past, death rates were higher in general, and first encounters with death occurred early in life. Under such conditions, death itself was more routine, and so the sense of loss attendant on any individual's death was lessened. In the contemporary world, where many people experience their first significant death when their grandparents die, death is a more shaking event simply because it is so unfamiliar. With a greater emphasis on the individual in modern life and increased opportunity for solitude and privacy, which encourages the elaboration of grief and restricts the opportunities for its expression, the emotional impact of death and the sense of loss that attends it may be greater now than in the past. Metaphorically, death tears a hole in the selves of those left behind. This is where the linkage between social experience and physical sensations occurs. The loss of a significant other, by disorganizing our social worlds and conceptions of self, creates many obstacles to ordinary, routine conduct. At every turn, people face habitual actions that cannot be completed as before because a significant other is not there. The sensations associated with grief—depression, frustration, anger, and so forth—are normal and spontaneous responses to the fact that the loss blocks our everyday actions.

Although cultures differ in their definitions of which individuals fall into the category of important, close relationships, the death of someone in such a category will provoke feelings of sadness and depression. Yet all cultures do not label the resulting feelings in the same way. One may treat the feelings in terms of a concept of grief, while another downplays the sense of personal loss and treats those feelings as illness. The existence of cultural vocabularies of emotion is a clue that people have expectations about who will have what emotional experiences under what circumstances. In U.S. society, for example, a woman whose husband dies is supposed to grieve. Not only is there a term to cover her experiences (a *widow*), but also her friends and family act toward her on the basis of the status of being a widow. They indicate their expectations about how she should behave and feel. They treat her as someone who is expected to grieve, and their actions are oriented toward helping this grief find appropriate expression and providing social supports.

Many social situations are arranged as regulators of emotion. In weddings and funerals, for example, the spontaneous and genuine emotions of some are managed and kept within bounds as they interact with others. At the same time, those who bring to such occasions only the appearance of proper emotional involvement may find it necessary to "act" so as to create the appropriate actual emotions. In both cases, emotions are integral parts of social life. Like all other forms of behavior, they are not matters of unconscious responses to stimuli, but of socially constructed meanings.

Constraint and Social Interaction

Symbolic interactionists are accused of painting too fluid a picture of the social world, of overemphasizing the freedom of individual actors or groups of actors to resist or overcome the influence of society and culture. By stressing the processes of role making and role taking, and the need to define situations, critics argue that symbolic interactionists overlook the many ways that conduct is constrained. Symbolic interactionists do acknowledge that there is both freedom and constraint in social life. Human beings are not merely social and cultural automatons, but thinking, acting creatures that use the social acumen they have as members of society to address the problems that confront them. Nonetheless, they must recognize that there are limits to what humans can do to act in ways of their own choosing.

Constraint is everywhere in social life. People must form definitions of situations and interpret others' conduct in order to construct their acts, but they are usually limited in what definitions they can consider and in the interpretations that they can make. They are constrained by limits to their knowledge of others and their purposes, by the power that others hold over them, by obligations to roles or to individuals who are not a part of the present situation, and by others' responses to their acts. The capacity to define a situation as one sees fit and to make a role as one chooses is highly limited. Individuals continually bump into others, their definitions, and their purposes. In the remainder of this chapter, we will consider several important constraints on our actions.

Altercasting

The aligning actions that we considered earlier in this chapter focused our attention on what Erving Goffman called the presentation of self—that is, on the things that people do in order to enhance or protect their conceptions of themselves and their status in other's eyes. Thus, we might describe a disclaimer as an individual's effort to avoid negative typifications for a particular act. The focus is on how the disclaiming person attempts to maintain a desirable self when he or she seeks to pursue a discrediting line of conduct.

Self-presentation is just one aspect of role taking and role making. Roles are reciprocal. One person's role has to "fit" another person's role. For example, in interactions between patients and physicians in the examining room, the two attempt to fit their respective lines of conduct to one another. They imaginatively take one another's roles and make their own roles accordingly. In studying the presentation of self, we focused on one side of this interchange—namely, the efforts a particular individual makes to perform a role and at the same time to put forth a self that the others present will regard favorably. Now we turn to examining the effects that one individual has on the other's capacity to make a role and preserve a valued conception of self. This process, whereby one person's acts constrain and limit what the other can do, is termed *altercasting*. Altercasting refers to "casting" the other person into a particular role that the altercaster prefers.[38]

A familiar example of altercasting is being (or putting someone) "on the defensive." In a formal debate, for example, or in political campaigning, an effective strategy to control the definition of the situation is to force others to defend positions they do not want to defend or to force them into a position of having to answer charges. A candidate for president may complain vigorously about an opponent's "tax and spend mentality" or call his or her character into question. Doing so forces the other candidate into a defensive position, and thus indirectly confirms that the charge is worth discussing. By creating an issue, a politician forces an opponent to respond and thus implicitly to be associated with alleged negative characteristics.[39]

Altercasting constrains people to act in certain ways. They are forced into roles of a particular kind because other people treat them as if they did occupy that role. A politician treats an opponent as someone who does "tax and spend" or who is of dubious character and by this treatment the other is forced to deny the charge and defend or explain his or her conduct as if he or she had actually engaged in that role. The moment the other candidate defends or explains his or her conduct, he or she can seem to accept the issue—to agree implicitly that what is charged is worth talking about and might actually be true.

Altercasting relies on a key feature of all social interaction: The imputation of roles to individuals. The "casting" in the term refers essentially to typecasting the other, thus constraining their potential to act to free themselves of the role expectations associated with the typecast role. A common form of altercasting in everyday life happens when one individual treats another as a more intimate friend or ally than either is accustomed to thinking of the other. Treating someone as a special friend, confidant, or intimate is a common form of interpersonal Machiavellianism. Although sometimes the intended victim of this altercasting recognizes its insincerity and knows, for example, that an employer is bestowing special favors and treatment only in an effort to cultivate a spy and thus find out what the employees are thinking, the victim also may be completely unaware of what is happening.

Why does altercasting work? For example, why should an employee be more inclined to squeal on coworkers if the boss begins to act in a friendly way? One simple explanation of the employer/employee example is that the subordinate perceives an advantage in responding reciprocally to the boss's overtures—perhaps anticipating a raise or promotion as a possible reward and thus acting without thought to the interests of fellow workers. Another explanation is that the employee is responding to a general norm of reciprocity. Alvin

Gouldner defined such a norm as the belief that one ought to help those who have been helpful, or at least avoid doing them harm.[40] By reducing interpersonal distance, the employer confers something of value on the employee and the latter feels obligated to reciprocate.

A more fundamental explanation of altercasting occurs at a cognitive level. The employer who acts in an intimate, friendly fashion toward a subordinate is defining a situation in a particular way, as an occasion in which formalities can be put aside and people can treat one another as equals, not as superior and subordinate. In so defining the situation, the employer influences the objects that are present and toward which conduct will take place. In particular, the boss indicates "friendly social intercourse" and "friendship" as main social objects of the occasion. Once the situation has been so defined, the subordinate would have to work very hard to define the situation differently. One typical altercasting is to use first names. One might refuse to address a superior by a first name, which calls attention to the formal relationship between the two. That act carries risks. To change the encounter's object from "friendly social intercourse" to "boss talks to wary employee" requires a self-conscious effort. The employee actively resists the boss's preferred definition, acting in the role of wary employee rather than in the role of friend. That relationship is accurate in a workplace hierarchy but to pretend that there is a friendship, benefits the boss more than the employee. The employee is not only induced to act in the role of friend by the very considerable press of implication in the situation. The employee knows that the boss has control and can reward or punish the worker's role performances.

Just as repeated self-presentations shape the character of self-concept, so, too, the repeated altercasting of one person by others affects self-concept. In many families, for instance, one individual—often, though not always, a child—is repeatedly treated as the scapegoat for everything that goes wrong. When someone is systematically blamed and regarded as responsible for undesirable events and calamitous circumstances, he or she is likely to develop a self-concept and a social identity that reflects that treatment.

Altercasting and the presentation of self are two sides of the same coin. Both involve efforts to define situations by establishing identities and roles. The concept of presentation of self centers on people's attempts to define situations in ways they think desirable by showing themselves in a favorable light to others. The concept of altercasting reminds us that what one individual does in a situation places limits on the roles and self-presentations of others. Impression management does not occur in a vacuum. Just as people attempt to present their own desirable image, they must counter the efforts other people make to paint them into a corner. The effects of altercasting and the presentation of self are not limited to manipulation, Machiavellian schemes, or negative consequences for self-concepts. People can also use them for benevolent purposes. Thus, the teacher who believes that a child's performance will be improved by positive rewards and encouragement is altercasting every bit as much as the employer who seeks an employee's confidence.

Power

Sociologists generally define power as the capacity of one person to achieve purposes without other people's consent and despite opposition.[41] Successful altercasting is an exercise of power. A successful altercaster can induce others to make a particular role without their realizing it or being able to resist doing so. Like all forms of power, altercasting involves controlling resources; in this case, control over the role of the other. The exercise of power depends, in part, on one party's control of resources in social interaction. What goods, tools, knowledge, and money do they have that others value and desire? When people interact, they pursue individual and collective ends and they cooperate to pursue common goals. However, they also compete for scarce resources or engage in conflicts over decisions and actions. For example, businesspeople might cooperate with one another to further organizational goals, but they will also compete to advance within the company. Sometimes they fight over issues such as whether to produce a new product or enter a new market.

In such contexts, managers, vice presidents, and department heads have more power than those whom they employ. That is, they have the power to hire or fire, make unilateral decisions, withhold information from some and share it with others, and increase the budgets for some projects and cut them for others. Superordinates also possess authority—that is, they claim the right to exercise control over the actions of others, who concede that they have this right.[42] Other inequalities of power exist in addition to different levels of authority. Some employees have been around longer than others and know more about how the organization works; others have close relationships with their superiors and can get them to hear their proposals; some work in key departments, such as research or marketing, and can make their influence strongly felt.

Exercising power involves the same processes of defining the situation, role making, and role taking as more cooperative forms of social interaction. For example, the more powerful person must role make—craft a performance that will convince others that here is someone to be reckoned with, someone who will not hesitate to use power ruthlessly if necessary. Likewise, the weaker individual also must role take and role make, discerning whether the other's power is real or a bluff.

When you can accurately gauge how another person will react to a contemplated act, you can assess how to secure the best advantage for yourself with the contemplated act. If I know that an associate will abandon a plan at the slightest hint of resistance, I can influence his or her conduct with a minimum use of my own power. If I can accurately anticipate spirited resistance, I can deploy my own resources to greatest advantage to counter that resistance. The more accurately I can role take—imputing intentions and the definition of the situation to the other—the more leverage I have over that person in our interactions.

Although role-taking ability enhances power, having power and authority to some extent lessens the need to role take accurately. The person who exercises authority can generally get away with less accurate role taking than the person over whom it is exercised. Parents, for example, are in a position to command their children's compliance, at least within certain limits. They can afford to be less sensitive to their children's evaluations of them or even to their children's definitions of various situations. The parent does not have to be too concerned with how the child will respond. The child, in contrast, has to learn accurate role-taking skills in order to predict how powerful parents may act toward him or her.

This link between role taking and authority should not obscure the basic fact, however, that social interaction always involves some degree of role taking. When a parent punishes a child for a forbidden act, and forbids the child from doing it again, role taking occurs. The parent's interpretation of the child's act is more powerful than the child's. Thus, the situation is viewed from the parent's perspective. Has a child deliberately broken a rule, or did the forbidden conduct occur by accident? The answer to this question—even the act of raising it—rests on parental role taking and on how the parent imputes motives to the child.

A less obvious way that people exercise power in everyday life is through controlling the physical setting where interaction occurs. Role making and role taking do not occur in a vacuum, but amongst props, physical objects, machines, locations, buildings, and habitats that have human meaning and are usually human creations. People interact in the social spaces provided by roles, such as in banks, stores, homes, physicians' offices, schools, parks, automobiles, beaches, factories, halls, and a myriad of other places, each with its own objects, colors, sounds, and other physical attributes. People act in and toward such physical settings on the basis of habit. Some people are put at ease by soothing colors and canned music in a dentist's office, made to feel a sense of awe as they sit amidst the grandeur and ritual of a large cathedral, or impelled to feel somber by furnishings, casket, dress, and the serious demeanor of attendants at a funeral home. Even the route by which a person customarily drives to and from work generally is a setting in which many habitual responses occur—stopping at a particular traffic light, for example, or being especially alert at a dangerous intersection.

To the extent that people do respond habitually to certain settings and physical conditions, whoever controls the physical elements of situations has considerable power to control how people in that situation will respond. Indeed, this is the rationale that underlies the widespread use of canned music, controlled lighting in factories and offices, and similar practices. In this view, to influence conduct, one must control the stimuli to which people habitually respond. We will take up this issue later in this book as we explore the relationship between themed environments and consumer behavior.

Although habitual responses doubtless figure to some extent in shaping people's definitions of situations, interpretations are more important. The dental patient knows that he or she will soon face discomfort in the dentist's chair, and that no matter how soothing, music is no substitute for anesthetic. The congregant participating in a Mass at the Notre Dame Cathedral in Paris sees the same architectural grandeur as the casual tourist, but the former is apt to feel a sense of mystical connection with the deity, while the latter keeps quiet out of respect rather than religious devotion. Indeed, social settings of a variety of kinds—medical offices, churches, funeral homes, banks, executive offices are designed to foster interpretations, not merely unthinking responses, by those who enter them. The rituals of donning rubber gloves and masks or breaking open packages of sterile instruments in a medical setting have an obvious practical justification—protection of the patient and physician from the transmission of disease. But they also have symbolic import, as means of conveying to patients the impression that everything possible is being done to safeguard the patient's health.

Awareness Contexts

Many people assume that we present ourselves genuinely and role take with reasonable accuracy. For example, parents and children, doctors and patients, teachers and students—most of these people, most of the time, interact in a context where roles are mutually and accurately understood and taken for granted. People trust others to be who they appear to be, and they act genuinely from the perspectives of their own roles. However, plenty of situations in everyday life involve ignorance, suspicion, and pretense. People deceive one another about their true intentions. Spouses are unfaithful. Seemingly dedicated government employees turn out to be spies. How does social interaction work under such conditions? Do the same fundamental processes of defining the situation, role taking, and role making operate in such contexts?

Barney Glaser and Anselm Strauss approached this topic through the concept of the awareness context, which they developed in a study of the interaction between dying patients and their families, physicians, and hospital staff. They defined an *awareness context* as "the total combination of what each interactant knows about the identity of the other and his own identity in the eyes of the other."[43] In an open awareness context, each participant knows the others' true identities—that is, the roles others intend to make in the situation—and his or her own identity in their eyes. In a closed awareness context, one interactant is ignorant of either the others' identities or his or her own situated social identity. In pretense contexts, interactants are aware of one another's identities but pretend not to be; in suspicion contexts, participants suspect that one another's identities are not what they appear to be.

There are numerous examples of awareness contexts in the real world. When friends suspect one another's loyalty, for example, they are in a suspicion awareness context. A married couple, each of whom is carrying on an affair and knows the other is also doing so, but who pretend that everything is normal, are sustaining a pretense awareness context. Descriptions and analyses of awareness contexts are essential to a full understanding of how people interact and of the outcomes of their interaction. The operations of a confidence scheme, for example, depend on a particular kind of awareness context. From the con artist's standpoint, the task is to keep the mark unaware of the ongoing deception while also ensuring that the mark is not really a disguised police officer. Awareness—knowing who knows what about whom—is an object of prime importance to the scheme's success, whether the scheme involves bilking an Internet surfer with a 419 scam or persuading a business executive to buy worthless or stolen securities.

In general, when awareness contexts are closed, considerable energies are devoted to opening them up or keeping them closed. Thus, in the hospital context that Glaser and Strauss describe, the staff put a considerable effort into engineering a closed context. Physicians and nurses talk to dying patients as if they were going to live; they control their outward manner in order to keep from giving away the show; and often they minimize their contacts with the patient so as to reduce the risks of discovery. Moreover, patients who suspect the worst about their true condition may become devoted to the task of discovering their actual prognosis.

Suspicion and pretense awareness contexts represent occasions in which a great deal of interaction is focused on the definition of the situation. Although such situations are marked by doubt or pretense as to whether others are actually who they seem to be, it is the definition of the situation itself that is at issue. If one's partner is a con artist and not a helpful new friend, then one is a victim of a con, not a beneficiary of friendship, and the situation is a con operation, not an exchange of benefits. If one is being conned, one acts toward the object of getting back one's money, or of going to the police while enduring the embarrassment of having been deceived. If a friend is helping you, the object is to think of a way to reciprocate. It is the situation, and objects and identities within it, which is being defined.

Awareness contexts constrain interaction. That is, what people know, do not know, suspect, or pretend with respect to one another constrains how they will interact. Wives who suspect their husbands of philandering will concentrate their efforts on discovery and proof. Nurses seeking to deceive a dying patient will guard every word lest they disclose information that would reveal the patient's true condition. Con artists who think the mark may be an undercover police officer are careful about what they promise. Ignorance, suspicion, and pretense shape definitions of situations and set the conditions within which role making and role taking occur.

Conventional and Interpersonal Roles

A final consideration in our analysis of constraint and social interaction requires a distinction between two fundamentally different kinds of roles. As Tamotsu Shibutani pointed out, people interact with one another in two capacities.[44] On the one hand, they interact on the basis of standardized, known, and labeled positions in various situations. People are mothers, physicians, store clerks, assembly line operators, police officers, men, women, and so on. In the myriad of situations in which people act, they have a grasp of the situations as wholes, and of the positions of various participants expressed in terms of such conventional roles. Much of our sense of the structure of routine situations in everyday life comes from our capacity to identify one another as acting from the standpoint of those roles.[45]

On the other hand, people do not interact with one another merely as makers of conventional roles, but also as unique human beings. A child does not relate merely to a "mother," but to "my mother"—a specific and in some ways unique human being with whom the child has had sustained contact. When people engage in repeated interactions with one another, networks of interpersonal relationships develop in which people have a sense of mutual position that reflects individual peculiarities and their history of contact with one another. That is, they come to define and make interpersonal roles. When two friends meet, each is responsive to a set of expectations, claims, and obligations with respect to the other. Each has a sense of position—and of the structure of the encounter as a whole—that is informed by the interpersonal role of friendship rather than by a particular conventional role.

In some situations, people simultaneously make conventional and interpersonal roles. Parents and children respond to one another on the basis of fairly standardized expectations of how parents and children typically behave. At the same time, children and parents make and take roles on the basis of a unique set of relationships that are built up over time and are a central part of their interaction. Similarly, coworkers in an office assume conventional roles assigned to them in the hierarchy of office life; at the same time, they are also friends, enemies, rivals, colleagues, lovers, shirkers, stooges, partners, and the like.

The overlay of conventional and interpersonal roles is responsible for much of the complexity of social life. People simultaneously typify one another's acts on the basis of the two sets of roles, and they must decide in any given situation, which is the controlling typification. Is my partner in interaction acting as my enemy? Is my partner in interaction acting as my subordinate? Such situations provide the basis for office intrigue, warring factions, academic politics, love triangles, and a great many other forms of interaction that, although often painful and embarrassing for people, also add spice to their lives.

Each type of role is constraining, but in a different way. Conventional roles constrain us not only because they pose a set of obligations that we must meet but also because they shape our view of social reality. They are the source of our most basic images of social structure and of our location within it. In some instances (e.g., gender roles) conventional roles generally seem to be natural and inevitable features of the social world. Moreover, they are also so deeply merged with the self that they seem to be the essence of the person.[46] Indeed, gender roles can be so constraining that they override other roles in a situation, as, for example, when a male cannot see past gender roles in order to interact appropriately with a female physician or manager.

Interpersonal roles also constrain. Like conventional roles, they present us with duties and obligations—but to individuals rather than to abstract conceptions of what we should or must do. They are likewise sources of our images of social structure. They point to our sense of structure as composed not just of the formally labeled roles of a group or society, but also of the unique way in which, over time, we come to see ourselves in relation to others within that structure.

Endnotes

1. The approach to the definition of the situation taken here is influenced by the work of Peter McHugh, *Defining the Situation* (Indianapolis, IN: Bobbs-Merrill, 1968), which in turn depends on George II. Mead, *The Philosophy of the Present* (Chicago: Open Court, 1932) for its emphasis on emergence and relativity.

2. Stefanie Cohen, "Fan-Tastic Gig: Sports Fan Paid to Fire Up Crowds." *New York Post,* March 1, 2009, p. 3.

3. G. H. Mead, *The Philosophy of the Act* (Chicago: University of Chicago Press, 1938), p. 6ff.

4. McHugh, *Defining the Situation* (Note 1).

5. See McHugh, *Defining the Situation* (Note 1); Harold Garfinkel, *Studies in Ethnomethodology* (Englewood Cliffs, NJ: Prentice-Hall, 1867); and Alfred Schutz, *On Phenomenology and Social Relations,* ed. Helmut Wagner (Chicago: University of Chicago Press, 1970).

6. Schutz, *On Phenomenology and Social Relations,* pp. 111–122 (Note 5).

7. Gregory P. Stone, "Appearance and the Self: A Slightly Revised Version," *in Social Psychology through Symbolic Interaction*, 2nd ed., ed. Gregory P. Stone and Harvey A. Farberman (New York: Wiley, 1981), pp. 187–202.

8. A. Tversky and D. Kahneman, "Judgment under Uncertainty: Heuristics and Biases." *Science* 185 (1974): 1124–1131.

9. See Tversky and Kahneman, "Judgment under Uncertainty," p. 1124 (Note 8).

10. For an excellent review of many ways that people attribute qualities based on perceptions of beauty, see Samantha Kwan and Mary Nell Trautner, "Beauty Work: Individual and Institutional Rewards, the Reproduction of Gender and the Question of Agency," *Sociology Compass* 2 (2008). www.blackwellcompass.com/subject/sociology/article_view?article_id=soco_articles_bpl179

11. See Peter Berger and Thomas Luckmann, *The Social Construction of Reality* (Garden City, NY: Doubleday Anchor, 1967), p. 42ff.

12. Randall Stokes and John P. Hewitt, "Aligning Actions," *American Sociological Review* 46 (October 1976): 838–849.

13. Stokes and Hewitt, "Aligning Actions" (Note 12).

14. See Erving Goffman, *The Presentation of Self in Everyday Life* (Garden City, New York: Doubleday Press, 1959); Goffman, *Stigma: Notes on the Management of Spoiled Identity* (Englewood Cliffs, NJ: Prentice Hall, 1963); Goffman, *Strategic Interaction* (Philadelphia: University of Pennsylvania Press, 1969); Goffman, *Frame Analysis: An Essay on the Organization of Experience* (Cambridge, MA: Harvard University Press, 1974).

15. Marvin B. Scott and Stanford M. Lyman, "Accounts," *American Sociological Review* 33 (1968): 46–62; Randall Stokes and John P. Hewitt, "Aligning Actions," *American Sociological Review* 46 (October 1976): 838–849; Hewitt and Stokes, "Disclaimers," *American Sociological Review* 40 (February 1975): 1–11; Pestello, P. Frederic, "Discounting," *Journal of Contemporary Ethnography* 20 (1991): 26–46; Sykes, M. Gresham, and David Matza, "Techniques of Neutralization: A Theory of Delinquency," *American Sociological Review* 22 (1957): 664–670; Robert L. Young, "Misunderstandings as Accounts," *Sociological Inquiry* 65 (1995): 251–264; C. Wright Mills, "Situated Actions and Vocabularies of Motive," *American Sociological Review* 5 (1940): 904–913.

16. See William L. Benoit, *Accounts, Excuses and Apologies: A Theory of Image Restoration Strategies* (Albany: Suny Press, 1995); Immo Fritsche, "Account Strategies for the Violation of Social Norms: Integration

and Extension of Sociological and Social Psychological Typologies." *Journal for the Theory of Social Behavior* 32 (2002): 371–395; Terry L. Orbuch, "People's Accounts Count: The Sociology of Accounts," *Annual Review of Sociology* 23 (1997): 455–478.

17. Stokes and Hewitt, "Aligning Actions," p. 40 (Note 15).

18. Stokes and Hewitt, "Aligning Actions," p. 847 (Note 15).

19. Mills, "Situated Actions and Vocabularies of Motive," pp. 904–913 (Note 15).

20. Mills, "Situated Actions and Vocabularies of Motive," p. 907 (Note 15).

21. Scott and Lyman, "Accounts," p. 46 (Note 15).

22. M. Pogrebin, E. Poole, and A. Martinez, "Accounts of Professional Misdeeds: The Sexual Exploitation of Clients by Psychotherapists," *Deviant Behavior* 13 (1992): 229–252; Reiss, J. Albert Jr."The Social Integration of Peers and Queers," pp. 181–210 in Howard Becker (ed.), *Outsiders* (New York: Free Press, 1964); Michael Benson, "Denying the Guilty Mind: Accounting for Involvement in a White-Collar Crime," *Criminology* 23 (1985): 583–607; Diana Scully and Joseph Marolla, "Convicted Rapists' Vocabulary of Motive: Excuses and Justifications," *Social Problems* 31 (1984): 530–544; Sykes, Gresham, and David, "Techniques of Neutralization: A Theory of Delinquency," pp. 664–670 (Note 15).

23. See Terry L. Orbuch, "People's Accounts Count: The Sociology of Accounts," *Annual Review of Sociology* 23 (1997): 455–478.

24. Hewitt and Stokes, "Disclaimers," p. 1 (Note 15).

25. Scott and Lyman, "Accounts," p. 46 (Note 15).

26. Lawrence Nichols, "Reconceptualizing Social Accounts: An Agenda for Theory-Building and Empirical Research," *Current Perspectives in Social Theory* 10 (1990): 113–144.

27. Christopher H. Hunter has extended the concept and classified the forms of aligning actions. See his "Aligning Actions: Types and Social Distribution," *Symbolic Interaction* 7 (Fall 1984): 155–174.

28. Nicholas Tavuchis, *Mea Culpa*: *A Sociology of Apology and Reconciliation* (Stanford, CA: Stanford University Press, 1991).

28a. Hunter, "Aligning Actions: Types and Social Distribution," pp. 157–158 (Note 27).

29. Barry Schlenker, "Impression Management," *The Self Concept, Social Identity, and Interpersonal Relations* (Monterey, CA: Brooks-Cole, 1980).

30. This description is drawn from Jonathan H. Turner and Jan E. Stets. "Sociological Theories of Human Emotions," *Annual Review of Sociology* 32 (2006): 25–52.

31. Phrases and elements of this analysis are drawn from Arlie R. Hochschild, "Emotion Work, Feeling Rules, and Social Structure," *American Journal of Sociology* 85 (November 1979): 551–575.

32. See Arlie R. Hochschild, *The Managed Heart: Commercialization of Human Feeling* (Berkeley: University of California Press, 1983). See also Hochschild, *The Second Shift: Working Parents and the Revolution at Home* (New York: Viking-Penguin, 1989), and Hochschild, "Ideology and Emotion Management: A Perspective and Path for Future Research," in *Research Agendas in the Sociology of Emotions,* ed. Theodore D. Kemper (Albany: State University of New York Press, 1990), pp. 117–142. For a discussion of ways the concept of emotions contributes to sociological explanation, see J. M. Barbalet, *Emotion, Social Theory, and Social Structure: A Macrosociological Approach* (Cambridge: Cambridge University Press, 1998). For a historical analysis of changing standards of emotional expression in the United States, see Peter N. Stearns, *American Cool: Constructing a Twentieth Century Emotional Style* (New York: New York University Press, 1994).

33. See Amy S. Wharton. "The Sociology of Emotional Labor." *Annual Review of Sociology* 35 (2009): 147–165; Robin Leidner, *Fast Food, Fast Talk: Service Work and the Routinization of Everyday Life* (University of California Press, 1993); and D. Orzechowicz, "Privileged Emotion Managers: The Case of Actors," *Social Psychology Quarterly* 1 (2) (2008): 143–156.

34. Jack Katz, *Seductions of Crime* (New York: Basic Books, 1988).

35. Kathy Charmaz, *The Social Reality of Death* (Reading, MA: Addison-Wesley, 1980).

36. Dale A. Lund, Michael S. Caserta, Margaret F. Dimond, and Robert M. Gray, "Impact of Bereavement on the Self-Conceptions of Older Surviving Spouses," *Symbolic Interaction* 9 (Fall 1986): 235–244.

37. Lyn H. Lofland, "The Social Shaping of Emotion: The Case of Grief," *Symbolic Interaction* 8 (Fall 1985): 175.

38. Eugene Weinstein and Paul Deutschberger, "Some Dimensions of Altercasting," *Sociometry* 26 (December 1963): 545–566.

39. M. Hall, "A Symbolic Interactionist Analysis of Politics," *Sociological Inquiry* 42 (1–2) (1972): 35–75.

40. Alvin W. Gouldner, "The Norm of Reciprocity: A Preliminary Statement," *American Sociological Review* 25 (February 1960): 161–178.

41. For an analysis of various processes of power, see Peter M. Hall, "Asymmetric Relationships and Processes of Power," in *Foundations of Interpretive Sociology: Original Essays in Symbolic Interaction. Studies in Symbolic Interaction, Supplement 1,* ed. Harvey A. Farberman and R. S. Perinbanayagam (New Haven, CT: JAI Press, 1985), pp. 309–344.

42. Darwin L. Thomas, David Franks, and J. Calonico, "Role-taking and Power in Social Psychology," *American Sociological Review* 7 (October 1972): 605–614.

43. Barney G. Glaser and Anselm L. Strauss, "Awareness Contexts and Social Interaction," in Stone and Farberman, *Social Psychology,* pp. 53–63 (Note 7).

44. Tamotsu Shibutani, *Society and Personality* (Englewood Cliffs, NJ: Prentice-Hall, 1961), pp. 324–331.

45. Ralph H. Turner, "The Role and the Person," *American Journal of Sociology* 84 (July 1978): 1–23.

46. For empirical studies see Louis Zurcher, *Social Roles: Conformity and Creativity* (Beverly Hills, CA: Sage, 1983).

CHAPTER

5 Understanding and Constructing Social Order

What if we could be as good in the real world as we are in our imaginations? We'd write a great novel before hitting 25, win *American Idol,* and be one of *People Magazine's* 50 most beautiful people. We could win the World Cup with a last minute goal, just in time to prepare our Nobel Peace Prize acceptance speech. Unfortunately, these accomplishments must occur in the real world, which tends to constrain achieving outlandish dreams. No matter how much we fantasize, or how great we think we sound singing in the shower, we ultimately have to prove ourselves to others, particularly strangers. We live within a larger framework of groups, organizations, social classes, institutions, and societies as a whole. Not only our close friends and family judge us; that larger social world does as well.

To sociologists, a person's biography is in part a product of media, government policies, economic position, and religious influences. These social institutions have significant impacts on people's identities and actions, and they also tend to operate beyond a person's immediate context. However, people tend to underestimate the impact of social forces and situations in explaining outcomes. We tend to understand and think about outcomes in people's lives, for example, jobs that they get or do not get, as if an individual's actions alone determine success. Yet, the larger social context has a tremendous impact on individual outcomes. If a labor market has shrunk or a company moves jobs overseas, there is little isolated individuals can do to get or keep affected jobs. However, people still tend to apply individually based explanations to many of those people being unemployed, ignoring their social situations.

Lee Ross identified this tendency as making a fundamental attribution error.[1] This error occurs when people explain individual outcomes by thinking of an individual's disposition as causing an outcome rather than considering the social situation that impacts a person. For example, we can view people on welfare as people who don't want to work (dispositional attribution) or explain their status as the product of labor market dynamics (no jobs) or lack of childcare (situational attribution). People also can be biased in an opposite way when evaluating their own performances. We are vulnerable to an actor-observer bias, in which if we commit mistakes, we tend to blame the situation; if someone else makes a mistake, however, we tend to explain his or her failure as being his or her own fault. For example, if we lose money in the stocks that we choose to invest in, the companies should have been successful but were poorly managed. If other people lose money in the market, they picked poor investments. Sociologists view how we attribute outcomes either to individual agency or to social forces as an important distinction, because people often overemphasize one cause or the other and do not consider their interrelations. The interrelationship between agency and social forces in how they impact people's lives must be examined carefully.

Doing so means taking C. Wright Mill's injunction to cultivate a sociological imagination, in which people learn to connect "private troubles and public issues" seriously. People develop a fuller appreciation for their circumstances and can potentially change them, if they know more about how the impact of social forces helps explain the situations in which they find themselves. The biases people have to favor individualized explanations over situational ones hinder this effort. This is not to state that people are naïve. People do not somehow miss that "connections" or having money can influence individual outcomes. We know, for example, that having the money to pay for an expensive lawyer will help you in court. However, while people acknowledge social influences and social order, they do not think enough about how they actually intersect with social order and its many subtle effects. In this chapter, we examine how these social forces, and the social order, become meaningful in everyday social life.

Social Order at a Microlevel

People take the existence of a more or less orderly social world for granted. What does social order actually mean in a sociological sense? First, social order does not refer to an Orwellian world of *Big Brother,* where security personnel use violence to control people's everyday actions and make them conform. Instead, sociologists view *social order* as comprising the many predictable and coordinated social activities that occur in everyday life. Consider the sheer multitude of mundane activities that organize everyday actions in ways that we don't really question. We engage in these activities, and in many ways, they control our collective behaviors. For example, we share a common knowledge of informal instructions about how we are supposed to wait in lines. We follow those instructions in conjunction with others, such as stating "would you hold my spot while I use the bathroom," or not cutting in line, or allowing a person's companions to join that person when he or she, anticipating their arrival, holds a place for them in line. There is social order evident in how people act in an elevator. We avoid making eye contact with each other, stare at the floor or fix our gaze on the changing lights as the elevator ascends or descends.

Though we are conscious of this social order, we do not really stop and articulate all the ways that we conform to the social order in getting through daily life. We follow folkways or informal norms, almost without conscious thought. We comply, as if on autopilot, with completing required steps in those interactions. By acting in accordance with the folk-ways of social order (from eating with a fork and knife in particular settings to giving people a certain amount of personal space when walking by them), we also fulfill and sustain the power of social order to induce our compliance. We walk into social settings full of strangers, and following the social order, complete coordinated actions successfully. For example, we enter restaurants surrounded by strangers and know how to order, eat and drink, to not interrupt adjacent diners, and to ask for a check when we want to pay the bill. We follow these perceptual shorthands in infinite mundane ways, from how we behave in public bathrooms or classrooms to boys carrying their schoolbooks at their hips while girls clasp their schoolbooks to their chests. This level of interaction is social order and a clear venue for examining how social influences impact us.

The social order appears as something external to us, as a seemingly natural feature of how things are. Many forces do ingrain social order in us. We obey those dictates much more often than we transgress them. Sociologists understand that people consent to social order willingly, not involuntarily. We acquiesce to everyday social order because doing so enables social life to function more smoothly and efficiently. Millions of people conform to expected behaviors, such as waiting in lines, and where they stare in elevators, with some variations depending on cultural context. Because we know what is expected of us and what to expect in others, we can engage in meaningful and predictable social exchanges. Social order emerges from this repeated and collective compliance, which occurs often enough to form predictable actions for most individuals in most situations. This compliance begs many sociological questions.

A first critical question is why do people take social order for granted? One answer is that people often do not articulate the work that they do to create social order and just take the existence of ordered behaviors for granted. Harold Garfinkel explored how people work to create social order. In doing so, he helped establish a field of inquiry now often referenced to as ethnomethodology.[2]

Ethnomethodology examines how people are "constantly engaged in a process of creating sense, making it appear that their behavior is correct or appropriate." To observe ethnomethodologically is to look at how "what everybody knows" is actually minutely built and sustained as real work that is exposed easily when people breach everyday social order. Unlike symbolic interactionists, ethnomethodologists do not assume that people actually share common symbolic meanings. What they do share is a ceaseless body of interpretive work that enables them to convince themselves and others that they share common meanings.[3] Studying this process of sense making is the task that ethnomethodologists have set for themselves.

To ethnomethodologists, people live in a world full of illusions of normality, in which they constantly create social order by imposing order on otherwise random or unassociated events. Garfinkel engaged in a number of groundbreaking experiments to examine this idea. For example, he designed a study in which a random response of yes or no was given in answer to questions in a simulated therapy session. If a person asked whether she should accept a marriage proposal, she would be told yes. Then if she asked whether the person who had proposed loved her, she would hear no. The randomly given answers were provided in no rational relation to the questions, yet the person interpreted the responses as if they were sequentially and logically related to the questions by trying to make sense of why she should accept a proposal from a man who didn't love her. Garfinkel noticed that people took steps to make sense of what they heard, even when sense was irrational in that context.

When a person behaves "strangely," the natural appearance of order is broken, and observers become agitated. They create interpretations to make sense of any breaches and they resent violations of the "invisible" order in which they are embedded. To examine this tendency, many sociology classes involve class assignments that ask students to violate the social order in order to expose how many examples of social order surround them that they take for granted. In David Shulman's classes, students have (1) started a conversation in a public bathroom stall by knocking on the door of the adjacent stall; (2) placed a folding chair in a public parking spot, put a quarter in the meter, and told people that the parking space was taken; (3) put on a three-piece suit and panhandled; (4) worn pajamas or clothes inside-out all day; (5) ordered dinner in a restaurant by asking to be served in reverse order with dessert first; (6) had women go out of their way to open doors for men and had men ask women or elderly people for help lifting very light objects such as soda bottles; (7) sat down on an elevator floor when riding the elevator; and (8) tried to negotiate the price they would pay for the *National Enquirer* at a supermarket. Each involves transgressing the social order and asks students to identify the violated folkways of the social order, such as that we pay one price in the supermarket for goods or wear distinct clothes when we sleep.

Students rendered these transgressions sensible to observers by explaining their actions as a "class project." However, they felt very uncomfortable when engaging in actions that violated the microsocial order of everyday life. This discomfort helps enforce social order and keeps people in line. People do not want to feel out of sorts with people around them, whether friends or strangers. A sociologist named Howard Becker once told a class of graduate student sociologists (Shulman among them) that much of the effectiveness of social control comes from people not wanting to look like jerks. The fear of "looking like a jerk" keeps us in thrall to and compliant with social order, and is obviously consonant with the symbolic interactionist perspective of self. As a result, men are clean-shaven when they might prefer to go unshaven, women wear uncomfortable pantyhose, people nod politely when strangers bore them, they try not to expel gas in public, and so forth. People maintain social order through fear of what others might think of us, not primarily by fearing that violence will befall them if they do not.

Ethnomethodologists share with symbolic interactionists an emphasis on how context shapes meaning. According to the idea of *indexicality,* people make interpretations based on context. A teenager will interpret the purpose of rules in high school differently than teachers. Further, familiarity with one's context is part of people's sense making. For example, many couples have conversations consisting of short exchanges that actually have complex meanings that are easily recognizable but hardly ever stated completely. Consider how people compact meaningful information in simple statements. When Shulman and his wife disagree on an issue, and one will concede on a point only reluctantly, they have learned each other's code words for begrudging concession. Mrs. Shulman will say, "Fine," and Mr. Shulman will say, "Suit yourself." However, each knows that the other is really stating almost the exact opposite, which is "I really disagree, but I am going to give in rather than continue a frustrating fight." If the Shulmans bug their teenage son to go to the supermarket with them, he might sit silently and then eventually answer their repeated requests with "Whatever." His parents understand that "whatever" is one word standing in representatively for a contextually rich longer set of words. What "whatever" actually means is, "Well, if you are going to make me go, I guess I will have to go, but don't think that my acquiescence is willing, or that I will forget that you are being so unreasonable and unfair in making me comply when I would rather do something else."

Imagine as a thought experiment, duplicating one of Garfinkel's studies, where subjects write down spoken words on the left column of a page, and then on the right column, they write out the actual full range of knowledge and meaning that was encapsulated incompletely in those few spoken words. What "background expectancies" and interpretive work do people do to make social order possible, such as in cases when we say "fine" or "whatever"? Garfinkel and other ethnomethodologists note that when people communicate, they create social order almost on the fly, acting on unstated and unarticulated understandings that people can interpret well enough to enable them to act in coordination.

Ethnomethodological sense-making processes make organized social life possible. Social order emerges when people understand and make collective meaning without having to articulate each aspect of that meaning out loud. However, how we make social order possible through sense-making work is one question; how social order emerges as a cumulative product is another. How do the activities of interacting individuals produce larger social units? How do these larger realities, in turn, constrain the conduct of interacting individuals? Our individual actions do not emerge from a vacuum or purely from our biological makeup. They also result from socialization and myriad social influences.

Symbolic interactionists propose two complementary answers to the emergence of social order. First, they argue that social order is a constructed reality. A more or less orderly and predictable social world arises out of the naming, classifying, interpretative, and discursive activities of participants, such as that identified by the ethnomethodological tradition. Second, they argue that social order is the product of social coordination. Social order arises from organized, self-conscious efforts of people and institutions to coordinate their activities and influence how others will define and act in particular situations. These answers are complementary in stating that both social construction and social coordination are required to create and maintain social order. We now focus on social order as a coordinated activity.

Social Order as Coordinated Activity

What we call a society is often a broad collectivity of social institutions. Society consists of extensive interlinkages of joint actions and collectivities that form myriad institutions such as the Internet, military actions, national identities, globalization, political campaigns involving millions of voters, synchronous religious services every Saturday and Sunday, stadium concerts by pop stars, and banking transactions worth billions. These activities combine diverse peoples and actions, all of which are interconnected across space and time, and organized in complex and highly systematic ways. Economic, religious, educational, military, and political institutions—each with its own complex network of joint actions and societies unto themselves—relate to one another in many ways. Religious beliefs justify economic activities, for example, and military activity influences political affairs. How is society, as a complex of joint actions, collectivities, and institutions held together? How do patterned and stable joint actions, collectivities, and institutions persist over time?

We usually see joint social action rather than chaotic, self-interested disaster all around us. Why?

Investigating the coordination of a whole society and its component parts and activities is a task that transcends the social sciences alone. However, sociologists and symbolic interactionists have conceptualized some of these large aspects of social integration and social order. Sociologist Emile Durkheim developed the concept of social facts to characterize the coordination involved in maintaining the larger social order. *Social facts* are "ways of acting, thinking and feeling, external to the individual and endowed with a power of coercion, by reason of which they control him. . . . [They are] beliefs and practices which are transmitted to us ready-made by previous generations. We receive and adopt them, because they are invested with a particular authority that education has taught us to recognize and respect."[4]

Durkheim sought to explain the web of social influences that constitute the cumulative social order. These social institutions are external and independent of individual biology. We are born into systems of education, religion, taxation, interpersonal greetings, and cultural heritages that are embodied in sets of practices that exist independent of us but which influence us. These social facts are collective and inculcated in people to a point where internalization is unconscious. To this point, Durkheim wrote: "Society is something beyond us and something in ourselves." Social facts constrain us into practicing them. By practicing them, we sustain them. For example, we learn gender norms; we then take them as our own, sustain them through our actions, and teach them to new members of society.

We tend to think of society as external to us rather than thinking of society as being something we actively maintain. From the individuals' standpoint, a society is a thing with an existence independent of them. Society has a name—the United States, Canada, India—that establishes its existence. Members of distinct societies view themselves as possessing a more or less distinctive way of life expressed in particular values, practices, beliefs, and political institutions. Society is there when we are born, affects our life chances for better or worse, and continues to exist after we expire. A society, in short, is an object toward which its members act. For example, Americans act toward the United States in a variety of ways that serve to constitute it as a stable, persisting object. Reciting the Pledge of Allegiance, arguing about the role of the United States in the Middle East, talking about "what is wrong with this country," or extolling "the American way of life" in political speeches—all are ways that people constitute and act toward a particular kind of object, a nation-state. These practices are social facts; ways of acting toward the object in question. These activities are also collective behaviors—actions that people do together. In large part, their acting toward the object of being an American defines, constitutes, and causes a sense of being American to persist. People are born into identities that help orient us to those behaviors; those behaviors, in turn, perpetuate the society around them through renewing the actions that constitute the society.

In the symbolic interactionist view, social order is achieved when people strive to coordinate their conduct and produce the great variety of joint activities that make up the society. People coordinate their actions in many ways to produce the social world in which they live. The countless situations in people's everyday lives, even among people who do not know one another and are separated by time and space, are nevertheless sewn together into a complex social fabric. Below we detail some ways in which people achieve this social coordination. The overall theoretical framework that we will use derives from the well-known symbolic interactionist Herbert Blumer's ideas.

Keep an example in mind, such as banking transactions, religious services, lectures, wars, or congressional debates. Each involves what Blumer called a *joint action*—an organization of several different acts by many participants that accumulate into a single whole. The joint action is identified as such and may be spoken of and handled without having to break it down into the separate acts that comprise it.[5] A lecture to a university class, for example, consists of many articulated acts of a professor and several students—speaking, listening, taking notes, asking questions, answering questions, and the like. However, the joint action is called a "lecture," rather than being named by any one of the specific acts in which individuals engage to make up the lecture.

Just as we (both as social scientists and as participants in social activities) can speak of various joint actions and thus constitute them as objects in our experience, we can speak of and constitute the collectivities that engage in such joint actions. We speak of bankers and their customers, priests and congregants, professors and students, the Iraqi Army, the United States Congress, workers at Microsoft, or John Jones's family, each of which is a named collectivity comprising—but also more than—the individuals that make it up. Just as the interlinkage of individual acts is what constitutes a joint action, so the interlinkage of individuals, rather than the specific persons themselves, is what constitutes a collectivity. What basic social processes help accomplish these social coordinations? From a social psychological point of view, *influence, the social bond, trust and problem solving, negotiated order, boundaries,* and *social movements* are all useful concepts for studying social coordination.

Influence

Psychologists explore the efforts that people make to get others to comply with their wishes. Tactics of influence or persuasion are a key mechanism in coordinating action and creating social order through directing people's actions in particular ways. For example, we seek to influence people to coordinate their actions to our preferences by casting a vote for our candidate, or by buying our products, or by praising us. Robert Cialdini is a prominent expert on social influence and has identified six principles of influence: reciprocation, scarcity, authority, commitment and consistency, liking, and social proof.[6] As a thought exercise, think of how often you can spot these techniques of influence being employed in everyday life.

Reciprocation refers to influencing others to act as we wish by appealing to their aversion to indebtedness. People like to reciprocate kindnesses or concessions. By maneuvering people into feeling that they "owe you one," you can influence their actions. For example, grocery stores give free samples. Sometimes, people use a technique called the "door in the face" to make use of reciprocity. In this maneuver, people first make an unrealistic demand and then upon refusal, reduce their demands by so much that the person being influenced feels that they have to reciprocate a concession. So one might start with asking for a thousand dollars, expecting a no, and then drop the demand to "just" a dollar a day. When infomercials keep stating that a price of $99.99 a month is being "slashed down to" $49.00, and finally to $19.99, along with a free book and tools, the idea is that people see that steep concession in price as a reason to leap at the final offer.

The *technique of scarcity* influences people to act because they view their compliance as earning them a rare reward. Con artists, for example, succeed because they promise people the scarce reward of something that sounds too good to be true, so people fall for the con. A chance to share a winning lottery ticket won by an illegal immigrant (who can't cash it in without you fronting for him or her) and all you have to do is show good faith by putting up $10,000 before getting a million dollars? Who could resist this temptation? Businesses make frequent use of this strategy, with one-day only super sales. Cialdini also noted that *perceived authority* is a technique of influence. When we perceive someone as a legitimate expert, we are more likely to accede to his or her influence. The influence technique of *commitment and consistency* relies on a tendency people have, that once they make an initial commitment, they often are consistent in following through on that commitment. Hence we ask people to "put it in writing." Or we might make use of what is called the "foot in the door," in which by asking someone to help out just for a few minutes, because of that initial agreement to help, the commitment can evolve into the person helping for a few hours.

Two other techniques of influence are social proof and liking. *Social proof* relies on the idea that many people are followers. When people observe the "evidence" of others doing a desired behavior, they will tend to view that as affirming that pattern and be influenced to take that action. This technique is particularly effective when groups of people are observed that are similar to the ones that you want to influence. *Liking* operates as a technique of influence by appealing to likability. Here, the issue is not just that the influencer is likable, but that part of that likability is based in the influenced person feeling that the influencer likes them. This type of liking occurs through flattery or when particularly physically attractive people are attempting to influence others. For example, conventions may hire particularly attractive people to populate sales booths. Walking in Manhattan, you may have passed Abercrombie and Fitch clothiers. They hire male model types to stand outside their Manhattan stores to influence shoppers to stare and then hopefully, enter and shop. Abercrombie and Fitch have also been sued for hiring people with a particular "look" to work inside their stores with the intention of using physical attractiveness to encourage people to buy. All of these tactics of influence are intended to gain the compliance of others to enter into coordinated actions and bind them to social order.

Creating Social Bonds

People also coordinate social activities through establishing stable interpersonal attachments or social bonds. Thomas Scheff argued that a main quest underlying human actions is maintaining intact, healthy social bonds. In Scheff's view, the need for social bonds is never completely filled and may be uniquely frustrated in contemporary society.[7]

A healthy social bond balances an individual's needs with the group. On the one hand, social bonds involve closeness and knowledge of the other's point of view. Bonds of friendship, or those between siblings, for example, entail a sense of intimacy between people and mindfulness of the other's values and beliefs. A healthy bond between parents and a child, for example, requires that each respect the other's differences even while feeling a sense of closeness.

Human social bonds must be constantly tested and renewed, for they do not endure merely through inertia or because of built-in genetic mechanisms. Each encounter with another provides an opportunity for the bond to be strengthened, repaired, or undermined. A married couple, for example, does not form a bond that subsequently maintains itself without help. Rather, each occasion of interaction between them—at the dinner table, working side by side in the home, at a party with friends, or in the bedroom—is an occasion that strengthens or weakens a bond.

The basis for a social bond is that each member recognizes the other as a legitimate participant—as someone who belongs and has the right to interact with the other. This mutual granting (or withholding) of legitimacy involves both actions and feelings. The members of a bond coordinate their actions, often harmoniously, but sometimes in conflict. Adult children cooperate in caring for their aging and infirm parents, for example, although sometimes they disagree about what to do. Their actions, cooperative or not, act to legitimize the other's presence and participation. Participants in a social bond also demonstrate feelings toward one another—respect for one another's contributions, admiration of the other's special abilities, and sometimes, disapproval of the other's actions. A feeling that one has a legitimate rewarding bond generates feelings of pride; a sense that one has let the other down creates shame.

Social bonds provide not only motivation but also some of the most important contexts within which human social activities are coordinated. Much of what people do, they do with friends, family, coworkers, and others with whom they develop attachments. Over time, these attachments produce interpersonal roles that shape people's conduct toward one another, as well as their identities. Nonetheless, contemporary people also live in a more impersonal social world in which they interact with others whom they scarcely know and with whom they feel no direct bonds. As we will see, then, the establishment of social bonds is only a part of the story of social coordination. We must also solve problems together and trust others, including impersonal organizations, to meet obligations.

Solving Problems and Trust

Sociologists generally emphasize the patterned and repetitive nature of social life. They stress that the vast majority of problems that arise in everyday social life have predetermined solutions established by previous generations. These answers are codified in a common social stock of knowledge. From this vantage point, the typifications, causal propositions, and other forms of knowledge that we discussed in Chapter 4 are more or less routinely applied, and nothing much is new or different in day-to-day life. However, modern life is not as routinized and prescribed so as to cover all decisions and actions. People are not tied to a limited set of responses to an environment (as they might have been in historical and less technologically complex times).

Today people must interpret more in the world and respond creatively to unprecedented choices. Many cultures are now more inherently open rather than closed. They can be defined in terms of problems of uncertainty and risk in decisions rather than by fixed and immutable behaviors. Put in more applicable terms, in the context of contemporary U.S. culture, we can decide to abide by religious doctrines or not, live in different areas, take on a variety of jobs, engage in a variety of belief systems, and choose between 500 channels on cable. As Blumer argued, areas of "unprescribed conduct are just as natural, indigenous, and recurrent in human group life as are those areas covered by preestablished and faithfully followed prescriptions of joint action."[8]

Symbolic interactionists see a problem-solving orientation as inherent in the contemporary organization of human conduct. Just a moment's reflection will suggest the extent to which attention to problems is a constant feature of everyday life. Problems of diverse kinds arise and are solved in everyday activities. Cars do not start, people fail to show up for meetings, tasks seem difficult to understand, others' feelings are hurt, bored children want to be entertained, parties have to be organized, athletic games are cancelled and rescheduled, unexpected deaths occur, marriages dissolve, people disappoint us, employers are unfair, and people get sick. Social coordination is accomplished in part by means of the joint orientation of people to addressing and solving these everyday, practical problems.

A great deal of joint action and order occurs in forming conduct around problems that confront people. Some institutions and organizations, of course, are particularly concerned with organizing responses to problems; science, medicine, other helping, and teaching professions. Safety and security forces are also problem-centered. Their everyday work routines regularly call on them to respond to conditions that others define as problematic. Even in the most routine activities and occupations, people have to overcome difficulties and solve problems.

People's efforts to solve their problems in a practical way are just as important to social order as is their routine conduct along culturally established and predictable lines. Family is a social unit that is fundamental to social order. Families require a set of roles, rules, and social relationships that focus on bearing and raising children and caring for spouses and kin. Yet people in their everyday lives experience and conceive of their families to a great extent as a series of situations where they must confront and solve practical problems. In this sense, a family (depending on one's age, religion, ethnicity, social class, and the like) is changing diapers on a child who ought to be toilet trained, struggling to feed a family on a limited budget, achieving some kind of mutually satisfactory companionship with another person, coping with the occasional rebelliousness of children (or of oneself or one's spouse), deciding whether one can afford a new house or how to pay a child's college tuition, and responding to a host of other problems. That people organize in the face of the problematic situation is fundamental to the coordination of conduct and social order, above and beyond any particular organized solution.

The complexity of choices and the need to solve problems collectively in everyday life also make trust vital. Who can we trust? When can we trust them? These two issues are critical in collective life and for coordinating social action because trust is essential to maintaining social order. Trust reduces uncertainty and complexity. When we trust others, we feel that we can predict and rely on their future actions and that they can depend on us to fulfill obligations to them. Thanks to trust, most of us do not worry about whether restaurants will serve spoiled food, or whether an employer will pay us for last month's work. However, there is a problem with trust. To trust always involves some risk that a partner will fail to meet his or her obligations. Unfortunately, restaurants and employers (among many others) are not always what we trust them to be. Organizations ranging from families to large bureaucracies all have formal and informal sets of agreements, based on trust, regarding which obligations partners must meet in order to earn reciprocal rewards. These trust relations always carry a risk of exploitation from people seeking to get "something for nothing."

Social structures also sometimes accentuate these ambiguities of trust by forcing relational dependencies that would not otherwise arise naturally. We sometimes have to engage in trust involuntarily. Acrimoniously divorced parents may need to trust one another in order to finance their children's college education. Coworkers who distrust each other may be assigned to the same project and have to set aside their reservations. Voluntary and involuntary trust also serves to coordinate social action and social order.

Functionalist social theorists also argue that trust is important in additional ways besides coordinating responses to social problems. From their perspective, trust strengthens group solidarity. When groups feel threatened by people that are unlike them, they circle the wagons and extend trust to those within their group, in case of potential conflict with outsiders. Trust also plays a crucial role in an advanced society where we have a complex division of labor and people's lives depend on the actions of many people and organizations that are impersonal, such as food producers in other states, insurers, airplane mechanics, and financial regulators. We are involuntarily bound into trusting relationships with others in order to engage in coordinated social actions and to maintain social order. We depend on bus drivers to not be drunk, on construction companies not to use substandard materials to make more money, on other citizens not to attack us on the streets, and on people doing their different jobs that keep our collective social life humming. The theorist Georg Simmel noted that the ascendancy of these impersonal trust relations has increased the severe consequences that lies and secrets can pose to contemporary social order:

> *Our modern life is based to a much larger extent than is usually realized upon the faith in the honesty of the other. Examples are our economy, which becomes more and more a credit economy, or our science, in which most scholars must use innumerable results of other scientists, which they cannot examine. We must base our gravest decisions on a complex system of conceptions, most of which presuppose the confidence that we will not be betrayed. Under modern conditions, the lie therefore, becomes something more devastating than it was earlier, something which questions the very foundations of our life.[9]*

Trust's importance in contemporary life also requires people to develop means to control trust. Social order is threatened by the self-seeking advantages that people might want to take by violating trust and not meeting obligations. The Bernard Madoff ponzi scheme scandal that came to light in 2008 showed how breach of trust ruthlessly victimized investors. The aftermath of such disasters demonstrates the critical importance of trying to ensure trustworthiness and social order. In an era of perceived threats to social order from a recession, terrorism, and white-collar crimes, scholarly interest in exploring the nature of trust, the consequences of broken trust and the social control of trust, is increasing.

The Negotiated Order

Social order is often presented in an oversimplified way. In this framing, social order comes from people obeying rules, enacting their roles appropriately, and using standard procedures for dealing with the problems of everyday life. These coordinated activities result from adequate socialization because people have mastered their roles and have the relevant stock of knowledge. Hence their activities mesh smoothly—men will know how and when to be fathers, breadwinners, or husbands and so forth. When, for one reason or another, conduct is inappropriate, mechanisms of social control take over: People are sanctioned for their departures from norms and corrective resocialization will occur.

As the previous content of this chapter demonstrates, however, this simplified account scarcely does justice to what actually happens in everyday life. Coordination and social order are as much the results of people's self-conscious efforts to produce them as they are spontaneous, unconscious products. Everywhere in social life we see bargaining, negotiation, deliberation, agreements, temporary arrangements, suspensions of the rules, and a variety of other procedures in which attaining social order and coordinated activity is a deliberate undertaking. We can describe the life of a middle-class family in U.S. society, for example, as an effort to negotiate an orderly set of relationships among people who sometimes have conflicting interests, competing demands on their time, and divided loyalties. Keeping peace among the children, finding time to do things around the house as well as earning a living, agreeing on where the family will vacation or whether the husband's or wife's job will take precedence in determining where the family will live—organizational tasks such as these are the stuff of everyday life. We consciously negotiate these tasks—we don't just fall into some blueprint for resolving them in a mindless way.

Anselm Strauss and his colleagues developed the concept of the *negotiated order* to account for how the ongoing activities of a complex organization such as a hospital are coordinated so as to pursue its paramount goal, which is to help sick people get better.[10] Although this concept pertains explicitly to organizational life—hospitals, schools, corporations, government agencies, universities, and the like—it can, as Peter Hall suggested, be extended to a societal level, as it provides one useful model of what social order is like and how it is attained.[11]

Theoretically, organizations such as hospitals develop rules and formal procedures to coordinate the activities of their members. The official rules specify the activities of various personnel so that they can coordinate their efforts on behalf of their patients. They describe duties, obligations, rights, limitations, and other requirements pertaining to the various organizational roles. They specify who has what kind of authority over whom, and presumably give members a fairly comprehensive picture of the work that they are to perform.

However, work situations are much more complicated. Even though all members may agree in theory on the abstract value of making sick people well, they conduct their everyday organizational lives amidst a myriad of details that can seem remote from this lofty objective. Individuals and subunits may hold a number of additional values or goals that are juxtaposed against that chief goal of the organization. Nurses and physicians are interested in their pay and social status as well as in curing the sick; department heads are apt to think of their domain as more beneficial or important than others, and so compete with one another for a larger budget; physicians are private practitioners and researchers as well as affiliates of the hospital, and so must divide their time; some support personnel, such as orderlies and aides, often are overworked and badly underpaid, asked to do jobs that go beyond their training, and so forth.

The important point is that in an organization's ongoing operations, no simple, easily unquestioned achieved coordination of activities surfaces. There are too many competing aims, individual interpretations of organizational goals, divided loyalties, internal disagreements over resources, and other complexities. Although organizations formulate rules and procedures to cope with those problems, no set of rules can comprehensively dictate what lines of authority, responsibilities, or rights will actually emerge. Constitutions, bylaws, procedural rules, "the book"—none of these can cover all possible contingencies that may arise, and so—by common consent—people break rules from time to time, even people who pledged to uphold them. Also, rules are sometimes made to deal with situations and then forgotten as new personnel and problems arrive.

Strauss argues that we attain social order in these chaotic circumstances through an ongoing process of negotiation, one in which agreements, contracts, and understandings among various members of the organization—made from time to time and occasionally renewed or allowed to lapse—serve as basis for coordinating activities. Since rules may be ambiguous or even absent, members agree in practice on certain interpretations, exceptions, or new rules to attach to changing circumstances. If jurisdictions seem to overlap, as between physicians and nurses, participants develop understandings about who is entitled to do what and when they are supposed to do it. If the responsibilities of several categories of personnel directly responsible for patient care—registered nurses, licensed practical nurses, nurses' aides, and orderlies, for example—are ambiguous, working agreements will be created to specify each responsibility.

Such negotiations do not occur in the same ways in all contexts, nor are they equally important in different kinds of organizations. On the basis of research in public schools and a review of other studies of negotiation, Hall and Spencer-Hall have identified a number of circumstances that influence how much negotiation occurs and how important those negotiations are.[12] First, they argued, when teamwork and coordination are required and activities are public and novel, more negotiation occurs than under circumstances where people work alone and in routinized ways. Special education teachers, for example, who move from classroom to classroom or who must coordinate their work with that of regular classroom teachers find they must engage in more negotiation than regular teachers, whose work is isolated in one classroom and tends to be quite routine. More negotiation occurs when organizational size and complexity is greater (the larger and more complex the organization, the more likely there will be competing subunits that must negotiate); when power is more broadly dispersed, when people feel more equality or effective (teachers are more likely to negotiate with one another than with superiors); when actual or planned changes in the organization require existing arrangements to be renegotiated; and when professionals (such as physicians or psychologists) who think of themselves as autonomous, and as entitled to negotiate the terms and conditions of their work are present.

Symbolic interactionists often analyze work and work settings. They ask: How do workers interpret the work that they do, how do they identify with or disavow that work in connection to their sense of "self," how do they do things together, how do they strategize their actions as "calculating and experiencing persons" within a set of formal and informal expectations for performance, and how do patterns of interaction constitute negotiated orders that shape how work is accomplished? Symbolic interactionists should view work as locally constituted through institutional arrangements and cultural assumptions, and practiced through negotiated group dynamics. Though formal bureaucratic relations and rules can determine the form of work, interactionists explore how people, with all the attendant messiness of lived experience, define, negotiate, and do (or shirk) their work in practice.[13]

Negotiation is ubiquitous, not only within many organizations that make up society as a whole, but at the societal level as well. Given that a complex society such as the United

States or Canada comprises regions, ethnic and religious groups, social classes, organizations, groups, social movements, and many other units with like, common, and competing interests, social order depends on an ongoing negotiation of orderly relationships among groups. Two elements of a societal level of negotiation are noteworthy. The first is self-interest. The units and individuals that make up a society rarely feel that their interests coincide with each other, nor with the perceived interests of the society as a whole. The second is power. Individuals and collectivities are not equal in their capacity to influence one another or to pursue their interests successfully.

The pursuit of self-interest, along with a need to negotiate between competing interests, is inherent to maintaining social order. Self-interest manifests itself in a variety of ways and contexts. City officials, for example, may oppose changes in the distribution of state or federal assistance to cities if such changes will reduce their control over how the money is spent or eliminate its value as political patronage. In such situations, various processes of negotiation are employed to reach agreement among contending parties.

In negotiating, individuals and groups attempt to exercise power over one another—that is, to bring to the negotiations whatever resources they can in order to achieve their goals, at the lowest cost or without the consent of others. The resources of power are varied, ranging from naked force to the control of information and knowledge, the dispensation of rewards by controlling jobs and financial resources, and the manipulation of symbols. However, power is exercised and no matter by whom, power is an important determinant of social order. Power influences who can bargain successfully, whose definitions of the rules prevail, and how individuals and collectivities will define and pursue their self-interest.

To provide a fuller analysis of the negotiation of social order in the political process—or of the nature of the groups that together form any given society as well as their interests and the distribution of power—is beyond the scope of this book. What must be stressed here is that power, negotiations, and self-interest are central to interactionist conceptions of social order and that such phenomena are important concerns in social psychology. When we examine the situations people define, the roles they make and take, the objects toward which they act, and the routine and problematic circumstances they confront, we discover that these elements of social life are inextricably bound up with inequalities of power, the pursuit of individual and collective interests, and the ongoing negotiation of social order, whether in any of the numerous units that make up a society or at the societal level. One cannot, for example, understand either the dynamics of U.S. society as a whole or the lives and selves of individual members without grasping the patterns of competition, conflict, and cooperation that have developed among various ethnic and religious groups. In ethnically and religiously diverse societies such as the United States and Canada, a negotiated order among such groups is a crucial aspect of the structure of the society that shapes individual lives. For example, a major shift has occurred in these negotiations with the election of Barack Obama as America's first African American president. Members of various ethnic and racial groups in the U.S. are now changing their views of what is possible—whether long-held racist attitudes among other social groups are waning and whether the example of Obama's election will influence countries where skepticism exists about the ability of less powerful minority groups to win elections. A certain racial social order has been dented, though how far-reaching this change will be remains to be negotiated through the self-interest and power of different groups.

Boundaries

Creating and maintaining social boundaries that divide various categories, groups, and communities from one another also helps to sustain social order. One boundary that we have already considered is ascribed statuses. Gender is one such ascribed status boundary. Using the minimal biological facts of sex differences, culture classifies people as male and female and constructs gender differences. These gender differences then cause people to act in predictable ways within the social order. The ethnic and religious divisions that we referred to earlier in this chapter also form important boundaries, as do race and social class. Gender, race, ethnicity, religion, and social class constitute fundamental lines of division in modern society. Sociologists refer to these boundaries as "structural," since they are intrinsic to the very organization of society.

Other boundaries are more ephemeral. Social controversies over capital punishment or abortion, for example, also create criteria of classification that separate one category of person from another. These boundaries are typically the product of social movements, a topic we consider later in this chapter. Even such media creations as the "gangsta" or "geek" provide a basis for classifying people according to character or lifestyle, thus creating boundaries between them.

A social boundary is akin to a fence or border that governs relationships between people on opposite sides. The existence of a boundary establishes as fact that there are two worlds and regulates the contact between them. Likewise, boundaries of race, religion, or ethnicity shape interaction across such lines and establish the existence of separate social worlds. The boundaries established between those on opposite sides of an issue govern their interaction. Previously existing social relationships, such as friendship, may be undermined when an issue such as abortion comes into play. Those who are pro-choice may regard people who are pro-life with suspicion. They may be wary of interacting with them and find that when they do interact, they act as representatives of their causes rather than on some other basis.

There is an important connection between boundaries and a social process called *labeling*. Sociologist Howard Becker is credited with the most influential formulation of labeling theory.[14] This approach examines how a label for being "deviant" emerges. In this perspective, some social groups develop the power to impose a label of being deviant onto selected others. Labeling theorists research the social processes through which social groups create and apply definitions for being "deviant" to individuals, groups and particular behaviors. If an individual or group is labeled, that label stigmatizes them. Rather than being seen as an individual, they are seen as a representative of the particular deviant group or behavior. From this perspective, boundaries are a source of labeling others. From this view, the pro-choice person labels the pro-life individual as a pro-lifer, rather than as a person. The label becomes what is called the "master status" of the person.

Labeling theorists believe that social groups work actively to enshrine some definitions and boundaries. Social groups that advocate particular constructions of what are deviant or normal are called *moral entrepreneurs*. Moral entrepreneurs work to define what others will accept as being real, or they will consider being real or an accurate definition of a situation. According to Becker, acts and individuals are not inherently good or bad until sufficiently powerful social groups can successfully define them to others as good or bad. We have already described the symbolic interactionist tenet that people define and construct their identities from society's perception of them. Labeling theory perceives groups as projecting rules and definitions onto otherwise neutral behaviors in order to create labels for particular identities, groups, and behaviors. Agents of social control who enforce the resulting standards—for example, by acting as police officers or simply by pointing out violations and embarrassing others—are called *rule enforcers.*

Labeling theorists research the motives and tactics that moral entrepreneurs use in trying to institutionalize their views for what should be considered deviant or normal, good or bad. With respect to boundaries, social groups work very hard to label other groups by defining them negatively or positively. Boundaries arise from conflict and negotiation within and between groups and organizations. Once in existence, stated labels for groups, at least for a time, are seen as natural features of the social landscape, rather than as socially constructed categories. If labeling is working on already existing boundaries, then differences become hardened. It may become obvious to people who accept the labels as true that men and women *are* "different" or that people who oppose abortion *are* all "extremists" and "fanatics" who are dangerous to society in general and think women have no rights. Boundaries provide points of reference in social life. They are inclusive of those who live on one side of the boundary and exclude those on the other side. They make it possible to distinguish between friend and foe, the virtuous and the evil, the like and the different. By highlighting labels and differences between social groups, we maintain social order.

Boundaries have four main characteristics in how they operate and help coordinate social activity. First, boundaries rest on the application of a principle of social classification— some criteria that divide into categories. Such principles of classification oversimplify the complex nature of human beings and exaggerate the importance or consequences of their differences. These labels end up sorting people into categories that are then treated in distinct ways. For example, we label many people by social class. We distinguish between "blue-collar" and "white-collar" workers, between "townies" and college students, between rich snobs and the "hard-working middle class."

As an example, a recent staple of reality television shows focuses on changing people that were considered "trashy" to become higher class. These shows, which are all in some ways contemporary revisions of the *Pygmalion/My Fair Lady* type, have titles like "From Gs to Gents" and "Charm School." People mock reality television stars such as Paris Hilton, Heidi Montag, and Spencer Pratt. Comedy books with titles like *Hot Chicks with Douchebags* are selling well, and viral video sensations like *My New Haircut,* are creating labels that serve to classify people into particular categories and cement differences between "us" and "them."

Second, boundaries count. Gender, race, and social class pervade almost every aspect of social life. Social interaction almost invariably requires participants to establish and enact gender, for example. As we have already noted, audiences inspect role performances for their conformity with specific and general typifications of being "male" and "female." A clear indication of the power of labels for "doing gender" is evident in the discomfort and awkwardness that people feel when they interact with someone whose gender they cannot conclusively determine, or their embarrassment when they misidentify someone's gender. We are embarrassed when, in speaking to a child's parents, we misidentify a boy with long hair as a girl, and a girl with short hair as a boy. Moreover, gender classification establishes an individual's credentials for entry into a variety of social situations, organizations, and roles—even to what toilets men or women can use.

Likewise, race and social class are consequential sources of labeling and subsequent classification and treatment. A black man jogging in a predominantly white neighborhood is very conscious that his color may end up labeling him. Residents or the police will use his race to typify him as a potential threat and not as the upstanding citizen he is. Likewise, membership in the working class, as evidenced by patterns of speech or dress, may affect an individual's life chances because "middle-class" people—potential employers, college admissions interviewers, or prospective mates—take class and associated labels for class into account in their perceptions of skills and qualities and in their decisions to employ, admit, or marry. Boundaries matter because they affect how the powerful or privileged treat the less powerful and privileged. They also are very important because membership in a category often entails loyalty to and acceptance of control by those group members and their labels.

A third characteristic of boundaries is that they promote self-identification. If a boundary is important in social life, people will regard it as an important basis for the construction of self and explicitly encourage others to regard the boundary similarly. Gender, for example, is a main component of biographical identity, because gender is situated in almost every social encounter. A sense of one's gender, of being a "dude," "biker chick," "bro," or "lady" becomes "second nature," a part of habitual attitudes toward others and ourselves. People are explicitly and self-consciously encouraged to identify with a gender category. Filling out an application form that requires checking a gender category or having a "boys'" or "girls' night out" constitute gender identity announcements that contribute in a small way to identification with gender. Even when men and women joke about the "battle of the sexes," they invoke the underlying idea that men and women owe loyalty to their respective genders.

Group solidarity and individual identification tend to thrive on creating boundaries and encouraging a sense of difference between oneself and "the other." Portraying or labeling some other as dangerous or deeply flawed helps to maintain the virtuous quality of the in-group. For example, media depictions of other countries may only highlight some negative feature that makes that society appear backwards or somehow inferior. The comedian Sacha Baron Cohen made a film called *Borat* in which he depicted life in Kazakhstan as a plethora of stereotypes of backward Eastern European and Asiatic societies. This caused the actual citizens of Kazakhstan no end of misery in trying to counter that depiction, which made many members of Western societies laugh at the "backwardness" of that country. Ironically, the comedian's underlying point that these stereotypes are shams might be lost on many audience members. In addition, many societies have long-term traditions of making jokes about neighboring countries (England, Scotland and Ireland; Mexico and the U.S.; Australians and New Zealanders) and about certain ethnic groups. By contrasting in-group virtues with an out-group's labeled flaws, members provide an explicit rationale and vocabulary for promoting identification with the group.

Finally, boundaries entail social controls that help maintain them, through applying sanctions for departing from them or efforts to transgress them. Here is where rule enforcers emerge. Members of a religious group who fear that their children will marry someone of another faith may go to some lengths to prevent the marriage. Parents may demand that their children date only coreligionists, send them to religion-based schools, or lecture them on the dangers of leaving the fold. Members of the in-group may publicly criticize those who seem to not respect boundaries. Prepubescent boys sometimes taunt their friends who play with girls. Working-class Americans may censure their fellows that attain middle-class jobs or incomes or adopt middle-class lifestyles. Some black Americans criticize peers for "acting white" and some whites criticize other whites for "acting black."

Techniques of social control and the application of sanctions form only a part of the explanation of how we maintain boundaries. Wherever people recognize and use a principle of classification, or wherever they take classification for granted, they create and sustain boundaries. Thus, to search for the men's room in a restaurant is to lend support to categorization by gender, as is a tendency to talk about cars or sports and thus exclude women who are not interested in these topics. (Indeed, even to write the preceding sentence is to reproduce the boundary!) To ask a Chinese American where to find the best Chinese restaurant is likewise to act to maintain a boundary (and to impose an identity on the other), because just posing the question contains the assumption that this individual will naturally know such things. Boundaries exist because people voluntarily recognize and take them for granted, and in doing so, they help enforce them.

Boundaries provide significant reference points in coordinating conduct and the construction of social order. Those committed to a particular boundary, such as gender, find in it a stable way of imagining and talking about the social order and standards for conduct. Boundaries, artificial though they may be, provide guidance in everyday life, specifying what is permissible and what is off limits. A good part of what goes on in contemporary society consists of struggles over boundaries. Strife, argument, contention, disagreement, cultural conflict, and other signs of such struggles are among the most stable and recurring features of life in the contemporary United States, and thus main features in its social order. The "politics of identity," or as they are more recently known, "the culture wars," are a prominent feature of contemporary life.[15]

Talking

A key way that members of a society constitute and uphold social order is by talking about social order. Everyday life is replete with chance encounters, coffee breaks, cocktail parties, formal conferences and seminars, speeches, religious gatherings, radio and television talk shows and interviews, informal get-togethers, and numerous other interactions where talking is the central and most observable form of behavior. These encounters may seem trivial. They also may appear to their participants merely as occasions for passing time and thus as unrelated to the real work of maintaining social order. Talk is so commonplace that we tend to regard it as of minor sociological significance.

Though talk is cheap, talk is nonetheless important sociologically. Talk's very ubiquity is important for making the social order more binding. Whatever the situations in which people talk, their talk is a primary means through which people sustain the world of objects in which they live. Talk is especially important for maintaining abstract objects—institutions, groups, values, principles, organizations, and society as a whole—which we do not experience in the same way as we do more tangible things. We can touch material objects like furniture and act toward them by sitting on them or moving them. However, people experience and act toward abstract objects, such as institutions, groups, and values, primarily by talking about them, until that talk leads to physical action in the name of those abstract objects.

Talk thrives on problems like bees to honey. A common form of talk, for example, takes the form of complaints, griping, and expressions of disaffection. The state of the economy, terrorism, corrupt politicians, the disloyalties of supposed friends, the difficulties people have with their cars and appliances, the character flaws of coworkers and employers, the high cost of medical care—such complaints about life constitute major topics of conversation, debate, and disagreement. People may occasionally state that the world is a delightful and perfect place, but they actually spend a lot of their time talking about problems, troubles, difficulties, and disasters.

Talk shapes our views of the social order, even though people do not discuss problems for the sake of maintaining the social order. People gripe, gossip, criticize one another, worry about conspiracies, argue, and in other ways confront the problems they face, not to construct social reality, but because they actually face real or imaginary problems. Other people do nasty things, ambition and effort go unrewarded, children misbehave, and employers and neighbors treat us unfairly. In dealing with and especially talking about these matters, we give shape and substance to our ideals, values, and conceptions of how things work in the society and how we think they should work.

How people talk about problematic events and situations are culturally and historically variable. One culture, for example, may encourage people to keep a stoic silence about personal problems, while another may encourage discourse about them. In the 1950s, for example, a number of books and articles appeared that expressed concern about a growing tendency in the United States toward conformity. Scholars such as David Riesman wrote books about the decline of inner-direction and the rise of other-direction. By the 1970s and 1980s, the attention of social critics shifted to narcissism, and they worried that Americans were becoming too wrapped up in themselves, too selfish, too inattentive to the needs and interests of others. Today, social critics worry that some youth are becoming too absorbed in fantasy and virtual worlds of gaming, movies, and the Internet, to the extent that they are decreasing their sociability, becoming more violent, and doing more poorly in school. Though the problems that social critics perceive have changed dramatically over the intervening years, the focus of their discourse remains on the problematic relationship between the person and the social order.[16]

People tend to take their activities for granted until something interferes with their capacity to attain their goals. They are apt to talk about the high cost of medical care when they experience it or see others whose savings have been eaten away by a major illness. They talk about the state of the economy when their aspirations for a better standard of living are thwarted by a market turndown. Under such circumstances, talk is a major means that people use to restore lines of conduct and redefine their goals.

People do not talk just about problems or merely about the present. Often they talk about the past—about important events, fond memories, places they lived or worked, their travels, and other items from the recent or distant past. Such talk is also significant in constructing the social order and linking the person to it.[17] A common way Americans talk about the past is by labeling decades and generations. Decade labeling entails naming calendar decades and assigning dominant or significant characteristics to them.[18] The "Roaring Twenties," the "Turbulent 60s," and the "Me Decade" of the 1970s are examples of the practice of decade labeling from the twentieth century.

Generally led by the mass media, people attribute distinctive qualities and characteristics to calendar decades. Thus, the 1950s are portrayed as a decade of boring conformity, the 1960s as a decade of social turbulence and upheaval, and the 1970s as a decade of excessive self-preoccupation. Likewise, generations acquire names and characteristics: The "selfish" and "self-centered" Baby Boomers were born during the considerable rise in birth rates that started in 1946, just after the end of World War II, and lasted until the beginning of the 1960s. The supposedly "aimless" and "bored" members of Generation X are said to have been born anywhere from the late 1960s to the 1980s, for there is no widely agreed definition of this generation. There is a more recently minted Generation Y or millennial generation, with as yet undetermined psychological characteristics. They are the children of the Baby Boomers.

The significance of these categories lies in the characteristics that are imputed to them. Labels for decades and generations provide what sociologist Fred Davis has called a "moral narrative." The "boring" and "conformist" decade of the 1950s is held in popular discourse to have been followed by the social protests of the 1960s, when people appeared to reject the materialism and conformity of the previous decade in exchange for serious efforts to make the society better. Later decades were constructed as ones in which people withdrew from social concerns, and turned exclusively to pursuing their own well-being or that of their families. Whatever the reality of these decades—which is far more complex than the labels imply—the discourse about them emphasizes important values, beliefs, and aspirations that members of society have.

Explaining Disorder

In addition to talking about problems or the past, people also talk about social order itself, often trying to explain disorder. In everyday conversation, people try to explain the causes of a problematic situation to their own satisfaction, whether from a participant's view or one that they observed from a distance. Such problematic situations take many forms. A married couple quarrels repeatedly; a riot or some other disturbance occurs; one's own or a neighbor's child is delinquent; a public official acts inexplicably—each of these situations may be viewed as problematic by somebody. Each may also be the topic of a conversation in which people seek to explain the nature and causes of the problematic occurrence or situation.

What makes a situation as a whole problematic? One mark of a problematic situation is that people label the situation as disorderly—as somehow falling outside the accepted tolerances and bounds of social experience. In nonproblematic situations, social order is taken for granted. Situations are defined well enough so that people can interact more or less routinely, even if some untoward event occurs that merits an account or a disclaimer. Problematic situations, in contrast, happen when social order cannot be taken for granted. The definition of the situation as a whole is called into question, and a special effort is required to comprehend and define what is happening. For example, mass unrest or disasters can produce disorder.

Suppose a crowd gathers on a street corner. That situation, for example, represents a problematic situation to a police officer, who must define the situation in order to decide what action to take. A sudden disturbance and rush to exit a large auditorium is also a problematic situation to those present, who must decide and define whether to call the police or fire department, or whether to leave the building, or to merely return quietly to their seats.

People construct explanations that focus on disorder, which they perceive exists when they cannot explain a situation in terms of their customary stock of knowledge. In making sense of one another's acts, people ordinarily rely on their conceptions of typicality, probability, causality, means-ends relationships, normative requirements, and substantive congruency. In role making, for example, the stock of knowledge enables people to know what is expected of them and how others will respond to their conduct. In offering accounts and disclaimers, the stock of knowledge guides the selection of a disclaimer or a particular account. Social disorder exists when the usual processes of motive talk, accounting, and disclaiming cannot sufficiently restore routine—when people persist in behaving in an undesirable way, for example, despite being repeatedly called to account for their conduct, or when they continue to act in ways that are unlikely to reach their stated goals.

Social disorder is a construction of reality, a belief that things are—for some reason—not working as they should. People perceive that something is amiss in social relations. A married couple, for example, may find themselves quarreling so much that the arguments themselves become a concern to others and to themselves. The frequent quarrels move from some threshold range of acceptable normality to becoming strange in several different ways—as atypical for this couple, for example, considering their past history of marital adjustment; as becoming too harmful to their children; or as improbable in light of recent accomplishments and successes. On whatever grounds a perception of disorder is based, the effect of that perception is to impel a search for an explanation—for some convincing statement of how this problem arose and what might remedy the situation.

Quasi theorizing is a process that people use to construct such explanations.[19] This explanatory process runs counter to commonsense notions about how we find explanations. Ordinarily, people begin with something to explain, and they then seek a plausible account of potential causes. In quasi-theorizing, however, people will identify a cause before the effect, and then construct the reality of the latter in terms of the former. In other words, they construct a set of conditions to match the cause they have decided on, rather than finding a cause that can account for the conditions that they actually observe.

Let's reconsider the case of the quarreling couple. At a certain point in their relationship, they realize that they are arguing too much, that they are unhappy with so much arguing, and that they ought to do something to fix things. Having arrived at the point where they define their level of arguing as problematic, they construct an explanation. That explanatory process occurs in a series of steps. First, they agree on a solution to their problem, like "We have to learn to communicate better." This statement becomes a tentative basis on which to construct the reality of their problem. If the other agrees, perhaps saying, "You're right, because sometimes I don't think you understand what I'm about," a quasi theory of communication is emerging to explain their arguing.

In the next phase of the process, the problem is now perceived to reflect the solution of communication issues on which they have decided to agree. In developing the quasi-theory citing communication, the couple now state that their disagreements are really problems of communication and understanding, that the issues that they fight about—money, sex, lifestyle, and so on—are really superficial. They now address the problem as learning to understand one another's views. In doing so, their points of agreement will outweigh the few topics on which they still disagree. At some point in their discussion, they will start to invoke generalizations about how important effective communication is in human affairs: "Failures of communication cause the fights," they may say, thus effectively classifying their particular case under this more general rule.

At this point, the couple can buttress their explanation in two additional ways. First, the couple will rewrite their history of fights, reinterpreting them in the light of their new insight about communication problems. They will reinterpret the past and find examples of other arguments in which they thought they understood one another's points of view, but, in retrospect, now decide that they did not. Second, they will introduce other values and beliefs to support their new explanation. They may agree, for example, that since they have stayed together despite their fighting, they must really agree that they really belong together, and that their communication problem is just temporary. The situation of the married couple is transformed from an undesirable and disorderly condition of too many arguments into one of unnecessary fights caused by a failure to communicate. The quasi theory reinvents the disorder in order to have the newly chosen cause shape the reality.

Paradoxically, the focus on explaining social disorder found in such forms of talk as quasi-theorizing helps sustain a sense of social order. These problematic situations give new life to important parts of the social stock of knowledge. Such talk affords an opportunity for exercising standards of social order, for applying familiar aphorisms that can once again be proven "correct" and for affirming important beliefs and values. Implementing distinctions between right and wrong, the typical and the atypical, the desirable and the undesirable preserves them. We can argue that occasional failures in social order play a positive role in its maintenance by affording opportunities for reaffirming values that sustain order.[20]

Quasi theories, along with disclaimers, accounts, and other aligning actions that we discussed in the previous chapter, are all important means whereby the members of a society reaffirm and preserve their culture. When people explain disorder, give accounts, or use disclaimers, they attend to and reaffirm important cultural objects. For example, the value placed on honesty is reaffirmed by an attempt to explain why a child is persistently dishonest; likewise, an excuse or apology for dishonesty calls attention to the significance of honesty. When people verbalize their values through aligning actions, they act toward their values as objects and thus bring them to life, even in circumstances where conduct violates them. As a result, these objects continue to form part of the landscape—part of what people notice, attend to, feel they must respect, and take into account in their conduct.

The social construction of social order depends on this continual reaffirmation of culture. Resolving disorder with affirmations preserves social order. Humans seem to want not only the sense that they can predict one another's conduct, but also the sense that the world is a more or less familiar and stable place. To construct social reality, therefore, they must continually reaffirm culture.

Social Problems

Talk about disorder and problems transcends day-to-day situations. We also construct social reality through discourse about societal problems. We may define a social problem as a collective object of concern; a condition that pertains to society as a whole or to important parts of it, something that we believe is undesirable and changeable. The collective construction of reality that moral entrepreneurs offer labels some condition—such as divorce, crime, homelessness, or child abuse—as a serious problem worthy of serious attention by government officials, the media, and the public. How we define specific conditions as social problems changes over time. Various social groups tend to demand and get a great deal of attention for a particular problem for a period of time before the public focus shifts to some other problem.[21]

Collective definitions of social problems are not objective responses to objective social conditions. For example, problems are "discovered" from time to time and moral panics ensue. Barry Glassner, in a book called *The Culture of Fear,* noted that Americans tend to be afraid of the wrong social problems—that we overestimate the dangers we face from some phenomena and end up having unrealistic fears, while we neglect more realistic problems and threats.[22] He noted that road rage suddenly became a widely perceived social problem despite statistics indicating that road rage incidents are not occurring on a wide scale. Recently, America was witness to fears of tainted food products, in which a numerically small number of incidents of *Escherichia coli* contaminations in one town led to a nationwide withdrawal of that food product. Contaminated spinach in a small town in Arkansas can lead people in Maine to refuse to consume spinach. Two shark attacks in Florida or California can produce widespread fear of becoming shark bait the next time someone swims in the ocean anywhere on the East or West coasts. As attention to one problem diminishes, another problem emerges to take its place. For example, fear of children on drugs seems to be perpetual, however the specific type of drug that is feared can also change over time. For a period, children were "sniffing glue." Now drug store chains forbid large-scale purchases of certain over-the-counter cold drugs, like Robitussin, because these can be transformed into a chemical mix that kids use to get high.

None of this denies the reality of many social problems. Poverty, environmental decay, homelessness, and child abuse are not figments of the collective imagination. However, social conditions are subject to many layers of definition and interpretation by moral entrepreneurs. Problem definitions are matters of intense social controversy. Many view homosexuality as a moral failing and a sin. Many others see homosexuality as an involuntary biological orientation that is not a moral choice. The subject of legalizing gay marriage has been a hot button issue for several years. A few American states have legalized gay marriage while the residents of other American states have refused to do so. Proposition 8 was a ballot proposition that passed in California in 2008. This proposition stated that only marriage between a man and a woman is valid and recognized in California. Opponents labeled this proposition as "Proposition Hate" and decried the passage of this proposition as an oppressive strike against human freedom. There is no middle ground in deciding (in proponents' minds) whether gay marriage is "okay," whether anyone has the right to even judge the "okayness" of homosexuality, or whether supporting this right is to endorse homosexuality, as opposed to allowing two consenting adults of the same sex to have the legal protections of marriage. Many people work to absolutely fix a particular take on this issue in the public mind. Whatever perspective one takes and acts on is significant. For example, many observers think that opposition to attempts to legalize gay marriage helped swing the 2004 election to former President George W. Bush.

Clearly, social problems are a focus of attention and action in several ways. Intellectuals and scientists theorize about them and conduct research. Government agencies are legislated into existence in order to address them. Social problems become important political symbols, usually lending themselves to diverse uses in the arena of political debate. At times, social problems take on a nearly universal symbolic value, appearing almost everywhere in society. For example, the need to act to help children is a universal statement of symbolic value. Whether the object is the environment, child abuse, or homelessness, the object is a ubiquitous social presence. News media are filled with statements about global warming and different proposals to wage war on it. Political debate focuses on the urgent need for action to deal with problems, and charges of inaction or overreaction fly back and forth. Advertisers promote "going green" and manufacturers put environmentally friendly stickers on their products.

Social problems come into existence when claims makers and moral entrepreneurs are successful in promoting their view that a particular social condition is a problem. They act to focus public attention on a condition by publicizing the issue through books, speeches, or television appearances, promoting legislation to deal with it, raising funds to support organizations that emphasize the importance of solving the problem. They do research to find solutions, or engage in collective actions, such as "Take Back the Night" marches by women's groups, "Black History Month," and various "Walks" to raise money for medical problems. Claims makers rely heavily on mass media, seeking out sympathetic reporters who they hope will write supportive stories. They stuff the blogosphere with commentaries; they post videos on Youtube and provide up-to-the-minute updates on Facebook. They also stage events that will be reported on television news, for example, using flash mobs or engaging in spectacle protests, such as those used by the satiric Internet site "The Truth Campaign" (*www.thetruth.com/*). Representatives of these moral entrepreneurs will appear on television, radio, Internet chats and talk shows. It is an open question whether a social problem is legitimate in U.S. society until the media grant it their seal of approval.[23] For example, the "War on Drugs" that the U.S. government wages relies heavily on media coverage of the drug menace—of efforts to rid neighborhoods of "crack houses" or meth labs, and of fighting against "medical marijuana."

Sometimes collective efforts to define social problems focus on the basic institutions of a society; alleging, for example, that poverty exists because an exploitative capitalist class benefits from perpetuating poverty and keeping wages low. More typically, however, people reject claims that the causes of social problems can be attributed to basic social institutions. Instead, they prefer to focus on more superficial aspects of underlying conditions, and to ignore the possibility that inherent faults of the social order are responsible for the problem. Rather than perceive poverty as a basic feature of the operation of the social system, the perception becomes that poverty is attributable to people not being motivated to take advantage of societal opportunities or being victims of a poor educational system. Of course, either view is a product of a particular kind of moral entrepreneurship.

Although social problems often focus on societal failings that generate considerable controversy, they also, and somewhat paradoxically, offer a basis for consensus on what society should ideally be. To agree that child abuse is evil and must be eliminated is also an admission that society is not all that it could be. This statement also specifies what a good society should be. That good society represents an idealization of social order, a collective vision of the kind of society we should seek. Social problems thus provide at least the potential for unifying diverse interests, ideas, and aspirations.

Social problems usually involve people agreeing more about end goals than means of attaining those goals. People see eye to eye on protecting the environment and ending homelessness. Exactly what to do, however, to achieve those goals—such as whether to raise taxes—causes endless disagreement. When people disagree on how to solve a problem, each person is free to identify his or her conduct as a potential solution. Some consumers can point proudly to their hybrid gas-electric cars, while others can take pride in recycling their goods.

Widespread discourse about social problems contributes in one additional way to conceiving of society as orderly and predictable. The conditions around which conceptions of social problems are built—drugs, crime, violence, urban decay, pollution, homelessness, and the like—remind us all that the world is an uncertain and sometimes hostile place, and that people have a limited capacity to mold their physical and social environment. Such conditions threaten to undermine the human sense of purpose, control, and meaning. The inherent optimism of social problem definitions—the belief that we can find solutions—reaffirms faith in human control. We treat crime and pollution as problems and organize actions against them, not only because they are objectively harmful, but also because our strategies of control and solution help to preserve a belief in human mastery over the world.

Creating and Joining Social Movements

Our final topic in examining the coordination of social activity is the social movement.[24] A *social movement* is a collective effort to change a part of society or to resist some changes that others might seek. Whatever their goals, ideologies, organizational form, or methods, social movements are oriented toward social change. They seek to restructure society, to alter its values, beliefs, practices, and modes of organization. Not only do social movements thus participate in the coordination of social activities; by their visible presence, they also shape the social construction of reality.

An understanding of the process by which people become attached to social movements is helpful in understanding the link between the social order that movements construct and the people who participate in them. Sociologists have examined this process in a variety of ways, including studies of those who become members of fringe religious movements. Joining social movements can be a function of finding others who share a similar orientation to solving a problem. However, membership in social movements can run the gamut between committing to social movement that comes to control identity and proposes very unconventional beliefs, versus social movements that involve dispersed people who will never met except in a virtual world. We shall examine each extreme as an example of coordinating action toward a particular end.

Why do people develop beliefs and engage in behaviors that others regard as bizarre, foolish, insane, or just plain tragic? What attracts people to groups whose ideas are so at odds with what most people think? How are people able to maintain such beliefs? How can people go to the extreme of suicide in defense of a group or in pursuit of its goals? Their commitment to extremity is also a commitment to coordinated action and a distinct form of social order.

There are many extreme groups and social movements, from those favoring racial or ethnic supremacy, to those that believe they are vampires, to those that have what many argue are odd religious beliefs. Of course, the perception of how extreme or insane a group is depends on labeling and moral entrepreneurship. Many adherents, for example, consider Scientology a religion as legitimate as any other. Others view Scientologists as crazy, based on Scientology's beliefs about aliens, thetans, and odd outbursts by famous members, such as actor Tom Cruise. As a label, "bizarre" is in the eyes of the beholder.

In a classic study, John Lofland and Rodney Stark studied, in its earliest form, a religious group now known as the Unification Church (the so-called "Moonies" named after their leader, the Reverend Sun Yung Moon).[25] At one point, the Moonies held a mass wedding of thousands in Madison Square Garden. Lofland and Stark's study offers a classic approach to explaining why people join extreme social movements. The two researchers proposed a general explanation of how conversion to such quasi-religious movements occurs. "For conversion, a person must experience, within a religious problem-solving perspective, enduring, acutely felt tensions that lead to defining her/him as a religious seeker; the person must encounter the cult at a turning point in his or her life; within the cult an affective bond must form (or preexist) and any extra cult attachments must be neutralized; and finally he/she must be exposed to intensive interaction to become a "deployable agent.""

People are motivated to join these religious cults by enduring problems or tensions in their personal lives. However, just feeling lost, anxious, or unhappy is not enough. The person must also define these tensions within a religious context and come to regard himself or herself as a religious seeker, someone who might find solace by joining a religious group. Further, the person must encounter the group at a turning point—that is, at some point of extreme tension or "hitting bottom" such that the person feels something must be done. If these conditions are met, then the following happens: the formation of a social bond within the movement, the neutralization of ties to family and friends who might oppose the person's membership, and intensive interaction within the group will convert the person to full membership. The individual will then believe and act as a member of the group.

Lofland and Stark's analysis of the process of becoming a "Moonie" provides a plausible explanation of conversion to cult membership. It suggests that when an individual cannot find a sense of meaning and a feeling of "belonging" in more mundane and widely accepted religious groups, the resulting "tensions" will motivate him or her to look elsewhere. If the person encounters a cult at a period of extreme tension and forms bonds with its members, then the stage is set for conversion to the cult and its perspective. That perspective will then create a very strong and compelling social order for the person, who has now found a new society to call home.

A theoretical explanation for joining an extreme religious cult may not serve well for understanding why people join racist, occult, or other religious movements. What is clear is that some process of an affective bond and self-identification occurs and the reflected self the person sees while with that organization motivates their affiliation. They have found others like themselves who see the world in their terms and orient themselves to problems in ways they favor. They can coordinate their action in a social movement with people that are rebelling against authority, that see threats from other races, or that see themselves as existing on a higher spiritual plane than others. That affiliation enables them to join a group of like-minded others with whom they can interact in the physical world and take joint action toward whatever is the object of their interests.

Social movements like the above form in order to advance particular lifestyle goals and agendas. They favor collective action and interaction with one another through sets of ritual practices, like religious or occult rites. Alternatively, some social movements operate on a very loose and less bounded basis, including resisting efforts to be boxed in by convention and perceived censorship. Such groups are now proliferating on the Internet, as is evident in Web sites that are dedicated to offering anonymous opinions through "freedom of speech." A social movement that is evident here is in a desire to express embarrassing or vitally held opinions without fear of sanction from people that the person knows. The groups share in guilty knowledge and those admissions and vow to protect anonymity at all costs. The coordinated action here is in advancing a complete freedom in sharing information without the accountability of excusing the expressed views to conform to convention.

As an example, consider these three popular Web sites: www.*4chan.com;* www.*fmylife.com;* and www.*textsfromlastnight.com.* These Web sites offer participants a chance to provide controversial opinions, embarrassing stories, and sexual adventures anonymously. The Web site *4chan* features different topics in which posters provide their true opinions on a range of controversial topics, from weapons and racial issues to sexual fetishes. *Fmylife* is a Web site in which people offer stories of personal mishaps and other posters rate whether the mishap is deserved or just unlucky. *Textsfromlastnight* is a collection of posted text messages that usually describe sexual desires or acts of drunkenness that were texted to friends while the texter was completely inebriated.

While people reading the posts on these Web sites can comment on the posted stories and opinions, all of the accounts are anonymous and the identities of the actual posters are unknown to acquaintances, friends, or families of the posters. These Internet groups thus constitute a community of anonymous strangers who have the common goal of wanting to preserve privacy and freedom of speech without worrying about in-person retaliation for their communications. They want to share discrediting views in concert with an appreciative audience without consequences. This goal culminates in a collective product of the constructed Web sites and their accompanying rules. The result is a social movement of strangers that are brought together by their desire to avoid identification while interacting with one another.

Many view the Internet community as a whole as a social movement oriented around freedom of information. Apart from those who seek to use the Internet to exploit children or to carry out cons, many people celebrate the Internet's unprecedented provision of freedom of access to information and behaviors that were previously unavailable or risky to attain in person. For example, people who might have wished to view pornography in the past might have had to visibly purchase pornography in a public place. Now, people can view or purchase pornography in private, without social shaming working against their interests. The availability of pornography, for example, in secrecy, may be a good or bad thing, but what is sociologically significant about that availability is that it is a result of coordinated actions by many strangers to make that material available either freely or for profit. Coordinated actions by strangers have produced a world where such information is available at people's fingertips. That Internet world has its own social order and rules, chief among them being anonymity and resisting regulation. Social movements can now work to produce coordinated actions and social order in the physical world as well as increasingly in the virtual ones.

Endnotes

1. Lee Ross, "The Intuitive Psychologist and His Shortcomings: Distortions in the Attribution Process," in *Advances in Experimental Social Psychology,* vol. 10, ed. L. Berkowitz (New York: Academic Press, 1977), pp. 173–220. See also Richard Nisbett and Lee Ross, *The Person and the Situation* (Philadelphia: University of Pennsylvania Press, 1991).

2. Harold Garfinkel, *Studies in Ethnomethodology* (Englewood Cliffs, NJ: Prentice-Hall, 1967). See also Hugh Mehan and Houston Wood, *The Reality of Ethnomethodology* (New York: Wiley Interscience, 1975).

3. This analytic description comes from Stephen Pfohl, *Images of Deviance and Social Control* (New York: Basic Books, 1985), pp. 292–293.

4. See Émile Durkheim, *The Rules of the Sociological Method,* ed. Steven Lukes and translated by W.D. Halls (New York: Free Press, 1982).

5. See Herbert Blumer, *Symbolic Interactionism: Perspective and Method* (Englewood Cliffs, NJ: Prentice-Hall, 1969), p. 17.

6. See Robert B. Cialdini and Noah J. Goldstein, "Social Influence: Compliance and Conformity," *Annual Review of Psychology* 55 (2004): 591–621.

7. Thomas J. Scheff, *Microsociology: Discourse, Emotion, and Social Structure* (Chicago: University of Chicago Press, 1990).

8. Blumer, *Symbolic Interactionism,* p. 18 (Note 5).

9. George Simmel, *The Sociology of Georg Simmel* (New York: Free Press, 1950), p. 313.

10. Anselm L. Strauss, D. Erlich, R. Bucher, and M. Sabshin, "The Hospital as a Negotiated Order," in *The Hospital in Modern Society,* ed. Eliot Friedson (New York: Free Press, 1963), pp. 147–169. Strauss, *Negotiations* (San Francisco: Jossey Bass, 1978) provides a major extension of the concept of negotiation.

11. Peter M. Hall, "A Symbolic Interactionist Analysis of Politics," *Sociological Inquiry* 42 (1–2) (1972): 35–75.

12. Peter M. Hall and Dee Spencer-Hall, "The Social Conditions of the Negotiated Order," *Urban Life* 11 (October 1982): 328–349.

13. This discussion is paraphrased from Hallett, Tim, David Shulman and Gary Alan Fine, "Peopling Institutions: The Promise of Classic Symbolic Interactionism for an Inhabited Institutionalism," in *The Oxford Handbook of Sociology and Organization Studies: Classical Foundations,* ed. Paul S. Adler, Chapter 22, (Oxford: Oxford University Press, 2009), pp. 486–509.

14. See Howard S. Becker, *Outsiders: Studies in the Sociology of Deviance,* Revised Edition (New York: Free Press, 1973) and ed. Becker *The Other Side: Perspectives on Deviance* (New York: Free Press, 1964).

15. For essays dealing with this topic, see *Social Theory and the Politics of Identity*, ed. Craig Calhoun (Oxford: Blackwell, 1994). See also John P. Hewitt, "Self, Role, and Discourse," in *Self, Collective Behavior and Society: Essays Honoring the Contributions of Ralph H. Turner,* ed. Gerald Platt and Chad Gordon (New Haven, CT: Jai Press, 1994), pp. 155–173.

16. For an analysis of this form of talk about the self, see John P. Hewitt, *Dilemmas of the American Self* (Philadelphia: Temple University Press, 1989).

17. For an analysis of the process of memorializing, see Stanford W. Gregory, Jr. and Jerry M. Lewis, "Symbols of Collective Memory: The Social Process of Memorializing May 4, 1970, at Kent State University," *Symbolic Interaction* 11 (1988): 213–233. For an analysis of the creation of a major political character, see Barry Schwartz, *George Washington: The Making of an American Symbol* (New York: Free Press, 1987).

18. See Fred Davis, "Decade Labeling: The Play of Collective Memory and the Narrative Plot," *Symbolic Interaction* 7 (1984): 15–24.

19. See John P. Hewitt and Peter M. Hall, "Social Problems, Problematic Situations, and Quasi-Theories," *The American Sociological Review* 38 (June 1973): 67–74; and Hall and Hewitt, "The Quasi-Theory of Communication and the Management of Dissent," *Social Problems* 18 (Summer 1970): 17–27.

20. This discussion bears a family resemblance to the classic position of Emile Durkheim that crime and its punishment arouse collective sentiments and thereby contributes to social order. See Emile Durkheim, *The Rules of Sociological Method,* 8th ed., ed. and translated G. Catlin, S. Solovay, and J. Mueller (New York: Free Press, 1964).

21. For a useful collection of studies of the construction of social problems, see *Images of Issues: Typifying Contemporary Social Problems,* 2nd ed., ed. Joel Best (New York: Aldine de Gruyter, 1995).

22. Barry Glassner, *The Culture of Fear: Why Americans are Afraid of the Wrong Things.* (New York: Basic Books, 1999).

23. For the classic formulation of social problems theory, see Malcolm Spector and John I. Kitsuse, *Constructing Social Problems,* Revised Edition (New York: Aldine de Gruyter, 1987). For an excellent review of social problems theory and research, see Joel Best, "Social Problems," in *Handbook of Symbolic Interaction,* ed. Larry T. Reynolds and Nancy J. Herman-Kinney (Walnut Creek, CA: Alta Mira, 2003), pp. 981–996.

24. For an analysis of social movements, see Ralph H. Turner and Lewis M. Killian, *Collective Behavior,* 3rd ed. (Englewood Cliffs, NJ: Prentice-Hall, 1987), Part 4.

25. John Lofland and Rodney Stark, "Becoming a World-Saver: A Theory of Religious Conversion," *American Sociological Review* 30 (1965): 862.

CHAPTER

6

Applications of the Symbolic Interactionist Perspective

What value does symbolic interactionism have in thinking about contemporary society? Having described this approach throughout this book, we now want to summarize some important benefits symbolic interactionism offers as a lens onto the world and to present some illustrative applications. We begin by reviewing some key aspects of the symbolic interactionist approach.

First, symbolic interactionism embraces the complexity of our social world, by avoiding depicting diverse human behaviors using narrow caricatures. Human beings are not just biological creatures with a fixed set of behavioral capabilities and a limited number of instructive instincts. People must learn more than a finite repertoire of conduct and they must also cope with a changing natural environment. We live in a cultural world that is also a human creation. We live amidst complexities of meaning and social organization, and they require us to rely on our capacity to interpret and use symbols. Although we must rely on habit for many of our everyday actions, if we are to act successfully in the world, we must also interpret and name events that confront us. We must recognize an insult or praise in order to decide how to respond; we pursue ambitions by naming our goals and continually reminding ourselves of those aims. Human beings are, in short, required to interpret the world in order to act.

The symbolic interactionist perspective orients us to a world of symbolic communications and contrasting definitions of reality. Human beings are intensely social creatures that create a complex symbolic world that we all inhabit together. We learn about that complex, abstract, and often distant or invisible world, including a host of names for material and abstract objects that we act upon and which act upon us. Symbolic communication and symbols articulate a complex physical world and also an abstract, and therefore, "unseen" material world.

Our intensive sociality has two consequences that bear significantly on how we understand the world. First, the stock of knowledge a society accumulates is constrained by how individual members know their world. An individual's knowledge depends on how social knowledge in any given society is distributed. Second, human sociality and socially created knowledge open up the possibility of discovering ways that our interactions both constrain and enable what we know and can be.

As an example, this book identifies several ways that people come to "know" the world, which inevitably incline us to notice some things and fail to see others. We have identified biases that persuade us to think that we know the world accurately when we do not. As an illustration, if we collectively "know" that people either succeed or fail in life according to their abilities and their willingness to work hard, then we buy into a meritocratic ideal and perceive people that fail to achieve important goals as lazy. Within this framing, we probably fail to notice that real obstacles exist that make success more difficult for some people than for others—we all do not start off in life with a pole position. This bias occurs because we have oriented ourselves to use individual dispositions for explanations, and we attend to a lesser degree to situational influences. Alternatively, if we "know" that people commit crimes because they lack legitimate alternative routes for economic gain, then we may ignore that some people want to commit crimes because they find the opportunities and excitements of crime to be more rewarding than those that are available to law-abiding citizens. Our everyday, shared knowledge of the social world is a basis for both blindness and insights into the world.

This important interactionist lesson is not to underestimate the extent to which "knowledge" of the social world also simultaneously represents some form of "ignorance." We must recognize the degree to which particular social classes, professions, or organizations exert unseen power on our thoughts by shaping the language that we use to grasp our sense of selves and the social world in which we live. As discussed in the chapter on social order, these forms of "power" are far subtler than the exercise of brute force. We are very conscious of events such as being forcefully drafted into military service or of police officers yelling at protesting crowds to disperse. However, we are less aware of the implications of "knowing" that women are "emotional" or that childcare is a woman's "natural" vocation or that "boys don't cry." These more diffused influences constrain us in far less obvious ways.

Human beings are capable of "knowing" their world as one where they may be deceived. They can make knowledge problematic and ask whether what they take for granted ought to be reconsidered. Put another way, we human beings can think about ourselves as the potential victims of our own assumptions, including that knowledge itself can be suspect when others want us to think in particular ways in order to further their own interests. This reflective quality is a hallmark of the symbolic interactionist approach.

Our grasp of social problems, for example, is always formulated relative to ideas, beliefs, and other forms of knowledge that we think are secure and can take for granted. Contemporary Americans, for example, use the term "alcoholism" to describe a problematic form of behavior as a disease. This disease occurs in "victims" who find a compulsion to drink alcohol to excess beyond their control, frequently with destructive consequences for the individual and for those around him or her. Embedded in the term *alcoholism* is a more complex set of attitudes toward the "alcoholic," attitudes that we may not fully realize are there when we use the term, even though they dispose us to act toward that person in specific ways. For example, this term inclines us to look for "treatment" and to apply to this "disease" the same assumptions that we might apply to any disease—namely, what steps can be taken to control it, if not to cure it?

We also are more empathetic to someone with an "alcoholism" label, and become more likely to perceive that the alcoholic is a victim rather than a person who makes a conscious choice to drink, no matter what the consequences. Once we learn and routinely use a set of terms to describe the world, those words act like an instruction manual that orient us to act in particular ways to the objects they denote and the forms of action that those objects invite.

Importantly, the labels that we use for the objects in our environment do not arise out of a collective and democratic process in which everybody participates equally. We do not use "alcoholism" because this term more or less spontaneously emerged out of various human efforts to match a perceived problem with a name and an interpretation. Instead, viewing excessive consumption of alcohol as a "disease" occurred because a variety of people, including physicians, convinced us that alcoholism is a disease. Medicine, with its particular conceptions of disease and cure, is one general way of "knowing" the world. We could have chosen alternative framings of uncontrollable urges to drink, such as drinking alcohol is a sin attributable to spiritual weakness or that this act is one of free will and marks a conscious decision to pursue self-indulgence.

In the course of the last century, medical practitioners and their allies have employed a perspective sociologists have termed the "medicalization of deviance" to frame a wider variety of phenomena than issues of bodily health. They have "medicalized" a variety of individual and social problems, including alcoholism, drug use, obesity, attention-deficit disorder, and many other behavioral difficulties. As these examples suggest, what people "know" is influenced by people and organizations that have vested interests in having others perceive the world in particular ways. The medical establishment has power over us because people regard their authority as dominant. Likewise, psychologists and psychiatrists exercise power over us because we learn to think of our behavior using the language they provide. People worry about their self-esteem or pursue self-actualization because they "learn" from psychologists that these are real and important phenomena. Being aware of labeling is an important contribution to take from symbolic interactionism.

Most dramatically of all, symbols give rise to consciousness of self by making it possible for human beings to become objects of their own experience and action. *Dramaturgy,* for example, is an expression of the apex of self-consciousness in describing the many actions people will take to shape the perceptions that others will have of them. The concept of the individual human being that George Herbert Mead developed is distinctive in portraying both the tension and the fine balance between the individual and the social world. On the one hand, this view of the person makes the self a product of the social order. Mead explains the emergence of individual self-consciousness as a product of membership and participation in the social world. We have consciousness of self because we are born into the stream of social life and come to share its names and knowledge and to apply them to ourselves. We learn to see ourselves as others see us, and we do so by adopting the language and the organized social perspectives made available in the social world around us. On the other hand, symbolic interactionism also views the self as a social force in its own right, which can take steps through, for example, dramaturgical actions, to alter its social conditions.

Socialization endows the individual with the capacity to cooperate in social acts with others. Yet, people are not automatons that unfailingly reproduce the meanings and actions that they have been taught. Joint actions—handshakes, cocktail parties, social movements, wars, and so on—exist because individual actors who share a conception of what they are doing come together and assemble their individual contributions into a social whole. To have a self, therefore, is not merely to be a thoroughly programmed agent of society, a "norm-driven robot." To have a self, just as importantly, also means to be one who chooses, who decides, who exerts control over his or her own conduct and that of others.

Individual actors also recognize and act in pursuit of their self-interest and conceive of themselves in opposition to the social world. The self is something we create and sustain jointly with others, and in that sense its "locus" is not strictly speaking within the body or brain, but in the social world that surrounds, nourishes, and often challenges us. The influence that the surrounding social world has on us depends on how we imagine it. When we engage in role taking in an effort to form our conduct, we respond to our imaginations of others, and our interpretations of their words and deeds. People respond to problems and opportunities that they can see and those that they cannot see and can only imagine. Thus, a spoken threat or insult from another human being can get our backs up, but so can an imagined slight that we did not hear but that we imagine that someone thought. The smell of fresh-baked cookies stimulates hunger. An athlete might train hard because the imagined future cheers of fans at next season's high school games motivates him or her. We throw ourselves into concrete tasks like cooking or writing books, as well as dedicating ourselves to more abstract tasks like "loving" or our "duty."

Moreover, individuals experience problematic situations and initiate knowing and problem solving. Human conduct, including efforts to confront and overcome problematic situations, is a thoroughly social affair because of shared assumptions and perspectives, shared knowledge, and some form of social coordination (whether cooperative, competitive, or conflicting). Yet, this intensely social and problem-solving conduct ultimately rests on what transpires *within* the single individual as much as on what transpires *between* individuals. Through the capacity to rebel, to innovate, to resist social influences, and to apply social knowledge creatively in an effort to solve problems, individuals can make their influence felt on the social world.

Moving Toward Applying Symbolic Interactionism

How does the tradition of symbolic interactionist social psychology seek to make a practical contribution to human affairs? What does this approach offer to those who study it and grasp its view of the social world? Symbolic interactionism proposes a method for the empirical study of social life and a distinct perspective on the social world. This method and perspective are also valuable because they produce specific solutions to social problems, and also because they offer a platform from which each of us can think analytically about our own lives and those of others.

Symbolic interactionists believe that we cannot study the social world from a distance. If we want to examine and understand social life, we must do so closely. The reason why, of course, lies in the interactionist view that conduct depends on meanings. If people form their conduct on the basis of meaning as they interact with one another, then we have to grasp meanings in order to explain why people act as they do. We must discover what is on the minds of people whose conduct we want to scrutinize. Doing so requires us to interact with them, to live cheek by jowl in their worlds, at least for a time, in order to see how and why they define situations, make and take roles, and interpret their worlds as they do.

Symbolic interactionism encourages people to enter and imagine the worlds of those whose lives they would understand. Symbolic interactionism exposes the social origins of the self, the nature of social constraints, and—crucially—how the social order depends on individual actions. In this sense, symbolic interactionism asserts that human beings share a dependence on symbols and a distinctive capacity for selfhood. We can use these shared abilities to transcend social and cultural barriers. So, a first move toward application is to appreciate that symbolic interactionism calls for attending to people's lived experiences—to pursuing insights into how different people interpret the world and under what constraints.

A second principle is that any form of knowledge—everyday, religious, and scientific knowledge—is partial and tentative. In our everyday lives, we act on the basis of what we know about driving cars or raising children, and we believe that we can generally regard that knowledge as sure and certain. To one degree or another, however, we can question that knowledge and learn new ways of behaving. Clearly, the rigor and care with which human beings scrutinize their knowledge, and the standards they use in evaluating that knowledge varies.

Symbolic interactionists believe that the body of knowledge we possess is always changing: Old "truths" are continually being shed as they cease to work and we discover new "truths" as we confront new problems. This transitional status of knowledge heightens the importance symbolic interactionists place on empirical knowledge. We believe that empirical knowledge is invaluable despite our knowing that such knowledge is incomplete. Interactionists believe that some knowledge is better than none, especially if that knowledge results from empirical study of the social world based on verifiable, public methods of inquiry that others could understand and check. Symbolic interactionism yields knowledge of social worlds and social processes that are open to empirical verification and revision. This knowledge provides us with some basis for acting in the world in which we find ourselves and for solving problems, particularly because we focus on the different ways that people can interpret these problems instead of assuming that only one version of the problem is universally applicable and true.

A third principle is that our knowledge of reality shapes that reality. We human beings seek knowledge in order to solve problems and then act on the basis of what we learn. Our actions, in turn, shape or influence the conditions under which we live. Symbolic interactionists believe that the relationship between human beings and their world is one of mutual determination: The environment—social or material—influences and constrains us, but our actions in return also influence or shape the world. If this is so, then in a general sense what we "know" about the world influences the "reality" of that world.

An example can clarify this important idea. One prevalent contemporary view is that public schools are not doing as good a job as Americans would like in educating many children. Standardized test scores are declining, many students do not read at grade level, and competence in science and math is lower than educators and parents want. Experts offer many explanations for this state of affairs and have suggested ways to change it. Some experts emphasize establishing national curriculum standards and holding schools accountable by having students take standardized tests to assess their knowledge. According to this argument, if schools are failing, it is because expectations for students are unclear or too low, and because teachers and principals are not held accountable for those failures.

Whether this view is true or not, this accountability and testing perspective is now established "knowledge" and enshrined in legislation. Curricular standards such as those embodied in "No Child Left Behind," with its subsequent periodic testing regimes have been implemented. What effect does this "knowledge" have in shaping reality? Critics of these educational reforms point out that where laws specify what must be taught to students at various grade levels and in various subjects, new educational consequences have arisen. Schools now spend considerable time and effort documenting how students are meeting standards. Teachers in some states, for example, must justify in writing the connection between any given day's lesson plan and the testing standard. Critics argue that periodic testing also encourages teachers to orient their lessons to the tests their students will take rather than to developing a deeper understanding of subject matter. In other words, teachers will encourage students to do well on standardized tests, but they will not necessarily do a better job teaching their students to understand or use ideas.

If teachers are successful in their efforts, test scores rise, and the "knowledge" that testing promotes accountability, which makes for better education, is "confirmed." However, is teaching a child to perform well on a standardized test an appropriate reality to construct to describe what a good education entails? Is being educated synonymous with scoring well on a timed multiple-choice exam? Further, the school system then becomes organized as per the new standards for accountability, so in effect, the new definition of what being educated means changes the reality of what the school experience is like for children.

This example illustrates that as we create explanations for problems, we provide people with a basis for acting to solve them, and we create new ways of actively interpreting their social worlds. Symbolic interactionists seek to understand the motives that form the basis of why people act, to understand how those motives for acting become powerful enough to influence behavior, *and* to encourage people to better understand their own actions. For symbolic interactionists, the social world is not a reality that is simply "out there," fixed and final. Rather, we must study how that reality is created.

Ultimately, the symbolic interactionist approach to knowledge is a humble one. We recognize that there are different versions of truth and that dogmatic adoption of some versions of the truth gives people blind spots. People do not know everything. Symbolic interactionists acknowledge the need to examine interpretations carefully rather than take reality at face value. Behind particular versions of truth may lurk particular interests and unequal power to pursue them. Sociology promises, stated C. Wright Mills, "an understanding of the intimate realities of ourselves in connection with larger social realities."[1] What the sociological imagination promises, however, is not easily realized. If sociology and social psychology represent potential contributions to advancing human intelligence—and to bettering the human condition—they do so only if we exercise them.

Applications: Total Institutions, Cathedrals of Consumption, and Celebrities

Having provided an introductory background into symbolic interactionist social psychology, we now want to present more comprehensive, concrete applications of those ideas and examine how contemporary researchers apply them in investigating contemporary life. A virtue of symbolic interactionist ideas like the definition of the situation and dramaturgy is how they orient people to notice complexity in individual behaviors and social institutions that they might otherwise overlook. We begin by analyzing how people label actions deviant, construct notions of what crime is, and create social institutions to control conduct.

In Chapter 5, we examined different boundaries that people create when they seek to coordinate their conduct. One important boundary distinguishes between conduct that is thought to uphold social order and conduct that is thought to undermine it. Sociologists have customarily described this boundary by using the terms "deviance" and "deviant behavior."

The sociological category of deviance encompasses a wide variety of conduct. Actions like murder, rape, assault, robbery, drug use, juvenile delinquency, homosexuality, securities fraud, price fixing, prostitution, and mental illness are all lumped into this category. The category of deviance is so inclusive that fine distinctions between kinds of acts can be lost. Both armed robbers and fraudulent securities dealers, for example, break the law and seize other people's valuables for their own use. But their social origins are often different. One uses force or the threat of force; the other uses deception. Some people condemn homosexuality as immoral or sinful, whereas others regard it as an alternative sexual orientation, neither better nor worse than heterosexuality or bisexuality. What possible basis can exist for lumping such diverse types of behavior together?

What makes the prostitute and the schizophrenic alike is neither their behavior nor their motivations, but rather the social treatment they receive at the hands of ordinary people, police, courts, social workers, psychiatrists, and other agents of social control. The symbolic interactionist approach to deviance is embodied in the labeling perspective, a body of research and theory created (in part by symbolic interactionists) beginning in the 1960s. Criticizing existing theories of deviant behavior, labeling theorists sought to emphasize the socially constructed nature of deviance. Howard Becker, a leading proponent of this approach, succinctly summarized its central tenets:

> *Social groups create deviance by making the rules whose infraction constitutes deviance, and by applying those rules to particular people and labeling them as outsiders. From this point of view, deviance is not a quality of the act a person commits, but rather a consequence of the application by others of rules and sanctions to an "offender." The deviant is one to whom that label has successfully been applied; deviant behavior is behavior that people so label.*[2]

Becker's approach sought to remedy some of the defects of the then-dominant theories of deviance. Existing theories treated deviance either as a distinctive quality of the deviant person himself or herself or of the universal vileness of his or her acts. Becker's definition proposed that deviance is a quality or qualities that social agents impute to the person and their actions, using processes of social classification. The successful application of labels creates deviance and those labels are applied differently depending on social context. As is often stated, one person's terrorist is another's freedom fighter.

When confronted by deviant behavior, people think that "something must be done," particularly when people violate formal laws and widely held social norms. Here is where applying the symbolic interactionist perspective starts to make this issue more complex. If deviance is constituted in the social reactions to an act, rather than in some inherent feature of the act, then researchers need to examine why some actions bring about greater reactions than others do. Further, we need to consider what answers people propose for problems based on the definition of the situation that they construct to explain deviant actions. Put practically, many people approach deviant behavior with one predominant frame of explanation. Crime is attributable to poor parenting, or to people being morally flawed or weak spiritually, or to drugs, or because of economic inequality, and so forth. There is an array of explanations for deviance. A symbolic interactionist then asks, what explanations are prevalent and with what social consequences?

Consider the problem as if you were a philanthropist interested in donating a billion dollars to lowering crime rates. Where would you donate your monies? What cause would you identify as the primary problem to address? You might believe that crimes originate in faulty biological impulses of people that ought to be controlled with drugs, so you might donate the money to pharmaceutical companies to develop drugs like Ritalin to control behaviors. You might see crime as a spiritual problem and donate money to faith-based organizations to encourage them to lead people to a more righteous and better path. You might think that a lack of jobs is the problem, so you might support jobs programs for wayward youth. You might think media images promote crime, so you might fund efforts against violent or sexist or homophobic images. You might think self-interest and weak punishments increase crime, so you might donate to politicians and lobbyists to produce legislation that lead to much more severe enforcement and sentencing. The symbolic interactionist examines how moral entrepreneurship operates in assigning culpability and investigates data to make sense of these different propositions.

Symbolic interactionists also attend to the implications of people's labeling of deviance. Deviance is not absolute but relative. We attach different weights to what offends us and in doing so, might not be aware of our blind spots or of contradictions in our judgments. People witness (or themselves engage in) many violations without arousing the feeling that something has to be done. They break the speed limit with impunity, cheat on exams or on their spouses, steal office supplies, lie, and violate many other norms without outrage, remorse, or guilt. Using accounts, people can do bad things and still see themselves as good people. Many students at elite colleges and universities are considered upstanding and the "best and the brightest," yet these students may routinely cheat on exams, break the speed limit, and engage in underage drinking. All of us can probably remember someone we knew in high school whom teachers, parents, and other authority figures thought was a moral paragon, despite this person having a secret life full of transgressions.

Even though some acts, such as physical assault, theft, or taking human life may more universally arouse concern, people may respond to these acts differently, depending on their social context. Not all members of a particular society exhibit the same degree of concern that something ought to be done in response to particular behaviors. Family violence—both child and spouse abuse—is a matter of public concern, but acts (such as the corporal punishment of children or wife beating) that nowadays are condemned in no uncertain terms were once widely tolerated and even supported.

A breach of social order entails a perception that the normal, usual, typical, and routine round of activities in the society is threatened. The issue is not the "reality" of a threat, but rather that one is alleged, whether on the basis of a violation of norms, laws, or the self-interest or power of a particular social group. Any conduct targeted as a breach of order may be placed in the deviance category, provided there is someone who is ready to do so and able to mobilize support for doing so. Mobilizing support is crucial because classifying conduct as deviant is not automatic. People do not always agree with any particular label or its application. Those who supply cocaine and other illegal drugs may see nothing wrong with their activities and insist that people who use legal drugs such as alcohol or tobacco are being hypocritical in making other drugs illegal. Alternatively, those who oppose using illegal drugs argue that society is endangered until we can eradicate that drug use. However, alcohol, tobacco or caffeine addiction or overeating is not consuming an illicit drug, and so does not ring the same alarm bells, despite the toll that partaking in too much of these substances takes.

There is another important point to consider in how symbolic interactionists conceive of deviance: They want to know how people understand and define their experiences. This view is counterintuitive to many traditional ways of understanding deviant behavior, which often emphasize trying to educate people out of deviant actions. For example, many scientific authorities argue that believing in ghosts is irrational and therefore wrong. A symbolic interactionist is less interested in whether ghosts are real or not, and more interested in why a person believes in them and under what circumstances they came to think of ghosts as real. Gillian Bennett has found that belief in ghosts is more frequent among the recently widowed.[3] She argues that believing that a dead family member has visited them is a means of sustaining a loved relationship beyond death. Rather than dismissing this belief as crazy, a better understanding of the definition of the situation improves how we see such a supposedly "irrational" practice. What makes an act or belief sane or insane is not the act itself, but rather how others interpret it. For example, whether a belief in ghosts indicates insanity depends on one's cultural surroundings. To believe seriously in ghosts or leprechauns in a culture where these beings are assumed to exist is to be sane, no matter what members of more skeptical cultures think.

Symbolic interactionists are also wary of being judgmental. For example, people often mock devoted science fiction fans like Trekkies or *Star Wars* aficionados who memorize and obsess over every detail of these stories, even to the point of dressing up in costumes to act as particular characters. "Normal" people mock the extensive dramaturgy of these fans, and tell them, as a skit with William Shatner made famous, that they ought to "get a life." However, if we consider being obsessed with a particular reality more objectively, then we might look at fanatical sports fans with new eyes, as just another variant of the science fiction fan. These sports fanatics memorize statistical accomplishments of professional athletes, and know their sports trivia down to minutiae, such as the batting averages of famous players in the 1970s, or free throw percentages of entire teams. They wear fake uniforms from their favorite teams, act as if they know the "heart" and "character" of particular players, and brag that if only they were the managers, they would know exactly what to do to win championships. College and high school football fans even paint themselves in colors and don odd costumes to attend games. At that point, how different are they, really, from the science fiction fans who they might hold in contempt as being so "odd?" Seen as dramaturgy, both groups qualify for a similar negative label.

Deviance, Socialization, and Total Institutions

People who address us in a babble of incoherent words, or who seem depressed when there is no "reason" to be depressed, disrupt our usual assumptions that we are living in a world where people understand one another and interact in an orderly fashion. We develop a sense that such people will harm themselves or others if they are not isolated and controlled. In such cases, the mentally ill are placed in institutions that are intended to control their behaviors, for their own good, in order to help them recover, or to manage their problematic conduct outside of daily life. When courts convict criminals, we also isolate and control them. Both the mentally ill and prisoners are housed in what are called *total institutions*. A total institution is a social facility where the staff is in complete control of the actions of the institutionalized population.[4] These staff control time and space in these areas, such as what and when people can eat, where they can go, what activities they can engage in, what they can wear, and when they can talk. Staff can even exercise physical control over inmates' bodies. Staff in some circumstances can use force to have people comply with orders, even against their will.

We often think of a definition of the situation or of a role from the perspective of an individual having some autonomy in choosing and enacting roles. Similarly, we may also think of individual identity as a social quality that people can very much choose. However, as we have clarified, there are some limits to individual agency. A total institution engages in what is called *resocialization* and represents an apex of social control over individual identity. The process of resocializing people in total institutions prevents them from being the unique individuals that they used to be—in many cases to the point of no longer even having their old names. Prisons, for example, refer to inmates using numbers, not individual names, and prisoners are made to wear uniform clothing. This process "depersonalizes" people, quarantining them for some amount of time from a heterogeneous society, and formally administering all aspects of their lives, leaving a minimum of individual autonomy. In his study of a total institution, Goffman described a process called "trimming and programming" in which the total institution shapes and codes new subjects into the "administrative machinery of the establishment."

In practice, a total institution has to manage the daily activities of a large number of people, some of them very dangerous or disturbed, within a restricted space. These people live in "batch" conditions and have tightly regimented lives. The total institution describes many different physical settings, but very importantly, signifies a social psychological process of identity transformation. The total institution is society acting to transform the old identity of a person into a new one, or holding the undesirable aspects of an old identity at bay until the period of institutionalization ends.

Total institutions are important to consider because of the vast number of people within them. As of summer 2008, for example, more than 2.3 million Americans were in prisons.[5] Many people also work as staff in total institutions like prison and mental hospitals. What role do they feel that they must take to control their involuntary charges? Another important point is that there are many voluntary total institutions. A total institution involves a process of resocialization that occurs through social organizations that are intended to produce a new type of person, like a "cured" drug addict. Basic military training is an example of a total institution in which the staff has complete control over the time, space, and action of people, but in this case, the total institution may be voluntary and aimed at producing a particular kind of soldier.

FIGURE 6.1   Total Institutions Flowchart

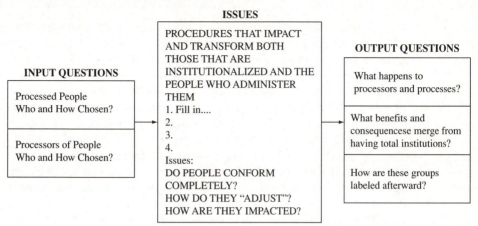

We can now move conceptually to think of a total institution as a matter of orientation and degree. There may be voluntary total institutions that people join, such as the army or drug rehabilitation centers, and involuntary ones, such as jails. Hospitals are a form of a total institution in controlling a patient's identity to act in order to help heal him or her. Brief periods of time in milder total institutions can be meant to be fun, such as in summer camps.

A total institution is an ultimate expression of social influence in taking over a person's identity. As an exercise to further understand this concept, fill out the total institution flowchart above through analyzing an example. Consider a jail, a drug rehabilitation facility, or basic training in the military. Consider how processors and processed people act and how context impacts them. What procedures occur as exercises of control? What outcomes emerge from time spent in a total institution?

People may experience the control of total institutions either as brutal or as a means of bettering their lives. Social scientists may argue that people who have fewer resources are more often exposed to total institutions and thus less likely to be able to pursue their own agency. Analysts also have written that the impacts of having to control people who do not want to be controlled is a psychologically destructive process; people in these roles become more authoritarian in order to fulfill their role obligations.[6]

As a thought experiment, we can also think of some ascribed statuses as being social boundaries that are as powerful as a total institution. A total institution is physically manifest in a locked facility with uniforms, regimented procedures, authority figures, and the people who are subject to that authority. However, there are also ideas that are akin to powerful total institutions, such as complying with notions of gender. Are some such statuses like total institutions in an analogical sense? Notions of beauty, race, and class may operate with tremendous power on people. That power might not be as overtly visible as that of a total institutional facility, but the ability of these less material forces and statuses to control identity and behavior is immense.

Variations on Total Institutions

A prison is an easily recognized total institution on the social landscape. There are formidable concrete barriers, jail cells, and armed guards, all clarifying that people are held against their will, can't escape, and must do what they are told. However, the definition of a total institution—viewed more generically—also characterizes other settings where staff controls the space and actions of people in both overt and subtler ways. Seen more broadly, we should examine how social settings constrain and influence people's behaviors, particularly in some locations where they are unaware of those effects.

We noted earlier in this book that people are profoundly social creatures that live in a new, increasingly complex world of symbolic communications. More and more named objects emerge everyday, and interpersonal interactions now extend well beyond face-to-face contacts into virtual and impersonal worlds of communication. An important force in this symbolic world is the power of the image.

At an individual level, all people work hard to manufacture and manage a personal image. Dramaturgy illustrates this work at both an individual and collective level. Our image making is aimed at persuading others to perceive us according to our wishes. We want to see a desired and idealized self reflected back to us through the affirmations of others. For example, we may want to be perceived as "hard-charging," "sophisticated," "popular," "witty," "iconoclastic," "right for the job," or "in a good relationship." Our images, at the individual level, are a public representation to others. Yet while individual images exist at one level, collective and public images are also pervasive influences on our constructions of self. Corporations, products, nations, media, celebrities, musicians, and other entertainment entities are all groups that illustrate image making on a grand scale. What does image making look like at the institutional level, as a mechanism working through advertising agents, entertainment products, industry groups, and political associations? If we consider the construction of reality as an industry, then we should attend to historian Daniel Boorstin's insight, when he wrote: "The making of the illusions which flood our experiences has become the business of America."[7]

Boorstin argues that images appeal to a facet in the American character that has extravagant expectations. Those expectations are of "what the world holds," of how sparkling and vivid life can be, of being able to achieve purposes easily and solve problems without delay. To keep up with the necessity to manufacture illusions that are more exciting than reality, we use images. A symbolic interactionist can argue that we have a new image-based society, in which large corporations, media, and state agencies work—sometimes at cross-purposes, sometimes together—in order to influence perceptions and to construct reality on a mass scale. The people responsible for this are image makers, whom Robert Jackall and Janice Hirota define as "interpretive experts skilled in the creation and propagation of symbols to persuade mass audiences to some action or belief."[8]

As a brief example, think about some of the products on your local pharmacy's shelves. Conduct a quick mental review of the countless advertisements that warn consumers about the spoiled identities they could have from minor bodily imperfections. For example, we encounter pressures to have idealized physical appearances—whether to avoid going grey, premature baldness, cellulite, excess pounds, wrinkles, and yellow teeth. It is unrealistic to assume that people can avoid all of these mild defects as they age. Yet the power to imagine those situations happening to us, abetted by advertisements, can hook us into consuming products that seduce us into thinking that we can attain the extravagant expectation of holding on to youth's physical benefits forever. We have skin products, pills to lose weight, diet industries, spray-on hair, and, for the hard-core image-seeker, plastic surgeries.

Are we aware of the full range of prefabricated definitions of the situation that present themselves to us in unbidden ways? Moral entrepreneurs may function openly in encouraging us to accept one advocated belief over another, such as choosing to vote for or against a state ballot initiative on medical marijuana or on preserving farmland. However, what about organizations that seek to persuade us but do not openly announce their intentions? How do they act to frame reality to lead us to behave in certain ways, without us thinking too deeply about our actions along the way? What about how retailers design buildings such as malls and casinos in order to encourage people to act in particular ways? Let's consider how such "persuasion entrepreneurs" work to induce behaviors in specific settings in order to encourage us to buy.

Images capture our attention, guide our consumption, and orient our thinking. The danger of images is that despite their having elements of unreality, they still affect our perceptions of what is or could be real. David Shulman's teenage son and his male friends know that the "Axe advertisements" for body cologne are exaggerations. These advertisements show normal appearing men dousing themselves with a scented body spray and then finding themselves attacked sexually by attractive and aroused female models. Though these young men know that this outcome is unlikely, they nonetheless are tempted into purchasing this body spray because that magical promise is implied, and if it is only a little possible, their desire to be impossibly attractive to the opposite sex can be realized. If advertisements are particularly clever, they can seduce us to their siren call.

Assuming the worst implications, we can depict people as puppets dangling on the strings of image-makers who can make their vested political and economic interests our own through clever interpretive framings. Assuming the best implications, we have a new complex world of choice of interpretive frames for events. Well-informed people need to understand this new world in order to make their own interpretive decisions. Writ large, our society is witness to innovative sets of instrumental techniques of image making and a set of image industries—advertising, entertainment, and marketing by colleges and universities, businesses and politics. We have professionals devoted to creating ready-made interpretations and eager throngs to join their ranks. Symbolic interactionists need to assess how people are affected, as individual and collective decision-makers, by this commercial interpretative and image work. How are we susceptible to clever technicians of imagery or particularly convincing advertisements, or the embodied persuasions in the designs of malls or casinos?

Sociologist George Ritzer has written eloquently about what he calls the new means of consumption.[9] In his argument, people now live in modern societies where they are tempted into consumption by being exposed to new constructions of reality that intoxicate them. He coined the term, "cathedrals of consumption" to describe how institutional structures like the Mall of America, themed restaurants, and Las Vegas destination hotels and casinos seduce and influence people into consumption. In his argument:

> [Las Vegas] . . . casinos and hotels are not "real" enchanted settings. There's a phony New Orleans, a phony Paris, a phony Venice. They get people in the doors

by providing huge simulated extravaganzas in an ordered, clean, controlled environment. The starting point for all of these undertakings is the question: How do you draw people in? You do it by creating a structure that overwhelms them, that causes them to say, "This is extraordinary." It is the spectacle that brings consumers back time and again. The people who designed the Mall of America in Minneapolis, or the Las Vegas casinos, or any of the other cathedrals of consumption understand and utilize this same principle, only they do it to take your money. The great advantage of artificial settings over natural ones is their controllability. If you want to use people's surroundings to control them, your settings have to be unnatural. The sad thing is that, in our society, increasing numbers of people seem more attracted to these simulated settings than to natural settings.[10]

Let's link the argument about extravagant expectations to Ritzer's points about cathedrals of consumption. People seem to want a reality that is better than the actual authentic reality that they can have, and they are content to ignore the difference. We could actually go to a jungle or go to Disney's Animal Kingdom. The old Times Square in New York City was seedy and not full of branded megastores, but disorder and seediness sell poorly compared to the cleanliness, orderliness, predictability, and sterility of Disney World like settings. We may not want to eat at a real Mexican restaurant such as would be located in a small Mexican town, but we are content with a fantasy-themed Mexican restaurant chain where some bullfighting posters and oversize cowboy hats will suffice.

Some experts now argue that we are in an experience/entertainment economy. The hallmark of this shift is that people no longer consume and buy in rote ways. Now, many people wish to shop and consume in locations that also offer a themed consumption experience, and marketers are doing their utmost to encourage that desire.

Cabela's, for example, is a leading retailer of outdoor products. However, their stores are not just warehouses with racks of their products on display. Instead, according to their Web site, a Cabela's retail outlet promises shoppers an "experience." These stores are: "as much wildlife museums and education centers as retail stores. Cabela's showrooms provide a truly unique shopping experience. True destination stores, Cabela's showrooms offer outdoor enthusiasts and their family an educational and entertaining shopping experience" (www.cabelas.com).

The Apple stores have also marketed themselves as a brand identity that extends into an experience in their retail stores and in consuming their products. Consumers can avail themselves of "genius bars" to learn about Macintosh computers in their stores, which are also designed to embed people within a sleek and chic shopping environment. Apple products, such as the iPod are considered to have innovative design features, and the company received a great footing from their "think different campaign," in which the Apple company implied that users of their products would be similar in nature to the innovative characteristics that famous historical achievers possessed.

In another example, think of changes that might be occurring in urban centers around America, where what some have called "Disneyification" has taken place. Disneyification is viewed as a type of remaking of urban neighborhoods into more sanitized and theme park-like environments. Some oppose Disneyification as a form of urban renewal that dramatically changes the character of a city for the worse and prices poorer people out of that environment. Others see Disneyification as the best means of urban renewal.

Times Square in New York City is cited as a recent example of having been Disney-ified. Once more of a red light district full of strip clubs and X-rated movie theaters, the Disney Company bought a block on Times Square and installed a theater showing the *Lion King* theatrical production. With the help of municipal authorities, more family friendly themed businesses moved in, such as the Madame Tussauds Wax Museum and ESPN-ZONE. The gritty character of Times Square suddenly changed from a rough area to having a plethora of retail "cathedrals of consumption." In a separate example, Carl Hiassen wrote that Disney World in Florida dyed the water color of a local pond because the pond's natural color of muddy brown just didn't meet the public's extravagant expectations that all bodies of water should appear in pretty colors.[11]

Future scholars should pay close attention to this trend around the world. Dubai is at the cutting edge of Disneyification as an attempt to encourage consumption and build their city into an economic empire. The city, which is located in a hot climate, contains a mall that built an indoor ski facility that can accommodate up to 1,500 people. A world famous hotel, the Burj Al Arab, is one of the most opulent hotels in the world, built to overlook the sea in the shape of a giant sail. One of the 10 best restaurants in the world is accessed in the hotel through a faux submarine ride, and there is a giant aquarium set in the middle of the restaurant. The experiences being built here are not based on historical realism—they are a new form of tourism based on artificially manufactured experiential qualities.

Of course, there is nothing wrong with preferring or liking Disneyified versions of the world. However, there is some danger of losing alternatives and variation in consumer choices because Disneyification makes everything everywhere more homogenous. As an example, New York City is home to some of the most varied restaurants in the world, yet some of the longest lines are for chain restaurants like the Olive Garden in Times Square. There is nothing different about the food at the Olive Garden in New York than in any other Olive Garden in another town; these dishes are served in exactly the same standardized way with exactly the same mechanized menu at all the chain's locations. Indeed, the standardization may draw people in, as they feel that they know exactly what to expect and experience in the restaurant. That construction of reality is familiar. Yet, while the Olive Garden chain pushes their authenticity as an Italian restaurant as part of their charm, the full range of Italian cuisine, such as distinctions between Northern and Southern Italian cuisine is lost and regional specialties or exotic versions of this cuisine are abandoned. In New York, one could expect to find that range at a local restaurant. The danger is that an image of generic Italian food will become the reality for what Italian food is, with consumers being none the wiser. We live in a world where a monoculture might emerge of image choices being the only emergent choices, not because of the quality of the product, but because of the success of the symbolic work done to promote one particular variety of the product.

Physical settings in cathedrals of consumption also shape our behaviors in programmatic ways, often without our full realization. Casinos offer good examples of such themed and organized environments. There is a two-part definition for a themed environment.[12] First, a themed environment is a socially constructed, built environment designed to serve as a container for commodified interaction. Second, a themed environment is the product of a cultural process designed to invest the space with symbolic meaning and to convey that meaning in order to induce a range of responses. How people actually consume and are consumed by such environments is important to consider. In taking on that question, we also can analyze the "consumer self"; namely how people seek to meet wants and desires within this constructed market. We can also, if we are feeling particularly ambitious, analyze the consequences of a consumer society, although doing so is beyond this book's scope.

Let's address the casino as a themed environment. In preparation of doing so, first consider how the casino's layout is designed to dictate behavior and consumer identifications with various themes. Note that we are not discussing why people gamble. Just as with many forms of deviant behavior, we can have many theories of why individuals gamble. Some theories view individual gamblers as a form of risk seekers who look for a high in gambling that is absent elsewhere in their lives. There are people who gamble to escape demands and pressures in their lives. Some gamble as entertainment and as a form of companionship. Other individuals—such as those who gamble as a profession—gamble as an "investment opportunity" that will eventually pay off. We can debate individual causes all day long. However, what is of interest here are not individual explanations, but to articulate organizational and social forces in designing the gambling experience and reality. Following the symbolic interactionist view, we ask, under what conditions are people encouraged, influenced, or halted in their attempts to gamble?

A first point to consider in this question is what some call the "servicescape." This term here refers to the setting where the service of gambling is provided, including the setting, dramaturgy, and emotional labor of workers. Anyone who has visited or even seen a picture of casinos in Las Vegas knows that each casino-hotel typically has a theme that is supposed to draw people in with its imagery. However, we need to look more concretely at the construction of the themed environment of the casino, design features that are similar across them, that in many ways help them to function as total institutions. Their physical settings influence behavior.

As anyone who has visited a Las Vegas casino knows, to reach all destinations a visitor must pass through the casino floor. After you check in, you must walk through a casino floor to get to the elevators to your room. If you want to leave your room and go to a pool, you will have to walk through a casino. If you want to eat, all the restaurants and entertainment are directly adjacent to the casino. The casino is omnipresent.

These casino floors have gambling opportunities embedded in designs and spaces approved by psychologists that have identified how people prefer to play their games. Hence table games are visible and prominent, where people—predominantly men—can play in front of a crowd, gaming visibly and collectively as a competitive spectacle. Alternatively, slot machines, which women favor more than men, are often lined up in little enclaves to allow those patrons to play more privately, because they favor the isolation, escapism, and self-absorption that playing slot machines offers. There also are no visible clocks in the casino and no one can tell whether it is day or night; all this contributes to a sense of timelessness, which encourages people to stay longer than they otherwise might. Attractive servers bring free alcohol to gamblers, combining the power of attractiveness with the loss of inhibitions that drinking alcohol contributes. Lastly, in a nod to labeling theory, people are not gambling, they are "gaming."

Slot machines themselves contain masterful influences at getting people to gamble, as they are replete with many psychological inducements. For example, there are bright flashing lights; the immediate reinforcement of small wins; frequent near misses as someone pulls two sevens and then a third wheel comes up blank. We have vivid depictions of all that we could win, and all the ways that we could win, and all the different levels of betting open to us. We have themed machines, so that we can play *Wheel of Fortune* if we like that TV show or we can play on a giant machine with a five-foot handle to pull the wheels. How can we not be seduced into playing?

Should these inducements not be enough, we can join a special club that tracks our points and awards us comps, or free privileges, depending on how much we gamble. We might get to enter a short wait VIP line for a free buffet or get free tickets to a show, all depending on how much we gamble. How these perks make us feel makes them work. That people end up spending much more than these perks actually cost in order to receive them "for free" is not a logical insight that many embrace. Instead, we applaud our own ability to get something for playing and ignore that we have been seduced to gamble on games where the house has a systematic and comprehensive advantage over us that ensures that they will take our money. Do we see the systematic influence of the setting on our behavior or appreciate the cleverness of the design in orienting us to consume? This total institution might be voluntary and far less comprehensive in determining our actions than a prison, but we should not pretend that the setting is free of influence or ignore that casinos manipulate us to buy what they sell.

We also are increasingly susceptible to paying more for image, and to consider image as the major factor in making consumption decisions, rather than, for example, considering the quality of the materials. Paying for a label is pure symbolic interactionism. To paraphrase a Mark Gottdeiner observation regarding themed restaurants, if a $3 hamburger at McDonalds is made from roughly the same quality of meat as a $10 hamburger at the Hard Rock Café, what explains the $7 difference? You are eating $7 worth of theme and atmosphere. The extra profit came from the value that the Hard Rock's image contributed, not the inherent quality of the meat.

Certainly we should feel free to consume as we wish, but we should do so with open eyes, and understand what we are really buying. Increasingly, we are buying an image with our money, such as thinking that a good meal is more of a sure bet at a chain restaurant than at a nonchain restaurant, or that because a celebrity uses a product, we can gain some of their magic by using that product ourselves. Air Jordans may be fine sneakers, and you can mimic Michael Jordan in wearing them if he also wears those sneakers, but you will never play basketball as well as "Mike" just because you bought the same sneakers. Still, that knowledge did not stop people from purchasing those sneakers in stunning numbers.

Other images exist that are not bound to physical structures, but are commodified in the body and in cultural products. Nothing epitomizes extravagant expectations more than celebrities. They are better looking, apparently lead much more glamorous lives than normal people, and they fulfill idealized images. They are also constructions of reality that serve purposes of consumption in many ways. Celebrities fulfill a need that the mass media have to fill space and to occupy our interests. Consider the presence of celebrities on the Web, where Web sites like Perez Hilton and E! Online have mass traffic. *People* magazine is a best-selling publication and many television shows are oriented to covering celebrities. Celebrities are personal brands that consume our free time: We go to movies to see celebrities, read their books, and wear their fashion lines.

Think of younger children who grew up on Pokemon, professional wrestling, Hannah Montana, or on movies like *Batman* or *Transformers*. Our children can consume these celebrities and entertainment products all day. A child can watch Hannah Montana on television, read about her in magazines, listen to her on an iPod, wear her clothing designs, hang her posters on her walls, and drink from a fast food cup with her picture. We live in a society where we can literally consume celebrities and have them be our everyday wallpaper. In doing so, we are consuming and speaking in a language of image, particularly in a language of extravagant expectations.

Nothing is wrong with liking celebrities as a value judgment. However, there are practical consequences to having the latest celebrity news or product be foremost on our minds: In thinking about them all the time, we are not thinking about other things. Shulman often asks his students if they can name 50 celebrities from the world of acting, music, and sports. Everyone always raises his or her hands. Shulman then asks them if they can name 50 United States senators, living or dead. No one raises his or her hands, including Shulman. Arguably, celebrities are more important in the daily consciousness and experiences of people who enjoy thinking about celebrities and their lives. However, senators and other political figures have more influence on the societal situations that characterize our lives, in terms of taxes, declaring wars, and the quality of healthcare and so forth.

An important danger of image is that we can come to prefer the simple, passive consumption of image more than doing the hard work of attending to detailed information. Why read long news stories when we can get witty summaries of daily politics from Jon Stewart's *Daily Show*? An image and construction of reality can inform us, but they should not be the only lenses that we use to look upon the world. A full appreciation of our social situation must come from a fuller awareness of the vested interests that exist in portraying what is real. It is our hope that this book can help.

Endnotes

1. C. Wright Mills, *The Sociological Imagination* (New York: Oxford University Press, 1959), p. 15.

2. Howard S. Becker, *Outsiders* (New York: Free Press, 1963), p. 9. For a review of sociological approaches to deviance and the symbolic interactionist response, including labeling theory, see Nancy J. Herman-Kinney, "Deviance," in *Handbook of Symbolic Interaction* (Walnut Creek, CA: Alta Mira, 2003), pp. 695–720 and Stephen Pfohl, *Images of Deviance and Social Control* (New York: Basic Books, 1988).

3. Gillian Bennett, *Alas, Poor Ghost: Traditions of Belief in Story and Discourse* (Logan, Utah: Utah State University Press, 1999).

4. This discussion draws from Erving Goffman's landmark study of St. Elizabeth's Hospital as a total institution. See Erving Goffman, *Asylums* (New York: Doubleday, 1961).

5. 2008 Bureau of Justice Statistics.

6. For an example of the psychological tolls of being a corrections officer, with particular attention to the impacts of a total institution, see Ted Conover,

Newjack: Guarding Sing-Sing (New York: Vintage, 2001). The "prison studies" that Phillip Zimbardo conducted are also important for insights into how perceived authority can corrupt and lead to brutality.

7. See Daniel Boorstin, *The Image: A Guide to Pseudo-Events in America* (New York: Vintage, 1961).

8. Robert Jackall and Janice Hirota, *Image Makers: Advertising, Public Relations, and the Ethos of Advocacy* (Chicago: University of Chicago Press, 2003).

9. See George Ritzer, *Revolutionizing the Means of Consumption: Enchanting a Disenchanted World*, 2nd ed. (Thousand Oaks, California: Pine Forge Press, 2005).

10. Quoted from an online interview with George Ritzer in *The Sun*, 2002.

11. Carl Hiaasen, *Team Rodent: How Disney Devours the World* (New York: Random House, 1998).

12. This definition comes from Mark Gottdiener, *The Theming of America: American Dreams, Media Fantasies, and Themed Environments*, 2nd ed. (Boulder, CO: Westview Press, 2001).

Postscript

Having read this book, you should now be familiar with the basic concepts and perspectives of symbolic interactionist social psychology. Knowing these ideas is a great start, putting them to use is the next step. What attracts us, and many others, to symbolic interactionism is that these ideas are so applicable to the world around us. People already use these ideas intuitively. We think about what makes other people tick, including our friends and families. We analyze other people's attempts at impression management and congratulate ourselves when we see through their pretenses. We recognize when people try to appear as "players" or as "perfect parents"; or when managers take their roles way too seriously and rookies try "too hard."

These informal analyses are different from, and less systematic than, doing scholarly research. However, our personal insights can sometimes lead to great scholarly questions. Even if we are not doing scholarly research at the time, we still engage in analysis when we appraise other people's actions—when we wonder what is happening in their relationships or when we are figuring out angles for how to deal with people at work. The more critical thinking that we do, the better. Transitioning individual insights into theories helps people predict and understand social action. You can build on your individual insights by linking them to symbolic interactionist ideas.

However, we urge you to think sociologically and to analyze beyond the level of just what individuals do. Start thinking, for example, about how certain behaviors aggregate around enacting a specific role, or about how a single individual acting like "a player" is representative of a set of dramaturgical activities that people use to enact that situated identity in many settings. Reverse the analytic direction: Instead of centering on the singular way someone acts, ask yourself how the role itself is constructed. For example, how do different people try to take on a situated identity of being an authority figure or a leader? When do people honor a performance in that role versus failing to accept a performance in that role? How do people account for failing to come across as a "leader"? In asking such questions, you are integrating symbolic interactionist ideas, as you are categorizing kinds of accounts, roles, and impression management. You also can develop deeper analyses, such as investigating what kinds of social contexts, ascribed statuses, and definitions of the situation help shape how people act as they do.

If you already think that you are skilled at figuring out what makes people tick and analyzing social situations, then these concepts will enhance your appraisals. Focus on categorizing kinds of roles and impression management. Strengthen your perceptions to see the intertwining of individual agency and social context in how people act authoritatively. For example, an individual may act bossy and give orders to friends on a rafting trip because he has been rafting before and has experience. This form of authority is different from a social context that inculcates authority. Training in a police academy, alternatively, teaches recruits the techniques and legitimacy that enable them to be figures of authority as police officers. Of course, differences in individual abilities may make some graduates more or less successful as authority figures. Yet, an individual thinking that he or she knows everything is a different sociological issue than analyzing how a total institution works that is dedicated to teaching people how to be authoritative. Examining the interactions between social forces and individual agency enhances your sociological imagination. To that end, we suggest several exercises below. Think of these exercises as drills in applying symbolic interactionist concepts.

Exercise 1: Explore Microorders

Conduct an observation of a social setting and identify the microorder inherent in what you see. Enumerate the rules that people must follow to carry out a set of social actions, from mundane behaviors to complex ones. For example, what rules do people follow in a cafeteria? How do people act as spectators at a sporting event? How do people know how to react to professional wrestling villains or good guys or backbiting on reality shows? What is the inherent typecasting on reality shows? How do people follow particular rules of being a "team" at a party? What is proper Facebook etiquette? What is the proper way to talk behind someone's back without getting caught? To send cell phone text messages during a class surreptitiously? The goal of this exercise is to understand and appreciate the sheer number of microorders and little-noticed norms that people follow in everyday interaction. Try identifying and naming those practices and rules. What do you call the look that people give when they steal a glance at someone they find attractive but then quickly turn away before that person sees them? How do they let that person know they are attracted without either coming across as creepy or being too understated? How do you get noticed when you work at hiding that you are noticing? What is a norm for acting in that situation? Describe situational contexts and how participants try to fulfill or do not fulfill what is expected of them in the scene. What happens if people do not conform? What accounts would they apply?

Exercise 2: Construct Reality

Invent some doublespeak or euphemisms. The chart next lists some less pleasant realities and some corresponding "doublespeak" that is intended to hide the harsh edges of those realities. Can you think of how you might transform reality with your own doublespeak?

Less Pleasant Realities	Doublespeak to Camouflage That Reality
Firing people	"Alternative Career Enhancement program"
Body bags	Transfer tubes
Salesperson	Relationship manager
Debt collector	Persistence specialist
Company losing money	Negative cash flow or deficit
Closing a plant	An "indefinite idling"
Unmotivated student	Gifted underachiever
Poor neighborhood	?
Obese	?
Doing poorly at a job	?

Exercise 3: Rehabilitate a Celebrity or Public Figure

Pretend that you are a public relations specialist hired to rehabilitate a celebrity's spoiled career. For example, you need to salvage Lindsay Lohan's or Amy Winehouse's reputations and get them back on top. Or think about how you would get a shamed politician back into the running or a disgraced public figure (O. J. Simpson, Michael Vick, or Tiger Woods) into the general public's good graces. What accounts could you use to help them? What dramaturgical advice would you tell them to follow to remove stigmas that have become attached to them? Would you try a "jailhouse conversion" storyline, or have them do community service or charity work in highly visible ways? Would you have them be unrepentant and go for a particular segment of the public that would be receptive to their current status? To do this work is to participate in an active construction of reality and moral entrepreneurship.

Exercise 4: Experiment with Conformity and Decide What Is Real

David Shulman sometimes takes a deck of cards to his classes. He finds playing a few hands of poker and some other card games helps him teach students about techniques of deception. In this exercise, take a deck of cards and bring them to a class or to a group of friends. Ask one to pick a card and identify that card out loud. Ask him or her to look again to confirm that the card is really that card (say a 10 of clubs). That person should agree. Then offer him or her a hypothetical proposition. Ask: "What if I give you fifty dollars right now to state that the card is not what you just said it was?" Follow up the $50 scenario by then asking the student to state if the card is still a ten of clubs. The student should say "no" even though the card is still visibly a ten of clubs. At this point, ask people, including the person, what is real—the original card or the new artificially influenced value for the card? At this point, Shulman tells the person that he also could have asked him or her to misidentify the card to avoid upsetting a relative, to let a small child think that a card trick worked, or to please an authority figure. If any of those scenarios occurred, then what is real? The point is, given the right inducements, how easy can it be to get people to see and state what you want them to see and state? Not all examples of conformity have to be as heavy-handed as in the Milgram experiment that we referred to in Chapter 1 or with as much initial need to absolve responsibility.

People are not blind sheep who willingly overlook the consequences of their acts. They have consciences and think about what they do. They may conform consciously (as in the above case of the card example) or unconsciously. Sociologists see conformity everywhere as the natural socialization of people into roles and institutions. Conformity is not primarily bowing to authority in extreme situations, but for the most part, going along with the demands of normal social life. In fact, social life often requires us to subsume private judgments in favor of agreeing visibly with a more public consensus. Consider examples of lying in the workplace to cover up for a coworker or lying within the family about the whereabouts of a sibling, or about "holding it for a friend."

In fact, conformity is so common that some sociologists think studying nonconformity is actually more critical. For example, it is a wake-up call to know that almost two-thirds of people conformed in the Milgram experiment, but importantly, what made the other third refuse to bow to the power of the situation? We may want to think hard about unraveling the mystery of nonconformity. Consider the example of whistle blowing. In this case, we are encouraging people to not conform, and a lot is at stake. Getting workers to blow the whistle is difficult when the message that workers internalize is that group loyalty is most important. However, as far as whistle blowing and criminal conspiracies go, that type of group loyalty is detrimental to the public good.

As a thought experiment, think about the role of accounts in the following question: How do people disassociate themselves easily from their own responsibility for negative effects stemming from their actions? For example, how can a group of students bully a weaker student in school, but still not see themselves as being at fault? What about when a white-collar criminal states that he or she had to do what he or she did or risk losing his or her job in a competitive environment? What about shoplifting small amounts of food from a school cafeteria or small items from a large retailer? Are those people thieves or do they state that the place will not miss it, or that high prices justify their taking a five-finger discount? Think about how accounts allow people to do bad things and still see themselves as good people.

Exercise 5: Deviance, Body Image, and Moral Entrepreneurship

People acutely recognize deviant identities around the issue of bodily imperfections. Keep a journal in which you question how people come to internalize or reject social pressures about their individual appearances. For example, how do people manage a "fat" identity? Many people switch from diet to diet and attempt to use clothing to camouflage excess weight as much as possible. For example, they may avoid wearing horizontal stripes or tucking in blouses or shirts, or use spandex fabrics and other modern day corsets.

There also are many television shows about empowering people through losing weight, while other moral entrepreneurs urge "fat acceptance." Many people argue that media images directly pressure people to have extravagant expectations regarding their appearance. Is that so? Are the media powerful enough to cause people to worry about weight and diet excessively? Given that many Americans are obese, and many in the developed world are growing increasingly obese (coined the problem of "globesity"), while the media parade around images of thinness, perhaps media images are less influential than we assume, or are they only powerful to some groups? While some decry skeletal models as encouraging many young women to fall prey to a "tyranny of thinness," most people—more than half at least—are capable of ignoring the pressures of these role models. What keeps people heavy in a world of propaganda that decries overeating? How does that propaganda encounter an American context in which highly caloric food is easy to acquire and fairly inexpensive? Why do so many magazines publish articles on diets while simultaneously listing recipes for fattening desserts? These issues are all connected to moral entrepreneurship.

As a thought exercise, consider how the social construction of reality is changing to accommodate heavier people. Are portions at restaurants getting bigger? Are there more buffets? Are whole new classes of diet foods emerging that promise great taste with fewer calories? Clothing sizes are changing, as waist sizes are no longer just in inches, but in a particular inch with three or four different fits that de facto mean that the pants are not just a specific size. For example, someone can buy a 38-inch pair of jeans in a slender fit or in a "relaxed" fit or with an elastic waistband that in essence makes the inch measurement variable. However, the person buying the jeans can think of himself or herself as wearing a 38-inch jeans when he or she is actually wearing a larger size. Are people with a heavy appearance mocked less than they used to be? Is the schoolyard easier for heavier children now than 30 years ago? Are "staring" rules relaxing about heavier people wearing tighter-fitting clothes in public than maybe they might have worn in earlier years? Is a consciousness of what is "fat" changing from being a little overweight to now only being "fat" if one is morbidly obese? Should it be anyone else's business if someone is overweight? These questions are not issues of fact. They are about definitions of reality and moral entrepreneurship.

Exercise 6: How Stores Use Entertainment Themes to Encourage Consumption

Assess how organizations create or manage an existing impression and theme to lure a particular market segment to purchase their products. Think of Disney World, a themed restaurant, the Mall of America, Dave & Busters, Cabela's, or a cruise ship. Ask yourself: What is the site's appeal? How is that appeal marketed, meaning how and why do you know about that place? What motivates someone to "purchase" the consumption experience of visiting and experiencing what the place offers? Incorporate issues of emotional labor. The theming in these places is choreographed and organized. People who work there must help maintain and enact the image associated with the site. Each site has different facets to fit into the theming, from security and souvenirs to costumed waitstaff and attractions. How are all these different facets integrated into a successful theme? How do they add up to an "experience"? What strategic choices can you spot in how an indoor mall— for example, the mall at Columbus Circle in New York City—is organized to influence consumers? Indoor malls have detailed architecture to cement their theming physically. How is the physical space commodified, just like we described in casinos in Chapter 6, to encourage people to spend money?

Exercise 7: Analyze a Total Institution

Pick an organization that controls an individual's identity and analyze how that organization does so. How does a prison depersonalize someone or military training resocialize groups of individuals into becoming soldiers? What total institutions might be voluntary, such as rehabilitation, versus involuntary, like jail? What limits should there be on the complete control of individual actions that characterize total institutions? How do people rebel against those controls?

Exercise 8: Watch Movies with an Analytic Eye

Watch some movies that illustrate symbolic interactionist ideas. A few starters (and this list is far from exhaustive) might include: *American Beauty; The Birdcage; City of God; Crash; Dark City; Europa, Europa; Fight Club; Full Metal Jacket; Gattaca; Glengarry-glenross; Hollywood Shuffle; Miss Congeniality; Mona Lisa Smile; Office Space; Ordinary People;* and *Shawshank Redemption.* There are also excellent documentaries that depict symbolic interactionist ideas, such as *The Farm; Paris is Burning; People Like US: Social Class in America; Trekkies; The Venetian-The World's Largest Hotel.* These films depict many different ideas from this book.

Consider the impact of roles, status, and impression management in films such as *American Beauty, Gattaca, Office Space,* and *Miss Congeniality.* Examine total institutions through the movie *Shawshank Redemption* or the documentary, *The Farm. Full Metal Jacket* is rightly famous for its harrowing portrayal of basic training for marines going to Vietnam. *Europa, Europa* depicts the story of Solomon Perel, a Jewish teen who poses as a German Nazi youth in order to survive World War II. He ends up being adopted by a German officer and sent to an elite boarding school for Nazi youth. Impression management is a life and death matter for him.

The power of gender roles is on exhibit in *Mona Lisa Smile,* as a progressive teacher tries to expand the options young women might pursue for themselves at Wellesley in the fifties. *Trekkies* is a documentary about devoted Star Trek fans who completely define all situations in their lives in order to conform to the role expectations of this science fiction show. This includes taking Klingon language classes and dressing in a Starfleet uniform at work. This documentary opens up the door to considering culture as a total institution as well as defining what is deviant or real. *The Birdcage* and *Paris is Burning* explore heterosexuality and homosexuality as constructions of reality that are enacted through dramaturgy. The documentary on the Venetian explores the theming of a large Las Vegas resort and the dramaturgical work and emotional labor that give life to that hotel's theme. Try exploring some of the other films on this list and discover their linkages to symbolic interactionist concepts.

Exercise 9: Surf the Web for Identity Construction

We have discussed various concepts of identity. Nowhere is identity more obviously a social construction than on the Internet. Explore how people present themselves in their virtual identities on Facebook. Note how the reciprocal relationship of defining one's self through how people respond to you is very evident in the give-and-take that people have with the people who write comments on their home pages. People clarify "who" they are on those pages for community appraisal. They also can assume identities, such as posing as singles when married on dating Web sites, or changing their genders when going on message boards. They can become objects of fantasy in online games or self-styled experts on cooking or in reviewing books, movies, and television shows.

The Internet is a playground for identity. People can test out different self-presentations anonymously. They can create wholesale new identities in *Second Life* and create avatars for themselves that are half-human and half-animal. Normal rules of appearance are out the window, as people can Photoshop their pictures and create biographical details that never existed. Without face-to-face interaction, consider how identity is constructed when there are few limits on how people can present themselves. Conversely, consider how on Facebook pages, particularly among different demographic segments, there is a convergence of what types of details people will present about themselves. Older people display a picture of their young children and themselves in a parenting pose. Younger people—say in college or high school—will present themselves with attractive friends or in a partying scene. Their links make them a small world or a large one. Some people have hundreds of "friends" that are tagged to their pages; others have a small number of friends in their online networks. There are many questions to answer about how people will present their identities when the flexibility of the Internet makes identity so complex a possibility.

Thank you for reading this book. We have a passion for symbolic interaction and have conducted research within this tradition for decades. We hope that our delight and enthusiasm for the usefulness of this approach is clear and productive for your own thinking.

Glossary

For the reader's reference, we define key concepts below that we introduced and presented in the previous chapters.

Act: An act is a functional unit of conduct, with an identifiable beginning and end. An act is related to an organism's purposes and is oriented toward one or more other objects. Acts comprise a number of responses to stimuli that move a person to accomplish goals. Interactionists argue that conduct is best understood as an ongoing process in which people try to adapt to or master their surroundings, accomplish tasks, and attain goals. For example, human beings want to care for their children, make a living, and get good grades in college. People constantly engage in activity, confront a variety of obstacles or interruptions, and they attempt to get activity back on track and keep it there. For example, students interrupt their studying to have a cup of coffee or to check their e-mail and then they return to their books. An act ends when its object is attained. The professor's act of answering a question ends when he or she provides what both the students and the professor view as a satisfactory "answer."

Aligning Actions: People sometimes pursue ends that they are ashamed of or that others censure. They may cheat on their exams, taxes, or partners; tell racist jokes to get a cheap laugh; or act belligerently when they are drunk. When someone's conduct contradicts culturally accepted values, he or she confronts a dilemma of having to make their activities seem sensible and reasonable in culturally legitimate terms. Aligning actions are efforts to address this dilemma through excusing, redefining, explaining, evading, justifying, and apologizing for one's problematic actions. For example, a philanderer can blame his or her infidelity on stress or alcohol, apologize to the partner, and promise never to do it again. Aligning actions include accounts, disclaimers, motive talk, apologies, acclaimers—indeed, any expression that functions to align discreditable conduct and cultural ideals. Aligning actions reflect a reoccurring dilemma in daily life, which is that cultural dictates and desired conduct often contradict one another.

Altercasting: People sometimes try to influence how other people will act by imposing a specific role and role expectations on them. Altercasting is the name of a social process in which a person constrains and shapes the acts of another by "casting" that person. An example of altercasting includes stating in public that someone is the most knowledgeable about a particular location in order to get that person to volunteer himself or herself to organize a trip to that place. Or a father might state that a mother is the "nurturing one" in order to get her to change a child's diaper. When a person is pigeonholed as a particular character, he or she may feel compelled to uphold that role, or be goaded into defending against that characterization. Either direction imposes a set of actions on the "altercasted" person.

Announcements: An announcement is any act or gesture that indicates or claims a particular identity in front of other people. Everyday situations are replete with announcements, as people intentionally and unintentionally indicate their social identities relative to one another. A young woman who leans earnestly toward a young man and reaches across the table to touch his hand may be announcing her romantic interest and potential availability as a romantic partner. She may, however, merely be announcing her readiness to listen sympathetically to a sad story. As this example suggests, the nature of an announcement depends on the situation: Are the two individuals on a date or is the woman merely consoling a friend on the loss of a job? Announcements may be verbal ("Good morning, I am Professor Hewitt") or behavioral (the professor hands out a syllabus and calls the roll). Frequently, announcements rely on appearance, such as wearing a company uniform and exiting a truck marked with the company's name.

Awareness Context: The awareness context is the total combination of what participants in a situation know about one another's identities and intentions. The concept of an awareness context applies descriptively to situations as a whole. Sometimes some people know more about a situation than others do. The different levels of knowledge create a different level of awareness that characterizes the overall knowledge and situation in which people find themselves. In a confidence scheme, for example, where unscrupulous securities dealers strive to rob an elderly widow of her life savings, the situation as a whole represents a closed awareness context. The widow does not know she is being cheated—she does not know the securities salespersons are crooks, and she does not know she is a victim in their eyes. An unequal and incomplete distribution of knowledge makes the situation a closed awareness context, and the context as a whole constrains the interactions that all participants can have. The widow cannot act in her own best interest precisely because she is being deceived; and the perpetrators of the scheme must exercise caution because they cannot be sure that the widow is truly ignorant, and they have to avoid giving any signs of their actual exploitative intent. Awareness contexts depend on whether people know the truth about others, and for that matter, whether the others know that other people know the truth.

Biographical Self: The self is an object created in interaction with others in concrete social situations. In this sense, the self is fundamentally a situated self (defined later). Yet the process of role taking that creates a situated self does not limit itself to spatial and temporal boundaries within the immediate situation. Rather, people act toward themselves and one another as people who have lives that extend beyond the immediate situation—as people who have pasts and futures, and who have other interests and responsibilities than those they presently enact. People engaging in everyday interaction in particular situations bring their whole historical selves with them, and sometimes their interaction focuses on those other aspects of their lives. Those situations involve people's biographical selves.

Boundaries: A boundary is a social line dividing the members of one social category from those of another, such as men from women, working-class people from middle-class people, members of one ethnic or religious group from another. In some instances, boundaries are drawn sharply and people are acutely aware of the differences that exist between one category and another. Gender in the United States, for example, despite improvements in the economic conditions of women, still remains a sharp boundary.

Other boundaries are less clear. People may find some boundary distinctions difficult to differentiate. In the case of social class, for example, they may sometimes deny that boundaries of social class even exist. The concept of a boundary emphasizes the importance that social divisions have in organizing social life. Concepts such as community or role signify ways that people identify themselves with social units or activities and with one another. Thus, to speak of the "gay community" emphasizes how a set of people is differentially bound together by identification with one another and a common sexual orientation. To grasp how such communities function in the social world, and in the identities of their members, we need to recognize that differences from others are as important as similarity with others. Distinctions between "gay" and "straight" guide the identities of both, as well as interactions between them. Such boundaries define how people visualize and talk about the social world, and they influence their coordination of everyday conduct.

Careers: In everyday language, a career refers to an individual's movement through various stages or levels of an occupation or profession, as in a "medical career" or "business career." Although a "career" is informally considered an individual property, occupations have typical career patterns, which specify periods of training, income expectations at various ages, and the pace at which people are promoted from one level to the next. People commonly measure their individual careers against these norms.

Symbolic interactionists use the term career more broadly as a metaphor to address temporal patterns and expectations in social actions. Thus, physicians have occupational careers, and they expect certain patterns of income, professional recognition, and influence over time. But from the perspective of physicians, illnesses also have careers or "trajectories," for treatment of a patient involves not only diagnosing a problem, but also arriving at prognosis—a prediction of the timing in which the patient will either recover or decline. Likewise, even a simple social act such as a conversation has a "career" in the sense that people share and communicate expectations about how long it will last and how to signal its impending end. Shared ideas about temporal progress or stages of development of illnesses, conversations, occupations, and a host of joint actions enable people to participate in actions in an orderly way. Thus, the notion of a "career" is an analytic category that sociologists use to organize the trajectory of social phenomena.

Communication: Communication is often—but misleadingly—defined as the transfer of information from a sender to a receiver. A newspaper informs its readers that the day's weather is cloudy and rainy; a sociology professor informs students that the middle class is shrinking and that the disparity of wealth between the richest and poorest segments of the society is growing. This approach to communication, although not completely wrong, ignores the most fundamental part of the phenomenon: influence. The essence of communication is not just the transfer of information, but rather the influence that the behavior of one person has on another through communicating information in particular ways. Symbolic interactionists argue that communication is a pervasive phenomenon and the most important social phenomenon that exists. Every act is communicative and influences the other, even if not always consciously intended to do so. Human communication is symbolic, which is to say that people base their responses on their interpretations of other people's acts and gestures. In symbolic communication, people predicate their responses on the designation of another's act as meaningful or purposive. Such interpretations can also be wrong sometimes—such as when a professor interprets a stretched arm as a raised hand and not a stretched arm.

Community: Community is an important concept in the social sciences. Most often, the term designates small towns, villages, neighborhoods, and other territorial social aggregates where people engage in a great deal of face-to-face interaction, know one another virtually from birth, and feel a sense of loyalty to one another arising out of their shared location. A contrast between community and society often accompany this usage. Society designates a larger, impersonal social entity where interaction with strangers is more common and people feel little loyalty to one another. These usages may also be evaluative in tone, with community regarded as good and society regarded as bad. In such cases, you encounter bemoaning the "loss of a sense of community."

George Herbert Mead used the term community in a broader sense. In his view, community refers to a social entity whose members share a common framework or universe of discourse. People are members of a community if they share a common way of seeing themselves and the world, even if they do not know one another or interact on a face-to-face basis. For the individual, a community in this sense comprises a generalized other—that is, a perspective others share from which the individual may view himself or herself, and by whose standards he or she forms a sense of self.

This book uses community in Mead's fashion. Even though communities based on territory (e.g., villages) are important historically, the grounds on which communities are established have widened. In the contemporary world, people often identify with and adopt the imagined perspectives of others whom they do not know and with whom they are not likely to have intimate contact. People identify with one another on the basis of age, generation, gender, social experiences, and similar grounds that do not have territorial linkage. Although communities are thus, in one sense, founded on similarity (e.g., all those who share a social characteristic such as age), they also cut across various social boundaries (e.g., those who identify with one another on the basis of age are likely to be diverse with respect to social class, ethnicity, or religion). Whatever the basis of identification and community formation, the importance of contemporary communities is in their provision for and support of social identities.

Conditioning: Conditioning is a process in which animals learn to respond to artificial stimuli that become associated with other stimuli to which animals have natural responses. For example, Pavlov's dog learned to salivate when a bell sounded. The dog became conditioned to treat a bell as though it were the stimulus of food. Although symbolic interactionists think that conditioning does not solely explain human behavior, conditioning is nonetheless important for understanding behavior. Human beings respond self-consciously to significant symbols (defined later).

Conventional Roles: Conventional roles are standardized, widely known, and labeled perspectives that people enact in a wide range of situations. These roles are standardized because they have commonly understood definitions and sets of associated behaviors and expectations. Most people in a society are aware of these roles and employ their knowledge of them in role taking, even if they may not enact the roles themselves. These roles have names that are widely recognized. Thus, father, mother, physician, professor, president, lawyer, student, and similar roles are conventional roles.

To say that a role is conventional is not to say that all who enact the role do so similarly or that universal agreement exists on how they ought to act. People's grasp of roles is general enough to encompass considerable variation, including disagreement about exactly how to enact them. This complexity exists because roles provide people with general perspectives from which to act, rather than an exhaustive specific list of activities or duties. People also understand conventional roles such as parent, child, father, mother, brother, and sister in relation to one another. There may be wide variation in how people enact these roles, with some siblings expressing and feeling strong obligations to one another, and others having more distant relationships. Yet both kinds of siblings would recognize their relationships as brother and sister and agree in many respects on what this relationship entails.

Culture: Although culture is defined in many ways in the social sciences, its definition almost invariably involves the idea that culture is a source of meaning. The ideas, norms, expectations, values, and knowledge that collectively make up culture are sources of meaning for individuals who participate in that culture. Culture, thus, defines what is important (success, honor, sex, education, and so forth), how people should achieve those valued things (through hard work, for instance), what they should know in order to achieve their goals, what will happen to them when they die, and so forth. Culture is a very encompassing term that covers what human beings learn as participants in a social world. Culture is another word people use to describe the complex, symbolic human environment.

Definition of the Situation: A definition of the situation organizes meanings through a shared interpretation of why people are present in a given situation, what conduct they should expect from others and what to do themselves, how events are likely to unfold over the course of that situation, where the situation is located in relation to other situations, and what goals are to be pursued by self and others. A definition of a situation as a "college class," for example, establishes that there will be students and a professor, that lectures and discussions will occur, that the class will begin and end at a fixed time, that the class is one of a series of other classes students take and professors teach, and that the situation's goals include such things as "understanding" and "answers." A definition of the situation provides an organized perception in which people assemble objects, meanings, and others, and know to act toward them in a coherent and recognizable way.

Two aspects of this important interactionist concept are especially worth remembering. First, a shared definition of the situation is necessary for organized and successful collective behavior to occur. Without a shared definition of the situation, people are confused or paralyzed, because they have no basis on which to anticipate the actions of others, or to know how they are expected to act. For example, drivers at an intersection where traffic signals have ceased to work will be confused and uncertain until they define the situation as "broken signals" or a "power outage." Only then will they usually improvise an orderly flow of traffic by taking turns, acting as if as an improvised four-way stop sign now controls the intersection.

Second, definitions of situations are external and constraining. Even though these definitions are in the minds of individuals, their reality is collective rather than individual. Each person's definition of the situation is a hypothesis about what is taking place and what he or she should do in response to the acts of others. People observe the acts of others and see how their acts fit with others. Moreover, once established, the definition of the situation is constraining because it is taken to be reality by those who create or accept it. Even those who doubt a definition's accuracy are constrained by it, for they are apt to feel there is something wrong with them if they do not see what others see. They may also be punished if they do not accept a particular definition of the situation, such as when a person does not go along with hiding a problematic behavior in the family, or they refuse to pretend that morale is high in an unpleasant workplace.

Deviance: Deviance describes categories of persons and/or conduct that are usually viewed negatively and that prompt responses of social control. Deviance is a product of social classification. Understanding deviance means analyzing the creation of social norms and rules and the circumstances under which social control is initialized. Examining the social construction of labels for deviance does not mean that all deviance is purely a judgment call. Undesirable conduct is not just an artifact of classification, but can be a matter of broad agreement and consensus, depending on the involved conduct. Like others, sociologists would rather avoid being mugged and would agree that frequent muggings are a threat to social order worth acting upon. That being stated, there are still many behaviors that should be understood as being neutral in character, in the sense that they may be seen as excessively deviant or not, depending on the variable social rules that people impose on how to perceive those actions. Often what is labeled deviant changes over time and place and is not absolute. For example, prostitution is a crime in some areas and decriminalized in others.

Disneyification: Disneyification is viewed as a remaking of urban or "sketchy" neighborhoods into more sanitized and theme park like environments. Times Square in New York City is cited as a recent example of having been Disneyified. Once more of a red light district full of seedy strip joints and X-rated movie theaters, the Disney Company bought a block on Times Square and installed a theater showing the Lion King theatrical production. With the help of municipal authorities, themed businesses moved in, such as the Madame Tussauds Wax Museum and ESPNZONE. The gritty character of Times Square suddenly changed from a rough area to having a plethora of sanitized and themed retail stores. Critics argue that Disneyification removes the authentic character of areas and replaces them with high-priced artificial experiences. For example, the Paris hotel in Las Vegas is a "Disneyified" version of Paris in France.

Emergence: Emergence refers to the peculiar yet crucial nature of meaning as something never final or finished, but always in the process of being created. Even in defined situations when roles and objects are understood and laid out in advance, meanings are still constantly in flux, being created, refreshed, and transformed. The emergent nature of meaning is important to the symbolic interactionist view of how the social world operates and for understanding how ongoing interaction works. If social meanings were absolutely fixed, to the point of leading to robotic ingrained behavior, there would be little or no room for variation, change, or novelty in social behavior. People would dutifully and invariably do what their roles tell them to do and they would not think of changing or even want to do so. While conformity is common, conformity itself is not a fixed property of social interaction and can be fragile. People do have impulses that make them want to act contrary to the ways their roles encourage them to act. They also make mistakes in role taking and so embark on lines of action that others find undesirable or at least unexpected. They think of new ways of accomplishing familiar tasks. Conduct depends on how people derive emergent meaning and is not just determined by automatic cultural programming.

Emotion: Emotion is one of three general ways—cognitive, conative, and affective—in which human beings orient themselves to their world and to themselves. Cognition refers to our perception and interpretation of objects and events in our surroundings. Conation is the experience of will or purposefulness. Affect refers to emotions and sentiments. Everyday experience blends these three elements together, and some scholars would argue that it is impossible to separate them. A craftsperson hard at work making a piece of pottery or furniture, for example, may simultaneously experience feelings of pride (affect), have a sense of purpose (conation) as he or she manipulates tools to shape a pot or smooth a surface, and engage in perceiving and interpreting the shape of a pot or the grain of a board (cognition). Even so, separating them, at least at an analytical level, is useful in order to call attention to the individual importance of each in social life.

Regarding emotions, they are an integral component of social life and the self. The same emotions that relationships with others arouse in us are also aroused when we perceive and act toward ourselves. We may be angry with ourselves, in love with ourselves, or feel detached from ourselves. Second, emotions are part and parcel of every individual and social act. Some emotions arise when acts are thwarted or blocked. We feel frustrated or upset when we cannot do what we want because of some obstacle. Emotions also arise during the course of our acts. In fact, emotions that arise during an act are important parts of being motivated to continue in those acts. Additionally, emotions accompany the consummation of acts, such as when one feels pride in a task well done.

Ethnomethodology: Ethnomethodology examines how people make sense of what they do. Underlying this approach is the belief that people are constantly engaged in a process of creating sense—making it appear that their behavior is correct or appropriate, that they are being sensible and normal human beings doing things in the usual way. The major contribution of ethnomethodology is in its insight that people construct meaning and sensibility through their conversations. Although symbolic interactionists emphasize the meanings that people share as they interact with one another, it is easy to overemphasize the extent to which meanings are fully and genuinely shared. Ethnomethodology emphasizes that shared meaning is often an illusion and not an actuality, that people have ways to convince themselves that they agree with one another or that they share the same motives when, in fact, they do not.

Gender: Sex refers to biologically defined characteristics, most notably the possession at birth of the genitalia of one biological sex or the other. Gender, in contrast, refers to what we learn to expect and take for granted about how males and females should behave. How to treat gender conceptually is not a settled matter. We argue that gender is a way of defining how a particular role should be performed and a role in itself. Many roles that are open to both sexes also seem to call for different performances from males and females.

The interactionist approach to role sheds some useful light on this issue. To symbolic interactionists, a role offers a perspective in a situation. It is a place or point of view from which the individual acts in concert with others. One role to examine is that of an "executive." To say that there is an "executive role" is to say that there is an "executive perspective" from which people in certain situations are expected to act. We can look at gender as a limitation imposed on the perspectives from which females can act in such situations. That is, in a world where women are denied access to executive roles, they simply cannot act from this perspective. But in a society where executive roles are open to women, there can be, and is still, uncertainty and conflict about how women are to act from the perspective of the executive role. In other words, those who censure women for "aggression" or "acting like men" are, in effect, showing their reluctance to accept females acting from an "executive" perspective, by treating them as if they should be acting from a different perspective—namely, that of "women." This constraint is a means to discriminate against women by forcing them into a bind that men do not face.

Generalized Other: The generalized other is an imagined perspective that people attribute to social others, whether this other is the whole society, the community that an individual belongs to, or some smaller category or grouping of people. The generalized other may represent the imagined perspectives of people as diverse as all members of U.S. society, one's fellow students or professors, all human beings, other African Americans or Roman Catholics, or all men or all women. The crucial point about this concept is that when human beings interact, they frequently, if not invariably, are influenced by a generalized idea of the expectations, values, beliefs, and standards of some category of human beings that they internalize and that guide them.

A more vivid way of portraying the generalized other is by thinking of each situation of human interaction as containing a set of imaginary others that are present in the mind of each interactant. Generalized others create both self-consciousness and constrain our actions. For example, a professor is aware of the lecture he or she is giving, is attentive to looks of understanding or confusion on his or her students, and thus gears his or her conduct toward the imagined meanings of their responses and gestures. However, the professor may also respond to the imagined expectations and standards of other professors. He or she may be thinking about how an off-color joke would illustrate a point perfectly, and that the students might think that joke is funny. However, he or she might not tell that joke because there is an imagined other, representing "professors" as a whole that would not approve of the joke. Someone might wish to be politically correct or incorrect but not pursue that goal because of how they imagine some "other" would respond. The generalized other constrains social behavior.

Horizontal and Vertical Linkages: Symbolic interactionists argue that conduct is situated, and that these situations themselves are located within larger and more encompassing social contexts—within groups, organizations, social classes, and other such social entities. Moreover, these social entities are linked to one another both horizontally and vertically. These concepts are meant to sensitize us to two key facts.

First, social entities have vertical linkages. Some groups, organizations, or social classes are in a position to exert control over others or are dependent on them. Large, increasingly global corporations, for example, can shift their manufacturing operations to countries with lower labor costs in order to increasing their profits. The implications for workers are clear: Their livelihoods, and the communities in which they live and exist are vulnerable to corporate executives in other parts of the globe. As other examples, poor people in the United States depend in various ways on the social policies of federal and state governments with respect to welfare rules and the generosity of private charities. Smaller, supplier companies are tied in relations of unequal power and dependency to larger companies who buy their products and services.

The power of large corporations over workers, of men over women or of the welfare bureaucracy over the poor, makes a great deal of difference to workers, women, and the poor. This power shapes their identities, their capacity to make roles, and their need to be accurate and perceptive role takers. In other words, the processes of identification, role making, and role taking do not occur in a vacuum but often in contexts of unequal power.

Horizontal linkages refer to a second key fact: That individuals whose actions constitute society are simultaneously members of several social interdependent entities. For example, people are simultaneously breadwinners and parents, voters and consumers. Companies sell products to one another, governmental agencies interact with one another and with the public, and charities cooperate in such fund-raising enterprises as the United Way. These linkages are horizontal in the sense that individuals and groups at roughly similar levels of power negotiate with one another. Many of the basic processes of self, social interaction, and conduct formation are situated in these complex horizontal linkages.

"I" and "Me:" The "I" and the "Me" are names for alternating phases of consciousness that human beings experience during their acts. The crucial fact to remember about these words is that they stand for different perspectives that the acting individual takes toward the self and toward others. One is an acting subject, an "I," whose attention is focused on taking actions. One also can be an object of one's own action, a "Me," with attention focused on one's own real or imagined actions in the eyes of others.

Following Mead, interactionists argue that people alternate between these two phases of consciousness. At one moment, the person begins to respond to a stimulus, and in doing so begins to form an object and develop a plan of action toward that object. At the next moment, the individual becomes aware of his or her response and does so by taking the perspective of another. At the next moment, the individual responds to this awareness of self.

An example will help illustrate these concepts. At one moment you can be in the "I" phase, still feel hungry, and want to get up to go back to a buffet for a second helping. At the next moment, you can be in the "Me" phase, and imagining your action from the vantage point of others around you, feel that they will think you are being a glutton. In the next moment, you will go back into the "I" phase, and respond to the "Me" action by sitting back down, and saying that you are full. You then revert back to the "Me" phase of consciousness and hope that others now imagine you as "not being a pig."

Identity: Identity refers to a person's social location relative to others in a situation, the community, or the society as a whole. Situated identity (defined later) is established generally on the basis of a person's role—that is, the perspective from which the individual acts and on the basis of how others act toward him or her. Beyond the immediate situation, a community of others with whom the individual identifies establishes a social identity. Personal identity (defined later) is established by a person's efforts to establish a particular life plan or project, and often involves a sense of distinction from others.

All forms of identity require the cooperation and affirmation of at least some other people. In a concrete situation of interaction, when a person enacts a particular role, announcements of intention to enact the role and actual enactments of the role must correspond with the placements (defined later) that others make. That is, others must act toward the individual as he or she acts toward self in order for the situated role to constitute a situated identity. A department store customer whom a clerk refuses to recognize as a customer may wish to have the customer identity but does not fully have it until the clerk places the customer in it. Likewise, announcements of a social identity require corresponding placements by others. If the identity involves membership in a community (e.g., the "gay community" or the "Jewish community"), these placements must come at least in part from other members of that community. Even personal identities require affirmation from at least some others, for an account of one's special abilities or difference from others requires others who will accept this account.

Because identity requires other people's cooperation, identity is never merely in the sole control of an individual. This point is tough to grasp but is central. To possess an identity fully and be able to act with energy and conviction in an identity requires a presence in a social world and a confirmation of that identity by others. To claim an identity is to express identification with that identity; to possess an identity is to have others honor that claim. Identity is a social and not merely an individual phenomenon.

Impression Management/Dramaturgy: Sociologists use the term *impression management* to describe the strategic actions that people take to manage both the impressions that other people will have of them and how other people will react to them. Thinking about occasions of self-consciousness clarifies the concreteness of impression management, since at such times we are acutely aware both of having to engage in impression management (a social process) and of our marked sensitivity to how much we think about ourselves as social objects. Sociologist Erving Goffman wrote a book, *The Presentation of Self in Everyday Life* that made a landmark contribution to advancing symbolic interactionist thinking. In this book, he analyzes how individuals and groups of people present images of themselves to others. To tackle the analysis of how people manage their impressions, Goffman suggests that we adopt a dramaturgical analogy. Doing so means examining individual and collective social behaviors as if people are actors performing characters onstage for an audience. These actions reflect how we locate ourselves to others and act out identities. Placed into the context of symbolic interactionism, *The Presentation of Self in Everyday Life* analyzes how people convey a personal identity and definition of the situation by managing the impressions that they express to others. Other people can only understand what we think of as individual and personal identity (the jumbles of characteristics that we think define us), when we enact them and put on a show to demonstrate them.

Interpersonal Roles: Interpersonal roles are perspectives that people create who interact repeatedly over a period of time, and who come to develop a set of mutual definitions and expectations that depend more on their history of interactions than on conventional expectations. Friends, lovers, allies, and enemies illustrate interpersonal roles. There are some standard ideas about these relationships, as participants in a culture share some basic ideas about friendship, how lovers should act, and how to deal with enemies. Interpersonal roles differ from conventional ones. The relationship between, say, student and teacher, is conventionalized enough so that strangers who have never encountered one another before can interact in terms of these roles. A professor knows how to interact with a new crop of students he or she has never met, and students can deal with a substitute teacher they have never seen. In contrast, interpersonal roles depend on a unique pair of interactants, and participants are not so interchangeable. If a teacher is absent, the school principal can find a substitute teacher. However, if a friend is gone, a new friend may be found, but there is no agency that will find a temporary substitute. Likewise, there are no substitutes for enemies and allies—their relationships of enmity or alliance are based on a specific history of doing one another harm or good.

Labeling: Labeling describes a process of social classification. A deviant label, for example, arises out of a process in which persons are classified as deviant. Labels are important, in the interactionist view, for the same reason naming more generally is important. Names define situations and their members, specifying how we are to treat them. Friend and enemy are thus as much labels in this sense as are murderer and thief.

Moral Entrepreneur: A moral entrepreneur is Howard Becker's term to describe a group or person's advocacy efforts to define various forms of behavior as deviant or nondeviant and usually to call for resources and authority to combat or defend those forms of conduct. This concept examines why certain kinds of behavior are singled out for scrutiny and classification as deviant or nondeviant. This concept illuminates that some rules arise not because people spontaneously experience fear or revulsion at the behavior that rules are created to prohibit, but because specific individuals and groups campaigned to create that fear and revulsion. Drug laws in the United States are a good example of moral entrepreneurship, not just in the original campaign against narcotics and marijuana, but also at present. There now exists a substantial antidrug industry whose economic and career interests depend on maintaining antidrug hysteria.

Motivation: The word motivation refers to the internal springs and motors of conduct—that is, to the internal sensitivities of the person as they exist at any given moment and shape a person's receptiveness to stimuli. If I am hungry—that is, my body is in a certain physiological state because I have not ingested food for a certain period of time—then I am particularly receptive to stimuli associated with food. I will be alert to things that I might eat, I will graze in the kitchen, and the sight of food will heighten my craving for food. Motivation operates beneath the surface of consciousness. That is, people are not conscious of being motivated in particular ways unless and until they encounter or find a stimulus that releases an impulse. A hungry person becomes self-conscious of his or her hunger when a food stimulus gives rise to the impulse to eat. That is the point at which the person begins to think of himself or herself as now acting from a hunger motive (defined later). Motivation is social as much or more than just physiological. That is, status or a need for recognition and approval can motivate every bit as much as hunger or thirst. Like physiological motivations, social ones operate initially beneath the threshold of consciousness. Moreover, like physiological motivations, social ones direct receptivity to stimuli. People become conscious of them only by formulating them self-consciously as plans of action.

Motive: A motive is a verbally formulated reason for conduct. A hungry person, for example, might explain finishing an entire bag of potato chips by asserting, "I was really hungry." A person eager for praise might respond to praise by exclaiming, "I was so anxious to learn what you thought of my work!" In these instances, people verbalize motives for their actions, and they do so usually in response either to real or anticipated questions from others. The situations people find themselves in, and the audiences that will judge their responses, typically govern what motives people cite.

Stated motives do not just reflect underlying motivations. A person who has just finished the bag of potato chips might be accurately reporting on a motivational state by saying, "I was hungry!" However, he or she may have no idea of what precipitated the action. Some people eat in response to stress, for example, but they are not always aware that they do so. They may, in fact, honestly believe they are hungry when in fact some other motivational state initiated their action. There is not necessarily a connection between what we say about our conduct and the motivational sources of that conduct. Nonetheless, the statement of motives connects people and their conduct to the social world and its expectations, and makes a kind of sense of their conduct for themselves and others, even if their statements could constitute a poor analysis of their internal states.

Negotiated Order: The negotiated order refers to a social order that emerges from negotiations. A union contract, for example, is a negotiated order that emerges from a formal process of contract negotiation, is signed by the parties that bargained, and subsequently governs relationships between labor and management for a specified period of time. Negotiation produces socially coordinated conduct—that is, labor agrees to work under certain conditions and management agrees to those conditions, such as pay, raises, and job conditions. Negotiation also produces a constructed sense of social order. That is, people who have negotiated a social order share a sense, officially or unofficially, of how their activities are and ought to be coordinated. A negotiated order is also an informal arrangement in a workplace that substitutes for official rules about how to conduct activity. In this sense, a negotiated order can just be "how we really do things around here."

Negotiation: Negotiation is a social process in which participants strike various kinds of bargains or agreements, of limited scope and duration that define the nature of their relationships to one another, as well as their mutual responsibilities. Negotiation occurs between individuals as individuals and also between individuals as members and representatives of groups and organizations. Negotiations can be highly formalized, such as contract negotiations between unions and corporations, which complex state and federal labor laws govern. Negotiation can also be quite informal, such as when various trades, such as carpenters, electricians, and plumbers at a construction site agree informally on how they will coordinate their work schedules.

Norms: Norms are expectations of what ought to be—of how people ought to conduct themselves and what they ought to or ought not to do. Symbolic interactionists approach norms in an unconventional way. Several features of their approach should be kept in mind. First, symbolic interactionists tend to take a somewhat ethnomethodological view of norms, regarding them as sense-making devices rather than as inviolable guides to behavior. In other words, people are more likely to invoke norms after the fact of behavior in order to make sense of it than before the fact in order to decide what to do. Second, the fit between norms and conduct is loose. In any given situation, it is possible to invoke a variety of norms to warrant or justify a particular act. Third, symbolic interactionists generally reject the idea that orderly social behavior is maintained because people learn to conform to norms and then go on autopilot following them. Instead, they view orderly behavior as depending on the maintenance of meaning in general, and norms are a component of meaning but not its only source nor the sole guarantee of social order. One of the orientations people can take toward the social world is to live up to norms, but this is only one orientation. More commonly, people act on habitual and practical grounds, making sense of the situations they are in and attempting to solve the problems they encounter. People may solve these problems in already available ways, such as norms, but that they will do so, or make sense in the same ways of what to do, is variable.

Object: An object is anything to which people pay attention and which orient action. There are several key points to keep in mind about objects. First, in symbolic interactionist usage, objects can be tangible and intangible. That is, an object may be a thing that is named and acted toward, such as a cup of coffee or a computer, but it can also be an abstraction, such as "love" or "truth," that cannot be directly grasped but that nonetheless is named and acted toward. Second, objects do not exist except insofar as they are named and acted toward. The thing we call a cup of coffee obviously has a physical existence that does not depend on our naming it or drinking it—the cup does not disappear from the earth when we do not think about it. But it is an object only by virtue of how we pay attention to and act toward it, and its physical characteristics do not determine its nature as an object. The "cup of coffee" can become another object, an "example," if someone uses it in that way, such as in a book on social psychology. Third, objects are linked to the goals of acts. Every act has an object in the sense that participants move toward some desired state of affairs—an object—such as "reaching agreement" or a "new house."

Phases of the Act: The phases of the act describe a process through which every act proceeds from start to finish (though not without interruption). Impulse is the initial phase in which the person feels a readiness or a need to act because some stimulus occurs. The telephone rings, a friend smiles, and a student sees a low grade written on his or her examination. In each instance, the individual is mobilized to act in some way. Perception is the next phase, in which the person grasps the nature of the stimulus that inspired the impulse. One hears the telephone, begins to interpret the smile, and realizes the significance of the grade. During this phase, human beings engage in a process of reflection, in which they gradually, and often very self-consciously, move from the initial perception of the stimulus to forming a plan of action—an object. The person sees himself or herself answering the phone, smiling in return, or asking the professor for an appointment to discuss the exam. Manipulation is the phase in which the person takes steps to move toward the object—answering the phone, creating a smiling face, or consulting the professor after class. Consummation is the phase in which the object is attained—a phone answered, a smile returned, an appointment made, and a grade changed.

Role: A role is a perspective from which the person acts in a defined situation. It is not a list of desired or expected behaviors or composed of a firmly written script that an actor merely memorizes and repeats. There are desired or expected behaviors but these are not necessarily the only chosen paths to enacting a role. Rather, a role contains several interlocked perspectives that the individual knows about and from which he or she can act or imagine others acting in the situation of fulfilling that role. A player in a baseball game knows the rules of the game as a whole and the part each player is to play, as well as the part he or she is called on to play, such as pitcher or outfielder. To know the role of pitcher or outfielder is to understand the perspective from which such a player should approach the game. People use such understandings to construct their own behaviors and to anticipate how others will behave.

Role Making: Role making involves constructing a performance that is relevant to the situation and appropriate to one's perspective within it. The image of role making emphasizes that people must often think hard in order to know what to do and that they must often invent new ways of acting in order to create a successful performance. Even though a student knows how to sit in a college classroom and act like an interested student, he or she must be able to respond to common events, such as being asked a question by the professor. Role making is often very routine, but sometimes it is not. Nonroutine instances of role making remind us that people engaged in social interaction must be attentive to the situations in which they interact and have a grasp of the perspective—the role—from which others expect them to act.

Role Taking: Role taking is the imaginative placing of oneself in the shoes of the other in a situation, so that one can grasp his or her perspective (role) and understand the other's conduct and one's own from that point of view. To take the role of the other is not to enact, play, or make the other's role, but rather to imagine that role, how the situation looks from its vantage point and what the other expects of one. Role taking is essential to role making, since constructing an adequate performance in a social situation requires the person to know how others in the situation view him or her. That knowledge does not generally come from questions directed to the other or from long-term acquaintance with them, but rather from knowledge of the situation as a whole and the perspectives (roles) that others usually take within it.

Personal Identity: Personal identity is based on a claim of special plans, projects, or purposes, and often entail a sense of difference from others rather than identification with them. As people proceed through the life course, acquiring and shedding roles, group memberships, and identifications, they develop a more or less autonomous sense of self. That is, they come to think of themselves as individuals with life histories and a future, and not just as role players or group members. The degree to which people seek such autonomy varies within cultures as well as from one culture to another. Even in a culture such as that of the United States, where people are encouraged to develop a strong sense of individuality and difference, many are content with a minimal sense of self as an autonomous agent. Such individuals prefer to identify with the various groups that they belong to or to think of themselves as incumbents in particular roles. In other words, their social and situated identities are paramount. Others define themselves strongly in terms of personal autonomy and resist strong identification with communities or with a particular situated role.

Placements: A placement is an act or gesture that assigns a person a social location within a situation, the broader community, or society. Placements may confirm the identities that a person claims—that is, placements may coincide with announcements or they may resist or ignore the person's announcements. For example, the airline passenger who accepts the flight attendant's smiling offer of a cup of coffee with thanks and a returning smile has confirmed the attendant's announcement of identity. The apartment dweller that invites the cable repairperson inside after looking at his or her uniform and identification card has placed the repairperson in the identity he or she claims. On the other hand, the prosecutor that casts a skeptical eye on a neatly attired defendant and remarks that a clean shave and tie do not change the facts of his crime has rejected the defendant's identity announcement of looking like a good, upstanding, and innocent citizen.

Power: Power is the capacity of one or more people to achieve their purposes without the consent of others or despite other people's resistance. This definition is broad enough to cover a great variety of forms of power and contexts. It is also broad enough to encompass the specifically symbolic interactionist approach to power as well as the approaches of other perspectives.

Virtually every interactionist concept must appreciate the exercise of power. Control over how a situation is defined and facility in role taking, for example, are sources of power in everyday social interaction. Likewise, awareness contexts, aligning actions, and emotions provide contexts where the exercise of power can be analyzed. Manipulating awareness contexts is a way to control others without their assent or even their knowledge. The rhetorical capacity to engage in effective motive talk gains legitimacy for actions that would otherwise seem to be unwarranted exercises of power and renders them authoritative. The capacity to arouse particular emotional states, likewise, is a resource of power.

However, power is a useful but slippery concept. This concept is best used to provoke a careful examination and detailed exposition of the means that people employ in various situations to exert control over how others behave. The power of professors over students, for example, is analyzed by showing how professors control the selection of reading materials, shape a classroom's emotional tone, define the situations of interactions with students, establish certain awareness contexts, and engage in altercasting. To explain complex social behavior merely by asserting that one party had the "power" to compel the other to behave in certain ways is to gloss over the actual processes of social interaction and to engage in mystification rather than analysis.

Pragmatism: Pragmatism is a predominantly American school of philosophy that views human beings, like all living things, as problem-solving creatures who create knowledge as they seek to live and persevere in the world. This approach to philosophy has several consequences. First, pragmatism views the world—social and physical—as an environment that presents both opportunities and obstacles to the organisms that live in it. Second, it emphasizes the active, goal-oriented, knowledge-seeking qualities of animals, including human beings, who must learn in order to adapt to the world. Third, pragmatism views knowledge as relative rather than absolute. That is, human beings do not discover "the truth" about the world, but rather construct "truths" of limited scope and duration. These so-called truths are true relative to the purposes for which they are sought, rather than in some absolute sense. In other words, pragmatists believe that we see and know reality through the lens of our collective needs and purposes.

Pragmatism is the philosophical approach most closely associated with symbolic interactionism. Mead, James, Dewey, and Peirce, on whom interactionists rely for philosophical insights, were pragmatists. The interactionist image of the world and its human inhabitants is a pragmatist image. Human beings are seen as striving to live in a physical and social world that presents them with opportunities but also imposes limitations and creates problems for them. Collectively, they strive to use the opportunities they see and to overcome problems of various kinds. Human beings are thus conceived as naturally active, using whatever practical means they can find and knowledge they can create, to select and achieve their individual and collective goals.

Problem Solving: Problem solving refers to human activities whose focus, or object, is to solve practical problems that arise in everyday life. Problem solving is important for social order in two respects. First, a great deal of the everyday coordination of social activities occurs in the context of solving problems—getting flat tires fixed, arranging to care for children, resolving problems in interpersonal relationships, and so forth. Second, a great deal of the everyday experience of social order (defined later) depends on the sense that problems have been or are capable of being solved. People achieve real social order by solving problems, and they achieve a sense of social order either by solving them or by talking about their solutions.

Schema: A schema functions as a loosely organized theory that people use to make sense of their world, predict the behavior of others, and decide on their own course of action. Schemas can focus on specific other people, situations, types of people, social roles, social groups, specific events, and even the self. Thus, a given individual might have schemas about a spouse, disciplining the children, office parties, workaholics, supervisors, fellow nurses, the war against terrorism, and self. A schema is a kind of "picture" of any of these things. Parts of this picture are quite abstract: An individual's schema for a supervisor might include such abstract traits as superior knowledge and wisdom, willingness to listen, and the capacity to make quick decisions. Other parts of a schema are more concrete, involving images of physical appearance, strength, clothing, or other material things. Thus, the schema for a corporate lawyer might include an expensive pinstriped suit, well-tailored shirts, and costly shoes.

Self: The self is a social object. The self is not a specific thing, nor is it equivalent to the body, nor is it mysteriously located somewhere inside the person. Rather, like any other object, the self is something named, to which attention is paid and toward which actions are directed. The self's importance lies in forming and controlling human conduct. Because human beings can name and thus objectify themselves, they have the capacity to take themselves into account when they act. That is, they can imagine themselves acting in a particular way, they can imagine others acting toward them, and they can consider the effect of alternative ways of acting on themselves, on others, and on the situation as a whole. Thus, the self is a key object that people use in their efforts to achieve control over their conduct. Our ability to imagine ourselves as a collection of particular characteristics helps guide our own conduct in a direction that will suit the situation as a whole and make sense to others. To sum, the self is both a product of role taking (previously defined), because we see ourselves when we imagine the perspectives of others, and a key object in role making (previously defined), because we have to see ourselves in order to make an acceptable performance.

Self-Esteem: Self-esteem is the affective or emotional dimension of the self. People become objects to themselves by attaching emotional significance to themselves and their actions. That is, they love or hate themselves, feel satisfied or dissatisfied, and manifest confidence or a lack of it. The concept of self-esteem summarizes the various positive or negative attitudes people may take toward themselves.

Self-esteem is influenced by mood (the person's position on a continuum that ranges from extreme euphoria to severe dysphoria). To be euphoric is to be energized, self-confident, positive, outgoing, and active in the extreme; to be dysphoric is to be the opposite, lacking in energy and self-confidence, negative, withdrawn, and perhaps even immobilized. Most people fall somewhere between these extremes, just as their self-esteem is neither completely assured nor totally lacking. The association of self-esteem with mood is evident in evident in the fact that depression, one of the chief ways that mood is disturbed or disordered, is associated with low self-esteem. Also, medications that relieve the symptoms of depression also raise self-esteem.

To associate self-esteem with mood and its disorders is not to say that self-esteem is a psychological or medical phenomenon rather than a social psychological one. How people feel about themselves—whether they have high self-esteem or low, elevated or depressed mood—also depends on their social experiences. The normal regulation of mood in the brain (i.e., responding to success or praise with pleasure and positive self-feeling and to criticism or failure with negative feelings and depressed mood) may well become disordered or disturbed. When that happens, people cannot respond positively to positive events, and they may become depressed and think negatively about themselves for no external reason. Even then, however, it is likely that such disturbances are shaped by the person's social experiences as well as by biology.

Self-Fulfilling Prophecy: A common means through which we experience constructing reality involves an important concept called the self-fulfilling prophecy. First coined by sociologist Robert K. Merton, a self-fulfilling prophecy refers to an "assumption or prediction that, purely as a result of having been made, causes the expected or predicted effect to occur, and thus confirms its own accuracy." In other words, when people have a prior belief about what is true, they interpret information or actions that pertain to that belief to be evidence that confirms the prior belief and "makes" it come true. For example, suppose someone believes that a person is antisocial and unfriendly. They may treat every action by that person as being intended to be nasty, and in turn, give off an unwelcoming vibe to that individual. Where the person might actually have not been an "angry outcast," how people act on the belief that the person is an angry outcast comes to make the person feel alienated and angry at being treated in an unfriendly way, such that the person retaliates by becoming antisocial and unfriendly.

Sign: A sign is something that stands for something else. In animal (and human) behavior, there are many instances where an animal learns to respond to a sign as a stimulus instead of, or in addition to, the actual stimulus for which it stands. The classic illustration is Pavlov's dog learning to salivate at the sound of a buzzer, a sign that it learned to treat as the stimulus of food. Signs are either natural or conventional. A natural sign is one that comes to stand for something else because an animal has learned that the sign and the stimulus it stands for are regularly associated in its world. A conventional sign is one whose meaning is established by some kind of agreement among those who use it and whose significance can be communicated from one to another. Another word for conventional sign is symbol (defined later).

Significant Symbol: In Mead's theory, the significant symbol is a gesture that arouses a similar response both in the one employing the gesture and in the others who perceive it. A gesture is anything to which an organism can respond. In gestural communication, it is the beginning part of the act of another that serves as the stimulus to which one responds. Significant symbols may involve such behavioral gestures, but for human beings, the system of symbols we call language is what we mostly employ. Human beings arouse responses in themselves and others by using words—by naming things and thus signaling their intentions or plans of action to one another.

The key to understanding Mead's concept of the significant symbol is that significant symbols arouse the same or a very similar response in the one using the symbol and the others who perceive it. The interpretation is shared. In a conversation of gestures, one animal's gesture arouses a response in the other animal. With the significant symbol, the symbol stimulates him or her at the same time he or she stimulates others. It is the significant symbol, in other words, that is the basis for shared meanings in human life. When I say to another that I am sad, I (hopefully) arouse in that person an attitude of sympathy toward me; I simultaneously also stimulate myself to feel sympathetic toward myself. By thus arousing the same or a very similar response in self and other, I cause us to see things in the same way—I cause both me and the other to take a certain attitude toward things.

Situated Identity: A situated identity is an identity that an individual has in interaction with others in a particular social situation. Situated identity is established when announcements and placements correspond—in other words, when a role and an associated identity that a person claims are confirmed or accepted by others with whom interactions take place. A person has the situated identity of an investor, for example, when he or she indicates to a broker his or her intent to purchase stocks, and the broker accepts the money and establishes an account.

Situated Self: The self is always a situated social object. That is, the self is an object that situated social interaction constructs. To Descartes's assertion that "I think, therefore I am," the symbolic interactionist might say, "I interact, therefore I am." In other words, people have an existence as objects in situations in which they interact with others and their self is situated within that set of interactions. This assertion does not mean that the interaction must be with real others. Even in solitary moments, the person frequently carries on imaginary conversations and other forms of social interaction with imaginary others, and these imaginings constitute a sense of self as surely as interaction with real people. When a person is with other people, he or she also may be imagining encounters with people that are not there and constitute a self in interaction with them. One way people occupy themselves in idle and solitary moments is by reflecting on and constructing a biographical self (previously defined).

Situation: A situation is a container of social interaction, a particular intersection in social time and space of people, objects, and acts, with a shared name and a shared definition that specifies an expected set and duration of activities. Situations have duration, that is to say, they have beginnings, a timetable of activities, and endings. They have a social location, since they exist relative to other situations, and they are usually located within the walls of organizations or the boundaries of groups or other human aggregates. They contain actors and their individual and social acts and objects. They are also defined, which means that people share ideas about what is going on, who is doing it, why they are doing it, when they will stop doing it, and where they are doing it.

Symbolic interactionists often focus on the definition of the situation, since that definition encompasses and predicts the other aspects of the situation from the standpoint of participants. If people define a situation as a cocktail party, it will have cocktail party consequences: They will see other participants as partygoers, perform acts that are performed at cocktail parties, and do so for the two or three hours that cocktail parties generally last.

This emphasis on the definition of the situation should not, however, be allowed to obscure the fundamental importance of the concept of the situation itself. Symbolic interactionists take the position that all human conduct is situated—that is, anchored in and attached to a situation of some kind. The "situatedness" of conduct is a crucial feature of the interactionist outlook, and one that makes them critical of other sociological and social psychological approaches that gloss over the situation in favor of abstract social forces of one kind or another. Thus, interactionists do not talk vaguely of "power" or "conformity." Instead, we want to know the details of how the exercise of power or the workings of conformity are specifically defined, manifest, and situated. Situations are complex—abstractions neglect that complexity.

Social Act: A social act is the coordinated activity of several individuals, who are jointly focused on and moving toward the completion of a social object. In a business contract, the various activities of people engaged in doing business constitute the social act: meetings, proposals, negotiations, offers, and counteroffers are undertaken in an effort to create "the contract," whereby they will do business together in the future. Just as an act is completed when its object is reached, a social act is completed when the social object is attained.

Social Control: The concept of social control refers to a variety of social arrangements that attempt to regulate and sanction the behavior of individuals and groups. The most obvious mechanism of social control is the formal mechanism of the legal system—that is, the laws, police, courts, and prisons that define, detect, adjudicate, and punish criminal behavior. Social control, however, exists in every sphere of social life and is informal as well as formal. Within friendship circles, for example, people exert informal social controls by criticizing, ostracizing, or gossiping about one another. Parents exert social control by "grounding" their children or by enforcing "time-outs." Social control can be positive as well as negative. Friends, for example, praise one another and thereby reinforce desired behavior. Parents may point to the accomplishments of other people's children to attempt to set standards for their own.

Undesired forms of conduct stimulate social controls. Parents respond to a misbehaving child by calling for a "time-out," and police respond to a robbery in progress by pursuing suspects, making arrests, and pressing charges in court. But social control also has a life of its own, sometimes creating deviance or even eliciting the behavior it is intended to regulate. Thus, agents of social control, such as drug enforcement agents, look for violations of the law in order to justify their employment. Parents may strive to regulate their children's lives for the sake of doing so (because they can) and not because their children's behavior is especially problematic. Indeed, in many circumstances, the existence of social control provokes rebellion, as when children consciously or unconsciously provoke their parents' ire by trying to get away with undetected rule violations to assure themselves they are not completely ruled by parental expectations.

Social Identity: Social identity refers to the person's sense of place or location in a community of some kind. Like personal identity, its referent is not the immediate situation where one has a role in relation to others, but rather a larger community to which one attaches oneself or with which one identifies. One can be a member of a particular religious faith while also being immediately involved in a nonreligious activity. Social identity, in other words, is an aspect of the biographical self. Social and personal identities do not vanish when situated identities are claimed, though they do recede momentarily into the background. Conversely, people do not surrender their right to lay claim to various situated identities when they are momentarily engaged in constructing or maintaining social and personal identities. Rather, one form of identity takes precedence over another for the moment. Indeed, social and personal identities make it possible to adopt situated identities, for the former provide a sense of continuity from one situation to another.

Social Object: A social object is an object created by the attention and action of several individuals coordinating their conduct toward it. Just as an object (previously defined) is anything that is an object of attention toward which people can act, so a social object requires attention and action. The social object just describes when there is coordinated behavior among interacting sets of individuals that is dedicated to that social object.

Social Order: The concepts of social order and disorder developed in this book rest on the basic idea that social life involves both the coordination of social conduct and the construction of images of that conduct. People coordinate their activities in everyday life with others. Employees punch time clocks and try to keep their bosses happy, or at least at bay. Purchasing agents try to find the goods and services their companies need at the best possible price and quality. Children try to decipher their parents' expectations, and parents try to keep their children fed and clothed and out of trouble. These same people also engage in talk about their experiences. Employees and employers gripe about one another, purchasing agents try to predict future trends in their industries, and parents and children talk about one another. These patterned activities constitute forms of social order.

Social order depends on both coordinated activity and the social construction of social order. From the vantage point of an outside, disinterested observer, parents and children act in highly regular and predictable ways, doing what countless other parents do and will do. In this sense, we could say that a social order exists, for it seems apparent that their activities are coordinated in predictable ways. From the vantage point of the parents and children themselves, however, things may seem different. First-time parents of adolescent children may be unnerved by their children's rebelliousness and feel that their world is falling apart when they are really just living the experience of other parents. Can we say that a social order exists in this situation? The answer really depends on whose perspective we adopt. From the parents' vantage point, the world is falling apart and they must do something to repair it. From the standpoint of others, they are experiencing what other parents have experienced before them, and they will probably live through the experience. Very importantly, social order is a collective enterprise in which people often chose to conform. Social order is not always imposed by brute force. Many people actually find comfort in social control and order as they enhance predictability. That stated, people who suffer from social control are not always among its cheerleaders. The ambiguity of benefits and tradeoffs of social order are important to study.

Social Problems: Symbolic interactionists have a distinctive approach to social problems. They emphasize the socially created definitions of social problems as important rather than assuming that there is collective agreement about what the exact objective conditions are that define a social problem. From the interactionist approach, a social problem is a condition defined as problematic and needing answers, regardless of the status of any "objective" conditions that may underlie the problem. Interactionists take this approach not to deny that there may well be objective conditions that create human unhappiness or misery, but because problem solving seems to be such an important part of the coordination of social conduct and the construction of social order (previously defined) and because the definition and awareness of problems, despite their objective qualities, is so variable given social influence and power.

Social Structure: Sociologists frequently use the term social structure, but what they mean is not always clear or the same. In general, to describe something in the social world in "structural" terms or as an aspect of "social structure," is to regard it as both external to the individual and as constraining individual and collective activities. To describe "social class" as an element of social structure, for example, is to say that the division of a society into more or less distinctive groupings on the basis of occupation, income, wealth, education, social origins, and other characteristics is external and constraining. People experience social class as external—that is, as a given and inevitable part of the social world; and they find that membership in a social class constrains their life chances. It affects how much education they can receive, what sort of medical care they can get, how vulnerable they are to economic downturns, and the like.

Social structure is sometimes used in contrast with culture (previously defined). Structure refers to the external and constraining facts with which a society confronts members (social class, for example or male domination in the workplace), whereas culture refers to the norms, knowledge, and beliefs that members of a society hold in common and that help sustain its structure. Thus, a structural explanation of occupational success emphasizes barriers to success caused by unequal access to educational opportunity. A cultural explanation would show how beliefs (in the importance of education, for example) could inhibit or encourage the pursuit of more years of education. These distinctions are not set in stone, though, as many scholars examine phenomena by integrating both cultural and structural perspectives.

Symbol: A symbol is a conventional sign. That is, a symbol is something—a gesture, a picture, and most often, a word—that stands for something else. Like any sign, a symbol stands in place of that which it signifies, and thus enables people to respond to it in place of what it signifies. Unlike natural signs, however, symbols have properties that give their users greater mastery over their worlds. Symbols are public rather than private. Moreover, because their meaning can be communicated, they do not have to be learned by trial and error by the individual but can be taught to others. Symbols have no natural connection with the things they signify, and so can be invoked even in the absence of that for which they stand. Indeed, symbols can be invented that do not stand for anything concrete—thus, symbols give rise to abstract objects. Symbols also make it possible for users to refer to themselves as a part of their environment, thus giving rise to the phenomenon we call "self."

Total Institutions: A total institution is a social facility where a staff controls the actions of an institutionalized population. These staff control time and space in these areas, such as what and when people can eat, where they can go, what activities they can engage in, what they can wear, and when they can talk. A total institution engages in what is called resocialization and represents an apex of social control over individual identity. Resocialized people in total institutions are prevented from being the unique individuals that they used to be—in many cases to the point of no longer even having their old names. Prisons, for example, refer to inmates using numbers, not individual names, and prisoners are made to wear uniform clothing. This process "depersonalizes" people, quarantining them for some amount of time from a heterogeneous society, and formally administering all aspects of their lives, leaving a minimum of individual autonomy. In practice, a total institution has to manage the daily activities of a large number of people, some of them very dangerous or disturbed, within a restricted space. These people live in "batch" conditions and have tightly regimented lives. The total institution describes many different physical settings, but very importantly, signifies a social psychological process of identity transformation. The total institution is society acting to transform the old identity of a person into a new one, or holding the undesirable aspects of an old identity at bay until the period of institutionalization ends.

Vocabularies of Motive: A vocabulary of motives is a set of situationally specific terms that people invoke (or that are imputed to them) in an effort to answer actual or anticipated questions about their conduct. The symbolic interactionist view of motivation and motive emphasizes the gap between these terms: Motivation is internal and unconscious; motive is public and verbal. Motives are avowed or imputed, both by self and others, and so a crucial question about motives is how they are chosen or selected. Symbolic interactionists argue that the choice of motives reflects the available vocabulary of motives. That is, what people say about their own conduct or impute to the conduct of others depends on their social location and on the situation in which the conduct occurs. Different institutional contexts and types of situations make available different vocabularies of motive.

Index

A

Accounts, 134–136
Achieved roles, 102
Act, 206
  phases of, 40
  and social acts, 39
Aligning actions, 132–135, 206
  classification by
    Hunter, Christopher, 137
  disclaimers, 135
Altercasting, 143–145, 206–207
Announcements, 207
Anxiety, 99–100
Apology 137
Asch, Solomon, 2
Awareness contexts, 147–149, 207

B

Becker, Howard
  theory of deviant behavior, 187
  moral entrepreneur, 125, 216
Bennett, Gillian
  theory on belief in ghosts, 189
Blumer, Herbert,
  symbolic interactionism, 25
  and grand narrative, 24
  symbolic interactionism, 23–24, 26
Biographical self, 207
Body image, 202–203
Boundaries, 207–208

C

Careers, symbolic interactionists view, 208
Cathedrals of consumption, 193
Child
  impact on his/her membership in, 62
  linking to social world, 62
Casinos, 195
Celebrities, 197
Classical behaviorism, 10
Classic communities, 108
Communication, 208–209
Community, 209
  Amish communities, 112
  experiential, 110
  contemporary 109–112
  identification, 112
  nature of, 111

persons and, 112
relationship to, 112
Second Life, 109
sense of, 111
Turner's view on, 111
World of Warcraft, 109
Conditioning process, 209
Conformity, 2, 3, 201–202
Conning consciousness, 69–70
Constraint and social interaction, 143
Construct reality, 200
Contemporary symbolic interactionism, 6
Conventional and interpersonal roles by
  Shibutani, Tamotsu, 149
Conventional roles, 209–210
Conventional signs, 43
Culture
  defined, 210
  and social structure, 4
The Culture of Fear, by Glassner, Barry, 175
Cumulative power, 137

D

Deep acting, 139
Deception, 90
Definition of situation, 49–50. *See also*
    Roles
  role structures and, 52
  sense making and predictive capacity, 53
Deviance, 202–203, 211
Disclaimers, 135
Discourse by Stone, Gregory, 128
Disneyification, 194–195, 211
Doublespeak, 200–201
Dramaturgical perspective/impression
  management, introduction to,
  66–70, 91

E

Ego, 11
Emergence, 211–212
  idea, 117
Ellis, Albert, 100
Emotions, 212
  antidepressant drugs, 58
  emotional demands, 140
  emotive dissonance, 140
  emotional labor, 140
  experience of, 58

Kemper, Theodore
  primary emotions, 57–58
  physical sensations, 57physiological
    responses, 57
  privileged emotion managers, 140 as
    role-making process, 58 sadness, 57
    self and social world, 56 and social
    interaction, 138–143 sociological
    conception of, 57
Entertainment themes and consumption, 203
Entitling acclaim, 138
Ethnomethodology, 16, 212
  ethnomethodological sense-making
    processes, 157 Garfinkel view on,
    155–156 symbolic interactionists, 17
Exchange theory
  assumptions of, 12
  consciously or unconsciously behaviors, 14
  exchange relationships, 13
  Molm and Cook
    psychological and economic
    principles, 15
  motivational premise of, 13
  stable relationship, development, 14
  valued things, 15
Excuses, 134
Explaining disorder, 172–174. *See also*
    Social order

F

Fear, 57–58
Feeling rules concept, 139
Freudian theory, 11
  symbolic interactionists, 12
Functionalist social theorists, 163

G

Garfinkel, Harold, 155–156
Gender, 212–213
Gendered expectations and social order, 102
Goffman, Erving, 66–70, 91, 133, 143, 190
Group solidarity and individual
    identification, 169
Guerilla marketers, 119

H

Healthy social bond, 160
Horizontal and vertical linkages, 213–214
Hochschild, Arlie, 139